FRENCH ODYSSEYS

VOYAGE PITTORESQUE

DE LA

GRECE

Par Choiseul-Gouffier

TOME PREMIER.

A PARIS,

M. DCC. LXXXII.

FRENCH ODYSSEYS

GREECE IN FRENCH TRAVEL LITERATURE FROM THE RENAISSANCE TO THE ROMANTIC ERA

OLGA AUGUSTINOS

THE JOHNS HOPKINS UNIVERSITY PRESS

BALTIMORE AND LONDON

The Johns Hopkins University Press
2715 North Charles Street
Baltimore, Maryland 21218-4319
The Johns Hopkins Press Ltd., London

Frontispiece: Greece Expiring among Classical Ruins. One of the first visual depictions of philhellenic sentiments. From the Comte de Choiseul-Gouffier, *Voyage pittoresque de la Grèce,* frontispiece, vol. 1 (1782).

Library of Congress Cataloging-in-Publication Data will be found at the end of this book.

A catalog record for this book is available from the British Library.

The General Research Division, the New York Public Library, Astor, Lenox and Tilden Foundations, generously granted permission to reprint *Greece Expiring among Classical Ruins, View of the Fountain of Chios, View of the Convent of Patmos, Reception of the Author by Hassan Tchaousch-oglou,* and *View of the Interior of a Khan or Caravansary* from Gabriel Choiseul-Goullier, *Voyage pittoresque de la Grèce,* Paris, 1782, and *Souli* from François Charles Pouqueville, *Grèce,* Paris, 1836.

The Art & Architecture Collection, Miriam and Ira D. Wallach Division of Art Prints and Photographs, the New York Public Library, Astor, Lenox and Tilden Foundations, generously granted permission to reprint *View of the Temple of Minerva in Athens, View of the Temple of Olympian Zeus in Athens, View of the Temple of Erechtheus in Athens,* and *View of the Lantern of Demosthenes* from Julien David Le Roy, *Les Ruines des plus beaux monuments de la Grèce,* Paris, 1758.

To Gerasimos, my mother Kleoniki,
and in memory of my father Chrysostomos

CONTENTS

PREFACE

Ever since the Renaissance, European intellectuals have engaged in the study and interpretation of ancient Greek civilization. One group of writers who contributed indirectly to the advance of knowledge of the Greek world was the travelers who began to visit the Greek lands in increasing numbers from the middle of the sixteenth century.

European travel literature on Greece, although it typifies in many respects the approach of Renaissance and post-Renaissance travelers to non-European peoples, has a unique dimension. The links with its classical past, real or imagined, made it seem closer to the West, while its subjugation to Ottoman rule placed it in the penumbra between East and West.

The interplay between the vision of classical antiquity and the image of modern Greece, with its rich array of comparisons and contrasts, was the overarching theme of all travelogues on prerevolutionary Greece. This book traces and analyzes this ubiquitous theme in French travel literature from the sixteenth century to the outbreak of the Greek War of Independence. In the process four aspects of this multifaceted genre are considered.

First, I endeavor to relate travel literature to the development of Hellenism by concentrating on the highlights of classical influences on French thought and letters from their humanist philological origins to the musings of the Romantic Hellenists. Second, I examine the image of Greece in modern times as portrayed by French travelers who came to know that world during their voyages to the Levant.

Since traveling is essentially an experience of cultural encounters, the travelogue is a discourse of representations. As such, it has a two-fold significance: it imparts information about the places visited and, at the same time, it is a mirror reflecting the reasoning processes, values, and perceptual framework that representatives of one culture use consciously or unconsciously in order to understand another. Thus I consider descriptions of the Greek physical world and its people in the light of the standards, criteria, and style of the various writers studied and their intellectual and literary milieu. Within this context, this work follows the development of the travel account as a literary genre, since its practitioners employed literary devices in order to render their narratives more vivid. Finally, I endeavor to delineate the literary and intellectual origins of philhellenism in its prerevolutionary phase and to interpret its development.

During the period examined in this book, the Greek world was part of the political and social order of the Ottoman Empire. Yet it was not perceived by Europeans as an integral part of the Orient. What distinguished it from its conquerors were its language, religion, and above all, its legacy from the classical world. By analyzing what that legacy meant to French travelers, and by extension to other intellectuals, this work attempts to understand their approach to the modern Greeks.

Not only did French travelers reflect attitudes toward antiquity prevalent in their culture but, at the same time, they also fostered the propagation of classical studies in their country in at least two ways. First, their visits to the lands of classical antiquity and the narratives they produced functioned as bridges connecting the abstract erudition of scholars with the physical setting of the events of their investigations. Second, the antiquities they acquired and carried back to Europe enriched private and public collections, stimulated the rise of the modern science of archeology, and provided a varied reservoir of themes and images for the visual arts and poetry. Indirectly, the appropriation of antiquities by Frenchmen and other Europeans is an example of the way knowledge became an instrument of power and control.

When they journeyed to Greece, Western travelers felt that they were entering not an alien terrain but a land whose legacy they had absorbed and integrated into the matrix of their own civilization. The contemporary Greek reality that confronted them, however, disoriented them because it diverged vastly from their expectations.

Part of this book traces the origins and the development of the efforts by French philhellenes to bridge this gap and see Greek culture reunified by resuscitating its Hellenic past and expelling what were perceived as foreign intrusions. This envisioned rehabilitation of the Greek world sought to reclaim and redeem it by purifying it and, consequently, by suppressing certain eras of its past. Seen from a wider angle, it reflected the general European concept of cultural integrity and identity. Cross-fertilization and mutual enrichment arising from the encounter and the admixture of different civilizations were not espoused by French writers before the Romantic era. The idea of Greece as the crossroads where East and West met would have been a distasteful proposition to them.

The reconciliation between the ancient and the modern Greeks advocated by French philhellenes was largely the outcome of observations made by a long line of travelers to the Ottoman lands. French and other Western commentators had a preconceived notion of what a Greek should be before they even set foot on Greek soil; in other words, the essence of Greekness preceded the existence of the modern Greeks. Concomitant with this fixed concept of Greek identity was the bipolar view of Greek history which divided it into the antipodal halves of the Hellenic (the preclassical, classical and Hellenistic eras were not yet clearly differentiated) and the post-Hellenic periods. The latter epoch was seen as a long hiatus during which classical Greek civilization had been progressively silenced. The advent of Christianity within the body politic of the Byzantine Empire, the Europeans believed, had plunged Greece into ignorance and superstition.

Sixteenth- and seventeenth-century French travelers, when describing the modern Greeks, limited their sympathy to a few expressions of commiseration for their state of subjugation, but they never proposed their emancipation from their Ottoman rulers. This would have been premature given the political and intellectual climate in their own country at a time when the legitimacy of absolute monarchy was not questioned. It was also untimely to think of the dissolution of the Ottoman Empire at a moment when it was still a great power and elicited respect mingled with fear from Europe.

But when the political and social thinkers of the Enlightenment challenged the authority of monarchs to govern according to the dictates of their personal will and interests, unhampered by the rule of law, then the subjugation of the Greeks to a foreign autocratic sovereign began to appear as a violation of natural human rights. Their liberation seemed not only desirable but also feasible because, by the end of the eighteenth century, the Ottoman Empire had fallen behind Europe militarily and politically, and signs of its decline were already visible. Thus, as this book demonstrates, it was not fortuitous that philhellenism—the vision of a reborn and liberated Greece coming closer to the West by virtue of its Hellenic lineage—emerged in France during the last decades of the eighteenth century.

The culmination of this book is the examination of the intellectual, artistic, and literary origins of philhellenism, which was the product of the convergence of the sensibilities of the romantic Hellenists and the political and social precepts of the Enlightenment. Although it has been seen primarily as an expression of good will and generosity on the part of Westerners toward the modern Greeks, classically inspired philhellenism was a much more complex phenomenon. It was above all a manifestation of the *mission civilisatrice* of the culturally superior Europeans, who sought to bring about the rehabilitation of the modern Greeks on their own terms, namely, through the efficacious imitation of Western-derived classical models. Ironically, although it proposed the reunification of Greek culture, in actuality it fostered its bifurcation because it pitted its more recent Christian-Byzantine-Ottoman legacy against its ancient past.

This book is based on a thorough reading of the major French travel accounts on prerevolutionary Greece. I have examined the themes and ideas expressed in them synchronically and diachronically. I interpret individual works in terms of their thematic, ideational, and stylistic aspects and then compare them with those of preceding travel relations, while pointing out their influence on subsequent works of the same nature. I have carried out the horizontal and vertical analysis of these travelogues in the broader context of the authors' literary and cultural milieu because a travel account is a two-way mirror: its creator, in trying to capture and engrave the features of a foreign land, leaves on it his personal and cultural imprint.

The ultimate purpose of this book is to contribute to a better understanding of the complex character of travel literature, the interplay between objective reality and subjective perception reflected in this type of writing, the persistent appeal of the ancient Greeks and their ineluctable authority on their modern progeny, and, above all, the dynamic, though unequal, relation between the representatives of one culture, the French travelers, and the epigones of their idols, the Greeks.

Research for this book was done primarily at the New York Public Library and the Gennadius Library in Athens. The Interlibrary Loan Department of the Thomas Cooper Library at the University of South Carolina was also very helpful in obtaining sources. I wish to express my appreciation to the staffs of these institutions for their courteous and generous assistance. I would also like to thank the Gennadius Library for granting me permission to use the unpublished papers and letters of Barbié du Bocage. The book benefited also from the valuable suggestions of the readers for the Press. Throughout the writing, my main source of advice, encouragement, and unwavering support was my husband. His incisive comments, probing questions, and critical appraisal helped to enhance this work.

I

THE USES OF HELLENISM
FROM THE RENAISSANCE
TO THE ROMANTIC ERA

The Efficacy of Imitation

It was during the Renaissance that Greece made an enduring impact on European thought first as an intellectual force derived primarily from literary sources and, later, as a specific physical location marked by the vestiges of its past. At this juncture of Western civilization, the rising prestige of the Greco-Roman world was one of the influences that gave Europeans a common cultural identity. Later this was reflected in the cosmopolitan character of the Enlightenment, which was to an extent the product of the infusion of the legacy of the ancient world into Western culture. Voltaire expressed this indebtedness when he wrote, "Since the time of the renaissance of letters, when the ancients began to be used as models, Homer, Demosthenes, Virgil, Cicero have in a way united the people of Europe and have formed out of so many nations a single republic of letters."[1] Renaissance humanists and poets found in antiquity models of intellectual discourse and literary forms and images. A return to the ancients meant that "the bards and philosophers of antiquity took precedence over the Medieval Christian schoolmen. The poet in his similes invariably had recourse to the attributes of the pagan divinities."[2]

Even though Renaissance humanists did not set out to attack "the

Medieval Christian schoolmen" or to repudiate their world, they introduced markedly different modes of thought. The complex web of ideas and crosscurrents which shaped Renaissance thinking was underlaid by the shifting emphasis from the "otherworldliness of the Middle Ages . . . to what has been characterized as 'this-worldly' age."[3] This changing focus affected the perception of the physical and metaphysical realms as well as humanity's relation to them. No longer was the pursuit of knowledge directed exclusively to supernatural things or the *regnum gratiae.* Now *scientia,* the study of the natural world, acquired primacy over *sapientia,* the knowledge of the metaphysical.[4] The former was viewed not as an imperfect reflection of the latter in the hierarchical scheme of creation but as a multiform entity for whose understanding theology was not the only source.

In order to understand the perceptible world as a complex system of natural laws and not simply as a way station to eternal life, science was constituted as "an indispensable tool, perhaps the only tool for the knowledge of truth."[5] Its interposition between the eternal world and the created one, although it did not make the two mutually exclusive, changed their relationship. This altered interdependence was pointedly expressed by Galileo when he wrote that "it is the office of the wise expositors to strive to find the true meanings of passages in the Bible that accord with those natural conclusions of which first the manifest meaning or the necessary demonstrations have made certain and sure."[6] Two themes are of paramount significance in this statement: first, Galileo wanted to make it clear to the church that it was not his intention to invalidate the scriptural explanation of the universe. Second, if contradictions arose between the biblical accounts and the conclusions of natural science, then the interpretation of the former should be elastic and figurative enough to conform with the propositions of the latter. In other words, biblical hermeneutics should be subordinated to scientific reasoning, not the reverse. The ecclesiastical authorities were not convinced by Galileo's argument because in his profession of faith to both religion and science they sensed a declaration of independence of the human intellect luxuriating in its power, which was all the more glorious because of its divine origin.

If the kingdom of God lost some of its omnipotence over the human mind—over some minds anyway—the kingdom of man saw its strength aggrandized. With the emphasis shifting from the metaphysical to the physical, sensual experience was valued highly for the making of the individual.[7] For the sensible material of the visible world to enter the human mind, it needed the conduit of the senses. Thus the external cosmos and the inner world were not at variance but in consonance through the intercession of the senses. It was perhaps this direct, one-to-one relation between sensory perception and physical nature which contributed to stripping from nature the legendary and fantastic attributes given to it by its medieval beholders. It was also faith in experience guided by reason which helped demarcate more clearly the boundaries between the earthly and the celestial, a distinction often beclouded in the Middle Ages.[8]

If sensory experience led to the internalization of the external world, it also contributed to the fashioning of the individual, with all his unique and idiosyncratic traits. The new station of the individual in the scale of values

> was linked with the dignity of man. . . . When we speak of Renaissance individuals, we do not mean the actual presence of great individuals who may be found at any period of history. . . . We rather mean the importance attached to the personal experiences, thoughts, and opinions of an individual person, and the eager or, if you wish, uninhibited expression given to them in the literature and art of the period.[9]

Montaigne's self-portrait in his *Essais* is a vibrant image of an individual always open to new experiences, always in a state of becoming, and never stationary.

> Others form man; I describe him and I am depicting a particular man quite ill-formed, and whom, if I could make over again, I would fashion quite differently. But what is done, is done. . . . I cannot seize my object. He is baffled and wavering, in a state of natural intoxication. I take him the way he is, at the moment when he piques my interest. I am recording not his state of being but his becoming.

Montaigne had a heightened sense of individual privacy and responsibility.

> I have my own laws and my own court to judge me by, and I address myself to them rather than to any other place. . . . Only you can know if you are cowardly and cruel or loyal and devoted; the others do not see you at all; they can only guess by certain con-

jectures; they do not so much see your nature as they see your artfulness.[10]

That a person could be his own judge was the apogee of individualism, and that "the portrayal of an individual man . . . could have a theoretical interest, was recognized by no philosophy before the Renaissance."[11]

The release and blossoming of mental as well as physical energies during the Renaissance encompassed both the realm of nature and the worth and dignity of the individual and also the pre-Christian past of the West embodied in the heritage of Greece and Rome. However, of the two ancient civilizations, it was Greece that was a relative newcomer. The language of Rome was the foundation of medieval learning whereas, with few exceptions, Greek language and literature were largely unfamiliar to the Latin West. Yet the study of Greek was not totally defunct in medieval Europe. One of its most remarkable students was the thirteenth-century English bishop Robert Grosseteste. Although originally his interest in Greek was prompted by his theological preoccupations, it soon evolved into a systematic philological and morphological approach encompassing lexical, syntactical, and grammatical analyses as well as textual criticism. He produced scholarly editions and translations of Greek texts with commentaries and variables, which reflected his interest in the structure of the Greek language. To achieve this, he used Greek grammars and dictionaries probably obtained through the Franciscans, who had been established at Constantinople since 1220. His two main sources were the Byzantine encyclopedic dictionary *Suidas*, or *Suda*, and the *Etymologicum Guidinianum*, another Greek dictionary of a linguistic and grammatical nature. Both were monolingual, which obliged Grosseteste to dispense with the intercession of Latin. His direct access to Greek texts was aided by Nicolaus Graecus, a Greek from southern Italy. The learning of this pioneer Hellenist evinces his abiding "interest in Greek culture [which] at times seems remarkably direct and independent of the filter of Latin tradition; and this is something altogether rare for a Westerner before the late sixteenth century."[12]

The systematic introduction of ancient Greek letters to Europe was a contribution of the early Renaissance humanists, whose revival of classical learning "was, if not the only, certainly the most characteristic and pervasive intellectual current of the period [fifteenth century]."[13] The term *humanism* was coined in 1808 by the German educator F. J. Niethammer. Derived from the Latin *humanista*, it was used during the Renaissance to designate a teacher of the humanities or *studia humanitatis*.[14] This program consisted primarily of the study of grammar, rhetoric, ethics, poetry, and history, and it stressed the memorization and stylistic imitation of ancient Greek and Latin texts.

Classical locutions and tropes entered the stream of Western scholarship first as models of correct written composition. Inevitably, the stylistic imitation of ancient writings led to the emulation of the ideas expressed in them, and, although humanism was neither a literary nor a philosophic doctrine, it had a direct influence on literature and philosophy by disseminating the entire body of ancient letters. This was the first example in European thought of the efficacy of the imitation of classical Greek and Latin models. The belief in the possibility of revivifying the spirit of a bygone era by successfully imitating its literary and artistic forms became one of the main tenets of Hellenism.

How did the humanists succeed in spreading classical literary, philosophical, and scientific ideas? By using the two most powerful instruments molding literate public opinion: education and the press. They incorporated the study of Greek into the curriculum of all universities—Latin had never ceased to be part of it—and they published almost the entire corpus of extant Greek literature. The diffusion of Greek thought was fostered as much or even more by Latin translations of original Greek texts, since the knowledge of ancient Greek was never coeval with that of Latin.[15]

The stage for the cultivation of classical letters in Italy was set in the second half of the fourteenth century. An important step in this direction was taken when a Greek from southern Italy, Leo Pilatus, was commissioned by Petrarch and Boccaccio to translate the *Iliad* and the *Odyssey*. It was also at that time, in 1361, that Pilatus, Homer's translator, was appointed to the first chair of Greek at Florence, which he held until 1363. Later the distinguished Byzantine Greek scholar Manuel Chrysoloras occupied it in 1396 and made Florence the center of Greek learning for European humanists.

The restoration of Greek letters which was undertaken by Renaissance humanists was invigorated by Byzantine Hellenists who arrived in the West, mainly Italy, fleeing the Ottoman occupation of their lands.[16] Their westward emigration began in the late fourteenth century and continued until the beginning of the sixteenth. Their contribution to the efflorescence of Greek learning in the main centers of humanist scholarship was manifold: not only was it the language of their schooling but they also had direct access to manuscripts of ancient Greek works. Their classical erudition and linguistic and philological skills made them invaluable as teachers, copiers, editors, and commentators of Greek texts. They imparted to their Western fellow scholars a philological approach to ancient works, which they had inherited from the Hellenistic tradition of textual analysis.

Last but not least, the Byzantine exiles brought with them whatever manuscripts they could carry, thus revealing to the West the richness and the complexity of ancient Greek literature. More manuscripts flowed to Europe from Byzantine and former Byzantine lands, sent by emissaries of Italian princes and noblemen. So feverish and zealous were the collecting, editing, and publishing activities of Western and Byzantine humanists that, by 1515 (the year of the death of Aldus Manutius, the foremost publisher of Greek works and founder of the Aldine Press in Venice), "his press had given to the world practically all the major Greek authors of classical antiquity."[17]

In retrospect, the favorable reception the Byzantine scholar-exiles were accorded by Renaissance Hellenists stands in contrast to the sweeping indictment delivered by eighteenth-century writers against Byzantium, which they saw as the sepulcher of classical Greece. Perhaps this disparity can be explained by the physical proximity, temporal parallelism, and intellectual affinities between the Western and Eastern fellow humanists, who put aside the religious conflict of their respective churches and united in their common faith in classical letters. Sometimes the Byzantine refugees were even flattered by their Western hosts as being the descendants of the ancient Greeks. "This is the second death of Homer and Plato," exclaimed the humanist pope, Pius II, upon receiving the news of Constantinople's fall to the Turks.[18] However, such utterances were fleeting expressions of commiseration at best, and anti-Byzantine sentiments in the West were already surfacing as early as the fifteenth century. Cyriac of Ancona, the first classically inspired explorer of the Greek lands, in a poem rhapsodizing the glories of ancient Sparta, bemoaned its demise under what he saw as its Byzantine captivity.

> Not Rome, not Philip,
> But now, in Mystra here, a lowlier age
> Has brought you to Byzantine vassalage.[19]

Until the last decade of the fourteenth century, signs of Greek humanism in France were very sporadic. The nascent humanism in Paris was still infused with "ideas of the Middle Ages and was groping to orient itself toward the new currents coming from Italy."[20] The first Greek chair in Paris was awarded to the Italian humanist Gregorio di Citta di Castello, known as Tiphernate, in 1457. His tenure, however, ended in 1458. Thereafter those few individuals who wanted to study the language had no choice but to take lessons from the Greek Hermonymos, who, his incompetence notwithstanding, introduced it to such distinguished future Hellenists as Budé and Erasmus.

A more inspiring and enthusiastic bearer of Greek learning appeared when Charles VIII brought Janus Lascaris with him on his return voyage from Italy. Lascaris, a descendant of a prominent Byzantine family with imperial connections, left his native land shortly after the fall of Constantinople. In 1465 he began his studies at the University of Padua, and in 1475 he went to Florence, the center of Greek letters at that time, where he sought his fortune at the brilliant court of the Medicis. Lascaris embarked on a successful and dynamic career in the service of noblemen, kings, and popes at a time when political power and cultural prestige reinforced each other. During his twenty-year stay in Florence, he actively engaged in the dissemination of Greek learning. In 1489–90 and 1491–92 he was sent by the Medicis to the Levant to search for Greek manuscripts. Upon his return, he resumed his scholarly activities, this time as a director of the Medici library, which he helped enrich with his new acquisitions.

His erudition, linguistic skills, and knowledge of affairs in the Ottoman Empire spread his renown outside the confines of Florence. In November 1494, when Charles VIII entered Florence, he decided to enlist Lascaris's talents and invited him to come to France. Three French kings, Charles VIII, Louis XII, and Francis I, used Lascaris's diplomatic and literary skills intermittently from 1494 to 1529. Lascaris died in Italy in 1535 at the age of ninety. Toward the end of his life, his finances declined and he was forced to sell part of his substantial library.

When Lascaris arrived in Paris in 1494, he was received enthusiastically in the fledgling humanist circles because he was seen as a representative of the Italian Renaissance and a direct heir of Greek
classical learning. Although Lascaris's diplomatic duties never allowed
him to stay in Paris long enough to establish a Greek program, he
was always eager to promote Hellenic studies and help students of
his native tongue. He made a lasting impression on Budé, who
remembered with gratitude his Greek mentor, whom he had met in
1494. "Lascaris, for all his goodwill could not give me much assistance, seeing that he was generally with the court miles away from
Paris. . . . But, being a man of the most obliging nature, he gladly
did what he could so that he gave me some twenty lessons, and when
he was absent from Paris, he entrusted me with the custody of his
books."[21]

The most powerful impact of Italian humanist scholarship was
made by the Hellenist Girolamo Aleandro, who is considered the
founder of Greek studies in Paris. He offered his first course at the
university in 1509, choosing Plutarch as his main subject. Soon after,
in 1514, he ended his teaching career in Paris after putting Greek studies on a sound basis there.[22]

Guillaume Budé was the first distinguished French Hellenist. He
was born in Paris on 26 January 1468 into a prominent family that
had served the kings of France for three generations. When he was
fifteen years old, his father sent him to Orléans to study law, a task
he pursued with considerably less zeal and dedication than his amuse-
ments. After three years he returned to Paris, and for the next several
years the only progress he made was in the domain of pleasure-
seeking diversions. Finally his father obtained an appointment for
him at the royal college of notaries and secretaries. At this juncture—
he was now twenty-three—the serious student awakened within
him. Budé developed a passion for antiquity which he pursued assiduously for the rest of his life. Soon his classical studies took on a
Greek orientation under the influence of Lascaris, and his interest
was further stimulated when he visited Italy in 1501 and 1505 as an
emissary of Louis XII.

By 1508, Budé had acquired an undisputed linguistic competence
in classical languages and was widely admired for his extensive and
profound erudition. In that year his first work, *Annotationes in Pandectas,* was published. Budé aimed at an integrated understanding of

antiquity embracing language, customs, and institutions. *De Asse,* also a study of antiquity but of a more comprehensive scope, appeared in 1514. Budé injected into it a note of national pride by dedicating it "à l'honneur et fortune de France" and urging his compatriots to emulate the ancients and prove themselves worthy disciples of Minerva. A third work, *Institution du Prince,* was written in French between 1517 and 1519 for the edification and diversion of Francis I.[23] A considerable part of this instructional treatise consisted of apophthegms from Plutarch, whose popularity during the Renaissance was widespread. Students and rulers were the two groups who stood to learn the most from Plutarch's characters, whose virtues as well as vices were seen as lessons for all people and all ages.

Budé's contribution to French humanism cannot be emphasized too strongly. Not only was he the first important French Hellenist, but his scholarship, even at this early date, combined the three salient traits of Hellenism in Europe: linguistic and philological analysis, the study of antiquity as a distinct civilization, and a belief in the universality of its cultural and literary models and the efficacy of their imitation. Furthermore, like Erasmus, whose contemporary he was, Budé was one of the earliest humanists to place an equal value on the study of Greek and that of Latin and to believe that Latin scholarship was deficient without a knowledge of Greek.[24]

In addition to engaging in erudite pursuits, Budé also was instrumental in augmenting the collection of Greek manuscripts in the royal library. The first holdings of this collection were two dozen manuscripts pilfered by Charles VIII from the library of the king of Naples during the Italian campaigns. Books and art objects have often been some of the most valued spoils of war and conquest among "civilized" states, at least since the time of the Romans. By the time Francis I died in 1547, the royal library at Fontainebleau contained 546 Greek works, thanks largely to Budé's efforts, an impressive number considering that the collection had been started only in 1496. The search for and acquisition of antiquities had begun in earnest.

Sixteenth-century humanists contributed to the development of French letters by promoting Hellenism as a field of erudite studies and as a source of literary themes and genres. Their translations of Thucydides, Xenophon, Homer, and Sophocles, to mention but a few writers, expanded the scope of French thought. The most cele-

brated translation of the century was Amyot's *Vies de Plutarque*, commissioned by Francis I and completed in 1559. It posed a considerable
philological challenge and even more importantly, presented to the
French literary public some of the most renowned figures of antiquity. Plutarch's significance as a moralist and chronicler of prominent men of Greece and Rome was noted by Montaigne, who praised
Amyot "for having known . . . to choose such a worthy and timely
book as a present to his country."[25]

One difficulty these translators faced was the faithful and at the
same time natural rendition of the original texts into the French language. To achieve this they had to explore all its resources so as to
make it a suitable instrument for the expression of classical concepts
and locutions. Likewise, the poets of the Pléiade, especially Ronsard
and Du Bellay, in their efforts to regenerate poetry—by introducing
new themes and images, adopting new forms such as the ode, the
elegy, and the satire, and perfecting the formal aspects of their
poems—followed the humanist tradition of written composition by
resorting to classical modes and metrical schemes. This desire to
enrich the French language in order to express noble ideas and subtle
thoughts was articulated in Du Bellay's *Défense et illustration de la
langue française* (1549).

The poets of the Pléiade not only imitated the prosodic devices of
Greek poetry but also found renewed inspiration and revitalizing
stimulation in its myths and legends. The first presentation of the
Greek myths in the West was Boccaccio's *Genealogy of the Gods*. Jean
Lemaire de Belges (c. 1473–1525), who was influenced by Italian literature, popularized classical mythology in France in his *Illustrations
de Gaule et singularités de Troie*, a fanciful composition of fabulous
narratives. Ronsard invested his treatment of mythological themes
with his characteristic intensity and enthusiasm. His divinities came
indiscriminately from the Greek, Roman, and Egyptian pantheons,
but his vibrant imagination clothed them in brilliant colors and
infused them with pulsating emotions.[26] The form and content of
the works of Ronsard and his contemporaries illustrate that the legacy of Hellenism as a fount of aesthetic, moral, and poetic guidance
and inspiration took root in France during the sixteenth century.
The conscious imitation of classical models was efficacious because
it combined with the exuberant dynamism of the Renaissance to produce works of creative originality.

The seventeenth century, heir to the vast body of Renaissance classical scholarship, made good use of it. The French dramaturgists of the classical era found in the myths and fables of the ancient world a powerful metaphor for the inner struggles, moral conflicts, and metaphysical quest of human beings. Racine in his tragedies made the legendary heroes and heroines more complex and therefore more human without diminishing their mythical aura. It was one of those rare moments of perfect harmony when the figures and images of one literary tradition expressed the psychological and artistic needs of another. This delicate balance, which was sustained in the masterpieces of Racine and Corneille, resulted not from the suppression of tensions but from the imposition of aesthetic harmony and moral order on violent passions, thus preventing them from exploding into chaotic disorder. This equilibrium "was a temporary pause, when a truce, wholly unlooked for, was entered into by the opposing forces, an entirely unpredictable reconciliation. This phenomenon was what is called . . . the revival of the classical spirit, and the fruit of it was peace and tranquil strength."[27]

The classical spirit of harmony, simplicity, and order inevitably pervaded the aesthetic precepts of that era. Their ultimate formulation and codification was Boileau's *Art poétique* (1674), in which he dictated the rules of poetic composition, emphasizing the conformity of artistic creation to the laws of nature, governed by clear and eternal principles. Boileau's poetics, however, is much more than technical advice to poets. It is the distillation of the classical concepts of the relation between poetry and nature and between art and science. "The genres and types of art correspond to the genera and species of natural objects; the former like the latter have their immutable and constant forms, their specific shape and function to which nothing can be added and nothing taken away."[28] Reason is the only arbiter of these correspondences and the surest means by which one can arrive at the essence of things behind the multiplicity of forms, at the universal constants behind the individual incidentals. Thus, two centuries after the energetic and systematic integration of classical works into the Western intellectual tradition by the Renaissance humanists, the seventeenth and to a large extent the eighteenth centuries conceived of classicism as the ordering principle uniting truth, beauty, and reason.

The consonance between classical literary forms and modern experience lost its vitality in the eighteenth century, however. Classical images and themes continued to be employed, and the theater adhered faithfully to the unities established by the preceding century. But gone were the convincing authenticity and the stirring poignancy of seventeenth-century drama. Intellectual discourse and inquiry into the individual's position in the universe and society, and not the poetic treatment of his passions, were the central concerns of the thinkers of the Enlightenment.

The eighteenth century displayed an ambivalent attitude toward classical antiquity, particularly ancient Greece, ranging from uncritical admiration to offhanded rejection. This seeming contradiction was the manifestation of the self-confidence of an age fully cognizant of its achievements and potential. The universality of classical forms so fervently espoused and codified in Boileau's *Art poétique* (1674) was disputed by Charles Perrault in his *Parallèles des anciens et des modernes* (1688–97), a four-volume comparative analysis of classical and contemporary cultures and arguably the first manifesto of modernism. Although Perrault did not initiate the debate between the proponents of the timeless validity of classical models and the defenders of the dynamism and complexity of modern culture, he gave it its most clear articulation and potent thrust, and he even baptized it as the *querelle des anciens et des modernes*.

In their arguments the partisans of the two camps explicitly and implicitly posed three pivotal questions: How could originality and creativity be reconciled with obedience to immutable rules? What was the relation between past and present? Were art and literature a reflection of nature? The proponents of the ancients equated culture with nature. Since antiquity had imitated nature the best, they argued, it was incumbent upon modern civilization to emulate it if it aspired to reach the same heights. Despite overt changes, the basic literary and philosophical structures, according to them, remain constant, and therefore what was best in the past continues to be so in the present, and the genius of today is not much different from the genius of yesterday. The moderns, on the other hand, saw humanity in an incessant state of transformation brought about by physical as well as historical forces. The present, in their view, was the direct beneficiary of the cumulative experience of the past, and consequently "human nature revealed in contemporary works was in fact much richer and more complex than that in the literature of antiquity."[29]

The polemics of the *querelle des anciens et des modernes* eventually subsided, but the tensions it unveiled remained and to a large extent were reflected in the ambivalence of eighteenth-century thinkers toward ancient Greece.

Still, a knowledge of the classics was deemed to be a necessary part of their education. Classical ideas and themes reached them through various channels, and even though they were committed to the present, they took pride in and received guidance from their knowledge of the past. They were "cultivated men [living] in a cultivated age" when learning, wit, and cultural refinement were a mark of distinction.[30] Their study of the classics, however, was not a mere display of erudition or an intellectual game. Their appreciation of the ancients may have lacked the zest and exhilaration of the Renaissance writers, but the questing spirit of the humanists lived on. In both cases the individual was assigned a central place in the world, and classical antiquity was seen as a milieu most conducive to the full development of human abilities.[31] The philosophes emphasized this even more than had the sixteenth-century humanists, who did not dwell on the differences between the pre-Christian and Christian modes of thinking and did not repudiate their Christian heritage.

During the Enlightenment this contrast was thought of as a historical reality. The philosophes saw the progress of civilization alternating between periods of asceticism, superstition, and intolerance, and epochs that affirmed the beauty of the human body and the power of the human mind. It is their merit to have perceived the distinction between the religious and the scientific, rational mentalities.[32]

History, as an investigative tool of the past, was refined by seventeenth- and eighteenth-century historians, who insisted on the authenticity of texts, supplementing their information with other sources such as inscriptions and coins. This became possible because the new humanism was no longer the exclusive domain of university teachers but was fostered by learned societies and antiquarians, who preferred traveling to the emendation of texts and who collected all sorts of items connected with the past.[33] At this time history as a vision of the past "was above all a means of freeing men . . . from superstition, from routine and, as far as possible, from the brute force of circumstance by revealing them to themselves as responsible agents, creators of themselves, of their institutions . . . and of all existing or possible explanations of the universe."[34]

Within this historical framework the Greeks were considered to
be the fathers of civilization, not because their accomplishments
were unsurpassed but because theirs was a model secular culture free
from the ordained thinking of scriptural dogma. For the philosophes the value of the Greeks meant the primacy of reason and philosophy and the individual's freedom to direct and shape one's personal destiny rather than to submit to a predetermined one. To the
Greeks belonged the honor of discovering the mind and harnessing
the irrational. Thus Greece, in Condorcet's words, became "the bene-
factor and guide of all nations, of all ages."[35]

While classical ideas and philosophy received a serious though not
always approving examination by the intellectual leaders of the
Enlightenment, themes and images from Greek mythology held a particular charm for the refined and urbane French society of that time.
In a milieu of social affability where the cultivation of wit and subtlety was accompanied by a search for pleasurable diversions, paganism found a new appeal. Its image was no longer that of an exuberant
force flowing through human creativity but a panorama of little
cupids, nymphs, and frivolous divinities draped in diaphanous veils
and engaged in amorous activities.[36] Venus was one of the most popular goddesses, and "she springs from blithe hearts as she did from
foamy waters in times past."[37] This visual depiction of pagan scenes
gratified the senses, pleased the aesthetic sensibilities, and enveloped
the viewer in an aura of glowing charm and discreet sensuality.

As in literature—especially tragedy, where the protagonists retained classical names but had very little or none of the forcefulness
and complexity of the characters of seventeenth-century drama—so
in the visual arts mythological figures were little more than decorative motifs. The function of art was no longer the affirmation and
glorification of central authority but the satisfaction of the caprices
of self-indulging patrons. The diminished, almost miniature size of
these figures was indicative of their reduced moral force. "The gods
of this art," in Starobinski's words, "have nothing mysterious about
them. What painters and sculptors sought to represent was not the
essence of any awe-inspiring divinity, but merely the outward attributes assigned them by tradition—a repertory of attitudes, clothing
and accessories chosen and arranged according to the requirements
of the decoration."[38]

The weakening of the primacy and uniqueness of classical mythology was also reflected in serious mythographical studies as they evolved in the eighteenth century. In these works the gods of the ancient Greeks were placed within the context of primitive religion, and thus they were equated with the deities of recently discovered aboriginal peoples. As travel accounts began to pour into Europe from the New World, the religious practices of the natives provided new material for comparative religious studies. The perceived parallels between ancient Greek idolatry and the contemporary practices of fetishism and magic reinforced the assumption that distinguished "between the superstitious mind and the enlightened mind, a timeless divide."[39]

This devitalized portrayal of Greek mythology did not signal its demise as a source of literary and artistic motifs. Imitation of antique forms continued unabated. The popular styles and tastes of the fashionable Parisian beau monde in the second half of the eighteenth century were replete with classical designs. Grimm, a reliable witness of his time, noted this phenomenon in a letter written in 1763. "For some years now, antique ornaments and forms have been highly sought after; taste has benefited considerably, and the fashion of antiquity has become so widespread that every thing today is made *à la grecque*. The interior and exterior decoration of buildings, furniture, fabrics, jewelry of all kinds, everything in Paris is *à la grecque.*"[40]

The excessive refinements of a polished society with the intricacies of its mannerisms and distractions caused an adverse reaction at the end of the eighteenth century, which led some individuals to seek a more frugal, simple, and virtuous way of life. To them Greek and Roman antiquity was not so much the polemical instrument it was for the philosophes as it was a moral force and a guide to ethical conduct. They envisioned a society made up of righteous and vigorous individuals dedicated to the common good, not to the satisfaction of personal needs and appetites.

Rousseau, the most articulate and impassioned exponent of this view of antiquity before the French Revolution, though not a stranger to the life of the salons, was never at ease with their set code of behavior and precious manners. Not a hermit by nature, he sought a direct and transparent communion with others unencumbered by dissimulation and artifice. Eager to denounce the distorting influences of luxury and affectation, he found comfort in such ancient authors as

Plutarch, Tacitus, and Seneca. Plutarch especially provided him with moral and intellectual nourishment from his childhood.[41] At a very early age, free and unconstrained by a rigid schedule, he indulged in the perusal of sentimental novels and then discovered the *Lives of Famous Men* of Plutarch. What an exaltation to find himself transported to the glorious days of the Greek and Roman republics and to imagine himself among their most renowned men.

> Plutarch especially became my favorite reading. My addiction to novels was somewhat cured by the pleasure I felt in reading him incessantly; and I soon began to prefer Agesilaus, Brutus, and Aristides to Orondate, Artamène, and Juba. These interesting readings and the conversations they occasioned between me and my father formed this free and republican spirit, this indomitable and proud character . . . which has tormented me my entire life. . . . Ceaselessly occupied with Rome and Athens, I myself the offspring of a republic, . . . I thought of myself as a Greek or a Roman; I became the character whose life I was reading.[42]

Plutarch's appeal was not merely a juvenile preoccupation; it was a lifelong pursuit: "It was the first reading of my childhood, it will be the last one of my old age," wrote Rousseau.[43]

For Rousseau, the didactic, moralizing influence of the ancients extended beyond the conduct of the individual and embraced the moral fabric and political character of the entire society. In this context the antithesis between Athens and Sparta was most instructive. These two poleis illustrated the opposition between a refined and cultivated city given to sophistry and the vain pursuit of luxury and pleasure, and a virtuous, simple, and temperate republic. In his *Discours sur les sciences et les arts*, the praise of the sober and frugal Spartans and the castigation of the effete Athenians reflected Rousseau's attitude toward his own social milieu and his search for true felicity for mankind. In his view classical Greece should not be emulated as the place where the arts flourished and philosophy and science developed. Rather, the early age, when heroes trod the earth, and later Sparta, where superfluous learning was shunned, were Greece's true contributions. Sparta alone, by the purity of its morals and the physical and military prowess of its citizens, did not succumb to this wave of decadence.

Should I forget that it was in the very heart of Greece that this City, as famous for its felicitous ignorance as it was for its wise laws, rose . . . ? O Sparta! eternal opprobrium of a vain doctrine! While the vices brought about by the Arts were penetrating Athens, . . . you were chasing away from your walls the Arts and the Artists, the Sciences and the Savants.[44]

The antithesis between the two ancient Greek poleis representing two opposed social systems was not a new one. The appeal of the Spartan ideal, with its insistence on military prowess, communal dedication and stern regulation of individual conduct, was strongest during times of cultural change and realignment of social and political forces. Two such eras were the Renaissance and the second half of the eighteenth century. The former saw in such Spartan figures as Agesilaus, Lycurgus, and Lysander, so vividly portrayed by Plutarch, admirable prototypes for the moral and political education of their rulers. For the latter half of the eighteenth century, particularly the revolutionary period, the most appealing features of laconism were its austere manners, its spirit of egalitarianism, the authority of the elders, the unforgiving treatment of those who dared to deviate from its dictates, and the education of the young in the hands of the state.[45]

The debate concerning the rivalry between mercantile, cosmopolitan Athens and militaristic, inward-looking Sparta became more intense during the second half of the eighteenth century. The ascendancy of the latter over the former in the estimation of such thinkers as Rousseau was emblematic of the reaction against the doctrine of progress according to which man advanced gradually from the tenebrous crudeness of the state of nature to the enlightened understanding and conscious control of himself and of his world. The opponents of this belief saw this same stage of the state of nature as "the golden age" of humanity "when man lived in harmony with the world, with his fellow men, and with himself."[46] Both camps, however, had this in common: in their endeavor to grasp the meaning of history, they went beyond the examination of individual events and made "the idea of civilization . . . the main theme of history";[47] they both used Greek antiquity to fortify their respective arguments about the origin of civilization.

Rousseau's tribute to Sparta expressed a desire for moderation and sobriety felt by many of his contemporaries. With the advent of the French Revolution, a more austere paganism emerged. The revolutionaries in their reforming zeal found in the example of the ancient republics models for emulation. The process of identification with the ancients, which had been a literary and philosophical exercise until then, now became a conscious moral imperative for them.

From the time of the *fêtes gallantes* to the clash of arms on the battlefields of the French Revolution, the Greek world provided a wide repertoire of themes, images, and standards whose appeal varied from generation to generation and from group to group. The pendulum of selection swung from an elegant and urbane Hellas to an austere and virtuous one, from Athens to Sparta. Pressed for time and unable to replace the old order with a new one, the revolutionaries looked to the Greco-Roman republics as prototypes of liberty and patriotism. Furthermore, their revolution was not going to create a brave new world by rushing into untried social and political schemes; rather, it would bring about a restitution of a nobler era in Europe's past. They did not indict and reject the past; rather, they affirmed its validity as a guide steering them away from corruption and toward the already charted path of liberty, justice, and fraternity; they were the builders and not the destroyers of history.

The revolutionaries' association with the ancients was based on a perceived—or rather, imagined—moral affinity with them. Their view, therefore, was predicated on their own self-image and sense of mission: they were not the inferiors of the Greeks and the Romans but their equals. After all, did they not win their own Marathons and promote excellence on the battlefield as well as in the exercise of justice and equality? Utilitarian and sublimating all at once, the cult of antiquity among the French revolutionaries served as a guide toward the realization of their envisioned new society, which combined elements of religious fervor and totalitarian regimentation.[48]

While they could no longer receive the benediction of the church—nor did they desire to—they nevertheless felt the need of the sanction of a higher authority for the founding of a new era. They believed that the symbols and emblems of the ancient republics, hallowed by history, would confer sacrality on the secular. "A society instituting itself must sacralize the very deed of institution."[49]

Echoing Rousseau's views, the revolutionaries placed Sparta above Athens in terms of moral stature and social organization. As such, it could serve as a model for educational and legislative reform. During a debate on education at the National Convention, Ducos praised

Lycurgus and his laws regulating the upbringing of the young. "It is not to the oath that Lycurgus extracted from Lacedaemon that this extraordinary people owed the stability of their happiness and laws; rather, it is to the attention he gave to the upbringing of the young, who, so to speak, sucked the love of their country with their mother's milk."[50] Aspiring to instill the same virtues in French youth, the Committee of Public Instruction proposed a program that would have children lodged together in *maisons d'éducation,* where they would be brought up under the aegis of the state.[51] Reaching out to encompass the whole body politic and create a virtuous citizenry, they undertook radical and stern reforms similar to those instituted by Lycurgus. In a politically tumultuous era, the stability of Lacedaemon was an enviable example, and it was often invoked in order to sanction harsh measures.

Despite the encomiums addressed to the Spartan tradition, however, these pronouncements were more impressive as rhetorical exhortations, which were seldom translated into a concerted effort to model the new France on the example of a small city-state. Athenian democracy, the criticism of its weaknesses and corruptibility notwithstanding, "becomes more acceptable than ever before," and "the detailed proposals appended are not very Spartan and indeed the education received by Solon is described as all that be desired."[52]

The revolutionary leaders, however, sensed that to mobilize as many people as possible and convert them to the new creed, they needed to appeal more to their emotions than to their reason. To this end they used art as a way of inculcating probity and arousing civic ardor. Episodes and figures from antiquity were chosen for their edifying value. Venus and her playful cupids gave way to the more austere divinities of Virtue, Truth, Innocence, and Victory. David fused perfectly these didactic and aesthetic precepts in his art. His rigid and proud figures emanating vigor and single-minded determination were enveloped by an unadorned and incandescent atmosphere of stark and icy colors. The sparse background of Doric columns and classical furniture was a fitting décor for his heroic personages. Not only did David borrow historical themes from antiquity, but also, he organized his subjects in vertical and horizontal planes similar in composition to ancient friezes and bas-reliefs.

David's artistic gifts were put to direct use by Robespierre in the planning and orchestration of the Feast of the Supreme Being, the most spectacular celebration in a series of public festivals. These communal gatherings, which were held in France in 1790 to arouse and galvanize dedication to the ideals of the Revolution, "would celebrate a new transparency; hearts would hide no more secrets, communication would be completely free of obstacles."[53] The enthusiasm generated by such spectacles of planned spontaneity was an attempt to sweep away established outward forms and replace them with a new but not original order reminiscent of "the fairest days of Lacedaemon." Although the participating masses were not consciously reenacting a classical institution, their leaders and organizers were purposely imitating what they imagined was the practice of the ancient republics. In this context, Greece was admired not for promoting individual excellency but for strengthening the civil bonds of its citizens through the display of collective dedication. "Greece was there," declared Robespierre, "one saw . . . the people who had been victorious over Asia, and whose republican virtues had raised them at times above humanity. One saw the great men who had saved and distinguished the country . . . whose mere presence was a lesson in magnanimity, justice and in patriotism."[54]

The early impact of these celebrations was powerful and uplifting. Immersed in an atmosphere of pomp and ritual reverberating with the sounds of martial hymns and suffused with the fragrance of burning incense, both participants and spectators were swept away by emotions heightened by what must have been felt as the moment of untainted beginning. The use of classical motifs and decorations was an attempt at a revival of both the form and the spirit of antiquity. It was a visual statement of the conviction that the form can and does create the essence. "In the public ceremonies," remarked Delecluse, "one could see the high priests like Calchas, young girls like those on the friezes of the Parthenon, and, more than once, I saw resin burning . . . in front of a cardboard temple copied after those at Paestum."[55]

The initial success of these festivals was such that it was deemed desirable to organize them on a more permanent basis. Rabaut offered a formal plan to the National Convention stressing their didactic function. He would have each canton construct a national temple where all citizens would assemble each Sunday. There the reading of the declaration of human rights, the singing of patriotic hymns, the performance of gymnastic and military exercises, and a constant evaluation of the young by their elders would establish the symbols and rituals of a new faith and hierarchy. Then France, like Plutarch's Sparta, would be assured of the dedication of its people.[56]

However, once these outbursts of patriotic zeal reached their peak, they quickly subsided and people had to cope with the harsh realities of life. It was soon realized that enthusiasm was but a fleeting passion and could not be institutionalized. Classically inspired festivals were an alien phenomenon and could not be transplanted easily onto French soil. Yet the demand for uncompromising devotion to the Revolution did not abate. As revolutionary fervor culminated in the excesses of the Terror, the exercise in republican virtue was to be pursued pitilessly. The more intense the fanaticism, the narrower the concept of classical Greece became. Solon, the Athenian lawgiver, was considered too moderate and indulgent. Lycurgus's unyielding measures, on the other hand, seemed more suitable. Billaud Varennes voiced this stand: "Citizens, the inflexible austerity of Lycurgus became in Sparta the unshakeable base of the Republic; the weak and trusting character of Solon plunged Athens again into slavery: this parallel encapsulates the whole science of government."[57]

Rhetoric and eloquence were highly prized as useful political instruments. Drawing on their classical education, based on the humanist tradition, many revolutionary orators embellished their arguments with images and figures borrowed from antiquity. The same imitative process was manifested in the adoption of classical names. Many revolutionary leaders changed their Christian names to those of illustrious ancients so as to disassociate themselves from the vestiges of royalism, aristocracy, and Catholicism. Such names as Aristides, Socrates, Phocion, Cato, and Brutus became more and more common. Those who chose them believed they were partaking of the qualities attributed to their Greek and Roman bearers. To complete the illusion of resurrecting the purity and simplicity of antiquity, the revolutionaries undertook to create around themselves a classical décor. Statues and busts of ancient lawmakers and republican figures decorated the Hall of the Assembly. Regimented discipline and solemnity in politics were paralleled by the adoption of a simpler apparel *à l'antique*. Instead of the elaborate, jewelry-laden costumes, the chlamys was displayed as the proper attire.

The cult of antiquity had of course preceded the revolutionaries. The philosophes had seen in it the triumph of reason and the preeminence of the intellect. But their critical spirit and belief in progress had steered them away from a slavish imitation of it. What was new with the revolutionaries was their desire to materialize what had preexisted as a vague state of mind. For them the classical past had a concrete function: it provided them with models whose prestige and unquestioned superiority fired the imagination and whose authority sanctioned harsh acts. Furthermore, now that the idols of the immediate past had been willfully shattered, a respectable substitute had to be found—and what could be more honorable than classical tradition? Perhaps more important was a perceived affinity with the classical republics: they both stood at the threshold of a new world, innocent, natural, and robust.

More thoughtful and prudent men perceived the fruitlessness of this attempt and its lack of historical perspective: "It is not enough for a system to appear escorted by illustrious names and to have as patrons Minos, Plato, and Lycurgus . . . ; it must first of all be informed by the immense difference that exists between the small city of Sparta, which contained perhaps twenty-five thousand individuals, and this vast empire, which has twenty-five million."[58] Different cultures interact and interpenetrate each other, but no culture can embody another one in its entirety.

The Aesthetic Appeal of Hellenism

The search for visual stimulation and the emphasis on sensory perception—on the "moment sensible," as Poulet characterized it—were important trends in the art and literature of the eighteenth century. When applied to the apprehension of the ancients, they fostered the presentation and reproduction of *l'antiquité figurée*. Artists and writers looked at it as a source of graphic and pictorial images. Moreover, within the context of science, which was constituted then as a systematic method for the exploration of the world, archeology became an important tool of investigation complementing historical and philological inquiries.

One of the leading figures in this field was Anne-Claude, comte de Caylus, a member of the Académie de peinture et de sculpture. Through his prestige and knowledge he exerted considerable influence on art and sculpture by advocating the imitation of classical sub-jects.[59] In his *Recueil d'antiquités* he gave exact reproductions of mon-uments to which he had access. The underlying principle of his theory was the continuous evolution of art and its integral relation to the literature and culture of its milieu; they are all facets of the onward movement of civilization. "The monuments of antiquity lead to the expansion of knowledge. They explain unusual practices; they clarify obscure facts, . . . they put the progress of the Arts under our eyes, and they serve as models to those who cultivate them."[60] Caylus's work embraced Egyptian, Etruscan, Greek, and Roman antiquity, in that order. His personal tastes and predilec-tions, however, led him to favor the Greeks. In acclaiming their artis-tic superiority, he distinguished them clearly from their predeces-sors, the Egyptians, and from the Romans, who followed them. "The Greeks moved away from the example of the Egyptians, who had a taste for the grand and the prodigious. They scaled down the massive in order to add elegance and harmony in the details. . . . Finally, the Greeks brought about the perfection of the Arts, whose object is to please by imitating nature."[61]

Like Caylus, Julien David Leroy embraced the idea of the contin-uous development of art and architecture which reached their perfec-tion at the hands of the Greeks. In his view, while they were indebted to the Egyptians, they applied different principles, which led to the establishment of a clear system of orders. The Greeks were superior to the civilizations of the Near East, Leroy maintained, and their ar-chitecture remained unsurpassed by the Romans. "In the end, it is apparent that the Romans lacked this creative spirit, which had enabled the Greeks to make so many discoveries; they imagined nothing of consequence in regard to the orders."[62] In placing the Greeks above the Romans, Caylus and Leroy articulated a changing perspective, which differentiated the two ancient cultures, associating the first with creative imagination and clear thinking and the second with legislative genius and a more mature historical consciousness.

Leroy's appreciation of Greek art and architecture was not purely textual. In May 1754 he set out on a journey to the Levant, which took him first to Constantinople and, in February 1755, to Athens. In visiting the latter city, he had a specific goal: to sketch its monu-ments from close up. His drawings constituted the pictorial aspect of his *Ruines des plus beaux monuments de la Grèce, considérées du côté de l'histoire et du côté de l'architecture* (2d ed., 1758). In the accompanying text he related historical developments to the evolution of architectural forms. His illustrations, despite their skill and grace, were fanciful recreations of the monuments. Although they were intended as visual records of the state of antiquities, they were at the same time a pictorial statement of the ubiquitous contrast between past and present. Groups of natives dressed in their picturesque costumes occupy the foreground. They are engaged in playful activities recalling the merry insouciance of the *fêtes champêtres*.

Whereas Caylus and Leroy traced the history and evolution of ancient art and architecture, Winckelmann formulated their aesthetic interpretation. His theories were received enthusiastically in France because they were confluent with current artistic views and tastes. Order, harmony, and nobility, key elements for the understanding of classical art in Winckelmann's opinion, were also qualities highly regarded by eighteenth-century French critics. Winckelmann's doctrine of the beau idéal embodied their own concept of beauty. This was not the beauty of energy, vigor, and movement contained within symmetrically proportioned figures but the beauty of smooth, undulating muscles, smiling faces, and polished surfaces. In Winckelmann's judgment the quintessence of Greek sculpture was *Apollo Belvedere*, a Roman copy of a Hellenistic statue. His encomium of it reflects the views of a whole generation of French neoclassicists on Greek art.

> To feel all the merit of this artistic masterpiece, one must be infused with intellectual beauty and must become, if possible, creator of a celestial nature, because there is nothing mortal in it, nothing that is subject to human need. . . . At the sight of this marvel of art, I forget the entire universe and my mind reaches a supernatural disposition, which enables it to judge it with dignity. My admiration is transformed into extasis.[63]

How did Greek sculptors achieve this expression of calm, almost transcendental nobility? In Winckelmann's view they exercised economy and discipline combined with a keen observation of nature. Absence of tension and agitation resulted in the portrayal of tranquility. If the Greeks were consummate artists, it was due, above all, to a process of idealization and abstraction which combined the most beautiful parts of individual bodies. Thus, "from this choice of the most beautiful forms, blended, so to speak, together, there arose a new conception in the mind of the artists, a kind of a nobler being, whose supreme idea, fruit of the contemplation of the beautiful, led to that of permanent youth" (1:368).

Classical Greece was associated with harmony, grace, and nobility in art and with a pristine and vivid imagination in poetry. In the age of Louis XVI, however, poetic inspiration was overshadowed by philosophical discourse and scientific inquiry. Emotions were expressed more stirringly in prose than in poetry. *La Nouvelle Héloïse* and *Paul et Virginie* explored the realm of feelings and unfulfilled yearnings more poignantly than contemporary poetry. In this general weakening of the poetic impulse, André Chénier was a fresh and refreshing voice of genuine lyricism. Because of his untimely death at the hands of the revolutionaries in 1794 at the age of thirty-one, his poems remained largely unknown during his time. It was Chateaubriand who first brought them to the attention of the public in a note in his *Génie du christianisme*. Sensing an aesthetic and emotional kinship with the poet, Chateaubriand discerned and admired in him a delicate sensibility and a melancholy solitude.

Although the Romantics saw in Chénier a kindred spirit tormented by moral isolation, fear of death, and the despair of love, he was not a stranger to his own time.[64] His vision of antiquity made him a part of his age. In his poetry many of the diffuse elements of eighteenth-century Hellenism crystallized. Of the two prevalent currents of Hellenism—one envisioning a polished and sophisticated Greece and the other a moral and austere one—Chénier was attracted to the former. He imagined an enchanting and glittering setting where poetic imagination communed directly with nature. His was a Hellenism that combined poetic emotion with erudition. For this reason he chose to emulate not the Greek lyricists but the Alexandrian poets of elegies, idylls, eclogues, and epigrams. Some of the Hellenistic poets whose works he admired were Theocritus, Moschos, Bion, and Meleager, all of them distinguished for their learning and subtlety as well as for the harmony and regularity of their verses.

Chénier's affinities with Greece were not merely literary but more intimate and personal. He was born in Constantinople in 1762 where his father was a commercial attaché to the French embassy. His mother, Elizabeth, although of Levantine origin, thought of herself as a Greek, a heritage she identified with and was exceedingly proud of. André inherited from her a lasting love for things Greek and yearned to see the place of his birth, which he had left at the age of three. In the fall of 1785 he visited Italy in the company of some friends with the intention of going on to Constantinople. He expressed his excitement and anticipation in verses that show how deeply conscious he was of his double heritage.

> Let's leave, the sail is ready, and Byzantium is calling me
>
> . . . .
>
> Greetings, Gods of Euxine, Hellespont, Sestos, and Abydos,
> And Nymph of Bosphorus and Nymph of Propontis,
> Who today see the oppressive crescent
> Of the barbarous Osmanli reach its nadir.
>
> . . . .
>
> Greetings, Thrace, my mother, and the mother of Orpheus,
> Galata, that my eyes for so long have been yearning to see.
>
> [Partons, la voile est prête, et Byzance m'appelle
>
> . . . .
>
> Salut, Dieux de l'Euxin, Helle, Sestos, Abyde,
> Et Nymphe du Bosphore, et Nymphe Propontide,
> Qui voyez aujourd'hui du barbare Osmanlin
> Le croissant oppresseur toucher à son déclin;
>
> . . . .
>
> Salut, Thrace, ma mère, et la mère d'Orphée,
> Galata, que mes yeux désiraient dès longtemps.[65]

Although the anxiously awaited voyage did not materialize, Chénier's love for Greece remained undiminished. Mythological themes, images, and figures were the most persistent influences in his poetry. His imitation of ancient writers, however, was grounded more on aesthetic considerations than on a desire to resuscitate their era. He, perhaps more than any other literary figure of this time, was aware of the "cleavage between the rational and the aesthetic ways of apprehending and ordering experience which was widening through-out the eighteenth century."[66] He understood that different eras of culture bring with them new moral and artistic sensibilities.

> Everything has changed for us, morals, science, and customs.
> Why then must we so painfully try
> What we have read to tell and retell time after time?

[Tout a changé pour nous, moeurs, sciences, coutumes.
Pourquoi donc nous faut-il un penible soin,
Dire et dire cent fois ce que nous avons lu?][67]

Yet invention, progress, and novel ways of apprehending reality need not dictate a complete rupture with the past. Classical antiquity especially, with its aesthetic models, the amplitude of its literary figures and fables, could, if creatively used, be a vehicle for new sentiments and attitudes. By *invention* Chénier did not suggest a venture into new and unexplored horizons but a rediscovery of old forms adapted to new modes of thinking. Thus the past would not dominate the present, but the two would interact and enrich each other.

> Let's change into our honey their ancient flowers;
> In order to paint our ideas, let's borrow their colors;
> Let's light our torches from their poetic embers;
> On new ideas let's make ancient verses.

> [Changeons en notre miel leurs plus antiques fleurs;
> Pour peindre notre idée, empruntons leur couleurs;
> Allumons nos flambeaux à leurs feux poétiques;
> Sur des pensers nouveaux faisons des vers antiques.][68]

This declaration of faith in the enduring value of ancient, particularly Greek, poetic tradition places him within the literary framework established by the Alexandrians, who had absorbed the poetic composition of the ancients by studying and compiling their rhetorical formulas and prosodic devices. Like them, he was a derivative poet whose inspiration was guided and shaped by erudition.

Ancient literature lent him not only its metrical schemes but also a poetic landscape. If the setting was borrowed, however, the voice that brought it to life was personal and authentic. The ponderousness and pedantry that stifled the poetry of his contemporaries were absent from his. Instead of fatuous images and trite formulas tediously repeated, he created exquisitely fashioned verses tinged with glowing colors and reverberating with melodious sounds. His bucolic poems were complete scenes in which the drama of love was enacted. Mortals and immortals alike were engaged in amorous games and explorations. Their names were chosen for both their mythological associations and their sonorous qualities, which en-

hanced their delicate beauty. For Chénier, love was not the pursuit
of a transcendental ideal, placing its object on a pedestal, but a
source of pleasure leading to a fuller experience of life. The plastic
beauty of the human body fascinated him, and he attached no guilt
to the enjoyment of physical pleasures. However, the voluptuousness of his poetic characters, though well within the eroticism of the
eighteenth century, was always discreet and delicate because love was
depicted as an experience leading to physical as well as spiritual
maturity and fulfillment.

Chénier's admiration for nature was intense but not simple and
spontaneous. His response to it, as to art and poetry, was an instinctive appreciation of beauty conditioned and guided by learning.
Thus in his poems nature, whether used metaphorically or depicted
directly, participated in or at least echoed the human activities it witnessed. Its role was not that of an indifferent bystander or a pleasing
spectacle but that of an animated presence resounding the fleeting
utterances of passing beings.

> Flowers, resonant groves, swaying reeds,
> Where Zephyr murmurs in the murmuring waters,
> Speak, is fair Mnazile in your shade?
> I often listen and the wind wailing in your woods
> Brings his voice to my ear from afar.
>
> [Fleurs, bocages sonores, et mobiles roseaux,
> Où murmure Zephyre au murmure des eaux,
> Parlez, le beau Mnazile est-il sous vos ombrages?
> Souvent j'écoute et l'air qui gémit dans vos bois,
> A mon oreille du loin vient apporter sa voix.][69]

The landscape of Chénier's poetry consisted of pastoral scenes and
sea images as well. The setting of his voyages was the Greek Mediterranean. Those who undertook them had Greek names, and their destinations were solitary ventures leading to sudden death. This, like all
of Chénier's landscapes, was an imaginary *mise en scène* in which the
sea became a treacherous tomb engulfing young maidens, as in "Tar-
antine," or adventurous young men, as in "Dryas." In answering the
call of the voyage, Chénier's poetic characters were responding to an
inner yearning propelling them to seek completion in the outer
reaches of the universe. The sudden death that awaited them was a

poetic testimony to the impossibility of achieving this completeness and to the tragedy of human life, which is destined to repeat indefinitely this search without ever sighting its longed-for haven.

Although Chénier's fictional characters were complex metaphors for the predicament of human existence, they were not abstract, one-dimensional figures. The gods and goddesses, the shepherds and shepherdesses who populated his pastoral and elegiac poems were infused with a life of their own. Their tone was plaintive and soft, never abrasive and harsh. Their physical charm was drawn in vivid detail, and they were animated with a refreshing innocence and unaffected gracefulness. Nevertheless, they were ethereal beings gliding almost imperceptibly from the realm of love to that of death without a struggle against the realities of existence.

In a similar manner his Hellenism was not an attempt to replicate ancient Greece. His love and admiration for it enriched his literary world and satisfied his emotional and artistic needs. Since he did not aspire to resurrect the spirit of the ancients, he cannot be accused of falsifying and distorting the image of their civilization. Yet his vision was circumscribed by both current views of the Greek past and his personal predilections. What emerges from his poems is an elegant and refined antiquity, a combination of idyllic charm and glittering sumptuousness, not a dynamic civilization moving from primitive vigor to more subtle cultural forms.

Chénier's Hellenism belonged to the tradition initiated by the poets of the Renaissance, who viewed antiquity as a source of literary and aesthetic beauty. Like them, he rarely allowed the sad present of Greece to disfigure this timeless image. Although he was not unaware of or indifferent to the vicissitudes that had befallen it, he found solace in the belief that in the course of human destruction, the poet alone, with the magic of his word, can recreate and preserve the past.

> Temples, marbles, metals, where are you?
> Happier is your name, which through the bards' voice
> Has penetrated the darkness of envious night.

> [Temples, marbres, métaux, qu'êtes-vous devenus?
> Votre nom plus heureux, grâce aux chantres célèbres,
> De la nuit envieuse a percé les ténèbres.][70]

The blind poet in "L'Aveugle," obviously an allusion to Homer, personifies the destructibility of matter and the endurance of the word. Maltreated and ridiculed, the aged bard arrived on the Greek island of Syros. There he was received by three young, hospitable shepherds, who were anxiously waiting to hear his tales. Time and suffering had left marks of decay on his body, but his voice had remained intact. It seemed as if the essence of his whole being and his experience encompassing the past and present had been distilled in his voice. Gradually, a true metamorphosis took place: the vulnerable and perishable form was transformed through the power of the word and song, which conjured up a vision of the whole universe.

> Because in the long meanders of vagabond songs,
> He coupled the fertile seeds of everything,
> The principles of fire, of air, of water and earth,
> The rivers flowing from Jupiter's breast,
> The oracles, arts, and cities fraternal,
> And since the time of chaos all loves eternal.

> [Car en de longs détours de chansons vagabondes,
> Il enchaînait de tout les semences fécondes,
> Les principes du feu, les eaux, la terre et l'air,
> Les fleuves descendus du sein de Jupiter,
> Les oracles, les arts, les cités fraternelles,
> Et depuis le chaos les amours immortelles.][71]

Thus, men die, but their deeds survive. Likewise, civilizations are eclipsed after they have reached their zenith, but the memory of their accomplishments persists. The poet more than anyone else perpetuates this memory and indeed recreates the past and present through the power of incantation. Consequently, for Chénier, Greece the place was changeable, but Greece the idea and the literary tradition endured beyond the confines of time and space. In this respect he "granted the fundamental validity of the neoclassical reverence for the achievements of ancient writers."[72]

Greek mythology and the Hellenic pantheon influenced the works of other poets, but with less felicitous results. The abbé Jacques Delille, a descriptive and didactic poet of the Imperial school, exemplifies the superficial elegance associated with Hellenism. Attempting a vivid depiction of Greece, he succeeded only in creating a shadow of it in his poem *L'Imagination* (1806). A long and ambitious work, it aspired to embrace the processes of imagination and memory and their reciprocal relations with nature, art, and religion. What attracted Delille to Greek antiquity was the charm and beauty of its art, the liveliness and gaiety of its people, and the human proportions of its gods. The image of Greece that emerges from his verses is akin to that projected by Winckelmann.

Delille's acquaintance with Greece was not purely literary. When Marie-Gabriel, comte de Choiseul-Gouffier was appointed ambassador to Constantinople in 1784, the poet accompanied him as a member of his entourage. Their voyage to the Levant first took them to Athens, and, as with most visitors to this ancient city, they piously climbed the steep path to the Acropolis. Delille, like many a sentimental admirer of antiquity, expressed his wonderment in theatrical gestures. "We saw him kiss with respect," wrote one of his fellow travelers, "a Roman sarcophagus transformed into a fountain, fill his pockets with pieces of sculpted stones . . . kneel on the threshold of the Parthenon and embrace the columns with tears of emotion, under the stunned eyes of the Turkish guards."[73]

His personal contact with places that marked the rise of Hellenic civilization, however, elicited little more than melodramatic effusions in him. His muse thrived best in the comfortable atmosphere of the salons. There it was more receptive to stimuli reaching it from literary channels than from the immediate world of nature. The abstract and factitious character of his poetry attests to his lack of personal vision, a failing shared by many of his contemporaries.

In prose, just as in poetry, writers were attracted to Greek antiquity by the fictions of a gallant and idyllic life.[74] In the second half of the eighteenth century, there appeared a series of pseudo-Greek novels in which the Hellenic décor was banal, the prose full of platitudes, and the amorous adventures of the characters absurd. It sufficed to give Greek names to the hero and heroine, have the action take place in ancient Greece, and state that the Greek text was exhumed in some dust-covered library in Turkey in order to make the illusion complete. A sample of the titles of these works is indicative of their intrigue: *Les Amours de Lais* (1765), *Les Amours de Poliris et de Driphé* (1766), and *Les Amours de Choréas et de Callirhoé* (1763). The influence of *Daphnis and Chloe* was obvious.[75]

Montesquieu's *Temple de Gnide* and *Voyage à Paphos* were recre-

ations—or rather fabrications—of an eternally smiling antiquity.
More Roman than Greek in his tastes,[76] he was drawn to the Greek
myths not by their primal power but by their youthful charm and
playful enchantment. Diderot, on the other hand, was temperament-
ally more suited to grasp the complexity of the Greeks. He knew their
language and could read Homer in the original. He was stirred by the
intense and violent passions of the Homeric heroes and by their
imposing simplicity. He found Aeschylus "épique et gigantesque" at
a time when the Greek tragedian was little understood and even less
appreciated. In general, eighteenth-century Hellenism depicted ancient Greece as a curious mixture of pastoral bliss and simplicity, on
the one hand, and graceful, urbane refinement, on the other.

The same approach to antiquity was apparent in theatrical produc-
tions. From 1755 to 1780 about one hundred plays bearing classical
titles and exploiting classical themes were written and performed.
Lemercier's *Agamemnon*, performed in 1799, was a weak and soulless
reproduction of the Aeschylean prototype.

In the domain of criticism, eighteenth-century insights into Greek
literature and thought were circumscribed by the urbane predilections and the rational, analytical spirit of the time. Greek philosophical thought was often used as a source of arguments supporting the
principles of freedom of thought and secular humanism. Also, the
majority of the philosophes, who viewed Christianity with increasing suspicion, thought of the ancients as a people who, although
not free from superstition, had not experienced the intolerance of
a priestly class. Nevertheless, a lightness often characterized eighteenth-century views on Greek philosophical thought, and the philosophes "often spoke of the Greeks with great assurance without
really knowing them."[77] Faith in the progress of reason and science,
which had given rise to the *querelle des anciens et des modernes*, also
engendered a condescending attitude toward the Greek philosophers. Voltaire reflected this stance: "One must agree that reasonable
men who have just finished reading Locke's *Essay Concerning Human
Understanding* would ask Plato to go to his [Locke's] school."[78]

The rational spirit of the age also guided the appraisal of Greek literature. In it flowed two streams of thought: on the one hand, some
critics expressed the opinion that Greek literature was often marred
by mythological absurdities and a certain crudeness; on the other,
early Greek poetry was viewed as the fresh, direct, and natural crea-

tion of a youthful and limpid imagination. Homer, Greek tragedy, and comedy elicited different responses. Since a high priority was placed on the analytical faculties of the human mind, the mythic apprehension of reality was seen as naïve at its best and primitive and uncouth at its worst. Whereas Voltaire depicted the simplicity of Nausicaa in his *Henriade*, his approach to Homer ranged from occasional admiration to caustic irony. "Homer was not sleeping when he was singing the exploits of cannibals; he was feverish, and the Greeks were attacked by rage."[79] Only a minority of critics admired Homer for the primitive grandeur of his heroes, the dramatic structure of his epics, and the moral lessons of his ethos.[80]

Homer's treatment illustrates the ambivalence of the eighteenth century toward Greece. Although everyone who professed a classical education was familiar with and even enamored of his heroes and heroines, he was deemed inferior to Virgil, whose *decorum* and *gravitas* struck a far more responsive chord than Homer's primitive, unchivalrous, and often unabashedly crude and fierce characters. Like Shakespeare's, Homer's robust and seemingly undisciplined genius baffled the cultured sensibilities of the Enlightenment. In general, from the Renaissance to the end of the eighteenth century, "Homer stood like a giant who was visible enough but, on the whole, unapproachable."[81]

Adverse criticism of Greek tragedy was even more vociferous. What offended many critics and writers with a sense of propriety and *bienséance* was the depiction of terror, of man's primeval and untamed nature, and of his irrevocable destiny rendered even more implacable by divine wrath. Voltaire, once more, voiced these reservations and lauded the superiority of French tragedy over its Greek counterpart. He criticized the Greeks for having "dared to venture into revolting spectacles" and for not knowing "the shock of passions, the clash of conflicting feelings, the animated speeches of rivals." Faithful to the doctrine of progress, he stated that Sophocles, with all his renown, could learn "from our good tragedians."[82] Obviously, Voltaire and most eighteenth-century critics "found Greek tragedy philosophically defective and morally disagreeable mainly because of their reluctance or sheer inability to recognize the central role of religion in Greek life—perhaps especially . . . in the evolution of Greek drama."[83]

If the violence and forcefulness of Greek tragedy offended these littérateurs, the explicitness of Aristophanes incensed them. From Voltaire to La Harpe, he was treated with sarcasm and contempt. He was characterized as a vulgar and gross buffoon "who is neither a comedian nor a poet [and who], if he were among us, would not be allowed even to show his farces at the fair of Saint Laurent."[84] Marmontel, in his *Encyclopédie méthodique,* was more virulent in his attacks against the Athenian playwright, this "vulgar, unrestrained, and obscene comedian, without taste, morals or verisimilitude."[85]

Mme de Staël's views on Greek literature oscillated between admiration for its pristine beauty and deprecation of what she considered a lack of depth of feeling. In *De la littérature,* which appeared in 1800, she saw the development of literature not as an independent phenomenon but as an integral part of culture, mirroring its social and moral precepts. She devoted the first four chapters of her work to Greek writing. Her knowledge of it was based on such works as the *Cours de littérature ancienne et moderne* by La Harpe, not always an admirer of the Greeks, and translations of Homer, the tragedians, Aristophanes, and Plutarch.

A woman of the Age of Reason, Mme de Staël adhered to the belief in the progress and perfectibility of civilization and used it sharply as a criterion in her writing. Her criticism was also tinged with a flair for moral judgment. As for the Greeks, she presented them as an essentially happy, pagan people who used their free and vivid imagination to depict their immediate world. Since they came first, they were in the privileged position of having no models and no other guide than the élan and brilliance of their fresh imagination. They were indeed "the first people to have existed."[86]

What they gained in radiance and directness of perception, however, they lost in depth and subtlety of feeling. According to Mme de Staël, they lacked true lyricism since they treated neither love nor melancholy because of their contemptuous view of women. Their poetry offered colorful and dazzling images of nature but no emotive content. "There are two types of poetry: the first is the poetry of nature and the second that of the eloquence of passions. It is in the first kind that the Greeks excelled during the oldest period of their literature by the animated description of external objects" (48). Civilized people, though more mature, lost the joy, the exuberance, and the exhilarating surprise that the discovery of a new world brings. Early Greek poetry portrayed nature in all its primal beauty and external forms. Paganism, in Mme de Staël's opinion, had mellowed and humanized its more destructive forces. Religion, with its mysteries, oracles, mythology, and festivals, had transformed the credulity of the people into a poetic, artistic vision of the world. "The paganism of the Greeks was one of the main causes that led to the perfection of their taste in the arts; these gods, always near men and yet always above them, consecrated the beauty and elegance of forms in every genre of depiction" (56). Pantheism and mythology were regarded no longer as fanciful superstitions or extravagant illusions but as creative stimulants.

The superiority of their art and poetry notwithstanding, the Greeks, in Mme de Staël's eyes, were spirited, amoral pagans, strangers to feelings of intimacy and affection. "The moral uncertainty of these distant times is not at all a proof of corruption; it only indicates how few philosophical ideas the people of that time had" (58). Their religion was essentially theatrical and, like their poetry, relied on the visual and the concrete and was devoid of spiritual substance. Though death and suffering were not unknown to them, the exteriorization of pain and terror diminished the intensity of anguish and sorrow. Furthermore, she criticized Greek tragedy for what she perceived as a lack of contrast between vice and virtue and for the absence of familiar sentiments, which alone could stir the human heart. The visual representation of terror and crime made a powerful but short-lived impression because "the contrast between vices and virtues, inner conflicts, the mixing and the opposition of feelings, which must be shown in order to interest the human heart, were scarcely indicated" (68). Greek theater did not appeal to her because it spoke not to the heart, but to the senses. In her view it lacked genuine emotion because it conveyed neither sorrow nor pity.

This criticism reflected Mme de Staël's search for a more intimate and direct experience and a more delicate treatment of the passions of love and affection, with their moments of exaltation and melancholy yearnings. The Greeks gave further offense because they neglected women and the powers of the feminine psyche. "The Greeks never expressed and never knew the first feeling of human nature, friendship in love. . . . Melancholy, tender, and enduring regrets are alien to their nature; it is in the heart of women that long memories reside" (59).

Her attitude toward the Greeks became more favorable when she

visited Germany. She was particularly influenced by Wilhelm von
Schlegel and Winckelmann, who revealed to her the beauty of
Greek art and the greatness of Greek tragedy.[87] But in *De la littérature* she did not regret the eclipse of the Greeks because, since they
appeared at the infancy of civilization, they looked at the world
with the enchantment and amazement of a child. The Romans, on
the contrary, according to Mme de Staël, as the inheritors of the
cumulative experience of the past, added depth and gravity to historical consciousness.

Unlike Chénier, who believed in the validity of the imitation of
ancient literary models, Mme de Staël was opposed to their emulation because, in her view, they were alien to modern national literatures. "The poetry of the ancients is more pure as art; that of the
moderns makes us shed more tears; but the question for us is choosing not between classical and romantic poetry but between the imitation of the former and the inspiration of the latter. . . . Art is
petrified when it no longer changes; the Greek subjects have been
exhausted."[88]

Mme de Staël's inability or unwillingness to feel close to the
Greeks sprang from her conviction that all authors, in order to be
true to themselves, must delve into the problems of their own era.
Her relativism and the emphasis on the importance of national literatures was in the stream of nascent Romanticism. Her denial of the
universality of the Greeks presaged the Romantics' notion of the
uniqueness of each culture. This made it possible to see the ancients
in their own milieu before accepting once more the permanence of
their values. In the course of the nineteenth century, writers came to
understand that the Greeks were great not only because they created
works of stirring beauty but above all because they were true to
themselves and to nature.[89]

Alongside the aesthetic-literary and the republican-didactic influences of Hellenism in eighteenth-century France, the scholarly tradition of the establishment and editing of ancient texts, which had
begun during the Renaissance, continued with ever increasing momentum. Classical scholars throughout Europe cooperated in the
restoration, exegesis, and translation of ancient works through an
established network of personal contacts and learned societies. In
France such critics as Boissonade, Cousin, Korais, Quatremère de
Quincy, the famous cartographer Barbié du Bocage, and the Didot

publishing family raised the standards of scholarship, promoted the study of Greek, and helped increase the number of studies dealing with Greece. The Académie des inscriptions provided support for epigraphical, philological, and archeological studies of antiquity as it undertook actively "to maintain, in the face of the triumphant modern culture, philological and historical studies applied to antiquity."[90]

During the latter part of the eighteenth century, two trends can be discerned in the appraisal and perception of ancient Greece. The first was admiration and emulation, as was shown in the cult of antiquity during the French Revolution, in the imitation of classical styles and manners, and in the adulation of the beauty of classical art revealed by excavations and travel accounts. The second was a critical evaluation of Greek literature, oscillating between admiration for the beauty of its poetry and visual arts and reproval for its pagan rites and the unfamiliar and unsettling world of their poetic and dramatic characters.

A Panorama of Ancient Greece:
Le Voyage du jeune Anacharsis en Grèce

Critical evaluations of the literature of Greece, archeological and artistic examinations of its monuments, poetical evocations of its legacy—none of these efforts enjoyed the impact and the wide popularity of Jean-Jacques Barthélemy's *Voyage du jeune Anacharsis en Grèce*. In it he created a unified expression of the diffuse views on Hellenic civilization of his time and popularized the myth of the golden age.

A prominent numismatologist, epigraphist, linguist, and Hellenist, he is mainly remembered for his fictional history of ancient Greece. He made his way to Paris in 1744 from Provence, his birthplace, after completing his studies in a seminary. Within a short time he obtained a position at the Cabinet des médailles and became a member of the Académie des inscriptions. His position and abilities enabled him to acquire a vast knowledge of antiquity. Rigorous and painstaking in his study of coins, inscriptions, and texts, he used the results derived from each of these disciplines to elucidate the others. He proceeded from analysis and observation to synthesis and integration. Although these qualities informed his scholarly work, it was in his fictitious travel account that they made their lasting and widely felt imprint.

Barthélemy's romantic, idealized Hellenism reflected the neoclassical precepts of his time. But unlike the scholarly treatises of erudite Hellenists, whose appeal was very limited, his work reached a wider public, impressing upon it the image of an industrious, creative, and secular civilization. Furthermore, Barthélemy was a cultivated man and littérateur, and not averse to the amenities and civilities of high society. His Hellenism had neither the messianic fervor of the revolutionaries nor the polemics of the philosophes. Its purpose was not to convert but to instruct and to please. His pseudo-*roman* did not introduce new trends in the study of antiquity, nor did it propound any new interpretations of Greek civilization, but it rendered this distant world more palpable and vivid. "In this appealing novel into which one of the most ingenious popularizers has poured all the conquests of science, the public sees the emergence of a living antiquity and not an antiquity suitable only for dissertations."[91]

In 1788 the *Gazette de France* announced in its last number the publication of an important six-volume work by the respected abbé Barthélemy and explained that "it was offered to the public by the Debure bookstore . . . in two editions . . . each edition accompanied by an atlas."[92] Although it appeared at a time of great political agitation, the success of *Anacharsis* was almost instant. A second edition followed in 1789 and a third in 1790. In 1799 there appeared a posthumous edition revised by the author before his death. Finally, in 1821 it appeared in a six-volume edition illustrated with splendid engravings.[93] Its coincidence with the outbreak of the Greek War of Independence fostered philhellenic sentiments.

The work was translated into several European languages including modern Greek. There were four successive attempts to translate it into Greek. The first was undertaken by George Sakellarios in 1797, who, however, was not able to go beyond the introduction. There followed a second, by Rhigas Velestinlis, the Greek patriot, political activist, and author, who translated only the fourth volume. A third effort, which was announced in 1807, failed to materialize. It was finally translated in its entirety in 1819 by Chrysovergis Kouropalatis. These repeated endeavors by Greek authors to make *Anacharsis* accessible to their compatriots are indicative of the significance they attached to it. The edifying and instructional value ascribed to Barthélemy's work by the Greeks was expressed characteristically by the last translator in the dedicatory note to his readers. "I beg you to receive this work kindly, oh descendants of the glorious Greek race and most ardent lovers of the ancestral virtues, paying homage to its ever memorable author, who, with so many labors and so much earnestness, wanted through it to benefit all aspects of social life."[94]

In France the reception of the book was unanimously favorable. The crowning point was reached when the Académie française accepted its author as a member in 1789. The celebrated abbé, after having felt the elation of success and the dislocating effects of the Revolution, died in 1795.

Not unexpectedly, the popular acclaim of *Anarcharsis* inspired others to write similar works. Several imitations appeared, the best known among them being *Les Voyages d'Anténor* by the baron de Lantier. Presented as the translation of a work written on a papyrus excavated in Herculaneum, it was full of frivolities and sentimental adventures. It was successful, nonetheless, and was reprinted sixteen times from the end of the Directory until 1826. Its reputation as the "Anacharsis des boudoirs" was well deserved.[95]

The interest in Greek antiquity in France at the time and the desire to emulate it, particularly its styles and manners, are a plausible explanation for the immense popularity of *Anacharsis*. In this historical novel, Barthélemy managed to integrate a vast amount of material gathered over a period of thirty-two years. Moreover, as has been already noted, the *romans grecs* enjoyed a certain vogue at that time because they depicted a graceful Greece, a Greece that was an extension of French culture. Barthélemy did this more brilliantly than any of his contemporaries. He also responded to the more sentimental needs of his readers, who craved a closer acquaintance with the great men of antiquity and details of their intimate life. He satisfied them by portraying a gallery of renowned figures with all the nobility of their public careers and the touching episodes of their domestic life. Dacier, the perpetual secretary of the Académie française, expressed the indebtedness that a whole generation of the French owed to Barthélemy because he made Greece appear "complete in our eyes, or rather he has transported it among us, has made its institutions, mores, laws, and doctrines more familiar to us, and has enabled us to commune intimately with the great men of the great century of Pericles."[96]

Why were readers fascinated and intrigued and not intimidated by its inordinate length? Novels of considerable length were not uncommon at that time, and although Barthélemy cannot be called a novelist, he did make use of some fictional techniques. He had a central character, the young, prudent, and observant prince Anacharsis, whose journey to Greece was a pedagogic voyage. His long stay there—363 to 337 B.C.—gave him ample opportunity to meet some of its most celebrated men and probe every aspect of its social and intellectual life. His keen eye was always ready to record everything he witnessed. He was never alone; he was accompanied by an array of secondary characters, some historical, some fictional, who were dispensed with as soon as they had performed their role. The plot is a series of scenes unfolding with cinematic rapidity. Everything is in the foreground, paratactically juxtaposed, with no ambiguity or mysteries to be fathomed. The characters play their well-rehearsed roles with aplomb and deftness. Everything is controlled and there is no room for the unpredictable, the spontaneous, or the explosive. What we see is a free, enterprising, highly articulate, and cultivated people. The time of Anacharsis's visit was judiciously chosen because fourth-century Greece possessed a glorious past and a vibrant present. Everywhere nature and humans seemed to coexist in perfect harmony, the latter perfecting with their art and ingenuity the generosity and fertility of the former.

What images of Greece emerged from the pages of *Anacharsis*? Barthélemy's lengthy narrative dealt with an extensive part of Greece beyond the boundaries of Athens and Sparta. It encompassed places as diverse as Thessaly, the islands, Asia Minor. He even ventured into the more inhospitable and forbidding regions of Epirus and Macedonia. Though Barthélemy never visited Greece, he tried to reproduce the features of the land and capture the beauty of its landscape. To do this more effectively, he turned to travel accounts and the assistance of able geographers and cartographers, particularly Barbié du Bocage.

Barthélemy was one of the first French writers to picture the luminescence of the Greek landscape and the vividness of its colors. His story abounds in descriptions of sites famous for both their historical significance and their physical beauty. He portrayed the clarity and sharpness of their contours and the interplay of light and shadow. His knowledge of ancient poetry unveiled to him a tranquil countryside stirred form time to time by the song of birds and the murmur of waters. He described the Vale of Tempe, an inexhaustible source of poetical themes and mythological associations, beautifully, even if facticiously:

> The mountains are covered with poplar, plane, and ash trees of a surprising beauty. From their feet flow springs of pure, crystalline water; and gusts of fresh air, which one can inhale with secret pleasure, blow among their peaks. The river winds its course with tranquility, and in certain places it embraces small islands whose verdure it nourishes. Grottoes perched on the mountainsides are the refuge of repose and pleasure. . . . In a word, everything in these beautiful places is a smiling ornament.[97]

Living in a benign climate and being endowed with a happy disposition, the ancient Greeks did not expend all their energies in intellectual and artistic occupations. Barthélemy presented them not as a frugal, abstemious people, but as an industrious society actively seeking to secure prosperity and material well-being. Allowing for the traditional contrast between opulent Athens and austere Sparta and for a sense of moderation ascribed to them, the Greeks, as Barthélemy envisaged them, were either deft merchants inhabiting rich towns or hard-working laborers tilling their fertile land. Poverty and want were unknown. Theirs was a model secular civilization ministering to spiritual as well as material needs. Everywhere, "on the seashore, and in the interior of the mainland, rich prairies are covered with numerous herds; the well-cultivated plains display abundant harvests of wheat, wine, oil, honey, and fruits of all kinds" (6:260).

While the people in the countryside spent their days in pastoral bliss, the inhabitants of the cities were assiduously engaged in the material enrichment and the artistic embellishment of their polis. Though private residences were simple and unpretentious, public edifices were lavishly decorated. Cultural communication among the poleis was effected by orators, minstrels, and sophists, who recited in public their panegyrics of heroes and distinguished citizens.

Athens was presented as the pinnacle of urbane living and cultural accomplishment. The splendor of its art and architecture was matched by the keen intelligence and social graces of its people.

Porticoes, temples, statues—each was a masterpiece in its own right
and was animated by the creative spirit of its artists. Public meeting
places were adorned with loving care because they, rather than private homes, were the center of life for the gregarious Athenians.
Their daily activities and insatiable desire to exchange ideas brought
them together in public squares in the daytime and at banquets in
the evening. There, pleasure was exercised with moderation and luxury was enjoyed without decadence. A long cultivation of the art of
conversation and social affability gave them a refined and supple
demeanor. "Good company demands decency in expression and
comportment . . . It demands a certain ease of manners, removed
equally from levity, which approves everything, and from austerity,
which approves nothing" (2:292–93).

While the Athenians valued the pursuit of knowledge highly,
they did not neglect the development of the body and of martial
skills. In his all-encompassing portrait of Athenian society, Anacharsis paid particular attention to its system of education. Young boys
were exposed to a program of studies that was the ideal of liberal education first formulated by the Renaissance and then propagated by
the Enlightenment. The teaching of logic, history, rhetoric, law, and
politics developed the mind, while courage, temperance, magnanimity, modesty, and truthfulness were the ethical basis of their conduct.
Physical exercises and competitive games formed and strengthened
the body and made young men valiant defenders of their city.
Finally, the study of poetry, music, and rhetoric enabled them to distinguish themselves in society. The study of language, with its musical qualities and subtle expressiveness, was of great importance. An
Athenian who had had such an education would be a perfect example of the *honnête homme*, and undoubtedly many a Frenchman
who read *Anacharsis* liked to see himself mirrored in this picture.

Athens, as Rousseau and many others before Barthélemy had
pointed out, was not unblemished. Although the abbé's sympathies
favored this most civilized city, he perceived certain shortcomings in
the character of its people. Their desire to please and to achieve preeminence led them to vanity and superciliousness, and their volatile
temper and ceremonious manners made them frivolous.

Following the current precepts and at the same time injecting a
vivid contrast in his narrative, Barthélemy presented a tableau of
Sparta, where life was more somber and disciplined. Its houses were

small and plain, its public buildings modest and not ostentatious. Poetry, philosophy, and the cultivation of the arts were considered idle occupations detrimental to the formation of a robust body and sound moral character. Energy and conciseness of expression were prized, while rhetoric and oratory were shunned. Material wealth was of little or no consequence, and speculative activities were deemed unworthy of a truly free people.

Barthélemy admired the Lacedaemonians for their dignity, restraint, and legendary bravery. He pointed out, however, that their character was as prone to excess as that of the Athenians. Since public esteem and acclaim could be won on the palaestra or the battlefield, the exhibition of martial qualities verged sometimes on cruelty inflicted on others or oneself. Mothers came to demand of their sons either victory or death. Survival after defeat was a calamitous disgrace, and some of them felt perverse pride in counting the wounds sustained by their sons. Great honors were bestowed on the one whose son or sons had the greatest number of wounds.

All Greeks, despite their differences and contentions, had certain basic characteristic traits that were fostered by common institutions and beliefs. Barthélemy took Greek religion, mythology, fables, and legends more seriously than did most of his contemporaries, who either scorned them or simply found them charming and delectable inventions. In order to know the Greeks well, said Anacharsis, "it is good to envisage sometimes the fictions that embellish their annals. . . . Actually, one finds in the history of this people the character of its passions, and in its fables that of its spirit" (2:66). It is this mythology and religion that gave rise to festivals and celebrations and afforded Barthélemy the opportunity to produce some of his most vivid descriptions.

In this vast panorama where the whole of Greece is a *tableau vivant*, games, festivals, and processions occupy a prominent place. Being extremely sociable and communicative, as Barthélemy portrayed them, the Greeks swarmed to places of public assembly and delighted in spectacles. Thus their theater, local and panhellenic festivals, and contests were not only manifestations of religious and patriotic sentiments but also occasions of reunion. There all of Hellas congregated, and representatives from its various poleis vied with one another and strove for glory and excellence. The Olympic games were the culmination of these gatherings. Of course, Anacharsis attended one of the Olympiads and was awe-struck by the grandeur and sumptuousness that reigned there. When the games commenced, everything was enveloped in an atmosphere of solemn festivity, which gradually reached a crescendo of feverish intensity. The excitement and exhilaration were infectious. "Chariots were flying in the plain; the sound of the trumpets, the neighing of horses, mingled with the cries of the multitude"(2:509).

Barthélemy's extensive reading on ancient Greece had revealed to him that there was a darker side to its religious practices and ceremonies. During the celebrations of Bacchus, restraint and modesty were abandoned and the participants were in a state of frenzy. "I saw," noted Anacharsis, "troops of Bacchantes crowned with ivy, fennel, and poplar, dancing and howling in the streets . . . tearing with their nails and teeth the raw entrails of victims and clasping snakes in their hands" (2:514). The search for the unknown and the desire to communicate with the other world were not foreign to the Greeks. In the countryside, Anacharsis witnessed oracles, mysterious ceremonies, and incantations performed in caves. The irrational forces in man found an outlet during these processions. The terror they inspired had cleansing effects and gave a chance to the participants to release their secret fears and recover their equanimity and balance.

The exploration of these occult practices in *Anacharsis* befitted the all-inclusive scheme of the book and enabled the author to exercise his literary aspirations. They were described more to dazzle and surprise than to elucidate the complexity of the Greeks. Yet Barthélemy had the insight to perceive the purifying function of these rites and not to dismiss them as superstitious aberrations.

In the realm of poetry and drama, Barthélemy exhibited a sensitivity and appreciation uncommon for his time. The general disapprobation that surrounded the name of Sappho did not prevent him from admiring her lyricism. In her treatment of love he discerned the most delicate and moving feelings, and in her depiction of nature he saw all its loveliness and vitality. He greatly admired Pindar, whose greatness was obscured by his abstruse style, marveling at his vigor, his energetic style, and his elliptical metaphors. He saw him as the panegyrist of glorious feats and the eulogist of human excellence, inspiring men by singing the divine majesty and sublimity of gods and heroes. While most of his contemporaries felt distant from the heroic world of Aeschylus, he lauded his grandeur, seeing in his tragedies the unfolding of human destiny: crimes bringing divine vengeance upon their perpetrators and good fortune inviting blind fatality. He was moved by the forcefulness and passion of Aeschylus's language, by the precision and boldness of his expression, and by his rich imagery. He admired his innovations and elevated and noble style and ranked him among the best poets of Greece (6:14–16).

Barthélemy was even more at variance with his contemporaries in his appreciation of Aristophanes. He praised his works for the purity of their diction, the verve of their dialogue, and their true comic spirit, whereas most critics denounced them as scandalous and scabrous. Furthermore, he understood that poetry and even tragedy, because of their forceful and direct impact, could be understood by all Greeks, whereas "it is only among rich and enlightened people such as the Athenians . . . that the taste for Comedy can be born and perfected" (6:200).

Its merits notwithstanding, the limits of *Anacharis* soon became apparent, and its popularity did not extend beyond the first decades of the nineteenth century. Its narrative lacked cohesion and organic unity. Its copious notes, while attesting to the impeccable erudition of its author and adding historical authenticity and credibility to his narratives, were cumbersome and destroyed the fictional illusion he wanted to create.[98] The unifying theme was the voyage of the central character, Anacharsis. However, he acted purely as a recording device, and although he undertook this voyage in order to perfect his education, the author made little or no attempt to integrate the formidable amount of information with the intellectual and emotional development of the young prince. From the beginning to the end, Anacharsis remained a mechanical chronicler, who omitted no aspect and spared no detail of ancient Greece's history and culture, albeit recounting his experiences in a graceful style and elegant manner.

The author tried to introduce variety by using contrasts and comparisons, but the result was monotonous and repetitive. His preoccupation with refinement and correctness of expression suppressed spontaneity and personal feeling. Had he used a more direct and selective approach, he might have been able to recapture and convey some of the simplicity and energy of the Hellenic spirit. But, as a man of his century, he reflected the false idea of simplicity of his contemporaries, for whom the natural had to be cultivated and purified of the offensive and the unpredictable.[99] This tendency is best demonstrated in his reconstruction of the Greek landscape, where geography was fused with art and literature. Despite his descriptive abilities, his sketches of Greek scenery were a perfect setting for his image of Greek civilization: smooth and unruffled surfaces, regular and symmetrical lines, and smiling valleys sheltered by majestic mountains. The sparseness and austerity, the starkness and revitalizing unpredictability of the Greek land were foreign to Barthélemy, as they were to his contemporaries, not so much because he had never seen them as because they would have contradicted his vision of a harmonious and noble antiquity.

The complete and objective restitution of the past is an impossibility because each epoch projects on it reflections of its own self-perception. This was even more true in Barthélemy's time, when archeology was still in its infancy and the critical appraisal of antiquity was just beginning. Furthermore, there was a strong desire to identify with it and adopt its forms. As a result, in order to bring it closer to the present, writers distorted and refracted it. Barthélemy's work was the embodiment of these tendencies. Its inclusiveness satisfied the desire for encyclopedic knowledge; its descriptive passages responded to the search for visual and sensory stimulation; and above all, the Athens of the Greeks could be easily transfigured into the Paris of the French. Fontanes, a well known poet of the time, perceived this obvious parallelism and valued *Anacharsis* all the more for it. What was intended as a compliment sounds today like an inadvertent criticism:

> Whether you recalled culpable judgments
> Where heroes were immolated to envious hate,
> Whether you drew me into congenial circles
> Where sensible Greeks cultivated refined speech,
> I meet Paris, and in your unadorned sketch,
> In the Athenians I see the image of the French.[100]

> [Soit que vous rappeliez les jugements coupables
> Où la haine envieuse immole les héros,
> Soit que vous m'attiriez dans ces cercles aimables
> Où les Grecs au bon sens préféraient les bons mots,
> Je retrouve Paris, et vos crayons sincères
> Dans les Athéniens me peignent les Français.]

At the beginning of the Restoration a negative reaction to *Anacharsis* began to emerge. Barthélemy was reproached for presenting an artificial and one-dimensional image of a cultured and graceful Greece, instead of an energetic and more authentic Hellenic world. Stendhal's pointed criticism encapsulated the changing current of critical opinion. "The country of the world where the Greeks are the least known is France, and this thanks to the abbé Barthélemy. This courtly priest knew very well everything that happened in Greece, but he never knew the Greeks."[101]

Stendhal was unjust to focus his criticism on Barthélemy because the limitations of the learned abbé were the same as those of the other Hellenists of the neoclassical era. Theirs was a Hellenism that valued order, measure, and harmony and dared not penetrate the deeper strata of human experience out of which the first creative impulses emanate. By glancing only at the shimmering surface, they were magnetized by its brilliance and failed to explore the mysteries that lay underneath. Their understanding of the ancient Greeks, emphasizing either the rational-moralizing or the elegant and the noble, reflected their lack of religious experience and inability to grasp the tragic vision of life.

Despite these limitations, however, they did possess one characteristic shared by all Hellenists regardless of time and place: a longing for a distant time in the past viewed as the culmination of the development of all human faculties. "True literary and artistic Hellenism," remarked Henri Peyre, "is almost always accompanied by a sentimental preference accorded to Greece. We reserve in space and time a privileged place for this small country, and on the small knowledge we have of its history and art, we built a luminous dream, a veritable retrospective religion: the cult of Greece."[102] For the sixteenth- and seventeenth-century humanists and the romantic Hellenists who succeeded them, this reverential treatment of classical antiquity reflected their belief in the perfectibility of man and a nostalgia for an epoch that, they were convinced, had come tantalizingly close to attaining that ideal.

Eighteenth-century Hellenists wanted to experience antiquity more directly than their precursors and to identify with it spiritually as well as intellectually. Increased travel to the Greek lands, the growing number of archeological discoveries, and the search for a more intimate and even sentimental relation with the immediate and the historical made it possible to see Hellenism not only as a field of literary and philosophical study but also as an experience in reliving the past.

In the context of these developments, mythology served as a fount of motifs and images for artists and poets who saw in it a wide range of moods and tastes from the frivolous and capricious to the sober and didactic. The philosophes examined the political mechanisms and social institutions of the ancient poleis so as to gain an understanding of their own society and to prescribe remedies for its maladies. Less critically disposed and acting under the urgency of pressing events, the French revolutionaries, believing they were the true heirs of Rome and Sparta, tried to adopt the political institutions and moral standards of those long-vanished supremacies.

These varied approaches to the ancients rested on a common perception: that history was a progressive and cumulative process, with the past propelling the present into a better future. The ancients occupied a privileged position in this evolutionary scheme both because of the virtues attributed to them and also because they were the first and critical link in the tripartite chain — past-present-future — of this historical continuum.

The tension between past and present made its most forceful impact on French and other European travelers, who came to see the Greek lands from the Renaissance onward in slowly but steadily increasing numbers. By pointing out the differences and some latent similarities between the ancient and modern Greeks and by accepting their racial kinship, these travelers built a bridge linking the ancient land and the contemporary people. By describing ancient monuments in their physical setting, they also constructed a bridge connecting the abstract and academic Hellenism propagated through literary sources with the visual and tangible creations of the classical past. Thus the writers of travel accounts contributed significantly to the projection of an expanded and variegated image of ancient and modern Greece.

2

FIRST CONTACTS: FRENCH TRAVELERS TO GREECE, 1550–1750

Old Routes, New Voyagers

In their perception of Greece, those Europeans who came to know the country and its people had to reconcile its two contrasting images, one evoking its past splendor and the other its ignoble present. In evaluating modern Greece, Western commentators measured present realities against the achievements of an idealized past. Behind their observations on Ottoman-held Greece loomed the vision of antiquity that invariably conditioned their responses to the modern Greeks.

A direct acquaintance with the Greek territories of the Ottoman Empire became possible in the middle of the sixteenth century when diplomatic and commercial relations were established with the Porte. France was one of the first Christian powers to negotiate an alliance with the Turks, as a result of which Francis I took the important step of sending one of his secretaries, Jean de la Forêt, as the first ambassador to the sultan's court on 11 February 1535. Francis used this alliance to strengthen his country's position vis-à-vis his archrival, Charles V of Austria. A commercial treaty soon followed in February 1536. According to its provisions, the French were given trading privileges in the Ottoman Empire, which came to be known as capitulations. The French expanded their political presence by creating consulates in the main urban centers of the empire and the islands in the Aegean.

Diplomats and merchants were followed by missionaries, who organized and established permanent missions in various key locations of the Levant. A Jesuit mission was founded in Athens in 1641. In 1658, when the Jesuits moved to Negropont (Euboea), they were succeeded in Athens by the Capuchins.[1] These missionaries were neither crusaders fighting for the expulsion of the Muslims nor individual pilgrims seeking personal salvation. Their aim was to proselytize by working within the established political and social order. It was still an infiltration, but the means at hand were no longer the force of the sword but the power of persuasion and the promise of spiritual reward.

The primary task of these diplomatic and religious emissaries was the safeguarding and the promotion of the interests of the country and the institutions they represented. Of lasting importance was their direct and indirect role in promoting an interest in the peoples of the Levant. Not only were they themselves knowledgeable in their history and traditions, but they also served as invaluable guides to European travelers, offering them hospitality, protection, and information.

In addition to being inquisitive observers of the contemporary scene, many of these Westerners were avid collectors of art objects, manuscripts, and coins. This passion for collecting antiquities had its roots in the infectious fascination with the specimens of the fauna and flora of distant lands as well as with cultural artifacts proudly displayed by their Renaissance possessors in their *cabinets de curiosités*. Italy's ancient monuments were the first classical sites to experience the removal of antiquities destined for the decoration of palaces and wealthy residences, primarily in France and England. Francis I entrusted the Italian artist Francesco Primaticcio with the task of acquiring ancient statuary. As a result, the galleries and corridors of Fontainebleau were adorned with an array of Roman originals and Roman copies of Greek sculptures of the postclassical era. It is no exaggeration to say that it was Francis I who laid the foundations for the systematic collection of ancient works in France.[2]

With the increasing appeal of antiquity, the insatiable desire to possess its remnants gave rise to a veritable rivalry among agents of

European kings and wealthy patrons. The competition for the acquisition of antiquities continued unabated until the various peoples of
the Levant gained their independence and asserted their right to protect what they now called national monuments.

In the meantime, European monarchs and noblemen had ample
opportunity to enrich their collections, which benefited enormously
from the activities of diplomats, who were eager to serve their superiors while at the same time aggrandizing their personal possessions.
The marquis de Nointel, for example, French ambassador to the
Porte from 1670 to 1679, was a tireless traveler and passionate collector, who spent as much time and energy exploring the Ottoman
lands and acquiring art treasures as he devoted to his diplomatic
duties. His eventful career is a striking example of the dual European
thrust—political and cultural—in the Near East.

The establishment of a full range of ties between France and the
Ottoman Empire, including diplomatic, commercial, and religious
missions, prompted many Frenchmen to travel there. Their number,
limited during the sixteenth century to a few hardy and adventurous
individuals seeking to expand their knowledge of the world, rose
significantly during the subsequent two centuries, when classical antiquity and the Orient presented new and rich sources for archaeological, historical, and linguistic investigation as well as literary
inspiration.

Traveling of course was not a new experience introduced by the
explorers of the Renaissance. Its roots go back to Herodotus, whose
boundless curiosity and sheer delight in the discovery of new things
made him the first Western traveler to give a sweeping view of the
diversity and richness of human cultures in their natural habitat.[3]
No facet of human collective behavior was unworthy of his recording, and no ethnic group was beneath his observation. He felt the
need to go beyond the city walls "in order to understand the historical achievements of his own culture" by comparing it with alien cultures because he believed that "knowledge depends upon travel, . . .
upon a restless drive toward the margins."[4] The wide geographical
radius of his journeys was matched by the use of a variety of sources,
which enabled him to add the dimension of the past to that of the
present and to convey a sense of movement in space and time.

The Herodotean historical and ethnographic tradition, however,
was minimized by Thucydides, whose more staid and punctilious

insistence on accuracy and reliability saw current political events as the proper domain of history.[5] Herodotus's influence was further diminished during the Middle Ages, when the reordered relation between the perceptible and the transcendental worlds made the former appear as the geographical locus of the simultaneous existence of the seen and revealed reality.[6] In the spiritualized landscapes of medieval travel accounts, physical markers "function . . . as tangible materializations of sacred stories. . . . Mandeville [a mid-fourteenth-century traveler] and his contemporaries are saturated with such stories, circulating not as chronologies or sources but as radiances that attach to material existence."[7]

Within this perceptual framework the coexistence of the fantastic and the factual was accepted and the actuality of headless men, two-headed creatures, gorgons, and other prodigies was not disputed.[8] The deeply rooted predispositions of medieval men and women affected the way they saw things and conditioned the messages transmitted through their senses. As a result "in the Middle Ages, visions defined reality."[9]

A concrete expression of this interdependability is provided by medieval maps. They were not a mere attempt to reproduce the physical features of the earth but visual representations "of biblical, classical, and fabulous history mixed with the names of true places, cities, and peoples."[10] The primacy of theology over empirical observation was manifested in the designation of Jerusalem as the spiritual as well as the geographical center of the world.

As animated graphic representations of external reality, medieval maps also reflected contemporary beliefs about human diversity. Alien peoples, differing in appearance and cultural practices, were placed on the outer edges of the world in such faraway, mystery-laden places as India, Cathay, and Ethiopia. These "monstrous races" were not seen as primitive because "the very concept of a 'primitive' society as one at an earlier stage of cultural evolution was not a part of the medieval world view," which was predicated on man's fall from grace and his attendant degeneration.[11] Neither was human diversity interpreted as a manifestation of the variety of Creation. Rather, these alien beings, whose humanity was not doubted, were symbolically removed to the periphery of the world so as to suggest their physical as well as moral deformity and their distance from divine providence. It was, therefore, the duty of the holders of the true faith to bring them back to the center of the world, to Jerusalem.

It is easy to see how this commingling of theology and cosmology with physical and human geography gave rise to the missionary tradition, which became such a potent force in the relation of Western European Christian nations with non-Christian and even Orthodox Christian peoples. It is this proselytizing impulse, direct or suggested, which connects the medieval travelers with their Renaissance and post-Renaissance successors and differentiates both of them from the ancient Herodotus. No sooner were new lands discovered than missionaries armed with religious rectitude followed, with the mission of redeeming the people, who had strayed from the original plan of Creation.

The sense of wonderment and initial disorientation at the encounter of the new and the unfamiliar was felt very keenly by medieval as well as Renaissance travelers, particularly by the explorers of the New World. Although the impact of the direct contact with the natives of the Americas dispelled the belief in the existence of the "monstrous people," new wonders awaited the European newcomers.[12] Perhaps they would have been less nonplused if they had found the monstrosities they had expected. The cultural diversity they met was far more complex than the oversimplification and dehumanization that underlay conquest and colonization. Faced with the totally unexpected, especially at the sight of the rich and mighty pre-Columbian cities, the European beholders were temporarily immobilized by awe because "the object that arouses wonder is so new that for a moment at least it is alone, nonsystematized, an utterly detached object of rapt attention."[13]

The absolute absorption of viewers and their momentary suspension of judgment and moral categorization while beholding the unique are succeeded by a feeling of exclusion and alienation, which is quickly overtaken by an overwhelming desire to possess the marvelous. But for it to be fully possessed, it must first be destroyed and then refashioned by the invader in his own image. Destruction gives a sense of purpose, direction, and reassurance by removing the obstacles raised by wonder and by bringing the ungraspable into one's possession. The movement from dazed wonder to estrangement to destructive fever was expressed by Bernal Diaz when he recounted his reaction to Mexico. "I say again that I stood looking at it and thought that never in the world would there be discovered other lands such as these." But "today all is overthrown and lost, nothing left standing."[14] Thus for the explorer of the New World, wonder was the prelude to as well as the agent of appropriation.

The possession of the foreign, however, was more than the physical reenactment of the psychological projection of the self on the other. It was the result of a complex of motives and desires encompassing curiosity and a genuine search for knowledge along with greed and self-righteous arrogance. The travel account became a fascinating record of these psychological underpinnings and their physical manifestations.

As the frequency, the means, and the purpose of the voyage changed, so did the character of the accounts. The new travelogues, which made their appearance at the end of the fifteenth century, derived "their strength" not from "a vision of the Holy Spirit's gradual expansion through the world, but [from] the shock of the unfamiliar, the provocation of an intense curiosity," and the shifting of the focus from the cohabitation of the fabulous and the factual to the objective autonomy of the physical world, which gradually separated theology from geography.[15]

It is therefore evident that the importance of the voyage as an educational experience and a means of securing tangible and intangible gains became an ever increasing force in Renaissance Europe. Its instructional and utilitarian value was stated characteristically by Pierre Belon, a sixteenth-century French naturalist and traveler.

> Herodotus, Diodorus, Strabo, Arianus, and several other ancients have left us written accounts of their distant voyages, which have been of inestimable benefit to man, considering that their works have contributed to the comfort and ease of posterity. . . . It is therefore obvious that singular things taken from plants, animals, and minerals are for the most part sent to us as a benefit of peregrinations without which it would be very difficult and indeed entirely impossible for us to partake of the richness of foreign lands; I am determined to go and see them in the places of their birth.[16]

The urge to go beyond the confines of their native country and gain a personal knowledge of foreign places was a common theme in the accounts of these early travelers. Knowledge, many of them pointed out, was the product of the direct involvement of the senses which interiorized the external world. Of all the senses, they stressed visual perception as an irreplaceable channel for obtaining insights into nature and humanity. André Thevet, a sixteenth-century naturalist like Belon, equated seeing with learning. "Aristotle, whom the Greeks called Δαιμόνιος, that is, divine, because of his great and perfect wisdom, says that man has a natural appetite to see and to know. . . . But if one ponders and examines the statement of the excellent Philosopher, it is not without reason that he said first to *see*, then to know."[17]

Personal observations based on sensory perceptions would be greatly enhanced and rendered more sagacious if they were preceded by an awareness of the past, which, in Belon's words, "gives us knowledge of infinite things gained by innumerable works and incredible toils of others."[18] Thus in embarking on their voyages these travelers were aware that they belonged to a tradition that traced back to the Greeks and Romans. Though the impetus to travel stemmed from an irrepressible curiosity for novel things, their perceptions were conditioned to some extent by their humanist education, with its emphasis on ancient authors. It was in part the reading of these authors that guided the first Renaissance voyagers to the eastern Mediterranean.

A typical sixteenth-century traveler to the Near East would follow one of two courses: The first, taken less frequently, was by land, through Dalmatia, Macedonia, Constantinople, and then on to Asia Minor. The second was by sea, the voyage beginning at Venice, and later at Marseilles, where travelers would board a ship destined for one of the ports of the Levant, most often Constantinople. Sailing through the Adriatic and then the Ionian Sea, they would circumnavigate the Peloponnesus before traversing the Aegean. The islands, in both the Ionian and the Aegean waters, were natural stopping places for resting, replenishing supplies, and sightseeing.

In undertaking their eastbound voyages the early travelers were imbued with a sense of mission: they viewed them not merely as peregrinations intended to satisfy their personal curiosity and sense of adventure, but also as enlightening experiences worthy of being communicated. Upon embarking on his long and circuitous voyage to the eastern Mediterranean, the interior of Asia Minor, and the Arabian Peninsula, Pierre Belon hoped for no recompense other than the gratification of seeing these strange lands and gaining a knowledge of things "worthy of being communicated to our nation" (ey). Similar statements by other voyagers reveal a confidence in the power of the written word to inform and instruct. Consequently, the travel account was meant to be not so much a record of subjective experiences as a means of expanding the mental horizon of those who stayed home by exposing them indirectly to different modes of life.

To impress and to perpetuate the memory of their eastward passage, Renaissance and post-Renaissance voyagers had recourse to the written text. The book was an integral part of the voyage, serving as an indispensable guide to prospective travelers, who in turn produced accounts recording their own experiences. As such, it established a temporal link between present, past, and future and an intellectual bond between the voyager-author and readers. The primacy of the text was another distinction between modern travelers and their medieval predecessors, whose "pilgrimage to the Holy Land was part of life. The account was only accessory, and besides, it was destined for propaganda and conversion. The time would come when the account would take first place in the mind of the new pilgrim as the veritable goal of the voyage."[19]

Furthermore, the possession of the technology of writing gave Europeans a "literal advantage" over cultures that relied primarily on oral means to preserve and reproduce their traditions. Samuel Purchas, a seventeenth-century writer, expressed the expanded consciousness of human experience over time and space as a result of writing.

> By speech we utter our minds once, at the present, to the present, as present occasions move us . . . : but by writing Man seems immortall, conferreth and consulteth with the Patriarks, Prophets, Apostles, Fathers, Philosophers, Historians and learnes the wisdome of Sages which have been in all times before him; yea by translations or learning the Languages in all Places and Regions of the World: and lastly, by his own writings surviveth himself, remaines (litera scripta manet) thorew all ages a Teacher and Counsellor to the last of men.[20]

All the pervasive but diffuse ideas on travel expressed by Renaissance voyagers were epitomized by Baudelot de Dairval in his work *De l'utilité des voyages et de l'avantage que la recherche des antiquitez procure aux sçavans* (1686). Writing it in the form of a letter to a prospective traveler, the author expatiates on the numerous advantages offered by the knowledge of foreign lands. He emphasizes the value of personal experience, which, in his view, is the source of the arts and philosophy. The richer one's experience, the more fecund an imagination and the wiser a judgment one possesses. One's immediate surroundings, de Dairval maintained, are inadequate for the individual's growth.[21] An intelligent traveler will find that "the climate, the customs, and the peculiarities of each country are the objects of his study when he wants to enrich his memory and to enlighten his mind."[22]

Traveling satisfies one's curiosity for novelty by revealing the marvelous natural and human diversity of the world and also deepens the awareness of time by exposing one to the vestiges of a people's past. "It is certain that in the first times everyone was mindful to leave in his country on stone or on bricks the signs of sciences he had cultivated, as it can be seen in Herodotus and Josephus."[23] The ultimate proof of the indubitable instructional value of traveling, de Dairval pointed out, was the high regard the ancients had for it. Their greatest heroes, Theseus and Jason among others, as well as their most original thinkers, used the voyage to accomplish their tasks. He sensed that the first sparks of innovative and inspired change in a society are lit when some of its members dare break the bonds of the familiar in order to explore and learn from the unfamiliar. His exhortations are one of the first and most articulate defenses of the educational voyage, which, he believed, would be much more instructive if it were directed to the birthplace of antiquity.

The accelerated increase of travel accounts after the mid sixteenth century popularized a hybrid genre, the travelogue, which contained in an embryonic form elements of history, sociology, anthropology, and archeology, to mention but a few subjects, long before they became scientific disciplines. When these areas of human inquiry developed into well-defined bodies of knowledge, they found in travel accounts a repository of valuable data.

Useful though they may be as sources of information, travelogues are even more significant as documents showing the reasoning processes, criteria, and perceptual framework that representatives of one culture, in this case Western European, used consciously or unconsciously in order to understand and evaluate another culture. Implicit in any endeavor intended to render the unfamiliar familiar is a process of conversion whereby alien matter is passed through the grid of one's own standards and values. Whatever remains in the filter is of necessity unassimilable material, which is either cast away or enveloped by the aura of the exotic.

Thus the perception of one culture by the agents of another is a selective process. The foreign observer imposes, so to speak, a structure on the field of observation by fitting the mass of the fluid material that constitutes the living experience of a people, its history, and its natural environment, into certain predetermined categories. The observers and collectors of customs have to organize their material into structures and types that seem to them applicable to all peoples and enable them to report their findings to others whose mental constructs they share. Thus "the cultural themes, styles, and categories, the structural elements of the several cultures of the world . . . were already ordained."[24] The resulting images are to a certain degree exterior to the reality they describe because "in any instance of at least written language, there is no such thing as a delivered presence, but a re-presence or a representation."[25]

The Greek Scene: Neither East nor West

The monuments of Greek antiquity became known to the Western world much later than those of Rome. The geography of the latter and the key role of Italian humanists in the revival of ancient letters are a partial explanation for the belated discovery of the former. An equally important factor was the Ottoman conquest of the Greek lands, which severed their links, however tenuous, with the West. Shortly before the fall of Constantinople, however, Greece received its first visitors, both Italian, who showed an interest in and appreciation of classical antiquity. They were the Florentine priest Cristoforo Buondelmonti and Cyriac of Ancona. The first evinced fleeting intimations of admiration for the relics of antiquity, and the second, even at this early date, exhibited some of the salient characteristics of future antiquarians: curiosity, undaunted enthusiasm, collection of removable antiquities, regret for the eclipse of the ancients, and a condescending, often accusatory stance toward their modern progeny.

Buondelmonti moved to Rhodes in 1414 to explore the islands of

Greece. He was also commissioned by the humanist Nicolo Nicoli to collect Greek manuscripts. During his fourteen-year sojourn he learned Greek and toured several of the islands. He recorded his impressions and observations in two books, both in Latin, one a description of Crete (1417) and the other his itinerary of the islands of the Archipelago (1420). They were both primarily geographical accounts sprinkled with classical overtones. "You will see," he stated, "briefly told, numerous pleasant tales of the men of antiquity and of the exploits of heroes."[26] Although medieval legends, such as the Gorgon tale, were still interfused with factual observation, the passion for antiquity was already dawning.

Buondelmonti's contemporary Cyriac of Ancona was an even more avid and systematic explorer of ancient sites. Born into a family of merchants in 1391, he began his trading voyages in 1412 along the coasts of Italy, Dalmatia, Greece, and Egypt. Soon his interest focused on archaeological matters. From 1423 until 1453 he undertook several journeys, engaging mainly in antiquarian activities: he sketched important monuments, including the western front of the Parthenon, transcribed inscriptions, and collected manuscripts at the behest of Italian humanists, who often funded his travels.

The wide scope of his activities was matched by the broad span of his journeys: he visited the Ionian Islands, northern Greece, the Peloponnesus, many of the Aegean Islands, and in the spring of 1436 he went to Athens. He was more beguiled by Sparta, however, whose site was believed to have been in the location of Mistras. Following his stay in Athens, he visited this enclave of Byzantine civilization. While there, he became a friend of the Byzantine Hellenist Gemisthos Plethon and the Despot Constantine Paleologos, who became the last Byzantine emperor. Cyriac appeared last in Constantinople when the city was going through the agony of its final days as the capital of Byzantium. He was with Mehmed the Conqueror while preparations were made for the final assault.[27] Cyriac's death, which coincided with the fall of Byzantium, marked the end of the first phase of the systematic antiquarian exploration of the Greek space.

A century later, European naturalists and cosmographers, the French foremost among them, began to include Greece in their voyages. These early French travelers, unlike the explorers of undiscovered and unknown lands, were conscious that they were about to tread on ground where extraordinary feats of history had been enacted. "But I am convinced," wrote Paul Lucas, "that all reasonable persons will always declare for the second kind [antiquity]; there will be few who do not prefer to read elucidations on Greek and Latin Authors, the additions to Greek or sacred History, or the confirmation of ancient traditions, to the stupidity of a Savage of the Mississippi or the cruelties of an Iroquois."[28]

That Lucas would have found the idea of the noble savage ludicrous reveals an underlying belief dividing the world into two spheres, a civilized and an uncivilized one. The second category included the natives of the New World, as well as the modern inhabitants of countries with long historical records, who, however, had deviated from the course set by the great cultures that had antedated them.

After the discovery and conquest of the New World, Europeans emerged self-confident and aware of their power over a multitude of new peoples. "Such was the confidence of this culture that it expected perfect strangers—the Arawaks of the Caribbean, for example—to abandon their own beliefs, . . . and embrace those of Europe as luminously and self-evidently true. A failure to do so provoked impatience [and] contempt."[29] Diversity was intriguing, but divergence from the European norm strengthened the notion of Eurocentrism, which "in some cases segregated and classified as barbarians any people who failed to fit into the European scheme of things."[30] This perceived bifurcation of mankind stemmed in part from the dual heritage of Europe—the Judeo-Christian and the classical—which judged peoples outside this tradition either as heathens who should be proselytized or as barbarians ungraced by rationality and civility.[31]

The natives of the New World were deemed to be totally alien to the European experience because they were not part of the providentialist interpretation of history, and they certainly belonged to the second half of humanity first qualified by the Greeks as barbarians.[32] The peoples of the Orient, though not seen as savages, were not considered full members of the family of civilized nations. Their split from Europe was typically, though somewhat harshly, noted as early as 1550 by Iaques Gassot, who described the countries of the Levant as "very strange and barbarous, removed from every civility and humanity."[33] In the centuries to come, the idea of the dichotomy between East and West was expanded to include not only patterns of social organization and religious beliefs but also modes of perceptual and reasoning processes and aesthetic sensibilities.

Where did the modern Greeks fit in this binary scheme of East and West? By their religion they were closer to the Christian West than to the Islamic East. Religious similarities were paralleled by indirect cultural affinities established through the connecting link of the ancients, whose civilization had been transplanted in the West. This progressive connection—ancient Greece–Europe–modern Greece—was not clearly articulated, however, until the eighteenth century, when Greek antiquity was seen as an integral component of Western culture and nascent philhellenism envisaged a reborn Greece restored to its former glory.

However, sixteenth- and seventeenth-century travelers who commented on the modern Greeks evinced little inclination and had little reason to see them as part of Europe. Christians though they were, they were schismatics; however noble their origin might have been, they were hopelessly fallen. Yet neither did they see them as part of the Orient. Their religion, language, customs, and even dress set them apart from their rulers, with whom they did not fuse, if for no other reason than because of their subjugation. Although these early observers were not conscious of this ambiguous standing of the Greeks between East and West, their expressed views placed them in a twilight zone illuminated neither by the radiance of the West nor by the exotic glow of the East.

Yet judgments were made and evaluations were clearly articulated. In formulating them, the criteria used to measure the Greeks were not only the travelers' own values but, more importantly, norms set by the ancients as Europeans saw them. What is significant here is not so much the favorability or otherwise of these pronouncements as the inception of a process whereby models fashioned almost two millennia earlier were imposed on modern Greeks when they themselves were only vaguely aware of their classical lineage.[34] Long before they began to forge their Hellenic identity, European travelers, the French prominent among them, began to compare the modern Greeks to the ancients, a theme that was to be fully explored by eighteenth- and nineteenth-century philhellenes.[35] As early as 1553 the naturalist Pierre Belon observed that "the common people . . . whether from the islands or the mainland, retain something of their antiquity." The same author, in describing the funeral practice of the Greeks of lamenting the deceased by employing professional mourners, commented that "the ancient manner of the pagans to mourn their dead is still practiced at the present time in the country of Greece."[36]

Admirers of the ancients though they were, sixteenth- and seventeenth-century antiquarians were not romantic Hellenists. They measured and sketched the ancient monuments, but they seldom felt stir within themselves the spirit that had created their beauty. Rare was the instance when a traveler-antiquarian tried to recreate through the power of imagination a scene from antiquity.

However, an awareness of the past was not absent from the minds of these early explorers. It was precisely this sensibility that differentiated their perception of the relation between past and present from that of the medieval pilgrims. The latter were drawn by the timeless religious associations of their destinations. Modern, historically minded travelers, on the other hand, focused on both the physical and figurative aspects of places because in their eyes they were signifiers of a past, time-conditioned reality, which had left its imprint on the visible and the immediately perceptible world. Thus they felt that, for a clearer understanding of the past, historical chronicles had to be illuminated by direct contact with the places they described. In this manner the textual, abstract approach to antiquity was complemented by a knowledge of its spatial configurations.

A result of this development was the study of ruins. Ever since the seventeenth century these visible remains of antiquity have been the objects of painstaking examination and scrutiny. But they were not always approached with the same attitude. The seventeenth-century antiquarian, although sensing their artistic beauty and aesthetic merit, concentrated more on their external appearance and architectural features and "stood, as it were, in the immediate presence of the past."[37] Thus a ruin, although clearly the vestige of a distant past, existed less as an emblem of a vanished era than as an integral part of the immediately apprehended world and as an object to be measured and examined in its present state. Its evocative power, conjuring up a living presence, however dimly its image was transmitted through the opaque stretches of time, was keenly felt for the first time by the neoclassicists of the latter part of the eighteenth century.

Notably absent from pre-Romantic descriptions of the external world was an aesthetic appreciation and an emotional response to nature. For the naturalists, such as Thevet, Belon, and Tournefort, nature signified a life-giving force manifested in its plants and animals, but it was not yet invested with the power to elicit feelings of elation. This dispassionate stance toward nature ranged from the sixteenth-century view of it as a variegated spectrum of living forms to the seventeenth- and eighteenth-century concept of a perfectly functioning system regulated by immutable laws. Within this perceptual scheme one searches in vain for evocative descriptions of Greek landscapes.

A depiction of Mount Olympus by Robert de Dreux is indicative of this unsentimental approach and of the absence of mythological associations. Robert de Vantelet, known as Robert de Dreux, a name derived from the place of his origin, served as chaplain to M. de la Haye-Vantelet, French ambassador to the Sublime Porte. He spent the years 1665–68 in Constantinople in the service of his distinguished relative. When the latter was invited to go to Larisa, where the sultan was to hold his annual hunt, de Dreux accompanied him as a member of his entourage. Unavoidably, they came within viewing distance of Mount Olympus; this is his impression of the august mountain:

> The following day we had dinner on the bank of the river Sestelison in view of the famous Mount Olympus, whose summit, rising high above the clouds, we could see. This mount, the subject of so many poets, is admirable not only because of its height but also because of its expanse, which is so great that it took us two entire days to skirt it.[38]

The naturalist Tournefort, given even less than de Dreux to lyrical musings, and writing fifty years later, was repelled by the sight of another famous mountain, Mount Ida.

> There is nothing beautiful about this big mountain, which occupies almost the center of the Island, except its name so famous in ancient history. This famous mount Ida has nothing to show but a big, nasty spine of a mangy donkey: one sees neither scenery nor agreeable solitude, fountain or brook; one can scarcely find a foul well from which one has to draw water by hand to save the sheep and horses from dying of thirst. . . . From the top of mount Ida . . . one can see the sea to the north and south, but why should one submit himself to such a cruel fatigue in order to see it from such a distance.[39]

Myth and legend could not enliven and transform the austere contours of the mountain in the eyes of Tournefort.

Nature had to wait until the advent of romanticism to reveal its
hidden aesthetic and emotive powers. Among French writers it was
Chateaubriand who was captivated—and in turn captured—and who
enshrined the unique features of the Greek landscape. Until then,
the attention of most foreign travelers was focused on the social and
religious life of the people and the history and architecture of the
ancient monuments. At the close of the seventeenth century, the
scales began to tip in favor of the latter. Jacob Spon, the physician
from Lyon whose voyage to Greece in 1675–76 was one of the most
important developments in the history of foreign travel in that country, divided his observations between the two sides of Greece, the
ancient and the modern, but not equally.

> As for me, I did not really neglect all these details [of contempo-
> rary life], when I was able to learn about them with ease and little
> cost; but it will not be difficult to see, even if I were not sincere
> enough to admit it, that the greatest object of my research has
> been the knowledge of the ancient Monuments of the countries
> that I saw on this Voyage and that this has been my strongest
> inclination.[40]

The increasing prominence of antiquity in the latter part of the
seventeenth century is attested to directly and indirectly by many a
traveler. Joseph Pitton de Tournefort, knowledgeable in botany, medicine, and other natural sciences, spent considerable time on Crete,
a stage in his eastward voyage, which brought him as far as Persia.
Although his express purpose was to study people and their natural
environment, he would have been disappointed had he directed his
investigation solely to the former. "It is only the research of antiquities, the study of natural history and commerce, which can attract
foreigners. The travel accounts of the Levant would be very dry if
one were to limit one's descriptions to the present state of the Provinces subject to Ottoman occupation."[41]

Yet, on sixteenth- and seventeenth-century travelers, who were
avid observers of the immediately perceptible reality with little inclination for sentimental reveries and historical contemplation, the
present made a forceful impact. They examined and recorded the
social customs, physical appearance, religious practices, and character traits of both the Greeks and the Turks. Comments on the interaction of the two peoples show a keen awareness of the social and

religious barriers that separated them. Their differences were immediately apparent by such visible signs as their manner of dress. The
Ottoman rulers had imposed a dress code on their subject peoples,
which prohibited the use and display of luxurious fabrics and bright
colors. These regulations applied to the outer appearance of the
homes of Christians as well. Certain concessions were made to privileged individuals, who could wear rich garments with fur lining.
These concrete distinctions, many French travelers observed, were
underlaid by differences in language, religion, and character.

In comparisons between the two peoples and evaluations of their
relative merits and defects, it was often the Turks who drew words
of praise. Robert de Dreux discerned in them a certain probity and
sobriety. While visiting Chios, he noted "among the common Turks
a great frankness, a gravity akin to modesty, a great temperance in
drinking and eating, and an incomparable zeal for their religion."
He admired the charity and hospitality shown to strangers "in certain places called khans, which the pashas or other Turkish dignitar-
ies build superbly in order to lodge travelers regardless of their
quality or religion, everyone being welcome without being obliged
to pay for his bed."[42]

The Turks, however, did not always enjoy a uniformly favorable
reputation among Westerners. Guillet in his *Athènes ancienne et nouvelle* (1675) describes a scene in which a hypothetical traveler, Guillet's presumed brother, and his companions were entertained to a
sumptuous repast by a Turk while they were in Athens. Once their
initial surprise and discomfiture caused by unfamiliar table manners
and eating habits had passed, our imaginary traveler listened to the
venerable old Turk speak of his people: "Where you come from,
they take the Turks for savage beasts, and I am not sorry for the little
honor they give us."[43] Derogatory comments on the Turks must
have been fairly persistent according to another traveler, Sieur du
Loir, who tried to dispell them: "I will tell you then, in regard to the
Turks, you must not think that they are as crude and brutal as many
would have you imagine, and certainly if equity is more considerable than politeness in manners, they are no less worthy than we
are."[44]

Their reputation for backwardness notwithstanding, the image of
the Turks painted by sixteenth- and seventeenth-century French travelers was more often than not a complimentary one. They were no

longer seen as a menace to Christendom, nor were they declared to
be tyrants and oppressors, as they would a century later by philhellenes. Undeniably they were masters, and many a traveler witnessed
scenes of cruelty perpetrated on the subject peoples, but rare was the
voice demanding their expulsion from Greece. Le Sieur de Villamont, who toured Asia Minor and the Aegean at the beginning of
the seventeenth century, related the sufferings and the cruel treatment Cypriots received at the hands of their conquerors but
refrained from expressing protest and indignation. "I blame no one,
but I will dare say that it is better to die while fighting against the
Turks than to surrender to their hands trusting their word. . . . It is
God's doing and men's sins that cause the decline and overthrow of
cities and kingdoms."[45]

Although Villamont explained human injustice by invoking divine providence, he expressed pity and sympathy for its victims.
Tournefort, on the other hand, who witnessed similar incidents
almost a century later, viewed them with detachment and even a
touch of cynicism. "One must admit that the cane of the Turks has
some great virtues: a whole island trembles when they speak of can-
ing; the most prosperous inhabitants do not dare appear except in a
very humiliating posture, their head covered with a grimy cap; and
most of these wretches retreat into caves so as not to expose themselves to such a great shame."[46] The same author described with
almost clinical thoroughness two forms of execution used by the
Turks to punish their insubordinate subjects: one was impaling and
the other a form of strappado. The tone once more was objective and
impassive. Although there were some voices commiserating with
the Greeks for their misfortunes, the prevailing attitude was one of
acceptance of the existing symbiotic, though uneasy, relationship
between the two peoples, who, though separated by language, religion, and traditions, lived nevertheless in the same place and under
similar conditions.

The identity of the two, however, remained distinct in the mind
of their foreign visitors. For the Europeans the Turks belonged to a
different, non-Western world. They were part of the Orient, and as
such they were approached with a certain condescension and at the
same time a sense of fascination, enveloped as they were by the allure
of the East. Unlike the Greeks, they were not expected to conform
to a set of preestablished norms because they did not have to shoul-

der the burden of the past. While it was incumbent upon the Greeks to have a love of learning and to display signs of education, the Turks were rarely criticized if they failed to exhibit marks of what Westerners considered cultivation. Greece, on the other hand, not so much because of its geography as because of its ancient history, could not be a part of the Orient and, because of its decline, could not be the Greece that its Western visitors wanted to see. Thus, even as early as the sixteenth and seventeenth centuries, Greece stood divided against itself, its identity torn between its idealized, timeless image and its current state of decline.

It is not surprising that the Greeks, living in the shadow of their progenitors, appear in an unfavorable light even in the earliest modern travel accounts. When compared to the Turks, they were found lacking in those qualities that drew approbation for the latter: modesty, sobriety, and probity. Du Loir was quite generous in both his praise for the Turks and his castigation of the Greeks.

> Naturally, they [the Turks] are better, and one must not attribute this to the climate, since the Greeks, who are born in the same country, have such different inclinations; of their ancestors they have retained the worst qualities: namely, deceit, perfidy, and vanity. The Turks, on the contrary, give particular value to modesty and sincerity, and with the exception of courtiers, who are almost all and everywhere slaves to ambition and avarice, simplicity and candor reign among them with an unmatched frankness.[47]

The Greeks were denounced even more vehemently by the marquis de Nointel, the French ambassador to the Porte, who came into direct contact with them first in Constantinople, where he tried to extract valuable manuscripts by either cajoling or enticing them with gifts, and then during his travels in Asia Minor. The particularly acrimonious tone of his denunciations can be partly explained by the rebuffs he received in his personal dealings with them, but they are also indicative of the negative reputation the Greeks had had since the time of the Romans. In a letter written from Jerusalem on 4 April 1674, to M. De Pomponne, he launched into a long diatribe against them.

> The same duty that has engaged me until now to inform you with exactitude of the good treatment the Greeks received as a result of my honesty, founded on an effort to lead them to a secret union,

> obliges me unavoidably to assure you that the instability, ambi-
> tion, and vengeance that have an absolute hold on them are con-
> trary to any human address. All that remains from their past
> domination consists of their criminal ruses, whose use is the only
> consolation they have in their enslavement. It is for this reason,
> Monsieur, that there are seven living Patriarchs of Constantinople.
> . . . I already had the honor to inform you of one of their perfidies,
> and I can assure you that every day they do their utmost to harm
> one another, which makes them unworthy of any protection.
> Truth and the desire I have always had to make them gentle force
> me to make this assertion.[48]

Even though this invective seems to have been provoked by the
alleged offenses that piqued his pride, his stance was that of a disillusioned reformer, an agent of a superior culture, who had taken it
upon himself to rehabilitate a people who had gone astray.

The dichotomy between ancient and modern Greece became a
common theme in travel accounts as early as the sixteenth and seventeenth centuries. The higher the prestige of the ancients rose on
the Western intellectual horizon, the lower the esteem for their
descendants fell. Belon's view was characteristic.

> The authors of all beneficial knowledge and disciplines that we
> revere today came for the most part from Greece, which (thanks
> to fortune, which brings sudden changes), though in ancient
> times rich and opulent and endowed with learned men in all dis-
> ciplines by virtue of which it dominated a large part of the world,
> has now been reduced to such a state that there is not a single foot
> of land which is not tributary to the Turkish yoke or Venetian
> servitude. . . . All the Greeks in both areas are in such an amazing
> state of ignorance that there is not a single city in the entire coun-
> try that has a university and not a trace of pleasure in learning the
> arts and sciences. Without any exception, they all speak a cor-
> rupted idiom of the ancient language.[49]

Language was an important criterion in judging the deviation of
the Greeks from their ancient prototypes because linguistic decline
was linked with cultural degradation. Belon noted that the quality of
spoken Greek differed from region to region. Spon, who knew ancient and some modern Greek, concluded that the best Greek was
spoken in Athens, where the ancient form of some words was still
preserved. He interjected, however, that "one must not conclude

from this that they understand literary Greek, because when we were in Athens, there were only three Greeks who were learned."[50] Spon, like most French travelers who commented on modern Greek, considered the vernacular not an evolved form but a vitiated idiom of the ancient language. In their estimation it was just another aspect of the general cultural degeneration and abasement.

Modern Greeks had not only failed to preserve their classical heritage, but they had also strayed from the true path of Christianity in the eyes of their French Catholic visitors. At a time when religion was still a potent spiritual force and, in the case of the Greeks, the only significant link providing them with a common identity, it was natural that this aspect of their collective existence would attract extensive attention. Greek Orthodox priests and monks, who were deemed to be the spiritual leaders of their people, dismayed their European observers because of their superstitiousness and lack of learning. The caloyer became a stock character in travel accounts, and his ignorance was a constant motif echoing through their pages. Pierre Belon visited Mount Athos after having completed his tour of the Aegean Islands and spent some time among its monks. While he praised their hospitality and industriousness, he bemoaned their intellectual indifference.

> Among the six thousand Caloyers, who live on the mountain, in such a great multitude one can scarcely find in each monas tery two or three who know how to read and write. This is because the prelates and the patriarchs of the Greek church, enemies of philosophy, excommunicated all the priests and monks who possessed, wrote, or read books other than those of theology and made it clear to other people that it is not permissible for Christians to study poetry and philosophy.[51]

Belon's criticism was based not on theological grounds, his own expertise in this domain being rather limited, but on a secular concept of a clergyman, which expected him to possess knowledge beyond the confines of theology.

Whereas Belon stopped short of calling the Greeks schismatics and heretics, Robert de Dreux, a man of the cloth himself, had much harsher words for the Orthodox clergy. He visited Greece a century after Belon at a time when the Catholic church was actively asserting its influence in the Levant and was in charge of founding a mission in Neocaesarea in 1658. Hence his opinions are more revealing than those of a lay traveler because to some extent they reflect not only the prevailing biases of his time but, more importantly, the official views of his church. He reproved the Greek clergymen strongly because he felt it

> a deplorable thing to see the blindness of these so- called priests, the majority of whom are so ignorant that they are considered quite learned when they know only how to read. . . . The popes, having been informed of all the abuses committed by the schismatic Greeks, have tried to remedy the situation to the best of their ability by naming bishops known as *in partibus infidelium*, who, when unable to be present in the area of their jurisdiction, designate vicars-general, who try with the missionaries to instruct the faithful and administer the sacraments with all the necessary dispositions; this serves as a model of emulation to the schismatic Greeks and engages them to fulfill their duties with more circumspection.[52]

Although references to the Greek church abound in sixteenth- and particularly seventeenth-century travelogues, all of them ringing with the familiar tone of deprecation, they are casual remarks presented as they were occasioned by the authors' personal experiences. The first French traveler to give a systematic exposé of the state of the Greek church, its practices, architecture, and hierarchy, was Joseph Pitton de Tournefort. He was born in 1656 in Aix-en-Provence, where he attended the Jesuit College. His family destined him for the church and to this end sent him to a seminary to study theology. His inclinations, however, were not congruent with this goal. He was passionately interested in the study of plants, and he made botany and the natural sciences his lifelong vocation. In 1689 he went to Monpellier to further his study of anatomy and medicine. He arrived in Paris in 1683 with an already established reputation as a botanist. He obtained a position as a professor of botany at the Jardin royal des plantes, and in 1698 he was named docteur en médecine in the Faculté de Paris.

To expand his knowledge of the natural world and broaden the field of his scientific investigations, he set out in 1700 on a voyage to Greece, Asia, and Africa accompanied by a doctor and a painter. This was not an individual undertaking, however. It was done at the behest of the French government, which financed it. Tournefort was

to inform M. le comte de Pontchartrain of his discoveries and explorations. The purpose of his mission was to identify plants mentioned by the ancients as well as those not mentioned, and to gather
information on the natural history, geography, customs, religion,
and commerce of these places. A felicitous combination of official
support and personal drive and inclination ensured his success.
When he returned to France in 1702, he brought back 1,356 new plant
species. He died in 1708, having seen in print only the first volume
of his *Relation d'un voyage du Levant fait par l'ordre du Roy.* . . . Fon-
tenelle, perpetual secretary of the Académie royale des sciences, delivered the eulogy during the assembly of its members on 10 April
1709, extolling Tournefort's wide knowledge and erudition in the
fields of natural sciences and history.

Being knowledgeable in both of these spheres was the mark of a
truly learned man in an era when knowledge was viewed as a unified
body of principles and not as a domain divided into various compart-
ments presided over by experts. Tournefort's work mirrors this
multiple approach by combining the pervasive curiosity of sixteenth-
and seventeenth-century travelers and the encyclopaedic spirit of the
dawning century. He was a detached observer with an inquisitive
intelligence and a bent for irony. His narrative follows the course of
his explorations and journeys. It is a succinct, matter-of-fact record
of things seen, not a reconstruction directed by thematic and imagis-
tic motifs. Factual information is interjected with personal impressions, comments, and judgments. In this respect it is well within the
stream of preceding and current travel accounts. Given the nature of
his enterprise, the book is amply illustrated with drawings of plants,
birds, native costumes, and cities, maps of islands, and a limited number of sketches of antiquities. The pictorial aspect of the book
reflects its binary composition, which encompassed the natural and
the human facets of the places he visited. He organized and presented his material in a series of letters addressed to M. le comte de
Pontchartrain.

One of these letters, a lengthy one compared to the others, is a
treatise on the Greek church. Though in content it is more comprehensive than the information provided by previous travelers, its tone
echoes their denigrating spirit. He traced the decline of the Greek
church in terms of its intellectual standing back to the fall of Byzantium, or the Greek Empire, as it was then called, when the most edu-

cated Greeks left for various parts of Europe, leaving behind them misery and ignorance. Those who continued to live in the Ottoman Empire, in Tournefort's estimation, neglected literary Greek to such an extent that they were unable to go back to the original sources of Christianity, a disorder that led to complete ignorance during the centuries following the Ottoman conquest. Thus, he continued with a sweeping statement, in his day there were scarcely a dozen persons in the lands held by the Turks who knew literary Greek. This sad state of affairs among both clergymen and laymen stemmed, according to Tournefort, not so much from Turkish oppression, since the Ottoman rulers allowed the Greeks to practice their religion, as from the ignorance of those who ruled the Greek church. To make things worse, corruption and simony were pervasive in the higher echelons of the church as a result of the patriarch's practice of acquiring his position by paying a sizable sum to the sultan. This led to financial schemes and extortions, which were emulated by others in the hierarchy down to the village priest.

Tournefort placed the entire responsibility for this anomaly on the Greek hierarchy, whereas in fact it was in part fostered by the patriarch's obligation to pay a large amount to the sultan in order to assume his office. Intense competition for the patriarchal throne was not uncommon because the Turks awarded it to the highest bidder. Furthermore, they saw to it that the patriarch changed as often as possible so that more money could be accrued from the sale of the *berat* (an imperial warrant conferring special privileges).[53] This was one of the reasons for the rapid succession of patriarchs, a phenomenon Tournefort and other Catholic observers attributed solely to the Greeks' intrigues and machinations and not, even in part, to the status of the Orthodox church and its relations with its Ottoman rulers.

Ignorance and superstition were the lot of the priest and the caloyer as well as the common Greek. Echoing de Dreux's and Nointel's patronizing attitudes, Tournefort lauded the proselytizing activities of the Catholic church in that part of the world, seeing them as beneficent efforts intended to mend the Greeks' stray ways.

> Our missionaries find great difficulties in bringing the Greeks back to their true faith, especially in towns away from the coast which are not accessible to the King's charity. Their devotion to their Saints and particularly to the Blessed Virgin is not far from degenerating into idolatry; every Saturday they faithfully burn a

lamp in front of her image; they implore her incessantly and thank her for the success in their affairs.[54]

Tournefort interpreted the personal, intimate relation of the Greeks with their saints as a survival of their pagan past. He was one of the first French observers of modern Greece to explore the relation between paganism and Christianity, a theme that later writers examined more extensively. There is a qualitative difference, however: whereas for philhellenes, such as Pouqueville, this affinity between ancients and moderns was yet another indication of continuity affirming the descent of the latter from the former and therefore a positive attribute, for Tournefort and his contemporaries for whom Catholicism was the true form of Christianity, this was but an aberration, further proof of the Greeks' deviation from the right path, and consequently all the more reason for the Catholic church to enlighten them.

Belon, de Dreux, and Tournefort, spanning a period of a century and a half, reached the same conclusions regarding the Orthodox church by using the same criteria—learning and a command of literary Greek, not faith and religious fervor. If it continued to be schismatic, it was mainly because of the lack of enlightenment and the obscurantism of its clergy and not because of well-reasoned and philosophically established dogmatic principles. "A good mind though they may have," argued Tournefort, "they lack instruction, and they know only what they have learned from tradition, good or bad; thus it is not surprising that they are still in their *ancient heresy* regarding the Holy Spirit, which does not proceed from the Son, according to most of their [Church] doctors (1:137).

When examining the impressions and comments of these travelers, one must keep in mind their itinerary because their views were shaped by their observations of the places they visited. The Aegean Islands figured more prominently at first, and then, after the middle of the seventeenth century, Athens, the Peloponnesus, and the Ionian Islands. Among the islands, Crete and Chios were focal points. Crete had been under continuous Venetian domination from 1211 until 1669, when it fell to the Turks after a twenty-one-year siege. The Turkish conquest brought the cultural development of the island to a standstill at a time when it had reached a high level of attainment. The long and uninterrupted Venetian occupation, however oppressive it might have been, provided creative stimulation and intellectual nourishment by making cultural contact and exchanges with the West possible. European literary models assimilated by Cretan writers inspired such accomplished works of literature as *Erophile* (1637), *The Sacrifice of Abraham* (1635), and *Erotokritos* (begun c. 1646).

Intellectual conditions, however, are by their nature difficult for a visitor to a foreign land to grasp and assess because they are diffuse and do not find a concrete and immediately apparent expression in the daily life of the people. Only faint echoes of the relative prosperity of the island emerge in the pages of Belon, who was there in 1546. As a naturalist, he commented extensively on its benign climate, well-tended orchards and gardens, and rich plant and animal life. As for its people, they struck him as valiant warriors and hardy mariners. André Thevet, a contemporary of Belon and like him a naturalist, left a different portrait of the Cretans, which, although not unique in its negative tenor, is striking in the virulence of its tone.

> Several of the inhabitants of this nation call themselves Christians: but I do not see how: because they are great hypocrites resembling sepulchers, white outside and foul-smelling inside. And if the rustics and the village people are malicious and depraved, their Priests are worse. . . . Be it said, this nation is more spiteful, more vexing and more outrageous to strangers than any other in all of Greece.[55]

The dramatic events of the last year of the siege of Crete (1669) were related by de Dreux, who, after his passage through Macedonia, Thessaly, and Attica, was in the Peloponnesus waiting for a ship to take him back to France. This was to be an important voyage because de Dreux had been instructed by M. de la Haye-Vantelet to accompany Suleiman Mustafa Aga, the first Turkish ambassador to Louis XIV's court.[56] De Dreux reported the progress of the siege during its concluding stage as news reached him from various sources. However, it was not so much the destruction of the island that he bemoaned as the decimation of a French detachment and the death of its leader, the duc de Beaufort, who had been sent to support the besieged Venetians. From de Dreux's perspective, the embattled protagonists were the Turks, the Venetians, and the captain of the French unit. The native inhabitants, who stood to lose the most, were in the background.

Crete's surrender to the Turks was such a devastating blow to the island that thirty years later, Tournefort could still see its indelible marks. He described its largest city, Candia (Herakleion) as "the carcass of a big city, well populated during the time of the Venetians, trading, rich, and very strong; today it would be but a desert were it not for its business quarter, where its best inhabitants have settled; the rest is nothing but shanties since the last siege, one of the most extensive in our days."[57]

The ethnic composition of the city's population, based on Tournefort's estimate, is compelling evidence of the decline of urban life on the island: there were eight hundred Greeks, two hundred Armenians, three or four French families including a vice-consul, and two Capuchin friars. The Turks made their presence strongly felt: there were eighty-five hundred of them in the city, distributed among various military units permanently stationed there.

The people of Crete were of slight interest to Tournefort. They were a basically honest people, he thought. No more thieves, assassins, and highwaymen among them, thanks to the deterrence of punishment by hanging. Incurably curious like the rest of the Greeks, they were avid seekers of news and novelties. Foreigners, a rare sight after the departure of the Venetians, caused a sensation among them. Tournefort's attitude was in general a mixture of patronizing condescension and disdain. He could be amused by their quaint ways just as easily as he could be angered by what he perceived as duplicity and connivance. They were also of use to him as the unconscious transmitters of names of plants used by the ancients, thus providing a living link between past and present.

> I looked at the brain of these poor Greeks as I would at living inscriptions, which serve to conserve for us the names cited by Theophrastus and Dioscorides; although subject to diverse alterations, it will last doubtlessly longer than the hardest marbles, because it is renewed every day, while marble wears away or is destroyed. Thus this kind of inscription will conserve for the centuries to come the names of several plants known by those skillful Greeks who lived in the most learned and happiest of times. (1:87–88)

For Tournefort, then, the Greeks had little significance other than as passive recorders perpetuating antique linguistic forms.

Of all the islands of the Aegean, it was Chios, invariably the favored stopping place for travelers to the Levant, which drew general approbation. Its privileged position in the Ottoman Empire as the supplier of the aromatic mastic for the sultan's harems and its fertile lands and enterprising inhabitants ensured its prosperity, which lasted until its destruction in 1822. More importantly, as far as foreign visitors were concerned, frequent contacts with Westerners due to the island's key geographical and commercial position had given its inhabitants an urbane and cosmopolitan character.

The women of Chios especially delighted French visitors with their beauty, grace, and affability, qualities highly valued in their courtly tradition. In a region where women were secluded and unapproachable, the sociable ladies of Chios were an unexpected and refreshing change. Belon's comments were not atypical. "Their beauty, grace, and loving courteousness disarm all the visitors inclined to gallantry. Their appearance is such that one would judge them to be nymphs rather than mortal women or girls."[58]

In comparing descriptions of Chios and Crete antedating the Turkish occupation of the latter, especially the ones written by authors who visited both islands, one is discomfited by the universal acclaim accorded to the first while the second engendered mixed reactions. Why this discrepancy when in retrospect it is Crete that is recognized as having attained a higher cultural level? Partly because a traveler is impressed by appearances and concrete and observable realities. And when it came to appearances, Chios was the more prepossessing. There the French and in general the European travelers found the closest parallel in the Levant to their own society. For this reason they felt at ease because they did not have to cope with completely foreign and unfamiliar modes of life. Crete, although it had vital connections with the West through its Venetian rulers, had retained its indigenous character and had evolved an individual, autochthonous culture, which, although stimulated by Western currents, was far from being a mirror of them. It was perhaps this uniqueness and authenticity that made it less accessible to foreign visitors and at times baffling and disconcerting to them.

The Turks, who had ousted the Venetians from Crete and consolidated their control in the Aegean, were unable to penetrate the Ionian Sea, whose islands remained in the hands of the Venetians. Their physical proximity to the West and the Italian presence on their soil not only facilitated contacts with the Western world but also provided educational opportunities for their inhabitants, many of whom attended Italian universities, especially the University of Padua.

A combination of geography and political conditions contributed to the Western orientation of the Ionian Islands. European travelers noted this affinity approvingly and were quick to point out that there were marked differences between the Ottoman- and the Venetian-held Greek lands. Belon observed that these distinctions were readily perceptible in the manner of speech and dress. The Greeks under Venetian occupation dressed in a Western style while those subject to Turkish rule wore Eastern apparel. On the basis of these observations, one can detect even at this early date the two most influential and formative currents, the Western and the Eastern, which would eventually direct the course of the modern Greek nation in its search for identity and political and cultural orientation. That these two influences were perceived in their most rudimentary forms by French commentators is certainly testimony to their inquisitiveness. Not unexpectedly, they assigned a higher value to Western-oriented forms. Given this perceptual scheme, it is understandable why Chios and the Ionian Islands received their approbation.

What made the Ionian Islands even more appealing to their French visitors were the signs of learning and intellectual life. Spon, who spent some time there on his way to Athens, mentioned several learned men, most of them, not surprisingly, educated in Italy. Corfu, the administrative and the cultural center of the islands and the seat of the Academy of Belles Lettres, could boast a good many writers. Spon met some of them and reported on their intellectual occupations. There was Nicholas Voulgaris, of the prominent house of that name, doctor and theologian. Then, there was "monsieur le Docteur Capello," who had undertaken the compilation of a Greek, Italian, and Latin dictionary. Another scholar, Jerome Valach, of Cretan origin, who possessed a rich collection of old manuscripts on theology, had already published a dictionary in four languages—ancient Greek, modern Greek, Latin, and Italian. Spon remarked that the islands that were under Venetian rule had more men of letters than other parts of Greece. Their merit was relative, however, because, "in a country where ignorance prevails, one need not be a great savant to make some noise."[59]

Unlike the islands, Attica, and the Peloponnesus, northern Greece
remained remote and outside the scope of most travelers' itinerary.
Those few hardy souls who ventured through its mountainous terrain convey impressions of a desolate countryside, ruined churches,
and fear-ridden natives. One such daring traveler was Robert de
Dreux. He was an avid seeker of adventure and a tireless, if indiscriminate, observer of everything within his purview. His descriptions
convey an impression of incessant movement, daring, and exploration even at the risk of personal harm. Dangers enough there
undoubtedly were, but he exaggerated them intentionally to mag-
nify his own boldness and fearlessness.

One such event, which forced him to muster all his ingenuity and
temerity, was his witnessing of the preparations for the sultan's hunt
in Larisa, certain aspects of which were strictly forbidden to non-
Muslims. The scene he described, one of the more vivid in an otherwise prosaic and colorless narrative, recreated the opulence, pomp,
and mystery surrounding the sultan and his entourage and the haunting fear benumbing the subject Christian people.

According to Dreux, whose tendency to exaggerate must be kept
in mind, the villages adjacent to Larisa had to supply twenty thousand men, whose function was to encircle the woods reserved for the
hunt and force the wild animals to exit onto a clearing where a dais
had been raised for the "Grand Seigneur," who, seeing the game dash-
ing before him, could kill to his heart's content with a minimum of
exertion. There was no escape for the animals because they were
pressed from all sides by the clamorous noises of the villagers, many
of whom lost their lives when attacked by the desperate animals.
Upon gazing at the men's bodies, the sultan was reputed to have said,
"At any rate, . . . they would have died anyway, and if they had not
died here, they would have died elsewhere."[60] Such senseless loss of
human life would undoubtedly have aroused indignation had it been
witnessed a century later. De Dreux, however, was so overwhelmed
by the display of Ottoman splendor and power and his own boldness that he had no time for commiserations and moral indignation.

Although the era of active support for the emancipation of the
Greeks had not yet dawned, there were some vague appeals for their
freedom. They sprang, however, not from a compelling concern for
the rights of a subjugated people but from a sense of obligation to
ancient Greece. The feeling of indebtedness to the ancients, coupled

with the belief that Europe was their intellectual heir, led Europeans to adopt a patronizing and protective attitude toward the modern Greeks. If Europeans were to espouse the cause of the Greeks, they were to do so not only as the guardians of the Hellenic heritage but also as champions of Christianity. In the middle of the sixteenth century, Thevet voiced one of the earliest appeals made in the name of Christianity.

> Concerning the condition of the inhabitants of the so-called Greece, they have been slaves since the fall of Constantinople, their main city and capital, brought about by Mehmed II, an Emperor cruel in war. . . . Since then, all the Greeks have been sequestered and deprived of their own country, rights, liberties, freedom, and immunities: God permitted this to happen because of the great errors that they had committed and which still continue to blind them. . . . I pray that God will illuminate the hearts of our Christian Princes so that they may use their power to recover the aforementioned places tyrannically occupied by the infidel Turks.[61]

The vindication of both Hellenism and Christianity was strongly invoked by Fénelon, the famous prelate and author of the *Aventures de Télémaque*, who contemplated a voyage to the Levant to join the Catholic missions there. In a letter dated 9 October 1674, and probably addressed to Bossuet, he stated his intentions and expectations.

> The whole of Greece opens before me, and the Sultan flees in terror; the Peloponnesus breathes again in liberty and the church of Corinth shall flourish once more; the voice of the apostle shall be heard there again. I seem to be transported among those enchanted places and those inestimable ruins, where, while I collect the most curious relics of antiquity, I imbibe also its spirit. I search for the Areopagus, where St. Paul declared to the sages of the world the unknown God! But, after what is sacred, I am delighted with what is profane; and I disdain not to descend to Piraeus, where Socrates drew up the plan of his republic. I reach the double summit of Parnassus; I pluck the laurels of Delphos, and I revel in the charms of Tempe.
>
> When will the blood of the Turks mingle with that of the Persians on the plains of Marathon, and leave the whole of Greece to religion, to philosophy and the fine arts, who regard her as their country?[62]

To Fénelon, Christianity and Hellenism were in perfect harmony and not in opposition. But the implication in this rapturous declaration was that both had been vitiated in modern Greece by the evils of oppression and that the time must come when they would be restored to their pristine form.

Fortunately for Fénelon, his voyage never materialized, and thus his vision of Greece did not have to come to terms with the reality of it. Nevertheless, his emotionally charged statements, even if one takes into consideration his youthful fervor, presage in tone and content some of the axioms of philhellenism: the Turks were part of the oriental menace, which, although repulsed by the ancients during the Persian attempt to conquer Greece, had succeeded in its second advance under the banner of the Ottomans; now that the Greeks were no longer able to defend their own country, it was incumbent upon the West, symbolized by Fénelon, to drive them back; once rid of the intruder, the spirit of Greece would spring forth and blossom again. It was particularly the last expectation that became the main tenet of philhellenism. Its underlying assumption, the resurgence of classical civilization, was ahistorical because it ignored the developments in the centuries following its demise and regarded postclassical Greece as a vacuum ready to be filled by "philosophy" and the "fine arts" once its fetters were removed.

Antiquarians and
Pilferers of Antiquities

The pursuit of knowledge is in a sense self-propelled and self-generated because it contains its own momentum: books give rise to new books, old ideas are analyzed, evaluated, and synthesized to produce new ones, and old art forms serve as stimuli awakening new sensibilities and creating new aesthetic dimensions. The progress of knowledge through time is a process of choosing and emphasizing those forms and ideas of the past which respond best to present needs and concepts. Knowledge is also a form of possession because it is a mental projection endeavoring to capture, internalize, and integrate phenomena of both the physical cosmos and humanity. To bring these two complementary worlds under its control and make them yield to its demands, their products must be possessed, be they in the form of natural elements or human creations. The search for knowledge has not stood aloof from nonintellectual expressions of Western expansion and penetration of other cultures. Thus scholars and artists accompanied European diplomats and other political emissaries to the Near East. The diplomatic and antiquarian activities of Charles-François Olier, marquis de Nointel were one example of this combination of political and cultural penetration.

A persistent form of cultural exploration accompanying the political and commercial advance of Europe eastward was the search for antiquities and their acquisition. Italy had often been ransacked; now it was the turn of Greece and the Orient. Just as the Christian powers competed for political influence in the Ottoman Empire, so too they vied with equal eagerness for the discovery and removal, when possible, of antiquities. Kings and noblemen, ministers and diplomats sought to enrich their libraries and to decorate their palaces and châteaus with the literary and artistic remains of past civilizations. The monuments of Greece and those of the Orient, however, engendered different attitudes and reactions: Greece was already viewed as an integral part of European civilization, and therefore its relics were considered part of Europe's intellectual patrimony; the Orient was seen as an essentially different civilization, and therefore its artistic and literary works would provide a key to its decipherment and understanding. Nonetheless, both worlds were fertile fields ready to yield their treasures when plowed by antiquarians and collectors of antiquities.

It was during the reign of Louis XIV that the quest for antiquities became a systematic, well-organized, and centrally directed effort. Art was not merely a source of aesthetic pleasure, something to be contemplated and pondered, but also an emblem of central authority, irradiating its might and magnificence. Hence the possession of the masterpieces of the ancient world as well as those of his own would enable the *Roi Soleil* to project all the more brilliant and powerful an image to posterity. "The King," wrote Charles Perrault, "desiring that the sumptuous edifices he is having built in France serve as models for posterity, has sent several learned persons to Italy, Egypt, Greece, Syria, Persia—in short, everywhere where there still remain traces of the talent and boldness of architects; these persons are well qualified to make observations on them."[63]

These "savants" ranged from scholars and diplomats to professional agents. They all acted within a well-established network of
contacts consisting of coin and manuscript merchants—Spon had
witnessed approvingly their prosperous trade in Constantinople and
Smyrna—consuls, and even missionaries. Their task was to locate
owners of libraries, manuscripts, or other valuable items and then
approach them to negotiate their sale. No means was considered too
devious. Giving bribes, especially to monks and priests, was an open
practice. A gift was often nothing less than the bait to obtain old
manuscripts. Nointel admitted as much in a letter describing his first
meeting with the patriarch, on 9 February 1672.

> I made him a present of the entire Byzantine historical corpus; if
> I had the Greek Fathers, I would also give them to him at the
> appropriate occasion, and I will take the liberty to tell you in
> regard to this subject that if I had two or three Byzantine his-
> tories, . . . I would be able to make use of them with advantageous
> results; because, in addition to being the means of making the lib-
> erality of His Majesty radiate, I would also be able to obtain sev-
> eral manuscripts from Mount Athos and other places where I
> stay.[64]

Of the ministers of Louis XIV, Colbert was a most energetic and
enthusiastic collector of antiquities for his own possession and that
of his king. By 1662 he had already amassed a considerable collection
of books and manuscripts, which was further enriched after 1670
with new acquisitions from Greece and the Orient. That this coincided with Nointel's appointment to the embassy to the Porte attests
to the ambassador's intense activity. Colbert was very specific as to
the type and quality of articles he wanted. In a circular addressed to
the French consuls in the Levant in November 1672, he gave them
clear instructions:

> It being quite convenient to search for manuscripts for my library,
> I have no doubt that you will easily find opportunities to obtain
> them; you will give me great pleasure if you let no chance escape
> and if you inform me before buying anything. You must be partic-
> ularly aware that Greek manuscripts in parchment are preferable
> to others. . . . But, for greater precaution, it will be necessary to
> find someone, either a Capuchin or someone else, who is knowl-
> edgeable and therefore able to choose well. Moreover, be careful
> to obtain them at the best price possible.[65]

His directive to Nointel was even more precise and explicit. Constantinople and its environs, according to information received by Colbert, were a repository of ancient manuscripts, which were in the hands of either Turks, who had taken them from the Christians, or Greek monks and priests. Nointel should see to it that they were located, appraised, and purchased provided they were not church manuals and prayer books. Once obtained, they should be sent with all due circumspection to Colbert to be deposited either in his own library or in that of the king. If he performed this service, "the public would find in it a great advantage, because scholars would enrich by the edition of several unprinted works of literature the fields of their respective professions, and our France would be embellished with the spoils of the Orient."[66] A sense of mission aiming at the preservation and enshrinement of the cultural and historical heritage of the past is implicit in this letter.

Nointel could not have been more receptive to Colbert's exhortations. Duty and personal inclination conspired to make him a most avid collector.[67] Largely successful in his search for antiquities, he regretted only that he was not able to carry off the coveted sculptures of the Parthenon. He was one of the first Europeans, certainly the first Frenchman, to voice a desire for their removal, believing, as others would after him, that they deserved more protective and appreciative surroundings. What a marvelous addition to the holdings of the monarch they would be, he mused while beholding them.

> All that one can say of the most elevated of these originals is that they would deserve to be placed in the cabinets or the galleries of His Majesty, where they would enjoy the protection this great monarch gives to the arts and sciences that produced them: there they would be sheltered from the abuse and the affronts done to them by the Turks, who, in order to avoid an imaginary idolatry, believe that they are performing a meritorious act by breaking away a nose or some other part.[68]

The French sovereign was seen as the patron and custodian of arts and letters of both his own country and the world.

The king and the ministers who acted on his behalf did not depend solely on French diplomats in the Levant to enrich his collections. The services of merchants were enlisted, and expeditions were organized with the express purpose of obtaining manuscripts, coins, sculptures—in short, anything of artistic and literary value that could be carted away. One of these agents was Paul Lucas. Born in 1664 in Rouen, where his father was a jeweler, Lucas traveled to the Levant for the first time in the 1680s to buy precious stones for his father's business. He evinced a spirit of adventure and curiosity combined with the pursuit of gain and commercial astuteness at the very outset. Although he possessed little, if any, education and classical learning, he had an instinctive and perspicacious insight into the value of antiquities. Upon his return from his first voyage, he had in his possession a significant collection of Greek coins, which he sold at a handsome price to the court of Louis XIV. His business acumen was immediately recognized, and it was deemed expedient to employ it for the benefit of the monarch. He returned to the Levant three times as the official agent of the French king.

Supplied with money, diplomatic protection, and precise instructions, Lucas embarked on his first voyage to the Orient in 1699 as the king's agent with Persia as his destination. While serving his sovereign faithfully and obediently, he did not neglect his personal gain. His next journey commenced on 15 October 1704 and was not completed until four years later. He set out from Paris accompanied by a young boy of eleven sent by the king to Constantinople to study Turkish and Arabic as part of a program to train future diplomats and interpreters. They sailed from Marseilles on 8 January 1705, and reached Constantinople in February of the same year.

Upon his arrival, Lucas repaired to the residence of the French ambassador, Ferriol, who had already been notified by the minister Pontchartrain. Ferriol was to see to it that Lucas was provided with all the necessary documents and passports, which would facilitate and expedite his travels throughout the Levant. His true identity and mission should be concealed so as not to arouse the suspicion of the authorities. Instead, he would be presented as a doctor, a profession highly esteemed by the Ottomans. Lucas himself received detailed instructions from Pontchartrain: he should be thorough in his investigation; he was to exercise prudence and restraint in spending the king's money by striking successful bargains, and he was also to use utter secrecy in sending his acquisitions back to France. The king's interest and indeed his direct role needed to be screened in all his dealings. Lucas was to contact an intermediary, another royal agent, and all transactions were to be effected through him.

Lucas diligently followed the directives of his patrons while showing remarkable initiative. His search was directed primarily to the acquisition of coins, manuscripts, and inscriptions. His investigation combined personal visits to bazaars, monasteries, ancient ruins, and old buildings with the cultivation of friendly relations with local officials, priests, and notables as invaluable sources of information. When he visited ancient ruins, he did not try to identify them and trace their origins, nor did he concern himself with their fate. He was a merchant, not a student of antiquities. Yet his practical approach was not devoid of enthusiasm and exhilaration. Eager to communicate his zeal and hoping for more generous rewards, he wrote to the king: "To this end [to obtain antiquities], I have traveled more than once to Greece, Asia Minor, Persia, Syria, Egypt, and Africa. I have accumulated, at great risk, a large number of Coins, Engraved Stones, ancient manuscripts, and other useful curiosities, which have found their place in the Cabinet or the Library of YOUR MAJESTY."[69]

Inevitably, some of the antiquities fell into the hands of pirates en route to France. But, by the end of his second mission, which was particularly fruitful, hundreds of ancient coins, twenty-two ancient manuscripts, and fifty-two inscriptions had reached Paris. A third and fourth voyage followed in 1714 and 1724. But during his last voyage he found the Levant less fertile as a result of the intense competition among European nations, particularly France and England.

Lucas exemplified a new type of traveler in the annals of French voyages to the Levant. His prime motive was the exploitation of a new market offering a freshly discovered commodity, the monuments of antiquity. This was his main goal, but he also had a strong sense of adventure and exploration. While scouring the markets and ancient sites of Greece and Asia Minor for antiquities, he took time to observe and record the various aspects of contemporary life.[70] As he went along, he described everything without elaboration, effusion, or evaluation. Although he was in constant contact with the remains of the past, he rarely stopped to contemplate the civilizations that had produced them. Accordingly, his remarks on the people and cultures of his day were free of comparisons and the customary unfavorable judgments. His understanding of the past being limited, his perceptions of the present were conditioned more by immediate concerns and less by historical perspective.

The archaeological exploration of Greece and the Orient with a view to removing antiquities was not the exclusive domain of kings and noblemen. Religious organizations and ecclesiastics did their share. The Benedectines, known for their learning and literary interests, actively engaged in it. The proselytizing activities of the Jesuits and the Capuchins in the Levant were now complemented by a new crusade to save not the sacred monuments of Christianity from the Muslims but the equally sacred monuments of antiquity from the ignorance of the contemporary inhabitants. Obviously, the sacralization of antiquity had become well entrenched by this time.

Dom Vincent Thuillet, a leading Benedectine, could not emphasize too strongly the significance and the immense contribution to the cause of letters of the retrieval of ancient manuscripts from Greek monasteries. From the secure distance of his study, he envisaged these religious centers, especially Mount Athos, not as abodes of Christian faith but as storehouses of ancient Christian and pagan manuscripts. If only they could be taken away from the hands of their unenlightened possessors, they would be marvelous revelations and confer glory on their rescuers. "All these works still exist—we will soon prove it—and when they are retrieved from the oblivion into which they have sunk because of the barbarity and the ignorance of the modern Greeks, how many mistakes will be rectified! How many great names will be known! How many gaps will be filled! How much knowledge of geography, war, politics!"[71]

Thuillet was unrealistically optimistic about the reputed treasures enclosed by walls of Greek monasteries and the "libraries of Greece." His advice to prospective seekers of antiquities, however, was underscored by two central ideas, which had already taken root and continued to be adhered to throughout the eighteenth century: first, if the modern Greeks happened to be the possessors of the relics of the ancients, they were not their rightful owners because they had forfeited that right by falling into ignorance; second, the Orthodox monasteries were of interest only to the extent that they tantalized European antiquaries with their purported ancient manuscripts. Their religious function as places of worship was of little if any concern to the Western Christians, even though some of them were themselves ecclesiastics.

Another member of the Benedectine order, Dom Bernard de Montfaucon, who was also a classical scholar and paleographer, offered guidance and detailed instructions to antiquarians. Unlike

Thuillet, Montfaucon was less emotional and speculative and more practical and specific in his directions. In his "Mémoire pour servir d'instruction à ceux qui cherchent d'anciens monumens dans la Grèce et dans le Levant," he distinguished clearly among the different categories of antiquities and their varied destinations once they were in Europe. Under the general rubric of "monuments" he subsumed coins, busts, statues and bas-reliefs, inscriptions, and manuscripts. A hierarchical order was constructed to determine their place in their new shelters: "The busts, statues, and bas-reliefs are not for everyone. It is usually the princes and great lords who acquire them to decorate their cabinets and gardens."[72] As in literature, where the genre of tragedy treated the passions and revealed the destiny of elevated personages, so too it was in art: its loftiest creations and august monuments were fit only for the mighty. Inscriptions and manuscripts, on the other hand, as useful sources of historical and literary investigation, were the proper domain of men of letters.

Two other Catholic clergymen, the abbés Sevin and Fourmont, accepted a commission from a minister of Louis XV, Maurepas, to journey to Greece and the Near East "to obtain for the Library of the King everything that can be found in the Levant, in the form of Greek manuscripts or books written in the different oriental languages."[73] The great significance attached to this mission is attested to by the length and detailed assignments they were given. The monasteries of the Levant, particularly Mount Athos, were their main objectives. But they were to proceed with utmost secrecy and caution so that the true nature of their motives would be concealed. They were to present themselves as mere travelers and explorers seeking to satisfy their curiosity and thirst for knowledge, not only to allay the suspicions of the Ottoman authorities but also to divert the attention of the Greek monks and strike better bargains with them. After all, these possessions were considered to mean very little to them, ignorant as they were, and they would surely part with them willingly for a small price.[74] The success of their endeavors would contribute "to the glory of the King and the nation and the acquisition of many advantages for the sciences in general and His Majesty's Library in particular."[75]

The two abbés arrived in Constantinople in December 1728. Two months later they parted company; Sevin stayed on in the Ottoman capital, where he carried on his search for manuscripts, while Four-

mont, accompanied by his nephew Claude-Louis, left the city on 8
February 1729, with the islands of the Archipelago and Greece as his
destination. Before departing, he obtained a firman from the sultan
for the Turkish governor of the Morea and letters of recommendation from the French ambassador, Villeneuve, to the various French
consuls in Greece. Making full use of the diplomatic protection he
had been granted, Fourmont descended on the ancient monuments,
literally taking them apart piece by piece, and thus destroying them,
in order to extract the inscriptions they enclosed.

Both of these royal emissaries corresponded extensively with the
French officials who directed their activities, keeping them up to date
on their progress. If one allows for a certain exaggeration inherent in
their desire to please their sponsors, these letters are valuable documents because they show both the methods used to obtain and carry
off antiquities and the writers' attitude toward the native people.

A complex of motives underlay this dislodging and appropriation
of antiquities: a strong desire to possess the artistic and intellectual
patrimony of the past in the firm belief that they would be of value
only to Europeans, who were better equipped to serve and advance
the cause of civilization; a fear that, were these precious relics to
remain in their places of origin, they would be in danger of disappear-
ing completely because of either willful destruction or ignorance
and indifference.[76] They were convinced that their pilfering fulfilled
the higher ideals of humanity and that any and all means to attain
this end were permissible. The rules of conduct dictating respect for
another's property and forbidding deceit and theft were not applicable in this area. Sevin, in a letter to Maurepas from Constantinople
on 2 April 1729, openly stated his practice of enticing avaricious
Greek monks and priests with bribes in order to obtain manuscripts.

> There are many among them who like gold more than they fear
> excommunication. It is to them that one must address oneself
> without fear of being rejected. Knowing whether such ways are
> legitimate, I leave it to the casuists to decide; what reassures me in
> some way is the interest of the public good, which must always
> take precedence, as even the severest critics would consent. Be-
> sides, what would be more useless in the hands of the Greeks than
> these treasures; they have no use for them, and at every moment
> excellent pieces run the risk of perishing.[77]

Sevin's approach proved fruitful. He left Constantinople on 29 April 1730 with a harvest of 400 oriental manuscripts in Arabic, Persian, Armenian, and Turkish and 125 Greek manuscripts, among which there was a magnificent text of Strabo's *Geography*. The arrival of these acquisitions in Paris was greeted as an event of supreme importance in the annals of the "republic of letters." Sevin himself had seen to it that his services were acknowledged. Throughout his stay in Constantinople he never ceased to point out to his patrons his indefatigable efforts. His labors, though, were frustrated by competing collectors. Prominent among these was the Phanariot Prince of Wallachia, whose collection of manuscripts in Sevin's estimation could match or even surpass that of any European prince. Sevin's incidental mention of this Phanariot inadvertently acknowledges the existence of an active intellectual life and literary interests among at least one segment of Greek society of that time, the Phanariots.[78]

Fourmont returned to France shortly after Sevin, having completed a sixteenth-month sojourn in Greece. He embarked for Marseilles on 23 June 1730. His acquisitions were equally rich, not in manuscripts but in inscriptions. He brought back with him 300 bas-reliefs, coins, plans and views of towns, monuments, and copies of 2,600 inscriptions. But he was received less enthusiastically than Sevin because the authenticity of his inscriptions was questioned. This was the least of his transgressions, however. What made his travels in Greece a dark page in the history of antiquarian searches was the willful and merciless defacement and destruction of monuments. His letters to Villeneuve, Maurepas, and Bignon chronicle his devastating progress through Attica and the Peloponnesus. To compensate for the dearth of manuscripts, which he attributed to the ignorance and the gross indifference of the natives, he scoured the area for inscriptions. Discovering and copying them was not enough. In one of his letters to Maurepas, he pointedly expressed his single-minded and destructive search. "Every castle, every citadel, every old tower where I suspected there were inscriptions was overturned, and as luck would have it, I found a great number of them."[79]

Fourmont's method of investigation, as he described it all too often in his letters, was to hire a group of local laborers and have them demolish any structures that bore signs of antiquity and whose walls were imbedded with inscriptions. His role was not merely that of a supervisor; he often participated, being "the first and the most enthusiastic to set to work." Once the inscriptions were copied, he ordered his workers to break them, thus erasing every trace of their existence. His destructive fury gained momentum as he moved southward and reached its peak in Sparta. On 30 April 1730 he wrote two letters, one to the abbé Bignon and the other to the ambassador, Villeneuve, apprising them of the progress of his work and, more importantly, expressing his exaggerated and perverse pride in having dismantled and overturned the ruins of Sparta.

> Your Excellence, who knows my zeal, can well imagine my chagrin upon leaving this barbarous people without bringing back anything that would at least compensate for the expense. I vented this ire at old Sparta; I did not want anything to remain from a city built by the fathers of this rabble. I overturned it from top to bottom, and there isn't one stone left on top of another. What is the point, Your Excellence will tell me, of throwing oneself so furiously at a city because of the sins of its children? I will have the honor to answer that . . . no traveler had dared to lay his hands on it; the Venetians, although they had formerly been the masters of this place, had respected it. I did not deem it suitable to have for it such regard; I toppled it over, and with full authority.[80]

Fourmont's vandalism was invariably bemoaned and denounced by later travelers and writers, all of whom tried to explain the motives for his aberrant behavior. Pouqueville found his claims exaggerated, little more than the boastful fantasies of a man known to be given to inebriation. Michaud interpreted his destructiveness as an expression of religious fanaticism. Still others attributed his defacement of inscriptions to a calculated design to destroy the original texts so that his mistakes and fabrications would not be detected. Eventually, comparative epigraphic scholarship and early twentieth-century excavations in Sparta verified some of his finds, while many were judged to be forgeries. Perhaps the most measured assessment of Fournmont's antiquarian activities in Greece was pronounced by Edward Dodwell in 1819.

> It is conjectured by many, and perhaps not without good reason, that his principal object in obliterating the inscriptions was that he might acquire the power of blending forgery and truth without detection. . . .
> On his return to France he produced a vast mass of inscrip-

tions, many of which are authentic and have since been copied in Greece. . . .

Since the time of Alaric, Greece never had so formidable an enemy.[81]

Though it is certainly true that Fourmont was unique in finding joy in destruction, the existing cultural climate made it possible for him to realize these annihilative urges with complete "authority," as he wrote to Villeneuve. Although his patrons were aware of his activities, they did nothing to restrain him. On the contrary, Villeneuve's response to his bombastic letter broadcasting his obliteration of Sparta was one of appreciation for his services. "I saw with pleasure the important discoveries you have made in terms of monuments and inscriptions and the considerable advantages you believe the Republic of letters will derive from them."[82] Thus Fourmont was able to act with license and impunity not so much because French officials approved of his methods as simply because they were concerned with the outcome, and not with the means employed to achieve it.

Fourmont was an expression of the temper of his time in another respect: he wanted to satisfy his vanity by making an impression marking his passage through Greece. To achieve this, he chose the obliteration of ruins. "This was the only means I had," he wrote to Bignon, "of making my voyage to the Morea illustrious, which without it would have been quite useless and therefore unsuitable for France and for me."[83]

Even though he was proud of the way he carried on in Greece, Fourmont felt compelled to justify his actions. For this reason he invoked the prevalent belief that civilization had fled Greece and found a new abode in Europe. Since Greece was now populated by barbarians, one should not be expected to obey the strictures of civilized behavior. "I become a barbarian in the midst of Greece; this country is no longer the abode of the Muses; ignorance has chased them away, which makes me miss France, where they have sought refuge."[84]

Although Greece had ceased to exist as an independent world of high culture, its ancient history and civilization conferred on it a character distinct from that of the other Ottoman lands. The modern Greeks were seen as a separate entity set apart from their rulers by religion, language, and customs. Whether they drew sympathy or denigration, it was invariably on the basis of their affinities with or divergencies from their ancestors. This association, even though it was predominantly negative, paved the way for philhellenism, which envisaged their revival through the regenerative influence of Hellenism.

3

ATHENS AND
ITS MONUMENTS:
THE SEVENTEENTH CENTURY

Dim Reflections of a Distant Radiance

After the eclipse of antiquity, sealed by the closing of the philosophical schools by Justinian, Athens lay forgotten for centuries, enshrouded by a mantle of silence. For the medieval pilgrim it offered no sacred relics and held no promises of spiritual renewal or salvation. For the merchant and the diplomat, the centers of activity were to be found in other cities of the Near East. Athens's political and cultural ascendancy in the eastern Mediterranean disappeared with the demise of classical civilization and passed on to other urban centers as new societies appeared in the area.

From the fourteenth to the seventeenth century, Athens received but a handful of visitors. The two Westerners who came during the second half of the fourteenth century were both pilgrims who stopped on their way to the Holy Land. The first was the German priest Ludolf von Südheim, whose account of his brief stay in 1350 was full of inaccurate, fanciful information evincing not the slightest awareness of the city's classical past. The second was the Italian Nicolo Martoni, who spent two days in Athens in February 1390. He too recounted the wonders associated with the monuments in his *Liber peregrinationis ad Loca Sancta*. This work is useful as a record of the medieval legends about the city, not of the state of antiquities. He was moved by the beauty of the Parthenon, or the Church of Panagia (Virgin Mary), as it was known then, and admired its rich collection of gospels. But to him it was only a Christian church and not a pagan temple.[1]

In 1436, Athens received the first true antiquary, Cyriac of Ancona, who was fully aware of the classical origin of its monuments. He called the Parthenon the Temple of Minerva, although it still functioned as an Orthodox church (it was transformed into a mosque in 1460). After a hiatus of almost two centuries, Johannes Meursius made the first topographical study of the city, *Athenae Atticae* (1624). His information, however, was based on literary sources and not on personal observation.

The first serious attention and systematic observation of Athens's classical sites occurred in the second half of the seventeenth century when the legacy it bequeathed to the Western world was acknowledged and prized. Thus, as with Greece in general, the idea of Athens existed before and above the physical city, a product of many changes through time. The emergence of Athens in the consciousness of modern Europeans is unique. Unlike Rome, which continued to play a vital role almost uninterruptedly, Athens reentered the Western world, so to speak, more as a symbol of a bygone era and less as a place of current significance. In this instance cultural and intellectual considerations preceded political interests.

It was during the seventeenth century, especially the second half, that French travelers directed their steps toward Athens. Their descriptions of the town were at first vague recollections of its past grandeur combined with passing glimpses at its present. Then they became progressively more comprehensive and precise in their treatment of both the ancient monuments and contemporary conditions. The first post-Renaissance Frenchman to set foot in the city was Louis des Hayes, baron de Courmerin, ambassador to the Sublime Porte. He stopped at Athens on his way to the Ottoman capital in 1626 and recorded his impressions in his *Voiage de Levant fait par le commandement du Roy* (1632).[2] The significance of the following passage is not only that it is the first in a series of descriptions over several centuries but also that it shows the transition from the state of oblivion which had enveloped the city to its emerging importance. This is how the city appeared to the French ambassador:

The City of Athens is situated on the slope and in the surroundings of a rock, which sits on a plain bordering on the sea to the
south and on pleasant mountains that enclose it in the north. It
is not half as large as it formerly was, as one can see by its ruins,
to which time has caused less harm than the barbarousness of the
nations that have sacked and pillaged this city so many times. The
ancient buildings that remain testify to the magnificence of those
who made them; because neither marble nor columns nor pilas-
ters were spared. On the top of the rock there is the castle, which
the Turks still use today. Among several ancient buildings there is
a temple that is as whole and unscathed by the injuries of time as
if it had been just made; its order and structure are admirable; its
form is oval on the outside as well as on the inside; it is supported
by three rows of marble columns, complete with bases and capi-
tals; behind each column there is a pilaster of the same order and
proportion.[3]

This is the testimony of a man who, unlike Cyriac of Ancona two
hundred years earlier, had scant knowledge of ancient Athens, since
he was unable to identify even the Parthenon. Nevertheless he was
well aware and appreciative of its past splendor.

A more knowledgeable and inquisitive traveler appeared in Athens
three decades after Louis des Hayes. The Jesuit missionary Jacques
Paul Babin probed its monuments with an admiring eye and cast a
sympathetic glance on its inhabitants. When he had completed his
stay there, he returned to Smyrna, the base of his missionary activities, by way of Constantinople. While in the Ottoman capital, he
met the abbé Pécoil, who was in the service of the French ambassador, the marquis de Nointel. Pécoil asked the Jesuit father for a
detailed account of his impressions of Athens and received the promise that he would find it ready during his next visit to Smyrna. It
took somewhat longer than Babin expected, but finally the relation,
written in the form of a letter, was completed in Smyrna on 8 October 1672 and sent on to Lyon, where Père Pécoil was now the canon
of the church of Saint-Just.

Père Pécoil communicated Babin's letter to Jacob Spon, a local
physician well known for his classical erudition, asking him to have
it published if it met with his approval. Spon was very impressed
with the judicious critique and clear presentation of Babin's narrative, which gave a balanced view of the ancient city combining obser-

vations about its classical monuments, Byzantine churches, and contemporary social life. He accepted it without reservation and arranged for its publication. In 1674 he brought out an annotated edition of Babin's text with a preface and a general plan of the city.[4] For the first time the French public was presented with a visual delineation of modern Athens, which, although not a faithful representation of the city, provided a view of its expanse and topographical and architectural features.

In view of the scarcity—or, rather, the absence—of contemporary books on Athens, Babin had to rely on Pausanias and other ancient authors in his effort to examine and identify the confused mass of ruins lying about. As with all foreign visitors who came before and after him, his attention was arrested by the Acropolis and its monuments. The Parthenon, high above the city, summoned the abbé to its sacred precinct.[5]

In the course of modern times, the Acropolis and its monuments, especially the Parthenon, have been seen as the quintessence of the artistic achievements of the ancients. Countless visitors have been moved as much by their intrinsic beauty as by the images and values they conjure up. Those who recorded their impressions felt impelled to exercise their descriptive talents and expressive abilities. A comparative analysis of the literary portrayals of these fabled ruins covering the span from the seventeenth-century narrative descriptions to Renan's composite but evocative *Prière sur l'Acropole* (1876) shows the development of the sensibility, historical consciousness, and the meaning of Hellenism among French writers.

Babin was well within the mainstream of his time. Nurtured in the rising classicism of his era and not lacking in classical erudition, he expressed uncontained admiration at the sight of such beauty. However, no lyrical and rhapsodic evocations or moments of rapturous transport color his narrative. He made no attempt to mark his passage by composing an eloquent prose destined to stir the heart and fire the imagination of his readers. The driving desire to impress one's existence on the fleeting and constantly moving path of time through the power of the written word, thus ensuring a kind of immortality, came only with the advent of romantic Hellenism. Chauteaubriand and Byron were its two most characteristic representatives. For the seventeenth-century traveler-writer psychological and aesthetic quests of this nature were almost nonexistent. What mattered primarily was the transmission of information mingled with personal judgments and comments. Observation was more important than poetry. Because of this objective approach and the fact that the Parthenon was almost intact when Babin, Spon, and Nointel saw it, their descriptions are of the utmost importance for the reconstruction of its original form.

Being a man of the cloth, Babin took particular notice of the continuous religious function of the temple: paganism succeeded by Christianity, and Christianity by Islam. The successive cultural waves that swept over Greece were enshrined, so to speak, in this single structure, and the marks of all three were still clearly visible until its destruction by Morosini in 1687. After the explosion, almost all traces of the last two religious worlds were effaced forever, and thus the ruined temple was ironically cleansed of foreign intrusions, and classical antiquity could claim it entirely once more. This is how it appeared to Babin:

> I entered only one of the *Mosques of Athens,* which was first a Temple built by the Gentiles in honor of the Goddess *Pallas* before the coming of the son of God, and then dedicated by the Christians to the *Eternal Wisdom*, following the teachings of the Apostles. This Temple, which can be seen from afar, and which, placed in the middle of the *Citadel,* is the most elevated edifice of Athens, is a masterpiece of the most excellent Architects of antiquity.[6]

The Christian traces and the Muslim modifications and additions, although they had altered the interior of the temple, had scarcely distorted its external architectural form. Babin was struck by its beauty and perfection and expressed his admiration with refreshing wonderment.

> The Frontispiece of the Temple, which rises high above this vestibule, is such that I believe it is difficult to find in all of France anything resembling its magnificence and workmanship. The figures and the statues of Richelieu's Château, which is the marvel of France and the masterpiece of the workers of our time, have nothing to offer in comparison with these beautiful and grand figures of men, women, and horses, numbering about thirty in the frontispiece and as many on the other side of the Temple, behind the place where the Christians had placed the great Altar. . . . The upper parts of the walls of this Temple are embel-

lished on the outside with a beautiful marble frieze worked to perfection, on which one sees a quantity of triumphs representing in
a semirelief form an infinity of men, women, children, horses,
and chariots represented on these stones, which are so elevated
that the eyes can but with difficulty discover all their beauty.
(28–29, 30)

Under the shadow of the noble edifices of the Acropolis and in
marked contrast with them lay the modern town of Athens, small
and unassuming. Above it loomed the vision of the other Athens,
the ideal and eternal city. Babin was one of the first French travelers
to dwell on this antithesis and to juxtapose the two antipodal images.

> Most of the streets resemble those of a village. Instead of these
> superb edifices, these glorious trophies, and these rich temples
> that were once the ornament of this city, one sees nothing but
> houses devoid of any magnificence, made from ancient ruins, hav-
> ing for their sole ornament some pieces of marble columns
> embedded in their walls without any order, in the same manner
> as the other stones. (11–12)

Babin, a thorough and comprehensive observer, gave not only
classical ruins but also Christian churches and monasteries his undi-
vided attention. Not unexpectedly, his praise and admiration were
reserved for the former.

Babin's significance is twofold: he was one of the first French travelers to give an inclusive picture of seventeenth-century Athens and
also one of the first to voice views and opinions on the character of
the modern Athenians. In judging them, he could not but have
recourse to the ancients, singling out those traits that were seemingly derived from them. "They still show this inclination to tell or
hear news; this curiosity is not derived only from their ancestors' heritage; but they still have great self-esteem notwithstanding their servitude, misery, and poverty under the domination of the Turks" (53).
Like other European observers, he looked for signs of learning, but
whereas most of them saw nothing but ignorance, he was pleased to
discern some stirrings of intellectual activity among some of its
more prominent citizens. He was equally impressed by instances of
individual courage and virtue. Despite these redeeming features,
modern Athens was but a faint echo of its former self, and Babin pre-
dicted correctly that its subjugation would continue for a long time

"since they [the Turks] are masters of all Greece, which now suffers this servitude with as much timidity and silence as the grandeur, courage, and intrepidity it displayed in olden times in order to maintain its honor and liberty" (182).

Babin's account, though brief and in certain places cursory and incomplete, was an important stage in the depiction of modern Athens because it gave an all-embracing portrayal of the city which focused on both its human and physical elements. Written in a straightforward and unadorned prose very much in the vein of contemporary travelogues, it encapsulated and typified in many respects the stylistic and structural composition and the mental attitudes expressed through them.

Athens Comes of Age:
Spon's Voyage to Greece

As I noted, Spon saw in Babin's essay a reliable eyewitness account and judged it worthy of public attention. It was perhaps no mere coincidence, then, that the erudite doctor from Lyon decided to visit Athens one year after the appearance of Babin's book. Even before leaving France, Spon had assembled an extensive collection of ancient inscriptions, an avocation he pursued even more avidly in the Levant. He left his native city in the fall of 1674, stopping in Italy before embarking on his eastward voyage. While there, he met three Englishmen, the botanist George Wheler and the noblemen G. Eastcourt and Fr. Vernon. The first became his constant companion throughout his voyage, and the other two parted company with them on the island of Zante.

They all gathered at Venice, whence they set out on their journey on 20 June 1675. The ship they boarded was the same one that was transporting Morosini, former Venetian ambassador to France, to his new ambassadorial post at Constantinople. While sailing through the Ionian Sea, they visited some of its islands. Corfu and Zante figured most prominently among them. Spon used his brief stay there to observe their architecture and social life, taking particular note of the level of education, commercial activities, and religious practices. When he completed his voyage and compared the

Ionian Islands to Ottoman-held Greece, he concluded that the former enjoyed a far better level of existence because Venetian rule was unquestionably less oppressive and more beneficent than Turkish. The travelers then skirted the Peloponnesus and traversed the Aegean before reaching Constantinople, the destination of the first part of their voyage, on 23 September 1675.

When Spon and Wheler arrived at the Ottoman capital, they immediately contacted the French ambassador, the marquis de Nointel, and received from him, as was customary then, hospitality, guidance, and, more importantly, letters of recommendation and passports that would facilitate their voyage. Nointel, who had returned recently from his long tour of Asia Minor and Greece, proudly showed them his numerous acquisitions and the sketches of the Parthenon he had commissioned. This was Spon's second indirect introduction to the antiquities of Athens. From Constantinople, Spon and Wheler followed the land route to Smyrna, a thriving commercial center whose merchants dealt in, among other things, antiquities, particularly manuscripts and coins. Spon, who was as competent a numismatologist as he was an epigraphist, thought of these activities as honest and beneficial because they helped increase and disseminate knowledge of antiquity. The two travelers boarded a ship sailing for the Peloponnesus in December 1675. The first Greek mainland city to receive them was not Athens but Patras. From there they crossed to Lepanto, then they proceeded inland to Delphi and took the road to Athens, passing through Thebes.

Athens had been the objective of Spon's voyage from its very inception. "We had difficulty choosing the route that we could take in order to go to Athens, the real goal for which we had undertaken our voyage."[7] Spon, though not the first Frenchman to visit Athens, was certainly the first one to make it the true object of his travel. His predecessors had visited the city either en route to or returning from Constantinople, where they were engaged in diplomatic or missionary activities. Spon had no such commitments. He undertook his journey with the purpose of satisfying his intellectual curiosity, expanding his classical learning, and enriching his collection of inscriptions. What better place to realize these expectations than Athens? Its surviving ancient monuments would broaden and at the same time challenge his knowledge of antiquity by testing his ability to identify them.

Spon has been acclaimed, and rightly so, as the most important seventeenth-century traveler to visit Athens and Greece in general. He was a thorough and meticulous observer and a fair and reliable critic, and there was system and method to his observations, which relied primarily on classical sources to locate and identify the ruins of ancient structures and to a lesser degree on popular traditions. These sources, however—historical records, existing monuments, and current legends and traditions—had to be weighed by the observer before any conclusions could be formulated. Spon himself stressed the importance of critical judgment. "The surest way in these matters is to show no favor to common opinions, if one has not examined them on one's own, and if one has not weighed them on the scales of reason" (V, 2:168).

Spon's approach to the study of antiquity exemplifies the new methods of histriography, which emphasized the use of a variety of sources for the accurate reconstruction of the past.[8] Textual information, the careful observation of physical surroundings and the present state of the ruins, and the reading of inscriptions, if any were to be found, provided the physical evidence for the reconstruction of the monuments's past. The formulation of conclusions was the outcome of a comparative analysis of these findings, guided by reason. In this respect, Spon was within the scientific spirit of his time, which aimed at the discovery of permanent laws that lie behind the phenomena of observable reality. His method validated the paramountcy of the two key principles introduced by Renaissance humanism for the investigation of the natural and the human world: observation and reason.

This does not mean that he did not commit errors. For instance, he mistook the theater of Herod Atticus for the theater of Bacchus and the columns of the temple of Zeus Olympius (Olympieum) for the palace of Hadrian. If one thinks of the conditions under which he was working, however, one would find more than ample justification for his mistakes. Reliable travel accounts, except for Babin's brief work, exact topographical maps and sketches of antiquities, and critical studies of them were nonexistent. To complicate matters even more, the Turkish authorities restricted free movement and put obstacles in the way of Europeans because they suspected them of spying. Moreover, the state of the monuments was nothing like today's neat arrangements made by archeologists and ritualistically described and explained by tour guides. What Spon and his contemporaries saw was a disorienting confusion, which Spon conveyed in his description of Ephesus in one of his more contemplative moments.

> I believe there is not a City in the world which has so great and so sad remains of its ancient splendor. Everywhere one sees nothing but pieces of marble, toppled walls, columns, capitals, and pieces of statues piled one on top of the other, with inscriptions one can uncover in various places; and it is when one speaks of Ephesus that one can say that it is no longer more than the cadaver of a City, according to Cicero's thought when he spoke of some Greek Cities.[9]

In some places the appearance of the ancient monuments had been further altered by the erection of churches on the very same ground and with materials from the monuments' toppled walls. One need only make a mental reconstruction of the ravaged and neglected state of ancient sites to value the efforts of such a pioneer amateur archeologist as Spon. In the words of his critic Laborde, "Spon did more than one could expect of a single man: with a vigorous hand he swept away a host of errors, and if he did not always see well himself, he taught future travelers the sound method of seeing and describing."[10]

Spon related his findings in a matter-of-fact and orderly fashion. The course of the narrative followed that of his journey: a horizontal progression through space and time, with clearly focused stages, without digressions or graphic descriptions. His mind was not of a philosophical, pensive, or didactic bent. Nor was he inclined to emotional transports or lyrical musings. For him fables and ancient legends were fanciful stories, and the mythological memories associated with a place could do very little to alleviate present hardships. When he and his companion were forced to spend a night on the deserted island of Delos with scarcely enough food, they found no solace in recreating its dazzling moment in history. "Our sleep," he commented wryly, "was not very deep that night because of our anxiety as to what would become of us on this miserable reef of Delos, whose ancient renown could give us nothing to eat."[11] When one notes that similar nights spent by Chateaubriand on the banks of the Eurotas or under the solitary columns of Sounion, and fraught with similar physical privations, were transformed by the memory of the past, one can see clearly the evolution of both the poetical sensibility and the historical consciousness of French writers.

Spon's work consists of three volumes: the first deals with Italy, Dalmatia, Constantinople, and Smyrna; the second treats mainland Greece; the third is a long essay on transcribing epigraphy which comments on the inscriptions he collected. The book was dedicated to Père de la Chaize, the king's counselor and ordinary confessor. Its publication in 1678, two years after the author's return from Greece, marked, according to Laborde, "an epoch in the history of Athens." In it Athens received the most extensive treatment of all the places he visited, and for the first time a full portrait of the city was unveiled to the French and European public. In conducting his investigation, Spon had two invaluable guides, the consul Giraud and Pausanias. The former was a generous host to European travelers, and, as a permanent resident of the city, he had wide knowledge of its past and present which he imparted most eagerly. Spon expressed his gratitude to him by acknowledging that it was because of his unstinting cooperation that he was able to see all the sights of Athens.

What picture of seventeenth-century Athens emerges from Spon's pages? It was a small town of eight or nine thousand inhabitants, three-fourths of whom were Greek and the rest Turks. (The French consul Giraud estimated its population to be seven thousand, while Guillet gave the inflated figure of fifteen or sixteen thousand.) Most of the houses were huddled around the Acropolis. The monotony and modesty of the place receded when one came upon the ruins of its ancient prototype. Christianity too made its presence felt by the numerous churches, chapels, and monasteries, which dotted the Attic landscape. The most recent arrival, Islam, raised its monuments as well. The minarets of five mosques—the Parthenon being one of them—defiantly pierced the Athenian sky. The climate was benign and salubrious and had a direct effect on the temperament and character of the people:

> The air of the entire country is very pure and very good, particularly that of Athens: this was the reason that it produced subtle minds suitable for learning, as Cicero said: and although the Athenians rarely take pains over it since the Ottoman domination, one cannot fail to see in them a natural politeness and a great skill in all the affairs they undertake. (*V,* 2:120–21)

Whether the climate had the same influence on the Turkish inhabitants of the city is not explained. Spon and his contemporaries who
came to Athens had little to say about its Turkish residents. When
they used the term *Athéniens* they invariably referred to the Greeks
of the city, thus implicitly excluding its Ottoman dwellers. And yet
it was clearly the Turks who were in control of the town. Administrative authority was in the hands of the *voivode* (governor), the
kadi (judge), and the *aga* (military commandant) of the Acropolis,
which served as a garrison headquarters and arms depot for the
Turks. The Greeks regulated some of their own affairs through their
ecclesiastical authorities and council of elders, or *epitropoi,* representing the most prominent Athenian families. The town was the fief of
Keslar-Aga, the chief of the Black Eunuchs, who received its reve-
nues.[12] The ruler-subject relationship between the two peoples was
apparent in their dress. "The dress of the Greeks of Athens is quite
different form that of the Turks; because they can wear only narrow
black or dark jackets with black boots covering their legs, while the
Turks wear boots only in the country or in bad weather, and these
boots are yellow; they wear wide colorful jackets and a turban on
their head."[13]

Contemporary life was only one aspect of the city, and not the
most important one at that. Ancient Athens was far more enticing,
beckoning its visitors to come and restore its memory. To its written
monuments now could be added its physical ones, which were even
more disfigured and unrecognizable. Spon contributed to their identification by taking exact measurements, giving precise topographical data, and establishing correspondences between ancient texts and
the surviving structures. A good part, if not most, of his investigative efforts was centered on the edifices of the Acropolis. Having
obtained permission from the Turkish authorities to visit the fortified hill thanks to the intercession of Giraud, Spon and Wheler
ascended its steep incline.

There, before them, rose "le Temple de Minerve." Its arresting
view inspired them with respect and admiration. Passing through
the shattered columns of the Propylaea, victims of an earlier explosion, Spon paused momentarily to inspect the elegant Ionic temple
of Nike, which at that time served as a gunpowder magazine. Then,
under the surveillance of the Turkish militiamen, they approached
the Parthenon, which retained its full nobility and harmony even

under the guise of a "grande Mosquée." Spon, the meticulous and unsentimental observer that he was, immediately measured its dimensions and examined the sculptures of its frieze and pediments. He noted that time had already taken its toll: many of the sculpted figures showed signs of erosion and mutilation. Still, its exterior was in good condition; its architectural strength had successfully resisted the assaults made on it by its several invaders.

Its interior, which was plain and unadorned, had not been so fortunate. "Thus there is no ornament; on the contrary, the Turks by an incredible stupidity have whitewashed everything in its interior although it would be infinitely more beautiful if the marble from which the entire structure is made were visible" (*V,* 2:158). Noting the darkness inside, Spon, in one of his rare speculative moments, hypothesized that the ancients sought to create a dark atmosphere because they imagined that obscurity added majesty and inspired awe and respect. The interior features of the temple showed no marks of the ancient pagan rites for which it was created. Now Christianity and Islam shared it, the first only in a vestigial form and the second as an actively practiced religion.

> The Turks have left the dais of the altar which was there during the time of the Christians. It is supported by four porphyry columns with beautiful Corinthian capitals. They were taken from the débris of another Temple . . . and in the middle of the Temple on the left side there is a raised tribune resting on small marble columns, which must undoubtedly have been the pulpit. But on the other side there is another one made for the Turks, where the Imam explains the Koran; as for that marble throne that is in the back of the choir, it is not used for anything. It was the seat of the Archbishop when he officiated. (2:155–56)

Beyond the Parthenon stood the Erechtheum, which, however, was unapproachable because it housed the harem. Spon could discern the Caryatids, which he mistook for the three Graces. The ground between the two temples was covered by huts and other makeshift structures used by the soldiers of the garrison stationed on the Acropolis. Although Spon's descriptions are not evocative and graphic, they are precise and detailed enough to enable us to visualize its composite appearance at a particular moment of its history.

Before departing for France, Spon made two brief excursions into the surrounding area. Accompanied by Wheler, he visited the islands of Salamis, Poros, and Aegina. In his crisp and laconic manner, he described the desolate state of these islands and the plight of their inhabitants, beset by poverty and preyed upon by pirates. The travelers returned to Athens to replenish their supplies and on 15 February 1676 set out for Eleusis, then known as Lepsina, Megara, and Corinth. Eleusis, Spon commented, was an amorphous mass of ruins deserted by its inhabitants, who could no longer withstand the cruelty and rapacity of Christian pirates.

Like Eleusis, Piraeus was then known under a different name. It was called Porto-Draco by the Greeks and Porto-Lione by the Franks. The name was derived from a large marble lion on the shore crouched on its hind legs and raising its head high above the harbor, its gaze fixed in the distance out to sea. Also like Eleusis, the once bustling port was now completely deserted except for a warehouse, which also served as a customhouse. So forlorn and abandoned was the countryside that even the collected and undemonstrative Spon keenly felt the eclipse of the ancients. Delphi, so prominent in Greek myth and history, existed only as a mental image, its physical signs having all but disappeared. Spon and his companion felt obliged "to look for Delphi in Delphi itself," and when they discovered the outline of what appeared to have been a stadium, they had to make an imaginary reconstruction by consulting ancient texts.

Ancient monuments had already fallen under the destructive blows of war and conquest. Their ruins were now left to disintegrate, eroded slowly by time or dismantled by collectors of antiquities. Monasteries and contemporary communities, however, were often the targets of marauding bandits in the inland regions and merciless pirates along the coast. The latter roamed the Mediterranean with impunity. They preyed on wealthy monasteries, European travelers to the Levant, and the inhabitants of the islands and coastal areas, bringing about their depopulation. Piracy was an occupation as ancient as the history of the Mediterranean. Its practitioners in modern times were of various national origins: Saracens, the Arabs of Tunisia, Morocco, and Algeria, Greeks, and, as the western European presence increased in the eastern Mediterranean, Venetians and French. The Knights of Malta were a particularly redoubtable group. Vandal, Nointel's biographer, commented that they made piracy "their sole occupation, their *raison d'être*: the glorious order of Saint John was transformed into an association of pirates, who scoured the seas of the Levant and whose every member thought to possess the authority to wreak havoc in the Archipelago by virtue of the white cross he wore on his chest."[14]

Another group of pirates came from the ranks of the nobility, whose younger members, having no prospect of inheritance, looked upon piracy as an attractive and gainful occupation. Lured by adventure and the constant threat of death, against which they had to measure themselves daily, those belated and misplaced knights-errant outfitted their own vessels and launched themselves on a career of violence and bravado. They accrued their profits from pillaging, kidnapping for ransom, and the slave trade. They came down with equal fury and rapacity on Christian and Muslim, peasant and noble, native and foreigner. Nointel himself had a perilous encounter on Chios with a band of pirates from Tripoli. Not only did they assail and plunder his ship, but they attacked the place where he and his entourage had sought refuge. Luckily, they were repulsed and Nointel came out unscathed. Spon witnessed the physical signs of this ever present menace. On his way to Eleusis he stopped to see the monastery of Daphni. Once a prosperous establishment, it was now completely abandoned because of the frequent incursions by Turks and Christian pirates. This lurking danger was yet another burden added to the woes of peasants and islanders, forcing them to retreat to inaccessible areas for better protection.

After Eleusis, Spon visited Corinth, which was the last stage of his tour of mainland Greece. He returned to Athens and on 9 March 1676 embarked on his return voyage to France. Once in his native city he resumed his medical practice and set to work on his travel account. Its publication two years later enhanced his already established reputation as an antiquarian and epigraphist. His avocation, however, had detrimental effects on his profession, which suffered because his prestige as a classicist overshadowed his prominence as a doctor and because of alleged neglect.[15] He saw his clientele slip and his income diminish to the point of impoverishment. He left France for Geneva, where he was sustained for some time by contributions from friends before falling seriously ill. He died on 25 December 1685 at the age of thirty-eight. Such was the brief career of the doctor-archeologist whose name would henceforth be associated with that of Athens.

Did the ancient city fulfill his expectations? Neither he nor his

contemporaries were imbued with visions of an eternally radiant
Greece. In setting out on his voyage, he was linguistically and scien-
tifically as well prepared as was possible, given his time and position,
but emotionally he was neutral. Not that he was incapable of experiencing the joy of anticipation. When he entered the Greek space, he
felt that he was sailing not in strange waters but toward a long-forgotten ancestral home that stirred vague intimations of kinship and
affinity. "We began then to see ourselves at the entrance of Greece,
which gave us as much joy as Aenias once felt grief when he passed
through those quarters, because he considered the Greeks to be the
destroyers of his country. As for us, we looked at them as the people
to whose ancestors we owed the Sciences and the Arts."[16] The Europeans' voyage to their spiritual homeland, Greece, had begun, and the
triangular relation—Europe-ancient Greece-modern Greece—was
clearly articulated by Spon.

But there was little left of the ancestral estate. Pillaged and under
foreign rule, it spoke more to the memory than to immediate perception. By its very absence, the past dwarfed and overshadowed the
present. In his closing remarks about Athens, Spon abandoned his
reserved tone and insistence on factual information and drew the following conclusion:

> Finally, do not be surprised that I have not described a greater
> number of antiquities of a City about which, it seems, there
> should be so many things to say. This is all I was able to observe:
> and I believe that even if we had been able to stay longer, we
> would not have departed any more satisfied. . . . One could sim-
> ply say on this subject that Athens is no longer more than a big
> poorhouse, which contains as many wretches as there are Chris-
> tians under the Turks' domination. . . . Time has finished off
> what had been spared by wars. (*V*, 2:307–8)

The prestige of Spon's work brought to the attention of the public
the name of his companion during his travels, George Wheler, to
whom Spon gave due credit by mentioning his name in the title and
throughout his narrative. Although each of them had started out on
his own, they had decided to join company when they met in Rome
for the first time and took an immediate liking to each other. Their
destination was the same, but not their interests and qualifications.
Spon was unquestionably the one whose background and knowl-

edge had prepared him to study the ancient monuments with a critical and judicious eye. He had a specific aim in mind: the collection of inscriptions in order to expand and supplement the work of the Dutch humanist Gruter, *Inscriptiones antiquae totius orbis Romanae* (1603). He was able to bring back with him two thousand inscriptions from both Greece and Italy.

Wheler, by contrast, was neither an antiquarian nor a Hellenist. By training he was a botanist, and in the course of his voyage he learned the rudiments of cartography and topography. Not unexpectedly, then, his acquisitions consisted of one thousand plant specimens. Being in Spon's company, however, he was inevitably exposed to the same experiences and the same stimuli. This may have led him to believe that he had a right to his companion's work. Thus, when he was informed that Spon's book was to be translated into English, he deemed it proper to undertake the task and to be styled not as translator but as author. By translating verbatim whole passages, paraphrasing and transposing others, inserting some of his own, and finally, adding two plans of Athens, a map of Achaia, and some sketches of costumes and plants, he composed a one-volume work entitled *A Journey into Greece by George Wheler esq., in the Company of Dr. Spon of Lyon* (London, 1682). The authenticity of the work was not questioned, and in 1689 a French translation appeared in Amsterdam. Ironically, the title of this translation bore a close resemblance to that of Spon's work.[17] The publication of this rival work did not compromise or diminish Spon's reputation. If anything, it helped enhance it. Spon himself did not contest the appropriation of his ideas, and thus no dispute arose between the former travel companions.

A literary quarrel, however, did erupt between Spon and another travel writer, André Georges Guillet. In 1675, Guillet published a work entitled *Athènes ancienne et nouvelle,* followed by another, *Lacédémone ancienne et nouvelle,* in 1676. Although he admitted that he had not visited these places, he claimed that he acted as the editor of his brother's memoirs, who had gone to Greece in 1669. Guillet maintained that he gave form and literary character to this information so that it could be published and that he also supplied the historical background by consulting ancient sources. The alleged brother, Sr. de la Gulletière, according to Guillet, was born in Auvergne and entered a military career. Being at the mercy of the vicissitudes of war, he found himself in Hungary, where he was captured and imprisoned by the Turks. He was sold to a Tunisian pirate and, after enduring the ordeals and tribulations of a captive, was set free in February 1669. Being in the eastern Mediterranean, he decided to visit Greece and the Levant in the company of two Germans, two Italians, and an Englishman. While still in Greece, he kept a journal of his experiences and views, which he then sent to his learned brother in France.

What better way to excite and captivate the imagination of the reader than to open his narrative with a story about pirates, whose perilous adventures were a very popular theme at the time! Another literary device used often by writers was the adoption of borrowed or fictitious names under whose guise the author appeared as the editor of a discovered manuscript. Guillet employed these means with felicitous results. His *Athènes ancienne et nouvelle* enjoyed an instant success: within the same year it went through four editions, and in 1676 it was translated into English as *Account of a late Voyage to Athens with an Account of Ancient and Modern Athens*.

This popularity began to wane when Spon questioned the accuracy of some of Guillet's descriptions. Spon obtained a copy of *Athènes ancienne et nouvelle* when he was in Venice, he read it on his way to Greece, and thus was able to put Guillet's (or de la Guilletière's) observations to the test when he himself investigated the monuments of Athens. He detected some inaccuracies and erroneous identifications, which he pointed out with a tinge of irony in his *Voyage d'Italie*:

> You will tell me perhaps that it is quite useless to write about Athens after what M. de la Guilletière has so curiously researched in the Book that appeared two years ago; but, as I have made many observations that he did not give us, and as I have noticed that several of his are a little feeble and are in need of a Doctor, I do not believe I am undertaking an affair beyond my reach.[18]

He went on to say that despite its shortcomings the book should be appreciated for its many merits.

This palliative, however, did not appease Guillet, who took exception to Spon's critical comments and lashed back at him with a virulent critique of his work.[19] Resorting to an artifice once more, he set up a scenario in which the author, Guillet, and five friends initiated a discussion on Spon's book while taking a walk in the countryside. The friends, a numismatologist, a geographer, a historian, a mathematician, and a lawyer, were decidedly against Spon with the exception of the lawyer, who put up a rather ineffectual defense. The verdict was that Spon was guilty of several fallacies centered on historical and geographical facts and inconsistent spelling. More seriously, his scholarly competence was questioned when his reading and transcription of inscriptions were deemed incorrect. As the discussion continued, the criticism mounted until it verged on the absurd and the malicious. The mathematician suggested that Spon's erudition was dubious and his veracity questionable, and he even went so far as to insinuate that Spon had never visited Athens. Guillet was obviously piqued by Spon's implications that his brother's travel to the Levant was but a fabrication.

> The latter [de la Guilletière], who, as you know, gave to the public the Book *Athènes ancienne et nouvelle*, is treated as an impostor in a cavalier way. He is the object of twenty biting derisions strewn from the beginning to the end of the second volume of the Account. Time will show who will have the last laugh and what will be said of a man who deliberately sets himself up as a satirical and mocking Aggressor.[20]

Spon's response was quick and equally sarcastic and denigrating. The mild and reserved criticism he had voiced before now became a full-blown attack. He characterized Guillet's books as fictions compiled from information supplied by the Capuchin missionaries in Greece. Spon had met a Capuchin from the mission of Napoli de Romanie (Nauplion), who showed him a memoir sent from Guillet's friends in Paris asking specific questions concerning places ranging from Misithra (Mistras) to Salonika. Spon inserted this document in his *Réponse* as a further proof of Guillet's use of secondary sources. Spon's claims have since been corroborated by other evidence showing that the Capuchins helped disseminate information about Greece, especially Athens, in the form of either plans and sketches—notable among them was a plan of Athens[21]—or oral and written reports. Guillet chose to leave unacknowledged his debt to the Capuchins and instead invented his brother's adventures in the Mediterranean, which gave his narrative an aura of intrigue. Spon's exposure called Guillet's veracity into question, thus bringing to a halt the popularity of the latter's works. The polemics eventually subsided, but Guillet's reputation was never restored.[22] Had his brother appeared on the scene, the record might have been set straight. But even his existence was not proved.

This dispute illustrates two developments in the nature and scope of travel accounts. First, the urgency of direct experience and personal contact with the people and places one described was no longer a necessary prerequisite, as it had been in the sixteenth century. The existence by the end of the seventeenth century of a substantial body of travel literature made it possible for authors who were either unable or unwilling to subject themselves to the rigors of traveling to compose narratives by relying on the observations of others. Thus the question of literary borrowings arose among writers of travel accounts, some of whom preferred not to acknowledge or reveal their true sources. The boundaries between actual travel and imaginary travel experienced vicariously through the pages of a book became hazy, and by the eighteenth century travelers saw as much through the eyes of other travelers as they did through their own. Second, the success of Guillet's books attests to the spreading popularity of travel accounts and the rising importance of Greece, and especially Athens, as a center of attraction.

Despite his use of a subterfuge, or perhaps because of it, Guillet's works possess a certain value, less as sources of information than as reflections of current attitudes toward Greece and its people. He wove a composite narrative where the description of a monument prompted an excursus into its origin and history, and a comment on the customs of the people led to the search for similar practices among the ancients. The very titles of his books, stressing both the old and the new aspects of Athens and Lacedaemon, are indicative of this characteristic. Although the practice of comparing and contrasting the moderns with the ancients appeared at the onset of travel accounts, Guillet, being removed from the immediate and often disorienting impact of personal experience, dwelt on it more extensively.

His parallelisms are abstract and schematic, and in the case of Sparta they verge on the purely fantastic. Since there were no visible traces of the ancient city, he had to invent them. He located it in the Byzantine city of Mistras and envisioned streets, temples, and arenas, placing them at will here and there. From this imaginary geography he proceeded to reconstruct the games, contests, and public activities of the ancient Spartans. Clearly, personal observation was of little importance to him. Direct experience had been supplanted by the written word, which could recreate, rather arbitrarily, distant times and places.

Alternating between past and present was at the heart of Guillet's approach to his subject. "I intend to show you the relation and the difference of the ancient mores of the Country and present-day manners. In effect, I pass from one century to the next, changing examples without changing the subject."[23] Among the French writers on Greece, he was the first to use the device of parallelism in a consistent way. In this respect he anticipated Pierre-Augustin Guys, who a century later adopted the same method in a more systematic way in his *Voyage littéraire de la Grèce* (1783). Guillet's comments and conclusions, however, were more often than not superficial and speculative since they lacked the insight and perspective afforded by personal observation and experience. Furthermore, unlike Guys, whose purpose in drawing parallels between ancients and moderns was to prove the Hellenic identity of the latter, Guillet harbored no such philhellenic sentiments.

Though not altogether ill-disposed toward the modern Greeks, he stated the current belief that they were a fallen race. The Turks, who had experienced no such striking contrasts in their history stood in a more favorable light if only because they did not have to conform to preestablished models. "Whether they are Christians or Turks, they are still Lacedaemonians. But I will feel much closer to the Mohammedans. The Greeks, whose portrait you have seen elsewhere, bear like us the sacred name of Christians; however, it is better to deplore their degradation instead of displaying it and still better if someone could comfort them" (*L,* 20–21). Their abasement notwithstanding, the Greeks had retained certain patterns of the past. Athenians of both sexes, living in the same benign climate as their progenitors, had a prepossessing physical appearance and enjoyed good health. Did the Maniots, whose reputation as fearsome and violent brigands and pirates was well established by that time, possess the same love of liberty and intrepidity as the ancient Lacedaemonians?

In regard to mores, never have there been so many diverse views as there are on them [the Maniots]. Some present them as brutal, dark and perfidious, and naturally inclined to brigandage. Others consider them to be the true descendants of those magnanimous Greeks who would choose liberty rather than life. . . . However this may be, of all the people of Greece, it is only the Epirots, called Albanians today, and the Maniots, deplorable progeny of the Lacedaemonians, who have been able to hold their own against the Turks." (*L*, 32)

Not only had some ancient character traits filtered down to the present, but ancient poetry was not entirely dead. Guillet ventured to hypothesize that the folk songs resounding in the mountains of Greece echoed the poets of antiquity. The continuity of this poetic legacy, only lightly touched upon by Guillet, was explored more fully by nineteenth-century Hellenists and philhellenes and culminated in Fauriel's seminal work *Chants populaires de la Grèce moderne* (1824).

By focusing his attention on Athens and Lacedaemon, Guillet chose not only the two most prominent Greek cities but two contrastive societies as well. The antithesis in character and culture between the two, the one refined and cultivated and the other less sophisticated but more virtuous, was elaborated by Guillet. The Spartan way of life, with its emphasis on martial qualities, austerity, and discipline, won his admiration. "But it is easy to avenge the Lacedaemonians. Philosophy and the maxims of virtue were explained in Athens, but they were practiced in Lacedaemon" (*L*, 515). By subjecting themselves willingly to the rigors of virtue, the Spartans presented an alternative social structure and a different ideal from that of the Athenians. The notion of contrastive ideals exercised a strong fascination as they competed for precedence during the following century.

Although he was not an original thinker, Guillet should be seen, as with all minor writers, as a barometer registering the conditions of his milieu. In reading his account of Athens, one should not look for accurate and faithful descriptions of its monuments but should instead garner from his pages glimpses of the image of the ancient city, whose prestige had already begun to be compared with that of Rome. Guillet reflected this changing perspective. "If the power of arms made Rome triumph over a part of the Earth for a time, Athens found in the felicitous discovery of Sciences and Arts the secret of giving laws everywhere and of securing an Empire over the spirit of men, which will last as long as they have reason and gratitude."[24]

While Guillet stimulated interest in Athens, Jean Giraud provided hospitality, guidance, and information to those who came to see the town. Like Spon, he was born in Lyon and entered the diplomatic service at an early age. He served as a vice consul in the Morea and in 1658 was appointed French consul in Athens. He acted in this capacity until 1664, when an unfortunate incident brought this phase of his career to an end. Giraud was involved in an altercation with a captain from Provence, whose insults provoked him to such a degree that he struck him. The Conseil du Roi deprived him of his position and appointed Chastagnier to succeed him. Giraud's reputation and qualifications, however, were well known, and he was approached by the English to act as their consul at Athens. He accepted this offer, as well as one from the Dutch to be Holland's vice consul. Though he was now in the service of different governments, Giraud was able to continue his diplomatic career in the city that was to be his permanent residence until 1688. Married to a Greek woman from the old family of Palaeologos, he enjoyed good relations with the Greeks of the city, the Capuchin missionaries, especially Père Simon de Compiegne, who tutored his children, and the Turkish authorities.

Since Athens was not one of the main centers of the Ottoman Empire, Giraud's diplomatic duties were not very demanding. On the contrary, his position made it easier for him to explore Athens and Attica and acquire a wide knowledge of their condition and the state of the antiquities. Moreover, as with all diplomats at that time, he acted both as a political and commercial representative and as a cultural liaison receiving and protecting European visitors and responding to their requests, a task he performed most cheerfully.

It was in response to such a request by the marquis de Nointel, who visited Athens in 1674, that Giraud wrote an essay, *Relation de l'Attique*, intended to provide the French ambassador with information concerning the population, customs and manners, government, and the commerce of the place.[25] His descriptions are concise, factual, and devoid of personal feelings and subjective reactions. Contemporary life is presented in sufficient detail: diet, dress, practices regulating marriage and inheritance, social and administrative structure, and trade relations—all receive their due attention. Nointel never used this material because his projected work on Athens was never written. Spon, however, was a direct beneficiary of Giraud's extensive knowledge.[26]

The last European whom Giraud accompanied on a tour of Athens was Anna Akerhjelm, a companion and secretary to Countess Koenigsmark, wife of Field marshal Otto-Guillaume Koenigsmark, second in command during the siege of Athens laid by the Venetian commander-in-chief Francesco Morosini. The success of the Venetian campaign against the Turks in Athens was ensured on 26 September 1687, when, after a three-day bombarment of the Acropolis, where the Turks had retreated, a bomb fell on the roof of the Parthenon and blew up the powder that had been stored there.[27]

Following the explosion, which she witnessed from a distance off the coast of Attica, Anna Akerhjelm and her patrons entered the city. "It is enough that we are now masters of Athens," she wrote to her brother from Athens on 18 October 1687, referring to the brief Venetian occupation of the city. Then, on a melancholy note, "How repugnant it was for his Excellency to destroy this beautiful temple, which existed for three thousand years and which is called the temple of Minerva; but in vain; the bombs did their job and never in this world will this temple be replaced."[28] Giraud, though in poor health, was with her as she gazed at the still smoldering remains of the ruined temple, but he refrained from making any comments or expressing indignation. Shortly thereafter the Venetian army, decimated by the plague and skirmishes with the Turks, retreated, leaving the city in a ruinous state. After that, all traces of Giraud were lost.

The Grand Tour Begins:
An Ambassador's Visit to Athens

One of the most prominent and memorable seventeenth-century diplomats to set foot in Athens while Giraud served as consul was Charles-François Olier, marquis de Nointel, French ambassador to the Sublime Porte. He succeeded M. de la Haye Vantelet, whose efforts to renew the capitulations and advance French interests in the Levant were rebuffed and frustrated by the Turks. Nointel's origins and personal qualities recommended him highly for this post: he came from an old, distinguished noble family, was well versed in foreign languages, was a seasoned traveler, and had a lively and abiding interest in the arts.

Highly conscious of the importance of his mission, he was determined to surround himself with grandeur and sumptuousness, a style befitting the glory of his nation and also his predilection for splendor and magnificence. Furthermore, he was convinced that in order to deal successfully with the Ottomans, one should address them from a position of strength. This meant ostentatious opulence, a quality greatly valued by the Orientals, in his view, and a stance of superiority and steadfastness. He attributed his predecessor's failure to his meek and passive ways in negotiating with the Turks. Nointel avoided any marks of deference and compromise, not too difficult a task, given his imperious temperament. On the contrary, if need be, he would return insult for insult and impertinence for impertinence.

To this effect, he made a grand entrance into Constantinople in the fall of 1670 attended by all the pomp and ceremony he could muster. When he was first received by the grand vizier, he was greeted with cold reserve and arrogance. This further entrenched his conviction that timidity and vacillation would be perilous. He presented the Turks with a choice: either the capitulations would be renewed, or the French diplomatic mission would leave and relations would be severed. Negotiations were stalled for a while, but finally the capitulations were renewed in 1672, and thus Nointel's firmness and forcefulness brought positive results.

Having concluded his mission successfully, and feeling confident that French interests in the Ottoman Empire were now ensured, he set out on a journey to the islands of the Archipelago, the Holy Land, Egypt, and Greece. This was not an individual venture, however. If anything, it was a veritable expedition intended as much to make an impression on the host countries as to explore and learn about them. To this end, he made extensive and laborious preparations, about which he was careful to inform his king.

The extravagance that marked Nointel's passage through the Near East was a display of national grandeur and personal flamboyance. His biographer, Vandal, noted, "There is in him a natural tendency for exuberance and profuseness, a seething and restless vigor, an ardor for description, the sense of the picturesque with a certain penchant for the burlesque, above all the taste and passion for local color, so rare for his time."[29] His expansive and restless imagination needed the stimulation of new horizons. And what could be more promising and enticing than a sweeping view of the Orient, whose very name conjured up scenes of dazzling splendor, mysterious intrigues, wild corsairs, and oppressed rayahs? In his entourage of janissaries, dragomans, and valets, Nointel included an orientalist, Antoine Galland, and two painters, Jacques Carrey and Rombaut Faidherbe, the better and more permanently to capture this scintillating image.

The presence of scholars and artists as part of the grand tour of highly placed personages was a new element. They were more than mere acolytes of the traveling dignitary; their expertise was being put to use so as to assemble, record, elucidate, and then disseminate a body of knowledge, which would be compiled, classified, and interpreted by contemporary and future scholars. They were in a sense cartographers of human cultures, charting their profiles and delineating their features. There was thus an emphasis on accumulating and disseminating of knowledge, capturing and reconstructing the past in the present so that it could be transmitted to the future. Nointel's progress through the Levant and Greece contained all these elements, masked though they were by the bedazzlement of his theatricality.

While he was in Cairo, Nointel received a dispatch from the grand vizier requesting his return to Constantinople. He had to cut short his sojourn in the Orient and expedite his return, but not before making a last stop, this time at Athens. On 4 November 1674 his frigate cast anchor at Porto Lione (Piraeus), and on the following day Nointel made his triumphant entrance into the city of Athena accompanied by the aga, who had come to welcome him. Nointel's own description of the procession from Piraeus to Athens expresses quite revealingly his overweening sense of self-importance.

> The Turkish officers led the procession, and I continued, surrounded by my staff members and others in Greek costumes, followed by the French and English consuls and fifty horsemen. My trumpets mixed their fanfare with the lugubrious sound of the native ones, which lasted for one hour and a half while we made our way through a plain and an olive grove with both the French banner and the red one unfurled. Near the temple of Theseus, I met the Athenian notables, both secular and ecclesiastic, in ceremonial dress, who paid me their respects, followed by a discharge of the cannon from the "château," and it was at its sound and in the middle of a great rush of people, after having passed under the beautiful remains of Pericles' palace and near the chapel or tomb

of Socrates, that I arrived at the palace that had been prepared for me, where I could not eat any of the Turkish dinner that was served to me.[30]

There were no palaces in Athens, so they had to be imagined because nothing less would befit the dignity of the French ambassador.

Fortunately, Giraud was there to ensure his comfort, guide him in his sightseeing, gather and provide information on contemporary conditions, and obtain permission from the governor of the citadel for Nointel's painter to make drawings of the sculptures and reliefs of the Parthenon. When that was accomplished to his satisfaction, Nointel set out to return to Constantinople, where he arrived on 21 February 1675, after having been away for seventeen months. This long absence had adverse effects on his career because it incurred the displeasure of the Ottoman government and his own and also put a strain on his finances, which eventually led to his bankruptcy. Upon his return, he found himself involved in financial entanglements brought about by his indulgence in luxury and grandeur, his love of the arts, which he pursued with extravagance, and bad management of his resources.

At that point, however, Nointel failed to perceive the impending catastrophe. His avocation as an art collector still absorbed his time at the expense of his diplomatic duties. He now had in his possession thirty inscriptions, four hundred drawings of bas-reliefs, edifices, and landscapes, and a rich assortment of costumes, sculptures, coins, and various art objects, all of which had to be sorted out, arranged, and classified. In the meantime, his debts mounted, as did the disapproval of his government. Finding himself in a desperate position, he made a last plea for financial assistance. In a dispatch dated 29 June 1678, he wrote: "I no longer know where I am, the plague keeps me four hours away from Constantinople, hunger, for lack of having enough to subsist on, attacks me every moment, and I have no news that might indicate, with sufficient authority, that I will receive adequate relief."[31]

The relief never came. Instead, Nointel was recalled at the end of 1679 and replaced by M. de Guilleragues. He met with a very cool and reserved reception at court in France, which made him feel even more keenly his "disgrâce." He retired to his estate in the country, where he set about working on the material he had collected during his nine years in the Near East, intending to compose an account of his experiences and recollections. With his finances still suffering from his excessive spending during his ambassadorial years, he had to sell part of his collection. His inscriptions from the Archipelago and Athens, some of them very ancient and rare, went eventually to the Louvre, where they became part of the collection of Greek antiquities. He died on 31 March 1685, never having completed the task he had undertaken. A restless and passionate man, exuberant and at the same time extravagant and self-indulgent,[32] he relished the excitement and exhilaration of traveling and constant movement but felt constrained and therefore fared poorly when faced with the discipline and the inescapable occasional tedium of his diplomatic duties. Intensity and enthusiasm he possessed in abundance, but patient persistence and sustained effort he lacked. This may explain in part his failure to realize his writing ambitions.

Nointel left only fragments in the form of notes and sketchy manuscripts recording his impressions of the Levant. These, along with his diplomatic correspondence, comprise a significant corpus of material disclosing the political and cultural activities of French diplomats as well as his personal predilections and idiosyncrasies. Of his stay in Athens there exists only one record, a letter to the minister Pomponne written on 17 December 1674. This is a valuable document because it introduces, even though briefly, themes that became recurrent motifs in the writings of European travelers to Greece during the course of the eighteenth century.

Not unexpectedly, the contrast between past glory and present abjection was constantly noted. Yet, in Nointel's eyes, the present was valuable, if not for its own sake, then as a reconstructive guide leading to a better apprehension of the past. "I have now been one month in this country, the memory of whose antiquity is so admirable and whose present state, however enshrouded in ruin and ignorance, merits nevertheless a strong admiration and an examination that gives many clues about the past through the consideration of the monuments that still stand."[33] Nointel exhibited a keen sensitivity to and an appreciation of the beauty of these monuments and placed their artistic value above those of Rome. Making no pretense of being erudite, he recorded his impressions in a vivid and fresh manner, injecting a personal and even emotional note, a novel element absent from the rather pedestrian narratives of his contemporaries. He was overwhelmed by the richness and variety of the sculpted figures that adorned the monuments of the Acropolis.

> The first time, I entered the treasury where these marvels are enclosed with pomp and at the sound of cannon, and I returned, incognito, four or five times the better to admire and know the beautiful drawings my painter was making of them, numbering more than two hundred figures . . . of men, women, and centaurs, their combats and victories, triumphs and sacrifices, and if it were possible to express now the rich confusion that such a beautiful array of different passions has left in my mind, I would undertake it with pleasure, but since I need to meditate on it again, you will allow me, Sire, to postpone this undertaking to a later time. (1:123–24)

A pity this promise was never fulfilled and we are left only with furtive glimpses and fleeting impressions.

Of more lasting value, particularly in view of the waves of destruction that swept over the Acropolis denuding its monuments down to their bare bones, are the drawings and designs executed by Nointel's painter.[34] Installed at the foot of the Parthenon and assiduously guarded by two janissaries, the artist painted, occasionally interrupted by the visits of his patron. Working without scaffolding, he had to strain his eyes to make out the contours and the details of the figures. Some critics found them inaccurate and too sketchy, a deficiency that can be explained by the conditions of their execution. Their value, however, lies not so much in their artistic merit as in their being the only pictorial record of the Parthenon before the explosion. Unfortunately, they did not survive as a collection because their owner had to dispose of them for financial reasons.

In addition to the sketches of the Parthenon, Nointel instructed his painter to depict various other aspects of the city. On the basis of these drawings, after his return from Athens, he commissioned a vast tableau portraying himself surrounded by a colorful crowd consisting of native men and women attired in their local costumes, janissaries, his own attendants in superb military dress, and the Capuchins of the Athens mission. The whole composition is irradiated by the commanding and striking figure of the ambassador. "Fur-lined coat made of red cloth open on the chest, green robe held with an ornamental belt; with this a wide-brimmed felt hat, a rich, unpowdered wig flowing to his shoulders and encasing his face, and a finely traced moustache: the head of a seventeenth-century Frenchman on the body of a pasha." What a fitting monument this painting is to Nointel's lavishness and theatricality, fancying himself as he did the personification of Western elegance and Eastern opulence.[35] He did not so much come to examine and understand the Orient as to impress upon it his own image by adopting some of its more dazzling fixtures. Seen in this light, Greece too was another scene in the vast and variegated tapestry, which formed the background for his blazing path.

With the exception of Nointel's vivid and colorful recollections of his brief visit to Athens, seventeenth-century descriptions of that city are straightforward, unembellished accounts. As literary creations, they are eminently forgettable; in vain would one search for an individual style trying to create an atmosphere and convey a mood. But one would be unjustly critical in this respect, because their authors made no pretense at literary creativity. As historical and social documents, they are useful when used in conjunction with other sources. As indicators of cultural encounters, they are invaluable records because they reflect the attitudes and values used by the representatives of one cultural tradition in judging those of another.

Antiqui adsiduus Meruit qui dicier æui
Cultor, Sæpe Manu Marmora prisca terens,
Moribus Antiquis SPONIVS, priscoǵ pudore,
Quem tabula expressit parvula, parǵ liber.

Jacob Spon (1647–1685). The doctor from Lyon who pioneered
the scientific investigation of the antiquities of Athens. From
Jacob Spon, *Voyage d'Italie, de Dalmatie, de Grèce et du Levant*
(1678).

View of the Temple of Minerva in Athens. Le Roy's representation of the Parthenon, his inaccuracies notwithstanding, shows the irreparable damage inflicted on it by Morosini in 1687. From Julien David Le Roy, *Les Ruines des plus beaux monuments de la Grèce* (1758).

View of the Temple of Olympian Zeus in Athens. Despite Le Roy's intention to dramatize the contrast between the old and the new, his illustration conveys the symbiosis of the two and the practical use contemporary Athenians made of the monuments. From Julien David Le Roy, *Les Ruines des plus beaux monuments de la Grèce* (1758).

➤

View of the Temple of Erechtheus in Athens. The exaggerated proportions of the Erechtheum in relation to its surroundings, the vegetation sprouting from the ruins, and the broad strokes and dark masses are intended to evoke a sentimental contemplation of past majesty. From Julien David Le Roy, *Les Ruines des plus beaux monuments de la Grèce* (1758).

View of the Lantern of Demosthenes. The dichotomy between the imposing ancient monument overlooking the residence of the Capuchins and
the merry insouciance of the dancers in front of their humble abodes is a
figurative representation of the contrastive cultures associated with these
images. From Julien David Le Roy, *Les Ruines des plus beaux monuments
de la Grèce* (1758).

View of the Fountain of Chios. The island's multilayered past and
prosperous present are reflected in the variegated architectural
background of the illustration and the picturesque foreground
animated by groupings of people, particularly the ladies of
Chios, who were famed for their civility and affability. From the
Comte de Choiseul-Gouffier, *Voyage pittoresque de la Grèce*, vol.
1 (1782).

View of the Convent of Patmos. A visual rendition of the author's chance meeting with an Orthodox monk, who astonished the French visitor by mentioning the names of Voltaire and Rousseau. From the Comte de Choiseul-Gouffier, *Voyage pittoresque de la Grèce,* vol. 1 (1782).

Reception of the Author by Hassan Tchaousch-oglou. Interior scene with the author meeting a Turkish official. From the Comte de Choiseul-Gouffier, *Voyage pittoresque de la Grèce,* vol. 1 (1782).

View of the Interior of a Khan or Caravansary. A vivid depiction of tra-
veling accommodations in the Ottoman domains, a scene that many
European travelers witnessed and described. From the Comte de
Choiseul-Gouffier, *Voyage pittoresque de la Grèce,* vol. 2 (1809).

Souli. The legendary resistance of the Souliots to Ali Pasha's relentless attacks was undoubtedly fortified by the forbidding ruggedness of their mountainous habitat. From François Charles Pouqueville, *Grèce* (1836).

4

THE RISE OF
PHILHELLENISM

Liberation and Revival

Philhellenism in its broad sense means love of and admiration for things Greek. During the last third of the eighteenth century and the first three decades of the nineteenth, a pivotal era for the making of the modern Greek nation, the content and scope of philhellenism can be defined more clearly because it had a specific focus and objective: the liberation of the modern Greeks and their cultural and spiritual renascence through the efficacious imitation of their progenitors. It was during that time that the concept of philhellenism was expanded to include the modern Greeks and elaborated so as to try and resolve the tension between past and present. Philhellenism taken in this limited sense was historical and ahistorical at the same time: historical because it was rooted in the perception of change through time crystallized in the concept of "rise and fall"; and ahistorical because it envisioned a return to the ancients and a return of the ancients.

The modern Greeks, however, could not rise alone in the estimation of their European advocates; they needed the guiding light of the West, which had become the repository of the legacy of antiquity. Thus philhellenism as a stance taken by Europeans in general and by the French in particular vis-à-vis the modern Greeks had, from its very inception, an element of mission, *la mission civilisatrice.* And as with all missions, it rested on the assumption of the superiority of the missionary and the dependency, at least in the initial stages of the conversion, of the proselyte. Philhellenism, then, viewed from this angle, was one instance of the self-confidence, assurance, and unity with which Europeans saw their own civilization and of their desire to mold another people's character in their own image.

The sentimental attachment the French felt for the ancients was not the only seed from which philhellenism sprouted. Of equal importance were the precepts of the Enlightenment, which posited a direct relationship between politics and culture. Only a people living under equitable laws administered by a wise ruler could form a progressive society and achieve cultural preeminence. On the other hand, a people dominated by an arbitrary government was doomed to suffer and atrophy. "Despotism is the abuse of royalty," stated Voltaire, "just as anarchy is the abuse of a republic. A sultan who, without justice and without due process of law, imprisons or kills the citizens, is a highwayman who is called *your highness.*"[1] The key phrase here is "without due process of law." Although Voltaire did not attack the institution of monarchy as such, he perceived law as a force restraining the personal whims of absolute monarchs. Of course, it had not yet been established as an impersonal body of principles whose authority transcended the individual ruler. If anything, the emphasis placed on the formulation and institution of just laws made the lawgiver a highly prized individual. "For eighteenth century historians barely liberated from the idea that Providence guided historical events, the legislator was an almost superhuman figure. They saw him as the embodiment of human energy, wisdom and rationality, as the founder of states, the preceptor of his country, the father of his people."[2]

The ultimate purpose of impartial and fair laws was the safeguarding of a person's physical integrity and general well-being, which alone could lead to social progress and justice. Thus the fate of the individual was seen more and more as the product of human institutions and socially elicited responses than as the unfolding of a providentially ordained chain of events. Humanity's fate, at least as far as existence here on earth was concerned, lay more with politics and less with religion.

Seen from this perspective, the modern Greeks were in the unenviable position of an oppressed people, a condition brought about by their subjugation to a succession of oppressive rulers. Their decline was interpreted as a progression of events set off when they lost their independence to the Romans; it continued under the theocratic rule of the Byzantine emperors and culminated during their centuries-long subjection to the Ottomans. To undo the harm inflicted on them during their long bondage, they would have to gain the right to live under a just government by freeing themselves from their foreign rulers. The political emancipation of the Greeks became one of the main tenets of philhellenism, from the first musings of philhellenes envisioning a reborn Greece to their commitment to struggle for freedom on the battlefield during the Greek War of Independence. Philhellenism, then, resulted from the convergence of liberal humanism and romantic Hellenism. Both of these developments reached their maturity in France during the closing decades of the eighteenth century.

By its nature philhellenism was idealistic, for it projected the dreams of the admirers of antiquity onto the modern Greeks. Its main impetus came from the writings and observations of travelers. Their number grew dramatically in the second half of the eighteenth century because of a growing taste for the visual and the picturesque in literature and the arts, expanded political and commercial interests in the Levant, and more numerous archeological explorations. Although the motives for their voyages differed, their attitudes and predispositions diverged only slightly. Whether amateur archaeologists, diplomats, or merchants, their voyage to Greece was an educational experience, a search for their spiritual roots, and a way to link their academic Hellenism to the place of its origin. Monuments and ancient sites conjured up vibrant images of the distant past. But the present intruded in their meditations. Efforts to reconcile the two or to explain the one in terms of the other became one of their abiding preoccupations.

To this end, the customs and manners, language, and religion of the modern Greeks were observed and analyzed. When these cultural forms did not conform to preconceived notions of antiquity, they were denounced as barbarisms. The perceived discontinuities in the evolution of Greek culture exemplify European attitudes toward cultural diffusion. With the onset of the explorations of foreign lands and peoples during the Renaissance and post-Renaissance eras, travelers and writers who laid claim to historical knowledge became aware of cultural diversity and diffusion among peoples. But, whereas the former stimulated their curiosity and fascination, the latter elicited two divergent responses: approval of the diachronic continuity of traditions and cultural patterns within the same people and disapproval of the transmission of traits from one people to another.

> The vertical transmission of traits over "tracts" of time, the maintenance of traditions with its end product, temporal cultural uniformity, was regarded universally as good. . . . It conserved the old in culture, and perhaps a few remnants of an ancient original. It was regarded as one of the best characteristics of the best peoples, the true source of their pre-eminence.
>
> On the other hand, diffusion proper, of the lateral, horizontal, or overland transmission of culture, was regarded as bad.[3]

In the case of the modern Greeks, the intermingling of what were seen as classically derived traits with foreign, mainly oriental, intrusions was neither charming nor exotic. The Orient was beguiling in its exoticism, but not Greece.

The allure of exoticism "consists especially of this feeling of diversity; it can appeal only when thinking, finally expanded, becomes capable of picturing aspects different from familiar landscapes, and of imagining modes of reasoning based on a model other than one's own."[4] But the civilization of ancient Greece was part of the Europeans' own inheritance, and its intellectual currents and aesthetic principles underpinned theirs. In these circumstances, to think of Greece as a crossroads where East and West met and where it might be possible for the two to coexist and engender new cultural forms was deemed impossible. For the Westerners, the penetration of the Turks into lands famous for their classical past signified above all a violation of the integrity of the legacy of ancient Greece and a contamination of its purity. Thus, if the modern Greeks were ever to revitalize this legacy, they would have to wage war on two fronts: on the battlefield against the Turks and in the cultural arena against the alien intrusions from the East.

French philhellenic sentiments during the closing decades of the eighteenth century are best exemplified by three writers: Voltaire,

Pierre Augustine Guys, a merchant and classical scholar, and a young nobleman, the comte de Choiseul-Gouffier.[5] The three shared an interest in modern Greece mainly as a result of their admiration for the ancients. Voltaire's philhellenism was abstract and academic. Never having visited Greece, and having had no direct contact with its people, he expressed sympathy for them during the Russo-Turkish War of 1770. He was primarily concerned, however, with the outcome of Catherine the Great's campaign against the Turks and what he perceived as her determination to expel them from Europe. This would benefit the Greeks because it would liberate them from Ottoman rule and place them under the tutelage of the enlightened czarina. At least, this is what Voltaire believed. At no time did he expect to see the Greeks autonomous. Unlike him, Guys and Choiseul-Gouffier envisaged an independent Greece and became personally attached to it, the former much more so than the latter.

Philhellenism as Liberal Humanism:
Voltaire

Voltaire's philhellenic sentiments reflected his literary predilections and must be viewed within the context of his century and his personal values. His attitude toward modern Greece was influenced by two considerations: first, his belief that Greek civilization had declined in the postclassical era and second, his aversion to tyranny and oppression. For him the modern Greeks were the victims of the unjust and arbitrary powers that impede the progress of humanistic values.

To begin with, Voltaire's admiration, even for the ancient Greeks, was not unreserved. I noted his ambivalent attitude toward Homer in chapter 1. On the one hand, he praised the noble passions of his heroes while, on the other, he derided their primitive manners and violent temper. The constant interference of the gods in the affairs of mortals struck him as absurd and childish. Like most of his contemporaries, he viewed the Greek myths as infantile fantasies. "With the exception of fables visibly allegorical, . . . all the rest are a pile of stories that have no merit other than having provided Ovid and Quinault with some beautiful verses and having exercised the brush of our best painters."[6] The acceptance of these fables led to erroneous beliefs, concluded Voltaire, which eventually became established religious practices.

Even though Voltaire thought of the Greek myths as naïve and irrational fabrications, he nonetheless acknowledged their merit as the products of a creative and poetic imagination.[7] He also praised the Greeks for their ability to refine and harmonize the artistic forms they had received from Egypt and Asia, for creating a language so melodious and precise at the same time, and for their cultivation of all aspects of human creativity, which set them above their neighbors to the east. The ancient Greeks, even though they did not invent everything or bring everything to perfection, transmitted to the world the basic elements of art, literature, and philosophy. "Beautiful architecture, perfected sculpture, painting, good music, true poetry, . . . even philosophy itself—even though unformed and obscure, all this came to nations only through the Greeks."[8]

Cultural superiority was not the only thing that distinguished the ancient Greeks from the peoples of Asia. More importantly, it was freedom in the realms of intellect, politics, and religion that allowed them to develop their faculties and perform feats of glory such as the decisive defeat of the Persians. "This superiority of a small, noble, and free people over all of enslaved Asia is perhaps the most glorious thing among men."[9]

To the philosophes, and to Voltaire in particular, classical Greece was a model of human freedom and dignity because it developed a secular civilization. In contrast, the ruling elites of India, Persia, and Egypt used religion as an instrument to control the people and deny them access to knowledge. "But in Greece, more free and happy, access to reason was open to everyone; all gave free expression to their ideas, and it is this that made the Greeks the most ingenious people on earth."[10] The absence of the domination of a priestly class made it possible for them not only to apply their critical faculties but also to exercise tolerance. Thus their religion, full of superstitious absurdities though it was, was "without dogmas, consequently, humane and tolerant."[11]

Unfortunately, in Voltaire's judgment as well as in that of his contemporaries, religious intolerance came to Greece too and signaled the onset of its decline. In his estimation the Byzantine-Christian legacy of the modern Greeks was a dark period in their history, just as nefarious as Turkish control. In his *Ode pindarique à propos de la guerre présente en Grèce* (1768), he denounced the Byzantines in a typically caustic manner. The opening stanza is a lament for the decay that had paralyzed Greece for centuries. Then, searching for the roots of this calamitous fate, he looked back at the time of the Byzantine emperors and found that they were the cause of this woeful state.

The reasons for which Voltaire disliked Byzantium were characteristic of the intellectual climate of his age. The eighteenth century saw the Eastern Roman Empire as a shadowy world embroiled in court intrigues, theological disputes, and religious fanaticism. It was perceived as a theocratic state where the influence and power of the church prevented the rise of a secular government based on reason and justice.

This was particularly disturbing to Montesquieu, for whom separation of church and state was a fundamental principle for the maintenance of civil tranquility. "The most poisonous source of all the misfortunes of the Greeks is that they never knew the nature or the boundaries between ecclesiastical and secular power; this is what caused both of them to go irrevocably astray."[12] Montesquieu's aversion for the Byzantines stemmed from both philosophical considerations and religious objections. Unlike Voltaire, who mistrusted all organized religions, Montesquieu placed the Catholic church above the Orthodox. He considered the latter both schismatic and idolatrous. He misunderstood the religious and spiritual significance of the icons, which he unhesitatingly dismissed as idols: "A crude superstition, which debases the mind as much as religion elevates it, placed all the virtue and confidence of men in an ignorant stupidity for the Images."[13] In comparing their hierarchies, he found the Catholic prelate superior to his Orthodox counterpart.

So intense was Montesquieu's dislike of the Byzantines that the sack of their capital by the crusaders of the Fourth Crusade aroused in him little protest. Indeed, he found no fault with the Franks, who, instead of fighting the Muslims as was their original plan, found it more profitable to plunder a city of immense wealth and dazzling treasures.[14] Montesquieu ridiculed the Byzantines for their defeat at the hands of their fellow Christians, who found them "as ill prepared for war as the Tartars found the Chinese during recent times. The French ridiculed their effeminate attire; they would stroll in the streets of Constantinople, dressed in their painted gowns."[15]

Voltaire was less lenient toward the crusaders. He saw their expeditions as a way to satisfy their greed and lust. In his *Essai sur les moeurs,* he exposed their violence and cruelty and concluded, "Thus the only fruit of Christians in their barbaric crusades was to exterminate other Christians."[16] One must not mistake this, however, as compassion for the Byzantines. He sympathized with them only to the extent that they were the victims of this "fureur épidémique," as he called the Crusades. Otherwise, he had few kind words to say about them. He interpreted the fall of their empire to the Turks as an inevitable result of their corruption, superstitions, and inner discords. In describing the siege of Constantinople, he evinced no regret for the fall and the devastation of such a great city and no pity for the anguish and suffering of its inhabitants in the last few days of their existence. Voltaire saw their flight to the churches, seeking refuge and praying for divine intervention to save them from the terrible fate that awaited them, as a last manifestation of their superstitious ways. "The Greeks' detestable superstition led them to seek refuge in Saint Sophia, basing their faith on a prediction that assured them that an angel would descend in the church in order to defend them" (*E,* 439).

Voltaire's insensitivity was even more pronounced when he described the forced entrance of the enemy into Hagia Sophia, where the faithful had congregated to listen to the Holy Liturgy for the last time. He minimized the horror of this scene by suppressing all the distressing details and swiftly shifting his focus from the vanquished to the victors: "They killed some Greeks on the square in front of the church, they made the rest slaves, and *Mehmet* went to thank GOD in this church only after having it washed with rosewater" (*E,* 439). Such a strict adherence to abstract principles, however rational and humane they may be, makes one impervious to human suffering and demonstrates "the depths to which a violent partisan can descend and the injustices that a *littérateur engagé* can commit for the sake of his cause."[17]

These negative views of Byzantium influenced the way in which many Westerners perceived the modern Greeks. Their subjugation to the Turks seemed to them little more than an exchange of masters. In Montesquieu's view these new masters did not mistreat the people any more than the old ones. "The people, instead of this ceaseless succession of vexations that the subtle avarice of the emperors had imagined, saw themselves subject to a simple tribute easily paid and easily collected: happier to obey a barbarous nation than a corrupt government under which they suffered all the drawbacks of a liberty they no longer enjoyed, with all the horrors of the present servitude."[18] Voltaire, too, thought that the condition of the Greeks under their conquerors, though abject and humiliating, was not unbearable. "The Greek families subsist in their country, debased, despised, but in peace: they pay only a light tribute; they engage in commerce and cultivate the land."[19] If he objected to the presence of the Turks in Greece, it was primarily because they occupied "the country of *Miltiades*, of *Leonidas*, of *Alexander*, of *Sophocles*. . . . The Greek language has been corrupted since that time" (*E*, 448).

These assertions notwithstanding, in the course of the eighteenth century, the Ottoman government became increasingly the target of attacks as a despotic system. This affected the Greeks, indirectly at first and directly later, because they began to be perceived as the victims of oppression. The idea that their decline was due to their subjugation eventually supplanted the belief that they were the perpetrators of their own downfall. The former view rested on the notion that a people's character is molded by its social environment and, more specifically, its government. The modern Greeks became an illustration of this principle. In Helvetius's words,

> The physical position of the Greeks is still the same: why are present-day Greeks different from the Greeks of former times? It is because the form of their government changed; it is because, just like the water that takes the form of the vessels in which it is poured, the character of nations is susceptible to all sorts of forms; in all countries the spirit of the government makes the spirit of nations.[20]

Voltaire, too, subscribed to the theory that the nature of government determined the character of a nation and the level of its culture. Therefore, he attacked the Ottoman government as a violator of human rights and an enemy of the spiritual legacy of Hellenism. He voiced these sentiments in his letters to Catherine II during the Russo-Turkish War of 1770. Voltaire hailed the empress's expedition as a momentous event because he expected her to liberate the subject peoples under Ottoman rule and redeem the lands of classical antiquity. Here was an opportune moment, Voltaire thought, for the

Greeks to rid themselves of their Turkish rulers and live under an enlightened monarch.

Although the insurrection in the Morea in 1770 was a minor incident in the conflict between Russia and Turkey, in the West it was greeted with a flurry of enthusiasm because it was believed that Greece's liberation was one of the issues. The inflated hopes that filled Western newspaper accounts were one of the first expressions of nascent philhellenism, which saw in this brief uprising the rebirth of the Hellenic ideal ready to shake off the fetters of subjugation.[21] Material considerations were of little consequence when the insurgents were Greeks animated, in the eyes of the romantic Hellenists, by the spirit of their ancestors. Not unexpectedly, these expectations were quickly transformed into disappointment and rebukes when the Greeks failed to reenact the ancients' glorious feats.

Voltaire's brief attention to the fortunes of the modern Greeks was occasioned by his more abiding interest in the activities of Catherine, who is his eyes espoused and promoted enlightened political ideas. Not surprisingly, then, he acclaimed her as the liberator of Greece and likened her to a new Amazon leading her armies down through the Balkans and striking terror at the heart of the Ottoman Empire. He viewed her war ventures not as maneuvers aimed at territorial and political aggrandizement but as a means to bring law and justice to places where none existed. When he addressed her, he compared her to such legendary lawgivers as Solon, Lycurgus, and, of course, the illustrious Babylonian Queen Semiramis. Once victorious, he thought, she would set aside her armor in order to don the mantle of the wise lawmaker. "Your Majesty," he wrote to her in 1771, "will put on again her legislator's clothes after having cast off her amazon's dress."[22] He was so removed from the real state of affairs in the Ottoman Empire, that he envisaged its imminent collapse under a superior Russian force and the coronation of Catherine at Constantinople, the fabled city of emperors and sultans.

Voltaire entertained the expectation that, once successful, Catherine would undertake measures to restore the Hellenic spirit in Greece by reviving some of the ancient institutions and cultivating the arts and sciences in their birthplace. Naïve as these expectations may appear, to Voltaire they seemed realizable because he believed in the strong reforming influence of an enlightened monarch. The congruence of national and state boundaries did not seem to him a prerequisite for a government to rule with reason, justice, and humanity. He envisioned Catherine enthroned in Constantinople, her second capital, and having under her aegis all the Greek lands. He hoped that one of her first tasks would be the creation of schools and academies and the education of her new subjects, the Greeks.

> Because if you were sovereign of Constantinople, Your Majesty would soon establish a beautiful Greek academy. They would call you Catheriniade, the Zeuxis and the Phidias would cover the earth with your images, the fall of the Ottoman Empire would be celebrated in Greek, Athens would be one of your capitals, the Greek language would become the universal language, all the merchants of the Aegean would ask for Greek passports from Your Majesty. (C, 76:142)

Exhortations of this nature abound in Voltaire's letters to Catherine, especially those written in 1770, the year of the Russians' first successes against the Turks. Putting aside the hyperbolic praise and the frivolous gallantries of these letters, and making allowances for Voltaire's misguided judgment based on insufficient or faulty information, "there remains something in his conception of Catherine's role that can be characterized only as a support of enlightened despotism."[23] For her part, Catherine responded to him by using equally flattering terms because, being fully aware of his stature and influence among the philosophes, she wanted to use him as a propagandist to promote her image in Europe.

However, in waging war against Turkey, she had the expansion of her empire uppermost in mind and felt little attachment to Hellenic ideals. Nevertheless, she seldom betrayed her true feelings to Voltaire. She replied to his entreaties with subtle wit tinged with irony. At times one senses annoyance on her part, but it never becomes explicit. To Voltaire's proposal that she make the Greek language the universal tongue of the Mediterranean, she responded with obvious scepticism: "I believe with you that soon it will be time to go and study Greek in some university. While waiting, Homer is being translated into Russian—it is still something as a beginning; depending on the circumstances, we will see if it will be necessary to go any further."[24]

During the first stages of the war, Voltaire urged Catherine repeatedly to hasten the liberation of Greece and supply its warriors with arms. In his fervent enthusiasm, he envisioned a general uprising against the Turks by the Greeks and other Balkan people as well. Catherine was less concerned with the fate of the subject peoples and answered his appeal by informing him simply that: "it depends only on the Greeks to revive Greece. I have done my best. . . . I do not know what will happen" (*C,* 76:103). In her letters to Voltaire she mentioned the Greeks only rarely, and then with indifference. When their ill-conceived uprising was swiftly put down by the Turks, she lavished harsh words on them, upbraiding them scornfully for their defeat. To a more impartial observer than Voltaire, it would have been clear that the Turks were Catherine's enemies not because they had conquered Greece but because they were an obstacle to her southward expansion.

Voltaire's hostility to the Turks was determined by different considerations. He called for their expulsion from Europe in the cause of arts and letters and the progress of humanitarian principles. "Politics is not my affair," he wrote to Frederick of Prussia in 1769. "I limit my small efforts to making men less foolish and more honest. It is to this end that, without consulting the interests of some sovereigns . . . , I limit myself to wishing passionately that the barbarous Turks be chased at once from the country of Xenophon, Sophocles, Plato" (*C,* 73:147).

This disavowal of politics refers to the transactions and conflicts among rulers, not to the fundamental principles underlying the influence of government on the governed. The relation between a people and its political institutions was one of the main concerns of eighteenth-century thinkers, who invariably arrived at the conclusion that enlightened governments would raise both the material and the spiritual level of their subjects, whereas authoritarian and oppressive regimes had the opposite effect. Within this framework, Voltaire and the philosophes in general viewed the Ottoman Empire as a violator of the natural rights of man.

> I have been accused of having little love for Moustafa;
> His viziers, his divans, his muftis, his *fetvas* [legal opinions]
>
> . . . .
>
> Yes, MADAME, I detest them, I must admit,
> I wish not that a Turk for his diversion play
> with nature's rights and men's days.[25]

On m'a trop accusé d'aimer peu Moustapha;
Ses viziers, ses divans, ses muphtis, ses fetfas;

. . . .

Oui, je les hais, MADAME, il faut que je l'avoue,
Je ne veux point qu'un Turc à son plaisir se joue
De droits de la nature et des jours des humains.

The Turks appeared even more objectionable to him because in his opinion they were ignorant of and indifferent to cultural principles valued by Europeans. "I am not at all accustomed," he wrote to Michel Hennin in 1769, "to see Greece governed by people who know neither how to read nor how to write, dance, or sing. If Greece were free, I would go to die in Corinth."[26]

In view of his denunciation of Ottoman rule on political and cultural grounds, it is not surprising that Voltaire hailed Catherine not as a conqueror but as a champion of liberty, tolerance, and civilization. Of all the European monarchs, he noted, she alone had the will and the courage to wage war against "the enemies of the arts" and the wisdom to institute just and equitable laws guaranteeing "universal tolerance."

Voltaire was referring to the *Instruction*, a project undertaken by Catherine at that time to devise legal formulas for the governance of church and state. To this end she had appointed a commission, and she herself wrote the introduction setting out the principles and procedures to be followed. Many of her ideas were based on legal concepts advanced by the philosophes. The project, however, was abandoned soon after its inception. Voltaire, after having read the introduction to the prospective code, surmised that these laws, once instituted, would apply not only to Catherine's Russian subjects, but also to those she would liberate from Ottoman rule. The initial deliberations of the commission charged with this task had preceded the outbreak of the hostilities against Turkey, and this perhaps led Voltaire to believe that Catherine intended to use the new code in governing her expanded empire.

Even if his idealism led Voltaire to misconstrue Catherine's motives and intentions, he was not carried away to the point of advocating Russian withdrawal from the territories freed from the Turks. Nor did he deem it desirable to have her grant independence to the inhabitants of those lands. His belief in tolerance and his defense of human rights stopped far short of advocating universal democracy and expressing faith in the ability of the masses to govern themselves. "When I was beseeching you to restore the fine arts of Greece," he wrote to Frederick II, "my plea did not go so far as to entreat you to reestablish the Athenian Democracy. I do not like the government of the rabble. You would have given Greece to M. de Lantulus, or some other general who would have prevented the modern Greeks from committing as many stupidities as their ancestors" (C, 86:75). He wished to see Greece free from the Turks, but not autonomous because centuries of enslavement had reduced its people to the same level as that of their captors.

> What has happened to this proud Greece,
> Crawling at the Tartar's knee,
> More languid and barbarous.
> And more contemptible than he?
>
> [Que devient cette Grèce altière,
> Rampante aux genoux d'un tartare,
> Plus amollie et plus barbare
> Et plus méprisable que lui?][27]

These pronouncements illustrate all too well Voltaire's pragmatic approach to political freedom: human rights, universal though they might be, had to be administered differently to different societies depending on the degree of maturity they had attained; for peoples under Ottoman and Russian rule, where conditions were almost primitive, benevolent autocracy seemed to be the best answer.[28]

Catherine's designs, of course, did not coincide with her mentor's wishes. Before the outbreak of hostilities, she had sent Russian agents to the Peloponnesus to incite the people to rise against the Turks, thus facilitating her attack against the Porte. At the beginning of the war, she sent a small naval force to the Morea under the leadership of Alexis and Theodore Orloff. The first attempt to liberate the Greeks was doomed from the outset. The size of the Russian contingent was far below the Greeks' expectations, and the Russians were equally disillusioned with the military unpreparedness of the Greeks. At the advance of the Turkish and Albanian forces, the insurgents disbanded and the uprising was promptly suppressed. The Greeks of the Morea suffered terrible reprisals and were at the mercy of roaming Albanian bands. As for the Russians, the Greek venture was but a prelude to their war against Turkey, and they proceeded with their plans of conquest.

During the latter part of 1770, Voltaire's expectations that Greece might be liberated received a setback. He was distressed to learn of the suppression of the insurrection in the Morea, and in August 1770 he wrote to Frederick: "Providence wishes . . . that the Turks recapture Greece; at least it allows that the gazettes say it. This is a mortal blow for me. It is not because I own an inch of land near Athens or Corinth; alas! I only have some in Switzerland; but you know what joy I felt at the prospect of seeing the grandsons of Sophocles and Demosthenes delivered from an ignorant pasha."[29]

Uncertain about the truth of the news, he wrote to Catherine urging her not to abandon "these poor Greeks." Catherine avoided the subject at first, but when it became clear that the revolt had been a fiasco, she attributed it not to poor planning but to the degradation of the Greeks. "The Greeks, the Spartans have degenerated; they like pillage more than liberty" (*C*, 77:33).

Voltaire, who did not know that the Russian aid was insufficient, and was unaware of the cruelty with which the rebellion had been suppressed, was quick to condemn the Greeks for not resisting. The severity of his criticism, especially if one contrasts it with his former sympathy for them, can be explained only by his excessive admiration for Catherine and his abstract approach to the problem. "My other regret," he wrote to the czarina in 1772, "is that the Greeks are unworthy of the liberty they would have recovered if they had the courage to follow you" (*C*, 81:109).

After their defeat, the Greeks ceased to receive Voltaire's attention. The only regrets he had were that the Turks had not been expelled from Europe and that the arts and philosophy had not been reborn in Athens. One of his last references to this episode was in a letter to Frederick written in September 1773. "I give up my good hopes of seeing the Mohametans chased from Europe, and eloquence, poetry, painting, sculpture, reborn in Athens; neither you nor the empress wants to run to the Bosphorus. . . . In short, you do not want to make a crusade" (*C*, 86:27). In his answer, Frederick justified his own indifference and recalled that Voltaire himself had not always been amicably disposed toward the Greeks.

I admit that the domination of the Turks is harsh, and even barbarous; I confess that of all the countries under this domination,
Greece especially is to be pitied the most; but remember the
unjust sentence of the areopagus against Socrates and the barbarousness with which the Athenians treated their admirals. . . . You
yourself say that it is as a punishment for these crimes that they
are subjugated and maltreated by barbarians. Does it depend on
me to deliver them? (*C*, 86:50)

Although not too much should be made of Voltaire's involvement
in Catherine's political affairs, his correspondence with her during
this period illustrates two things: his espousal of enlightened despotism and his denunciation of tyranny. Concomitant with the latter
was the advocacy of legal safeguards administered by a just and prudent ruler, which would guarantee a certain measure of political liberty to the individual. The application of these principles to the
polity of the modern Greeks made Voltaire's sympathetic pronouncements on their behalf the first truly philhellenic statements expressed
by a Frenchman. What their liberation signified to him, however,
was not the creation of an independent Greece but the victory of reason and human rights. These expectations were heightened by the
prospect of the rebirth of the classical spirit. He was primarily interested in the recovery of the Greek land and in the restoration of the
heritage associated with it for the benefit of the West. In his redemp-
tion scheme, the Greeks were to be the indirect beneficiaries of
Catherine's good will and generosity and not the protagonists of
their emancipation.

Short-lived though the uprising was, it set the stage on which the
modern Greeks were to perform for the next six decades. They were
assigned the role of impersonating their classical ancestors, and, if
successful in their performance, they would rediscover their true
Hellenic identity. While the stage was theirs, the text and the rules
of the play were written and directed by the Europeans, who were
at the same time the audience and the judges. Although the 1770
insurrection was of secondary importance historically, it was a landmark in the development of philhellenism because it gave rise to a
concerted expression of its fundamental principle: the emancipation
of the modern Greeks and their regeneration through the emulation
of their ancient progenitors. What makes this event even more
weighty in the unfolding of philhellenic sentiments and ideas is that

no less eloquent and prominent a figure than Voltaire articulated the exaggerated hopes of the philhellenes and their abrupt about-face when the Greeks failed to meet their expectations.

Five decades passed before Voltaire's momentary enthusiasm became a potent force that sent many idealistic and not so idealistic Europeans to Greece to fight for its independence. During that interval a transformation took place which made the attitudes of many Westerners evolve from a sentimental yearning for the past to a more active commitment to the present. Still, always mesmerized by the scintillating vision of antiquity, they hoped to see it revived in a free Greece. Their philhellenism was more complex and more ardent than Voltaire's fleeting concern. Yet they shared with him a common attitude: the modern Greeks were to be the instruments through which the dream of the "golden age" would come true.

Greeks of All Time: Guys

Unlike Voltaire's brief interest in the modern Greeks, that of Guys was more abiding and deeper, and he made them the exclusive object of his investigation. People, not political and philosophical concepts, were the focus of his interest. He was not so much concerned to see ancient Hellas resurrected as he was to observe the character and traditions of the modern Greeks, which, in his view, were a living proof of their glorious lineage. By demonstrating such a connection, he believed that he would help raise their sorely fallen dignity. "It is to ennoble the modern Greeks by comparing them to those who made the country they inhabit so famous and tracing the usages they have been able to preserve back to the Ancients."[30]

Pierre-Augustin Guys was born in Marseilles in 1720. A merchant by profession, he was known in the learned world as an amateur archaeologist and poet. In recognition of his erudition and extensive knowledge of antiquity, he was made a member of the Académie des sciences et belles-lettres of Marseilles in 1752. D'Ansse de Villoison, a prominent classical scholar himself, cited Guys in his *Recherches sur le grec moderne* as an important authority on antiquity. The commercial interests of his family brought Guys to Constantinople, where he stayed for twenty years. His earliest letters date from 1744, when he traveled from Constantinople to Sofia. In 1748 he visited the Aegean Islands, and in 1771 he published his *Voyage littéraire de la Grèce ou Lettres sur les Grecs anciens et modernes avec un parallèle de leurs moeurs.*

His work was received favorably and stirred enough interest to go through two more editions in the following decade (1776, 1783). The 1776 edition included two letters on Greek dances and funerals by Mme Chénier. Its appeal was undoubtedly bolstered by its publication one year after the insurrection in the Morea, the very event that had turned Voltaire's attention to Greece. The convergence of interest by both men on Greece at that moment was symbolized by Guys's dedication of his work to the venerable philosophe. Guys's close association with Greece continued to the end of his life. It was on the island of Zante, where his son was the French consul, that he died in 1796.

In Guys's book the Greek world emerges as a unified cultural entity distinct from the Orient. His systematic attempt to establish the affinities between the ancient and the modern Greeks had an antecedent in André Guillet, who, a century earlier, had used a similar approach. The latter's views were at best schematic and abstract because they lacked Guys's authenticity, personal experience, and commitment. Having absorbed the classical learning of his time, Guys adulated the ancients with all the fervor of the neoclassical era. However, he diverged from his contemporaries in one respect: he experienced no nostalgia for Greek antiquity because he felt that its vitality still lived on. The disfigurement of its monuments was irremediable, but its spirit had been preserved in the people. In his view archaeologists groped in vain for its vestiges in mutilated statues and dismantled edifices. Instead they should look at the people, whose customs and traditions embodied the legacy of ancient Greece. "I have already said that the present-day Greeks have been scorned too much because they have not been sufficiently studied. The respect shown for the age of cities and ancient monuments—would it be less meritorious for an entire nation, for a people whose very wrinkles of caducity will never be disfigured to the point of making them unrecognizable" (2:189–90).

Guys's arguments assumed that the Greek character had remained essentially unaltered throughout the centuries because of the tenacity of the people. "It is among the people that I always look for ancient customs, because the people, refining little and faithful to received traditions, are always attached to these usages, which are their main laws" (1:123). His conviction that ancient patterns had retained their integrity was so firm that he did not perceive any changes brought about by developments in the intervening centuries. For example, he interpreted the rituals of the Orthodox church not as the symbolic enactments of religious events and Christian beliefs but as a modified version of pagan rites. The religious feasts were more like the seasonal festivities of the ancients than gatherings of Christian celebrants. Even the various superstitions associated with many religious and social observances were a legacy of antiquity, in his view. For him, this was one of the less felicitous aspects of the Greek character.

To make his comparisons more convincing and his parallels more accurate, Guys used two methods of investigation: extensive references to ancient writers and close observation of the modern Greeks. He considered both approaches indispensable for a serious study of the Greeks. He described his system with an apt metaphor:

In any case, look at me as an Antiquarian, who, instead of neglecting a copper coin, as so many other travelers have done, because it is unpolished and badly preserved, takes the trouble to wash it, to clean it carefully, and finally discovers the characters that were believed to be entirely effaced. . . . I have all the satisfaction of this Antiquarian when, by observing the modern Greek step by step and comparing him to the ancient, all of whose signs I have, I recognize the one I am looking for. (1:384)

His mercantile activities, instead of being a hindrance to his literary pursuits, were an asset because he dealt with people on a day-to-day basis. As a man of practical affairs and a scholar who valued observation as a tool of research, he reproved writers who treated a people in an abstract and offhand manner. He was particularly piqued by travelers who formed their opinions of the modern Greeks after a limited and cursory examination. He maintained that they based their judgments on a passing acquaintance with the inhabitants of the islands, many of whom lived in poverty and ignorance. Had these travelers been more discriminating and had they known the Greek language, Guys argued, they would have found that cultivation and quest for knowledge still existed in some strata of Greek society. He asserted that higher ecclesiastics and European-educated Greeks had kept the tradition of intellectual excellence and the respect for learning alive.

In his study, Guys used as models the Greeks of Constantinople and its environs and not those of the Peloponnesus and the islands, where he felt foreign invasions had had a more deleterious impact. His long acquaintance with them and his knowledge of their language made it possible for him to probe deeply into their customs and character and appreciate their culture. Only Pouqueville, who came to Greece thirty years later, could claim a similar experience.

At the very outset of his sojourn, Guys expressed his partiality for the Greeks. Their past and their present aroused his interest and curiosity.

> I am mainly attached to the Greeks because this people will always be interesting, because one cannot read Ancient History without beginning with that of the Greeks; finally because it is good that Travelers, curious to discover in their country monuments that no longer exist, should know that in their absence the inhabitants of the places they used to embellish still deserve our attention. (1:2)

His decision to write about them was dictated by both intellectual considerations and subjective and emotional preferences.

However original he considered his approach to the study of the Greeks, he shared with his contemporaries more similarities than he would have liked to admit. Like them, he had a static concept of Greek history and valued only those characteristics that seemed to be derived from the ancients. Anything else he rejected as an undesirable intrusion. That Greek culture could be receptive to other influences, assimilate them, and give rise to new forms of expression was as alien to Guys as it was to most of his contemporaries. He attributed any manifestation of creativity in postclassical Greece to the survival of Hellenic traits. For example, the church of Hagia Sophia was proof in his eyes of the undying vitality of the Greek spirit. His esteem for Byzantium was obviously no higher than that of his contemporaries. His determination to trace everything creative back to the ancients was so firm that he failed to perceive that this magnificent edifice was as different from the ancient temples as the Christian God was from the Olympians.

What would this Temple have been then, if it had been built in the high age of Greek Architecture and of the other Arts? This monument that Travelers are never weary of admiring makes us see at least what the genius of the Greeks was capable of, since in the decadence of the Arts, or in the middle of the barbarism that reigned in the sixth century, it awakened but for one moment, and it produced a model that all the Great Masters have glorified by imitating it. (2:4)

Such comparisons and parallelisms were the essence of his narrative, which embraced all aspects of Greek life. Nothing was too trivial or insignificant. He deftly integrated costumes, domestic architecture and artifacts, daily activities, and communal festivals in order to validate his premises. His central idea determined the structure of his work and gave it cohesiveness. However, the prejudicial treatment of his subjects, even though favorable, made the Greeks conform to a preconceived scheme. Fortunately, his literary sensibilities were developed enough to steer him away from writing a compendium of facts and observations.

Guys recorded his impressions in a style vivid and at the same time ample and varied, so as to communicate the logic of his arguments and the intensity of his feelings. His sentences are well ordered and balanced, and their tempo follows the movement of the scenes he describes. His tone is warm and sympathetic without being sentimental and melodramatic. This subjective element was a novel one in travel literature and set Guys's work apart from the impassive and detached travelogues of the previous century. The interpolation of anecdotes and colorful scenes from daily life makes his impressive erudition less ponderous and adds animation to his narrative. In the words of a historian, Guys's book delights the reader "with this spontaneity, this passionate curiosity, this extreme finesse, and at the same time simplicity of style."[31]

In trying to establish the continuity of Greek identity, Guys felt compelled to explain the decline of the modern Greeks. Because of the stringent measures of a repressive government that viewed with suspicion any signs of wealth and prosperity among its subjects, he argued, the arts had declined. While old masterpieces decayed, no new edifices were erected to take their place. A climate of fear and suppression and the discouragement of free competition had stifled literary and artistic excellence.

In classical antiquity freedom of expression, relative prosperity, and above all the nurturing atmosphere of the polis, gave rise to the simultaneous and unified development of all the arts. Subsequent political developments destroyed this delicate balance, and gifted individuals could no longer seek glory and preeminence among their fellow citizens. Implicit in this reasoning is the conviction that a society is like a tightly knit fabric whose strands are interdependent. If one of them comes loose, then the whole pattern unravels. In the case of Greek society as it existed in antiquity, the loss of political freedom signaled its dissolution. Guys accepted the commonly held view that disintegration set in with the onset of the Byzantine era. He remarked that religious fanaticism destroyed invaluable art objects, and by imposing a ban on nudity, it placed a barrier between the artist and nature, the main source of his inspiration.

But Guys was a sensitive and receptive individual, who could see beauty and charm where others perceived nothing but the unprepossessing and crude fabrications of an ignorant people. In his eyes, artistic expression and creative imagination had not died in Greece but had retreated from the public domain to private abodes and anonymous works, from the realm of "high culture" promoted by the state to that of folk traditions. Furthermore, nature had lost none of its radiance and the Greek people themselves still possessed their physical beauty and graceful countenance. "I see," he declared joyfully, "natural scenes and living models that can still inspire talent successfully. . . . I see the most regular forms, black, bright eyes animated with a natural fire, elegant and majestic physiques, a simple and light dress."[32]

The decline of the arts and literature due to adverse historical changes, observed Guys, forced the innate talent and the predilection of the Greek people for visual beauty to seek other channels of expression. Domestic architecture, interior decoration, local costumes, and the cultivation of embroidery, metalwork, and pottery evinced the loving care the Greeks lavished on their immediate surroundings. The elaborate patterns, the charming motifs of birds and flowers, and the symmetrical designs of their handicrafts fascinated the viewer with the harmonious combination of shape and color and the precision of their execution.

Of all the French travelers of that time, Guys was the only one to conduct a careful examination of Greek arts and crafts. However, he would not have been drawn to them had they not reminded him of antique forms. They had a strong appeal because he viewed them as artistic creations transmitted from generation to generation which perpetuated in the collective memory of the people ancient modes and patterns. The Greek women were instrumental in this process of preservation. After all, did not the ancient poets speak of queens and noble ladies spending their time embroidering and weaving? The Greek ladies of his day, he pointed out, were equally adept at recreating old designs and scenes.

Guys's single-minded preoccupation with proving the direct affinity between the ancient and modern Greeks beclouded his vision and prevented him from seeing similar traits and motifs in other traditional cultures adjacent to Greece. His concept of Greek civilization can be visualized as a vertical line connecting the two peoples, not as a network of multiple influences expanding, enriching, and transforming post-Hellenic Greek culture. Moreover, although he has been praised for his discerning evaluation of popular traditions, his appreciation of modern Greek culture was not that of a folklorist.[33] The songs, dances, and crafts of the modern Greeks, had they been viewed simply as creations of the people reflecting their simplicity, their intuitive apprehension of beauty, their fresh imagination, and their long experience, would have elicited little admiration. Clearly, Guys was not enthralled by a folk culture but by what he perceived as the reflections of ancient forms and patterns that shaped and elevated it.

Guys traced the legacy of the ancients not only in the decorative arts, but also in the character, temperament, and manners of the modern Greeks. Their natural mirth, their verve and expressiveness, and their volatile temper and inquisitive mind were in his eyes traits that established their identity. The less commendable aspects of their behavior, such as vanity, cupidity, and frivolity, were also bequeathed by their ancestors. True, subjugation had accentuated these unedifying propensities, but their seeds existed already in antiquity. "As for me," he noted, echoing long-held stereotypes, "I found the Greeks just as their Historians, especially Thucydides, characterized them: dissembling, vain, supple, volatile, avid for gain, enthusiasts of novelty, unscrupulous on their oaths."[34] Their weaknesses notwithstanding, the Greeks captivated him by their conviviality and gregariousness.

Reflecting the views of his time, Guys looked at ancient myths as the creations of a lively imagination that animated the universe with ethereal beings, capricious gods, and outlandish monsters. Religious ceremonies dedicated to the worship of these divinities were intended to please the senses and arouse exhilaration with their outer pomp and glitter, not to induce a communion with hidden, transcendental forces. Likewise, Christianity did not modify these pagan practices significantly, nor did it make the Greeks more devout and spiritual. To Guys, Christian rituals and religious feasts brought the people together in a display of festivity and jubilation reminiscent of ancient rites. While making no claim to possessing a deep knowledge of Eastern Orthodoxy, he was quick to dismiss its formative influence on the spiritual life of the Greek people.

Guys dwelled extensively on Greek festivals and celebrations. He described them as communal gatherings where carefree merriment was tempered by dignity and decorum. He was impressed by their order and precise regulations: feasts began with the serving of roasted lamb and wine to the celebrants; preferential treatment was accorded to those guests who were distinguished by age and position; spirited conversation was succeeded by song and dance, which brought the festivities to their peak. How fascinating it was, Guys remarked, to behold the dancers decked out in their resplendent costumes, now moving with carefully measured steps, their countenances solemn and stately, and now quickening their tempo with swift and rhythmical leaps! Their mounting excitement and animation uplifted their whole being in a glorious moment of joy and self-abandonment.

Guys's appreciation of Greek songs and dances was a novel element in the travel literature of that time. In addition to the aesthetic and emotional pleasure he derived from observing them, he heard in the folk songs echoes of ancient legends and saw in the execution of dances "the figurative imitation of actions and mores" of olden times (1:166). For him these dances were the consummate synthesis of past and present. In their composition and configurations he perceived the visual representation of ancient myths and stories. For example, he interpreted the *candiot* dance as the enactment of the myth of Theseus and the Labyrinth, and the *pyrrhic* one as the ritual imitation of war scenes.[35] The people who performed them were not aware of their deeper historical meaning but found in their execution an outlet for their energy and a satisfaction for communal belonging. Thus for Guys the significance of folk songs and dances was historical and cultural as well as aesthetic and psychological.

A persistent investigation of the similarities between past and present led Guys to examine the nature and development of the Greek language. Knowledgeable in both idioms, the ancient and the modern, he found in the learned language of the church and the educated Greeks, the most convincing evidence supporting the uninterrupted continuity of the Hellenic heritage. On the one hand, there were the people who clung faithfully to their traditions without being conscious of their noble origins. The church hierarchy and the educated Greeks, on the other hand, cognizant of the higher cultural values of the classical past, preserved the Greek language as an instrument of erudition and as a concrete link with a loftier and richer civilization. Though Guys had little or no appreciation for the Greek Orthodox church as a religious institution, he emphasized its usefulness as the main repository of the Greek language and learning.

Guys was one of the few Europeans of that time to note the existence of a Greek intelligentsia, which had not severed its contacts with the West. In his view, the church and the upper stratum of Greek society, concentrated mainly in Constantinople, were actively engaged in the preservation and perpetuation of the scholarly tradition of Greek culture, a fact that Europeans all but ignored. "But consult the enlightened men of this Nation," he exhorted them, "those who received education, and who are distinguished by their language as they are by their birth. Go especially in their Churches . . . [where] the purity of the ancient language and pronunciation are equally preserved" (2:203).

Guys's comments on the Greek language would have been incomplete had he not pointed out its dichotomy. He noted that it had developed into two distinct idioms, the spoken one constantly evolving and subject to many influences, and the learned one used in ecclesiastical and scholarly circles. His classical predilections led him to favor the latter, but, like Korais, he did not condemn the language of the people as a hopelessly deformed amalgam. He maintained that the spoken idiom still showed the imprint of its ancient prototype and that "the language, disfigured in appearance, especially by Turkish expressions which they cannot help adopting . . . preserves all the essence, all the richness and all the smoothness of the ancient"

(1:99). Yet, in spite of these merits, it was the literary language that he advocated as a model of imitation, because in it he found the suppleness and the purity of ancient Greek.

Guys's sympathetic treatment of the Greeks and his vivid scenes appealed to his readers. His efforts to raise the Greeks' prestige and enhance their reputation drew favorable reactions. His son paid tribute to him for his pioneer work: "The Greeks in your scenes are no longer in chains; they have recovered their rights; they are free in the opinion of educated men; they make us recall what they were" (3:2). Voltaire, after receiving a copy of Guys's book at Ferney, thanked its author for dedicating it to him and for making Greece come alive in his pages.

Another enthusiastic reader of the *Voyage littéraire* was Mme Chénier. Proud to be Greek, she expressed gratitude on behalf of her compatriots. "In the name of modern Greece, I take it upon myself to pay you the highest respect of our gratitude, because by stirring the ashes of our fathers, you raised the Greeks from the oblivion where time, prejudice, and the barbarity of their conquerors had buried them."[36] She contributed to his endeavor by writing two essays on dances and funerals, explaining their function as transmitters of ancient customs.

Guys's erudite and vivid work was one of the first accounts to project a favorable image of the modern Greeks. It was unique among such studies written at the end of the eighteenth century because of its all-embracing scope and its approach and intention. Though his philhellenism was classically inspired and reflected current views on antiquity, his interest was focused on the modern Greeks. People and not ruins attracted his attention. Whereas other travelers uttered expressions of regret and despondency, Guys rejoiced in discovering in the modern Greeks the eternal appeal of Hellas. He did not openly advocate the overthrow of Ottoman authority, but he was convinced that liberation would come. For the moment it was enough to refute the aspersions cast on the Greeks by proving the continuity and the integrity of their culture despite the discontinuity of their historical experience. "Thus they are still the same Greeks, regardless of the side from which one looks at them. The men of today in Greece are the men of all time."[37]

The Greeks "of all time" were of course the ancients, whose indelible imprint had marked the Greek character forever. Guys's view of Greek culture was not evolutionary and assimilative but static and exclusionist. In tracing the similarities that linked the modern with the ancient Greeks, he singled out those traits that, in his estimation, were the constant dimensions giving inner cohesiveness to a society whose outer structure had crumbled. He considered all postclassical developments not as transforming influences, or as disfiguring intrusions, but as incidents of little import to the essence of the Greek character. His integrative efforts, however, intending to prove that modern Greek culture flowed directly from its ancient sources, were selective and, therefore, cut it off from its more immediate Christian-Byzantine past. This purifying approach, which either repudiated or discarded everything that seemed alien to accepted norms of what a Greek should be, was at the heart of philhellenism during the pre-revolutionary and revolutionary eras.

Ruins Astir with Memories: Choiseul-Gouffier

While Guys sketched the human profile of Greece, Choiseul-Gouffier engraved its monuments framed by its landscape and its modern habitations. Marie-Gabriel-Auguste-Florent, comte de Choiseul-Gouffier, was the descendant of an old family distinguished for its noble origins and service to the state. Born in Paris in 1752, he was nurtured in an atmosphere of learning and intellectual stimulation. His family possessed a substantial collection of works on the history and literature of Greece and Rome, which it had made accessible to Barthélemy when he was preparing his *Voyage du jeune Ancharsis en Grèce*.

The young count received a sound classical education under the tutelage of his able preceptor, who instilled in him an abiding love and appreciation for the art and literature of antiquity. Choiseul-Gouffier grew up at a time of heightened interest in the archeological exploration of classical sites, especially those of Greece, and in the critical appraisal of its art and literature. Caylus's *Recueil d'antiquités* (1761), Le Roy's *Les Ruines des plus beaux monuments de la Grèce* (1770), Winckelmann's studies of ancient art, Guys's *Voyage littéraire de la Grèce* (1771), the works of the English scholars Richard Chan-

dler, Richard Pococke, James Stuart, and Nicholas Revett, to mention a few, brought Greece closer to Europeans. In this intellectual
climate, marked by the confluence of romantic and scholarly Hellenism, Choiseul-Gouffier cultivated his taste for ancient art. He was
not satisfied with contemplating it from a distance through the
works of others but sought direct knowledge by visiting the places
of its origin.

The opportune moment arrived in March 1776, when at the age
of twenty-four he embarked on the royal frigate *Atalante*. Its captain,
the marquis de Chabert, was sailing to the Aegean to conduct geographical and astronomical observations. Choiseul-Gouffier intended
both to satisfy his personal curiosity and to produce a visual record
of ancient monuments and scenes from contemporary life. To accomplish this he took with him three artists and a personal secretary.
Their talents were put to use as soon as Choiseul-Gouffier set foot
on the Aegean Islands, the first stage of his eastward voyage. Their
task proved quite arduous, however, because they had to follow the
hurried pace of their patron, who was driven by impatience and a
desire to cover as much territory as possible.

Unforeseen problems interrupted the expedition of the marquis
de Chabert, and the *Atalante* had to sail back to France. Choiseul-
Gouffier, however, continued his journey with undiminished energy
and enthusiasm. His tour of the islands completed, he went on to
Asia Minor. He fell ill in Smyrna, a circumstance that necessitated
the curtailment of his itinerary and his return to France, but not
before visiting Constantinople and Athens. He arrived at the latter
city on 1 October 1776 and repaired to the house of the French consul Gaspary. After a ten-day stay in the ancient town, he started out
on his return journey to France. This was not a sea voyage, however,
but a long and at times hazardous trek. He traveled northward
through Thessaly and Macedonia, then on through Serbia to the
Dalmatian coast, arriving finally in Italy on Christmas Eve 1776.[38]
From there it was a relatively short and easy journey to Paris by mail
coach.

No sooner did Choiseul-Gouffier return to France than he began
to make the results of his voyage known to Hellenists and to seek
assistance for his projected *Voyage pittoresque de la Grèce*. He contacted M. d'Anville, first geographer to the king and a member of
the Académie des inscriptions et belles-lettres. But M. d'Anville was

advanced in years and rather infirm and therefore not especially receptive to Choiseul-Gouffier's observations on Greece. Although the young nobleman failed to impress the aged scholar, the meeting proved to be fruitful for another reason. During this interview, Barbié du Bocage, a student and assistant of d'Anville and a prominent Hellenist and cartographer in his own right, was present. He took an immediate interest in Choiseul-Gouffier's plans and descriptions of ancient monuments and offered to provide commentaries and explications relating them to passages of ancient authors. This encounter marked the beginning of an extensive collaboration between the two men, which spanned the rest of Choiseul-Gouffier's life.[39]

Following these first contacts, Choiseul-Gouffier undertook the task of preparing the first volume of the *Voyage pittoresque de la Grèce*. Anticipation and talk about the work arose even before its publication. The public was given a foretaste in excerpts that began to appear in 1778. The first volume was completed in 1782 and won immediate critical acclaim. Its popularity spread beyond the boundaries of France. Grimm sent a copy of it to Catherine II of Russia, and Reichard translated it into German. At home, the author's success was recognized officially by offers of membership in three bodies of literary distinction: the Académie des inscriptions made him a titular member in 1779; in 1782 the Académie des beaux-arts made him an honorary associate member, and in the same year the Académie française called on him to succeed d'Alembert. During the ceremonies at the Académie française honoring its new member, the poet Delille read an excerpt from his as yet unpublished poem *Imagination* praising Choiseul-Gouffier's dedication to ancient art:

> In order to see the august antiquity of these sites,
> He left everything: parents, friends, and delights.
>
> [Pour voir de ces beaux lieux l'auguste antiquité,
> Plaisirs, amis, parents, il avait tout quitté.][40]

While enjoying such wide praise and recognition, Choiseul-Gouffier had already begun to work on the second volume of his book. But, he felt that there were several lacunae in the material because his voyage to Greece had not covered all the ancient sites. To bridge these gaps, in 1780 he commissioned two artists, the architect

Foucherot and the designer Fauvel, to go to Greece and to make detailed plans and maps of ancient locations, copy inscriptions, and produce designs and plaster casts of statues and bas-reliefs. At the same time, Barbié du Bocage continued to assist him with commentaries and memoirs on ancient authors.

Work on the second volume was well under way when Choiseul-Gouffier was notified that he had been nominated to be ambassador to the Sublime Porte. Although this development necessitated the interruption of his literary pursuits, he welcomed it not only because of the prestige of the position but also because of the opportunity to conduct his archeological investigations on the spot. Like his compatriot Nointel, who had occupied the same post a century earlier, Choiseul-Gouffier combined the promotion of his country's political interests with the fulfillment of his personal, literary-artistic aspirations. He was the epitome of the *diplomate lettré*, who, in the words of his biographer Pingaud,

> appeared in Greece and Constantinople in a dual role, corresponding exactly to the double interest the people and things of these distant countries arouse. For eight years, from 1784 to 1792, he represented France to the Porte, and during his whole life, by his writings, his travels, his research, he became known as an intelligent and fervent admirer of Hellenic antiquity.[41]

Yet a dark cloud hovered over what promised to be an auspicious beginning to his diplomatic career. In January 1783 he published the *Discours préliminaire du Voyage pittoresque de la Grèce*, and in May he was appointed ambassador to the Ottoman capital. Imbued with philhellenic sentiments, the *Discours préliminaire* portended to be troublesome because it openly advocated the removal of Turkish rule from Greece. To minimize its effects and silence his enemies, who would undoubtedly use this document against him, Choiseul-Gouffier had it withdrawn and wrote a new preface to the *Voyage pittoresque*. He even sent agents to Germany and England to buy all remaining copies of the *Discours préliminaire*.

Despite these efforts, lingering criticism and certain key passages circulating in translation in Constantinople still imperiled his position. The attacks persisted for some time. As late as 1788, Choiseul-Gouffier had to clarify his stance vis-à-vis the Greeks. This was in response to a passage in Volney's *Considérations sur la guerre des Turcs*

(1788), in which Choiseul-Gouffier was characterized as an ambassador whose work, known throughout Europe, had publicized the vices of the Ottoman government and expressed the desire to see it overthrown. To dispel these suspicions, Choiseul-Gouffier disavowed the statements he had made in favor of the Greeks. Now, instead of advocating their independence, he simply wished to see them live as loyal subjects of the sultan.

Vexatious though this affair was, it did not delay his second voyage to the Near East. He embarked on the *Séduisant* at Toulon at the end of July 1784, accompanied by members of his staff and an assemblage of artists, men of letters, and classicists. It was a veritable archeological expedition, "a small, sailing academy," in the words of the embassy chaplain, the abbé Martin. Among his guests and fellow travelers were the poet Dellile, the painter Cassas, the astronomer Tondue, his agent Fauvel, and the Hellenist D'Ansse de Villoison. Choiseul-Gouffier had also invited the cartographer Barbié du Bocage, who declined because he was preparing the atlas for the *Voyage du jeune Anacharsis.*

Athens was the first stop on the journey. The Turkish authorities received the new ambassador and his entourage with all the pomp and ceremony befitting his position. After a two-week sojourn in August, they sailed on to Constantinople, where they arrived at the beginning of September. Choiseul-Gouffier's first task was to ensure the success of his diplomatic career by securing the respect and trust of the Ottoman officials. To achieve this, he was instrumental in obtaining French technical assistance to modernize the Turkish army. At the same time, keeping in mind the completion of the second volume of his *Voyage pittoresque*, he organized and directed the activities of his agents dispersed throughout the Near East.

His powerful position, wealth, and knowledge of antiquity enabled him to finance and coordinate the various aspects of this complex enterprise. Le Chevalier, using Homer and Pausanias as his guides, made topographical and geographical observations on the location of Troy. Cassas, a gifted artist, made superb reproductions of ancient monuments. Fauvel was commissioned by Choiseul-Gouffier to collect antiquities from Attica and the Peloponnesus. An extensive correspondence with European classicists, particularly Barbié du Bocage, gave the ambassador valuable historical and literary information. Whenever his official duties allowed, he explored sites in Asia Minor, focusing his attention on their archeological features. With the *Iliad* in his hands, he visited the plain of Troy, where he identified the Scamander and Simois rivers, located what he mistook as the tombs of Achilles, Patroclus, and other Homeric heroes, and collected many precious art objects.[42]

Diplomatic tasks and archeological explorations were carried out in perfect consonance until both came to an abrupt end with the eruption of the French Revolution. In 1791, after a series of accusations and insinuations that cast doubt on Choiseul-Gouffier's reliability, he was recalled and was named ambassador to England. He refused to accept the new position as a sign of protest against the revolutionary government. To make things worse, his correspondence with the brothers of Louis XVI, who were in Germany, was seized by agents of the Republic in November 1792. He was accused of conspiring to aid the royal family, and his arrest was immediately ordered. Fortunately, he was warned of the impending danger in time, and he escaped first to the environs of Constantinople and then to Russia, where he spent ten years in self-imposed exile. There he was well received by Catherine II, who made him advisor to her son Paul. When the latter succeeded his mother, he appointed the distinguished exile director of the Academy of Fine Arts and supervisor of the imperial libraries. Thus a successful diplomatic career and a widespread archeological mission came to an end. Though amateurish in many respects, his effort nevertheless was a pioneering step in the development of the new science of archeology.

In 1802, when he judged that conditions had become normal and that there was no longer any danger to his personal safety, he returned to France. It was far from a joyous homecoming. Bereft of many friends and relatives, deprived of his wealth and titles, and finding his precious collection of antiquities partly destroyed and partly confiscated, he experienced great distress and grief. A persevering man, he had learned to endure adversity and to suppress outcries of indignation. Completely withdrawn from politics, he found solace and meaningful occupation in the continuation of the *Voyage pittoresque*, which had been neglected during the time of his exile. Though a large part of the material had been lost, enough remained to make the completion of the work possible. With only the remnants of his research at his disposal, he rededicated himself to the study of antiquity, and in 1809 he published the first part of the second volume of the *Voyage pittoresque*.

Choiseul-Gouffier's fortunes improved with the return of the French monarchy, an event he greeted with deep satisfaction. His services to Louis XVI were recognized and his family titles and estates returned to him. Unfortunately, he did not live to enjoy his renewed status and see his work finished. He died in Aix-la-Chapelle in June 1817. The second part of the second volume was published in 1822, mainly through the efforts of the classicists Letronne and Barbié de Bocage.[43] It took exactly forty years for this monumental work to come to completion.

Although Choiseul-Gouffier's admiration for Greek antiquity was the most abiding and persistent influence on his life, his attitude toward it changed over the years. When he first visited Greece, his emotions were stirred by the anticipation of experiencing the nobility and charm of ancient Hellas evoked by the ancient poets.

> When I was leaving Paris to visit Greece, I only wanted to satisfy the passion of my youth for the most celebrated places of antiquity. . . . I was carried away by a consuming curiosity that I was to satisfy with the marvels I was going to see; I was tasting in advance the pleasure of going over this beautiful and illustrious region, a Homer and a Herodotus in hand, of feeling more vividly the rich beauties depicted in the Poets' images.[44]

Here he attempted to seize the emotions that he felt at a particular moment of his life. The passage also captures the mood of a generation of travelers to Greece, who wanted to experience in the present the grandeur of an imagined past. This sentimental dimension differentiated the voyagers of the eighteenth century from those of the preceding one.

Choiseul-Gouffier's second voyage to Greece was different in many respects from the first. No longer did he expect the dream of antiquity to come true. Greece no longer aroused his emotions and fired his imagination. Instead, it was a field of archeological research ready to yield its treasures and secrets to methodical investigation. The assumption of diplomatic responsibilities and the ensuing years of exile subdued his élan and idealism. When he first visited Greece, he wished to see the Greeks rise against their rulers. Ironically, it was in his own country and against his own class that a revolution took place. After the turmoil that wrought irremediable changes in his life, he found consolation in his scholarly pursuits. The sentimental yearnings of his youth had given place to more circumspect reflection on the past. Looking back on his early peregrinations in Greece and the work that recorded them, he contemplated them with mild reproval and sympathetic detachment. "More than twenty years have passed since I dared publish the first volume of the *Voyage pittoresque en Grèce*. This undertaking was a temerity of my age. What talent and at the same time what maturity of reflection one needed to possess in order to speak with dignity of these places charmed by Fable and consecrated by History."[45]

This altered perspective, not unexpectedly, left an imprint on his work, which was the only constant dimension in his life. Whereas the first volume, in both its pictorial and textual aspects, attempted to encompass the past and present, now delighting in their similarities and now bemoaning their polarity, the second concentrated on the state and history of antiquities. Contemporary life was not altogether neglected, but the focus was no longer mainland Greece. Constantinople figured prominently in the last part of the second volume in scenes capturing its rich and varied architectural and human character. The work concluded with only two views of Athens, one of "the remains of a temple dedicated to Zeus Olympius" and the other of a side of the Acropolis crowned with the Parthenon. The text in the second volume was little more than an accessory to the drawings, elucidating their archeological features and historical background. Consciously and deliberately, the author treated his subject in an objective manner almost totally devoid of the ardor and excitement that characterized the first volume.

It is in the first volume, then, of the *Voyage pittoresque* that one must seek glimpses of modern Greece. Here too the illustrations played a predominant role. Yet the narrative was not dry and factual like that of the second volume. Subjective reactions, personal comments, and episodes from the life of the modern Greeks alternated with historical and archeological explanations. They were related succinctly, yet vividly, with a swift tempo and at the same time with ease and smoothness. The style was clear and graceful. It was the style of a cultivated man conscious of the use of language as a literary instrument intended both to impart information and to elicit emotional and aesthetic satisfaction.

Through his ordered and harmonious prose, one senses a certain impatience and hastiness propelling him to make his visits as brief as possible. No sooner did he arrive at a place than he left his boat briskly, passed through villages hurriedly exchanging greetings with the natives, cast a sweeping glance at the surroundings, and quickened his step toward the antiquities of the area. This incessant movement is communicated to the reader by the rapid succession of landscapes, monuments, towns, and people. The alternation of text and illustrations presents a kaleidoscopic view of Greece, with its variety of superimposed strata of different historical eras. The colorful portraits of men and women in their native attire convey scenes that have all but disappeared. The faithful reproductions of ancient monuments picture them as they existed at a particular historical moment, seizing the changes that had befallen them over the centuries.

Choiseul-Gouffier's account documented many facets of prerevolutionary Greece. In conjunction with similar reports by other travelers, it provides a valuable record for the reconstruction of the life of the people at that time. Equally important is its interpretation and evaluation by the author. The startling contrast between the envisioned past and the experienced present had the same effect on him as it did on other European visitors. Disillusionment rose within him as he saw his images of antiquity gleaned from literature distorted by the present. The process was all too familiar: first the European traveler embarked on his voyage full of exalted ideas; then, upon his arrival, he was shaken by the reality that awaited him and refused to conform to his ideals. Dismay was his first reaction to this abrupt awakening. Choiseul-Gouffier expressed this psychological pattern pointedly. "If the enthusiasm inspired by the memory of great men produces the regret of not having seen them, of not having lived among them and of not having experienced the benefits of their century, it is even more distressing to find their memory enveloped in darkness."[46]

To the extent that Choiseul-Gouffier and others like him were caught in the web of contradiction between preestablished concepts and objective reality, that reality was bound to appear disconcerting. For the experience of Greece to be complete, objective circumstance had to be perceived so as to conform to preexistent schemas fashioned by literature. Thus observation was filtered through the channels of preconceived constructs shaped by reading. This development indicates a change in the balance between the book and direct experience as it was perceived by sixteenth- and even seventeenth-century naturalist-travelers. For them, the function of the book was to bring readers closer to the external world and to enhance their understanding and knowledge of it. For the romantic Hellenist, who visited Greece at the end of the eighteenth and the beginning of the nineteenth century, literature assumed preeminence over that world. Sometimes it even became a substitute for it. This rejection of objective reality, in this case contemporary Greek reality, was a sort of historical *bovarysme* induced by overreading, and—to transpose the definition of *bovarysme* from the psychological to the historical level—by the habit of conceiving Greece other than it was. In this respect romantic Hellenism and dawning Romanticism had a common characteristic: the drifting away of the immediately perceptible world from the imagined world of ideals.

To make the idea of Greece correspond to the reality of Greece, the Western traveler searched for vestiges of the past. After all, a voyage to Greece was not the exploration of a hitherto unknown terrain. On the contrary, it was above all an endeavor to experience through the senses what had already been envisaged through the imagination. Dacier, Choiseul-Gouffier's eulogist, estimated correctly this approach when he commented:

> It was not the Greece oppressed by the fierce and arrogant Muslim that he was burning to visit; . . . he would have bemoaned such great and crushing misfortune; he was asking from the captive and humiliated Greece more gentle impressions, some traces not entirely effaced, some weak signs of its past splendor; he was looking for the Greece of Homer and Herodotus, and, going back three thousand years, he wanted to meet the old people, the old divinities.[47]

Sifting through the débris, both literally and figuratively, Choiseul-Gouffier had some small satisfaction in finding some echoes of the past. A congregation of old men on the island of Siphnos eagerly asking the foreign visitors for news of the outside world evoked scenes from antiquity: "I thought I was transported to the fair days of Greece; these porticoes, this popular assembly of old men to whom one listened with respectful silence, their faces, their clothes, their language, everything reminded me of Athens or Corinth."[48] On the island of Tinos he beheld an idyllic scene that carried him to the world of the ancient poets. As the last rays of the sun were fading away before the advancing dusk and the warmth of the day lingered for a while before the cool of the night, the atmosphere began to reverberate with the lively voices of women, who began to emerge from their houses. While bent over their embroideries, a time-honored female occupation in Choiseul-Gouffier's eyes, the younger ones listened with fascination to the tales recounted by their mothers. Peels of laughter and merry songs suddenly arose from their midst and were carried by the gentle breeze to the distant valleys and hills. Such scenes made Choiseul-Gouffier exclaim with rapture that "the charming scenes the Greek authors offer us were less the product of their imagination than a faithful imitation of nature."[49]

The pleasure derived from the contemplation of scenes reminiscent of antiquity was dimmed by the intrusion of less agreeable aspects of contemporary life. Choiseul-Gouffier's initial contact with it was far from rewarding. He found the life of most islanders crude and primitive and their native costumes bizarre in their design and decoration. Unlike Guys, he was not enthralled by the motifs of folk art and did not discern in them patterns derived from antiquity. As for the character traits of the people, he often treated them with disdain mingled with pity. As was the case with most European travelers to Greece, he was quick to make judgments and evaluations despite his brief and cursory acquaintance with its people.

A case in point is his recounting of the 1770 insurrection in the Peloponnesus instigated by Russia. He first saw the shores of the Morea in April 1776, when the *Atalante* cast anchor at Coron. The memory of the 1770 debacle was still vivid, and its destructive aftermath was still visible in the ruined city and the devastated countryside. Choiseul-Gouffier gave an account of this episode whose factual errors and misrepresentations are understandable in view of his unreliable sources. What reveals his prejudiced treatment of this affair is his analysis of the causes of the suppression of the insurrection. He placed the responsibility for it on the Greeks, particularly the Maniots, who were more interested in looting than fighting against the Turks. Lack of coordination, discipline, and courage among the Greeks forced Count Orloff to send them away, according to Choiseul-Gouffier. At no time did he stop to consider the failure of the Russians to prepare and organize the Greeks, especially the Maniots, who were notorious for their fearlessness as well as insubordination and addiction to brigandage. Nor did he seem to be aware that the Russians had sent only scant military personnel and arms to the

Morea.[50] Obviously, Catherine's propaganda maintaining that the Greeks had brought about their own defeat was channeled successfully to France through her correspondence with Voltaire and other philosophes.

Choiseul-Gouffier reserved his most acerbic remarks for the Orthodox clergy. He applied the epithets *fanatic, ignorant,* and *superstitious* indiscriminately to all its representatives from the simple village priest to the higher ecclesiastics. The tone of these castigations was more acrimonious in the writings of eighteenth-century travelers than in those of the preceding era. This was paralleled by the increased criticism directed against Byzantium imputing to it the origins of the decline of Greek civilization. Although references to the Orthodox church as "schismatic" were now rare, a reflection of the diminished religious fervor of the French visitors, its role in the life of the people was deemed deleterious. Choiseul-Gouffier's treatment of this subject mirrored these pervasive attitudes. He described the Greek monks and priests as greedy and self-centered, preying on the people's gullibility and exploiting their superstitions. So removed were they from their spiritual mission, in his view, that they cooperated with and participated directly in acts of piracy, an age-old occupation in the Mediterranean. Some monks did abet or engage in such activities, but Choiseul-Gouffier overlooked the fact that this practice involved Europeans from all walks of life.

Choiseul-Gouffier's uncompromisingly negative view of the Orthodox clergy explains the astonishment he experienced when in 1776 he met a monk on the island of Patmos who asked of the foreign visitor for news about Voltaire and Rousseau. That this caloyer was even familiar with these names aroused in Choiseul-Gouffier no small consternation.

> As soon as my ship was brought to anchor, I hastened to step on land in order to go to the monastery. I was far from anticipating the meeting that, a moment later, was going to arouse my interest and my curiosity. I was heading toward the mountain when I noticed a caloyer who was descending from it and who approached me with eagerness, asking me in Italian from what country I was, where I was coming from, what had taken place in Europe during the last seven years when no ship had reached these rocks. No sooner did he find out that I was French than he exclaimed, "Tell me, is Voltaire still living?" One can imagine my

consternation. I asked him in turn: "Who are you?" I exclaimed. A monk, inhabitant of those rocks, and pronouncing a name one can hardly expect to hear in these places?[51]

Choiseul-Gouffier would have been even more surprised had he known that it was another ecclesiastic, Evgenios Voulgaris, who had translated some of Voltaire's works into modern Greek and that educated Greeks saw the famous philosophe as the champion of liberty, the defender of the weak and the oppressed, and the enemy of the sultan.[52]

Because of Choiseul-Gouffier's disillusionment when confronted by the dichotomy between the Greece of his day and the idealized Greece of antiquity, expressions of philhellenic sentiment are understandably sparse in the first volume of the *Voyage pittoresque*. However, also missing is the disdainful and sarcastic tone of Villoison and other, even harsher critics of the modern Greeks. Choiseul-Gouffier's criticism was tempered with pity and sadness, not so much for the fate of the moderns as for the eclipse of the ancients. The most telling expression of these feelings was the frontispiece of the first volume. This is how the author described it:

> Greece, depicted as a woman in chains, is surrounded by the funerary monuments erected in honor of the great men of Greece who devoted themselves to liberty; such as Lycurgus, Miltiades, Themistocles, Aristides. . . . She is leaning on Leonidas's tomb, and behind her is the stele on which was engraved this inscription that Simonides wrote for the three hundred Spartans who fell at Thermopylae. . . . Greece seems to summon the spirits of her great Men, and on the nearby rock these words are written: *Exoriare aliquis.*[53]

What was merely hinted at in the frontispiece was fully articulated in the *Discours préliminaire du Voyage pittoresque de la Grèce,* where Choiseul-Gouffier stated that the Greeks occupied a distinct position among the subject peoples of the Ottoman Empire. Humane principles dictated that one feel compassion for all oppressed people; but when these people happened to be Hellenes, their fate should receive special interest and active concern. However deplorable their situation appeared to be, it was not hopeless. He believed that since amalgamation with the conquerors had been avoided, it was still possible for the Greeks to regain their independence. The barriers of religion, customs, and language had averted an intermingling with the Turks. Moreover, the occasional uprisings and the fierce spirit of the Greek mountaineers were a sign that the desire for liberty was not extinct. Choiseul-Gouffier subscribed to the theory that the spirit of freedom had been preserved among the inhabitants of the mountains and that it was from them that the struggle for independence would spring.

Greece's liberation was, in Choiseul-Gouffier's opinion, a goal with wider implications. Diplomatic and commercial interests, as well as moral obligations, demanded that Europe assume an active role in its political future. Like Voltaire, he advocated that a concerted effort by the European powers to liberate Greece would be to their benefit because it would maintain a certain balance among them and forestall any conflicts arising from a unilateral intervention. France especially stood to derive substantial commercial and political benefits from an independent Greece. Clearly, political considerations went hand in hand with cultural and intellectual concerns.

In trying to explain the present condition of the Greeks, he supported the view held by contemporaries that decadence had set in with Byzantium. The Roman conquest that had preceded it was benign, since the Romans had emulated and absorbed Greek culture. The creation of the Eastern Roman Empire, though it signaled the return of political power to the Greeks, was no reason for jubilation. The Byzantines, Choiseul-Gouffier maintained, expended their energy in court intrigues, internecine struggles, and religious fanaticism. "Their character was a mixture of cunning, baseness, ferocity, and superstition; their minds, degenerating into craftiness, brought metaphysics to religious disputes and . . . plunged Greece into the last degree of degradation, which made their history a web of crimes and perfidies."[54]

Unlike the first part of the *Voyage pittoresque*, where disapproving comments on the modern Greeks outnumbered approving ones, the *Discours préliminaire* was clearly a philhellenic tract.[55] It treated them with sympathy, attributing their decline to their long enslavement. It pointed out redeeming traits derived from their ancestors, and, more importantly, it advocated their right to liberty as a prelude to their revival. This changed tone can be explained, at least in part, by the time span that separated the two works and by their different character. The first recorded the author's immediate reactions to the Greek reality as he experienced it, whereas the second was written seven years after his voyage, and the dislocating effects of the first impressions had faded away. The *Voyage pittoresque* mirrored the clash between the idealized past and the debased present, whereas the *Discours* was an expression of faith in the transforming influence of the former on the latter.

The *Discours préliminaire* was one of the first direct appeals for Greek independence addressed by a Frenchman to the European public. Support of the Greeks' right to gain their political freedom, however, threatened to compromise Choiseul-Gouffier's diplomatic position. In an effort to extricate himself from this rather embarrassing situation, he belittled the seriousness and significance of the *Discours*. Without denying his philhellenic feelings at the time he expressed them, he attributed them to his youthful enthusiasm and impetuosity and to his love for antiquity. These feelings, he argued, were purely romantic in motivation and nature and no longer had any bearing on the execution of his diplomatic duties, and it would be inadmissible "to recall today and present as a political system a purely literary bagatelle, a romantic idea adopted with the sole purpose of interesting those who cherish the arts."[56]

Did these denials spring from a desire to secure his position, or did they reveal a more sober disposition that no longer permitted spontaneous and emotional responses? Perhaps it was a combination of both. One thing is certain: once in Constantinople, Choiseul-Gouffier dedicated himself to his ambassadorial tasks and archeological pursuits. His interest in the modern Greeks was a thing of the past never to be rekindled. This altered stance was in consonance with his differentiated attitude toward the ancients, which was no longer sentimental and evocative but dispassionate and scholarly.

Choiseul-Gouffier's work marks an important stage in the development of French attitudes and reactions toward Greece, both ancient and modern. Its superb illustrations captured the magic aura of its ruined monuments and rendered antiquity more palpable. Delille's verses are an eloquent expression of the pleasure felt by a whole generation of romantic Hellenists in contemplating them.

> And still beautiful, despite the ravages of time,
> with its monuments, its gods, and its heroes
> Greece reappears whole before our eyes.

[Et belle encore, malgré les injures de l'âge,
avec ses monumens, ses héros et ses dieux,
La Grèce reparaît toute entière à nos yeux.][57]

Moreover, these engravings were an important contribution to the
developing discipline of archeology because they were and still are a
visual record of the state of antiquities at that time. By depicting
them in their natural setting, the *Voyage pittoresque* gave graphic
expression to the association between the idea of Greece and Greece
as a physical entity. Modern Greece made its presence felt because
the alternation between views of ancient sites and scenes from contemporary life suggested the coexistence of these two worlds in the
space that nurtured both of them. Thus, in the *Voyage pittoresque*
the connecting link between the ancient and the modern Greeks
was not so much the cultural continuity so painstakingly delineated
by Guys, but the sharing of the same space.

Dacier, in his eulogy to Choiseul-Gouffier, lauded his lifelong dedication to Greek antiquity and appraised his feelings toward the modern Greeks. Dacier's assessment encapsulates the essential characteristics of philhellenism as it evolved from the time of Voltaire until
the Greek Revolution. This critique is important because it is an eloquent testimonial reflecting prevailing philhellenic sentiments:

> Embracing in his ardent philanthropy all the people of Greece, he
> is indignant at their servitude and invokes the great spirits of Mil-
> tiades, Themistocles, and Epaminondas; . . . he would like to hear
> Greece cry out *exoriare aliquis* from her chains in the middle of
> their immortal trophies; but, he adds with sadness, the virile and
> ancient virtues of these heroes of liberty are no longer practiced
> by their descendents. He tries nonetheless to have them revived
> among them; he exhorts them to shake off the yoke that oppresses
> them, to recover their independence. . . . His wishes for the Greeks
> in particular are the outbursts of his heart; they are inspired in
> him by the passion for the arts and fair antiquity, by the regret of
> not recognizing Greece in Greece, by the ardent desire to see it
> reborn graceful, polite, powerful, as it was in the time of Pericles;
> and by the conviction that it would recover these advantages only
> after having gained its liberty.[58]

By the end of the eighteenth century, the basic tenets of French
philhellenism had already been established. They were formed in

the writings of Voltaire, Guys, and Choiseul-Gouffier. If the modern Greeks were to be restored to their former state as a civilized people, they had to regain their independence. The basis of this axiom was both emotional and intellectual. As such it reflected the gamut of feelings associated with romantic Hellenism, that is, the idealization of the ancients, a nostalgia for their world, and the desire to see it revived in the land where it was born and had flourished. Although emotions and rational thinking are more often than not at opposite ends, in this case they converged. The liberation of the modern Greeks was a noble cause not only because of their glorious lineage but also because it was dictated by the liberal humanistic principles of social justice and progress attainable only within the framework of political freedom.

Exactly what concrete form this political freedom should take among the Greeks was not as yet clearly elaborated. Was Greece to be an independent nation-state free to create its own mechanisms for the governance of its people? Voltaire, who defended the Greeks' right to liberty, was not in favor of granting them full autonomy. He would rather see them ruled by an enlightened monarch than by what he thought to be inexperienced and undisciplined native leaders. Choiseul-Gouffier, when he declared his rousing plea *exoriare aliquis*, was too young and impassioned to address such an issue. In his mature years, when he had disassociated himself from the modern Greeks, he wished only to see their lot bettered within the existing scheme of things. Guys, the most enthusiastic philhellene of the three figures studied in this chapter, was too intent on establishing the Hellenic character of the modern Greeks to examine the question of their political future.

Obviously, then, at this stage philhellenism existed more as a mood and less as a concerted plan of action. Its proponents were men of letters and travelers imbued with the spirit of romantic classicism. Though they shared similar views, they did not participate in an organized movement to liberate the Greeks. Only when the Greeks took up arms against their rulers did European philhellenes commit themselves to action. But action is often born after a period of gestation during which it is nourished by ideas and emotions. The philhellenism of the prerevolutionary era was such a period.

5

CHATEAUBRIAND'S GREECE:
THE ROMANTIC PILGRIMAGE

Past and Present:
The Unbridged Distance

It is perhaps symbolic that Chateaubriand's journey to Greece and the Near East coincided with the opening of the new century. His visit to lands immortalized by legend and history, both pagan and Christian, signaled the appearance of a new kind of traveler. For almost three centuries—from the time of the Renaissance, when energetic and inquisitive Europeans set out to explore the world beyond the confines of their continent, to the end of the eighteenth century—a common thread bound travel accounts regardless of their focus: a travelogue was a description of the external world, both natural and human, intended to impart information on the resources, history, and social and political modes of the countries visited and the state of their monuments. Although personal feelings and judgments were injected into these works, their objective was to reproduce as faithfully as possible perceived reality. Thus the rapport between the signifier, the verbal reconstruction of observable phenomena, and the signified, the field of observation, was direct and unambiguous. This correspondence became less distinct in the latter part of the eighteenth century, when emotions of nostalgia and reveries intermingled with the factual and informative aspects of the voyage accounts.

The shifting balance between the subjective and the objective in favor of the former reached its culmination in Chateaubriand's *Itinéraire de Paris à Jérusalem et de Jérusalem à Paris*. In it, as well as in Chateaubriand's recounting of his experiences in the New World, objective reality was transmuted through the author's imagination into an artistic and poetic vision, and then it was reconstructed through the medium of language. No longer was the travelogue a product of erudition and detailed observation; no longer was it an instrument of instruction and edification. Instead, it was the expression of a personal quest and of a yearning seeking fulfillment in a wider universe, away from the tedium of immediate reality. Hence travel was at once an escape and a discovery. It was not, however, an outwardly directed discovery displaying its findings for the world to see and learn from them, but an inward-looking revelation bringing the self closer to the universe by exploiting all its resources in order to attain personal completion.

The psychological urge to appropriate the visible world for the aggrandizement of the self was accompanied by the equally powerful quest to glean from it images and motifs that would stir and nourish the imagination. Stimulated by these impressions, the creative impulse of the writer-traveler was now ready to fashion a work of literature that obeyed the artistic dictates of inner structural cohesion, stylistic originality, richness of imagery, and lyrical élan. The ultimate aim of such a travel account was not to serve as a field guide to prospective travelers, sharing with them one's experiences of foreign lands, but to proclaim the uniqueness of these experiences and impart aesthetic pleasure. Thus the profile of a country and a people in this *littérature de voyage* produced by such writers as Chateaubriand, Lamartine, Flaubert, Gérard de Nerval, and Pierre Loti was a projection of their fantasies, yearnings, and visions rather than a descriptive statement approximating real conditions. In this respect external reality functioned more as a stimulus of the creative imagination and less as an object worthy of being studied for its own sake.

The emergent subjective, relativist perception of foreign lands affected the representation of their present state as well as of their historical past. This was true especially of Greece. Although the conception that the eighteenth century had of ancient Greece persisted, its image began to be transformed at the beginning of the nineteenth. The preceding century was attacked for its static and unimaginative academicism, on the one hand, and for its superficial and frivolous treatment of classical art and mythology, on the other. Moreover, the increasing appeal of the foreign literatures of Northern and Southern Europe among early French Romantics placed classical antiquity in a different perspective. Without belittling its accomplishments, they no longer accepted its standards as universal.[1] They felt that the tastes and aspirations of modern man had to seek other sources of inspiration. Mme de Staël disputed the universality and timelessness of the ancient Greeks because she believed that there was a gap between modern consciousness and their way of apprehending reality; since the Greeks lived in a constantly renewed present, she argued, full of wonderment for the natural beauty that surrounded them, they were foreign to feelings of sadness and melancholy that come with the awareness of the evanescence of all human experiences.

Chateaubriand too saw a barrier between modern man, who had to bear the weight of history, and the ancient Greeks, who were free of the burden of the past. For him the apprehension of the unbridged division between past, present, and future was the bitter fruit of a ripe civilization. How fortunate was the savage, he mused, "who does not know as we do that sorrow is succeeded by sorrow, and whose soul, which has no recollection and no foresight, does not gather within itself the past, the present, and the future by the apprehension of a dolorous eternity."[2] He felt that contemporary man could not experience the plenitude of the present moment because he could see it no longer as an organic link in the triadic chain of past-present-future but as an isolated signpost from where one contemplated the past ebbing away and the future fleeting away as soon as it materialized in the present. In his apprehension of what Poulet calls "la déficience infinie" of the finite moment, Chateaubriand heralded the attitude of the Romantics toward time because, like them, he apprehended "the nostalgia of this life that the soul can never experience fully at any given moment, and which, nevertheless, it discovers constantly before and beyond the moment in the evanescent domain of *durée*."[3]

The more isolated and incomplete the present moment appeared, the more intense the search for a unifying principle transcending this division became. That which gave meaning and substance to the individual moment and saved it from obliteration was memory.

Without it, Chateaubriand noted, personal and collective experience would dissolve into a confused assemblage of unrelated events without any sequence or pattern.

> We would forget our friendships, our loves, our pleasures, our affairs; the mind would not be able to assemble its ideas; the most affectionate heart would lose its tenderness if it no longer remembered; our existence would be reduced to a series of moments in a ceaselessly flowing present; there would be no longer any past. O the misery of us! our life is so vain that it is only a reflection of our memory.[4]

The significance of memory as an organizing force of personal and historical experience was clearly perceived during the eighteenth century. For the Enlightenment thinkers memory established the continuity between past and present. For the Romantics, on the other hand, memory was the consciousness of the barriers between these two chronological planes as well as an instrument of surmounting them. In both instances the objective was to find a connection with the past; the first, however, was underscored by the belief that the past had been absorbed by the present and so it could be reenacted in the external, objective world. The cult of antiquity during the French Revolution and the expectation of nascent philhellenism to see ancient Greece revived reflect this optimistic view of the relation between past and present. No such comforting belief was entertained by the pre-Romantics and the Romantics. The union with one's personal and collective past was a feat of the personal will to be consummated at a given moment, which, however, would be once more succeeded by the awareness of division. "Remembering, then," in Poulet's words, "is no longer abolishing the interval, uniting the present with a rediscovered existence; it is, on the contrary, becoming most keenly conscious of this interval."[5]

Within this perspective of broken continuity, classical antiquity appeared in a different light. Since its existence, like that of every human phenomenon, was finite, then it was possible to discern other forces that succeeded it and gave a new direction and content to European civilization. Thus Christianity, so bitterly denounced by the eighteenth century as an obstacle to rational and humanistic progress, could now be restored to its position as the successor to pagan antiquity whose pantheon could no longer satisfy man's spiritual needs. Chateaubriand was one of the first modern French writers to perceive this movement and to express it, first in his *Génie du christianisme* and then in the *Martyrs*.

The relativistic view of the classical Greek world affected not so much "its ideal form but its temporal presence"[6] in the land where it arose and which still bore its vestiges. The distance between the ideal Greece of literature and philosophy and the Greece of change and contingency, a ubiquitous theme in the writings of European travelers, appeared to Chateaubriand as an eternal divide. "Well, Monsieur," he wrote to M. de Baure from Constantinople in 1806, "I have seen Greece! I visited Sparta, Argos, Mycenae, Corinth, Athens; beautiful names, alas! nothing more. . . . Never see Greece, Monsieur, except in Homer. It is the best way."[7]

Chateaubriand's visit to Greece was the first stage of a long voyage that took him around the shores of the Mediterranean. Its avowed purpose was to enrich his imagination and to replenish his reservoir of images so that he could convey more evocatively and more convincingly the passing of paganism and the coming of Christianity in his *Martyrs*. "I went to search for images," he wrote; "that is all."[8] This declaration, simple and direct though it may appear, is pivotal in understanding the organic relation between sensory perception and artistic creation in Chateaubriand.

He stressed the value of the perceptible world and the senses that register its images in the human consciousness. Before embarking on his creative journey, the artist, whether writer or painter, should explore the external world in its spatial and temporal dimensions. The wider one's acquaintance with it, the more fecund one's imagination and the more profound one's understanding of the human spirit would be. Observation, however, was only the first step in the creative process; the primary elements it furnished would be transmuted by the alchemy of personal vision, which, after a process of association and selection, would refashion them in the objects of its creation. "Always screening and choosing, cutting and adding, they [the poets] gradually created forms that were no longer natural but were more beautiful than those of nature; and the artists called these forms the beau idéal. One can then define the beau idéal as the *art of choosing and screening*."[9]

This interdependence between the objective and the subjective in Chateaubriand's concept of the artistic elaboration explains in part the importance he attached to the voyage. His two long journeys, one to the New World and the other to the Orient, were a manifestation of his search to absorb external reality before recreating his artistic vision of it.

His Mediterranean voyage was in a way a sequel to his youthful explorations of North America. "Having been to the New World and seen its monuments of nature, he needed to complete his circle of studies by visiting the Orient and its monuments of knowledge."[10] At the same time, it can be considered as its antipode. In America, young, self-confident, and eager to shed the strictures of civilization, he sought a direct communion with nature in a world of unspoiled splendor still untrammeled by human interference. In his customary dramatic and theatrical manner, years later he recalled his feelings of liberation when, "intoxicated by a feeling of independence, I was going from one tree to the next, to the right and the left, saying to myself, 'Here there are no more streets, no more cities, no more monarchy, no more kings, and no more men.' An in order to prove that I had recovered my original rights, I would abandon myself to my will's fancies."[11] As his youth waned, he began to seek the roots of his own heritage, namely, Hellenism and Christianity, Greece and Jerusalem, which teemed with the memories "of the mind and of the heart." One of the prime motivations of both voyages was the search for the first sources of man, a creature of nature and the creator of civilization. "Next to the American paradise, he had to place another Edenic landscape, the Greek, or more broadly the Mediterranean, which holds analogous values."[12]

Chateaubriand first announced his intention to visit Greece in a letter to the poet Fontanes dated 16 August 1803. At that time he was serving as secretary to the French embassy in Rome, a post he considered inferior to his qualifications. Similar announcements appeared in letters written to other friends between 1803 and 1806, when he finally decided to put his plans into effect. At first the scope of his projected itinerary was limited in time and space. He intended to visit Greece and Constantinople and then return to Paris before winter. Then he expanded his tour to include Jerusalem. Writing to his cousin Mme de Talaru from Constantinople on 13 September 1806, he informed her briefly about the highlights of his visits to ancient Greek sites and then noted that he would return to France in December, after having seen Jerusalem.[13] No mention was made of Egypt, Carthage, and Spain. The improvisatory character of his itinerary reflects the pattern of his approach to the activities he undertook: he did not proceed according to an a priori design, but his ideas and plans received impetus from each successive experience. What mattered in essence was not "the completed thing, [but] a becoming that is always future."[14]

And yet completion was the thing Chateaubriand yearned for precisely because he knew it was unattainable. A constant theme in his letters dealing with his voyage to the Orient was his intention to make this his last grand journey and to put an end to his traveling. The image of the closed circle was a constant motif in these letters. "I had a real need," he wrote to Mme de Talaru, "to make the voyage so as to complete the circle of my studies. Presently, when I will have seen the most beautiful monuments created by men and nature, I will no longer have any desire to leave my hole."[15] But he knew very well that the circle would not close and that his voyage to the Orient would make it even wider.

The voyage described in the *Itinéraire*, from the time he left Paris until his return to France, lasted ten months. He departed on 13 July 1806 and reentered France on 3 May 1807. He sailed around the shores of the Mediterranean visiting some of the most renowned cities of classical and Christian antiquity, such as Athens, Sparta, Constantinople, Rhodes, Jerusalem, Carthage, and Alexandria. Although Greece occupies more than one-third of the book, his sojourn in Greece proper lasted only nineteen days. He arrived at Modon, the port town at the tip of the Peloponnesus where most foreign visitors disembarked, on 10 August 1806. He departed for Smyrna on 29 August of the same year. Highlights of his tour included Sparta on the seventeenth and eighteenth of August, Argos on the nineteenth and twentieth, Mycenae on the twenty-first, and Athens on the twenty-third and twenty-sixth of the same month.[16]

Three years later, on 18 May 1809, Chateaubriand signed a contract with Le Normant to publish the *Itinéraire*. Its appearance on 27 February 1811 was greeted with success and critical acclaim. This is how the author himself described this triumph: "The year 1811 was one of the most remarkable of my literary career. I published the *Itinéraire de Paris à Jérusalem*, I replaced M. de Chénier at the Institute, and I began to write the *Mémoires,* which I am completing today. The success of the *Itinéraire* was as complete as that of the

Martyrs was disputed."¹⁷ Malte-Brun, among others, gave it a glowing review in his periodical *Annales des voyages de la géographie et de
l'histoire.* Another contemporary reviewer wrote:

> But however eager they [the journalists] all were to review the
> *Itinéraire*, the sale of thousands of copies preceded their judg-
> ments. Since the publication of this work, one and a half months
> have hardly passed, and the demand for it is increasing daily. M.
> de Chateaubriand is being translated in Italy, Germany, and other
> Countries. . . . A more swift and complete success has perhaps
> never been seen before.¹⁸

A second edition followed in the same year, and a third, revised and
corrected, appeared in 1812.

The *Itinéraire* was a work of transition. It was within the mainstream of travel accounts, whose number had increased significantly
at the end of the eighteenth century. Chateaubriand was careful to
point out that it belonged to a tradition established before him. In
his long introduction he gave an exhaustive list of works by travelers
who had preceded him. He also prefaced his account with a historical essay to provide a better understanding and a broader view of the
places he described. Furthermore, his text was interspersed with references to ancient historians, whose authority he invoked to elucidate the history of the sites he visited.

The insistence on historical fact, authoritative sources, and objective details had two main functions in the *Itinéraire*. First, it placed
it within the tradition of erudition of the previous centuries and
gave it academic respectability and recognition. Second, and perhaps
more importantly, it was an integral part of his vision of the past and
its relation to the present. In his view, time—chronological time,
that is—means movement and change. A given fact, be it a historical
event or the life of an individual, cannot be objectively restituted
and recaptured. The constant flow of time places an insurmountable
barrier between that which was and that which is. But what is lost
in the external world survives in the memory of man. Thus a para-
dox takes place: the more acute the awareness of his finiteness and
contingency, the more intense his search for infinity and completeness and therefore the more precious the remembrance of things
past. This aspect integrated the historical narrative into the artistic
and subjective part of his work.

Although the historical, learned part of the *Itinéraire* placed it in the tradition of past travel literature, it differed in one important aspect: for the first time a travelogue aspired to be a work of art and not a mere record of places and events. As such, it was not a strict copy of the surrounding world but a refracted image of it. Whereas objective reality had undergone no essential transformation in the travel accounts of previous writers, the *Itinéraire* was stamped by the unique vision of the author, "whose soul made an imprint on things."[19] When we read Guys and Choiseul-Gouffier, we learn very little about their inner dimension because they made no conscious effort to connect their voyage with their intimate life. They were personally involved only to the extent that they identified themselves with classical antiquity. In Chateaubriand's *Itinéraire*, however, we see both the writer as the master craftsman and the man now lyrical and compassionate, now haughty and egotistical.

Thus the *Itinéraire* created in French literature "the personal, lyrical or better yet autobiographical voyage,"[20] which introduced Greece and Asia Minor to French lyricism.[21] In a broader sense it showed the vast psychological and literary possibilities of the voyage and paved the way for such future travelers as Lamartine, Flaubert, Gérard de Nerval, and Barrès.

In the *Itinéraire* and in Chateaubriand's work in general, the external world and the inner self coexisted in a dynamic relationship in which the one stimulated the other. Nature, with its shapes and contours, is there; its reality is not disputed. However, it is a reality perceived by the human eye and infused with the memory of human events. A landscape has a clear outline, a background and a foreground, and a movement and life of its own. Its features are accentuated by the interplay of light and shadow. Chateaubriand's tableaux resemble those Flemish paintings that, while portraying realistically the perceptible world, emanate an inner glow and a transcendental meaning of their own. Like them, Chateaubriand admirably used the technique of chiaroscuro and exploited its emotive suggestions. He did not simply react emotionally to nature and the memories it evoked, but he sought to find a structure and to reveal the hidden correspondences that unify it. In that respect he was indeed "the first to discover the play of light on things, the first to construct a landscape, to create a kind of impressionism."[22]

Chateaubriand's literary work is a multifaceted creation. Not a particularly humble man, he was aware of his talent and did not hesitate to display it. One can detect certain elements of the poseur in him. Some parts of the *Itinéraire* leave the impression that a scene is a literary creation, a masterful combination of words designed to enthrall the reader. Its undeniable beauty does not prevent it from being at times an artifice. This is especially true when the author, in recounting his experiences in Greece, treats Chateaubriand the traveler with obvious partiality and minimizes every other human presence. It is as if the world around him existed for his gratification and the stimulation of his imagination. He took from it what he needed in order to create his images. He was not an impersonal observer but an ever felt presence never letting the reader forget that he was partly the demiurge of the world he depicted. In his work "the ego dissolves itself in the contemplation of wonders it creates, and then is reborn, stronger than ever, more able to savor its powers and to enjoy its interpretations."[23]

In a travel account this approach creates certain problems. When the author-traveler, posing as a central character, appropriates the world he is presenting, the people of this world are robbed of their significance and individuality. This was the fate of the modern Greeks in the *Itinéraire*. In a way the presence of the dead was felt more keenly than that of the living, who were portrayed as shadows. His admiration for the former contrasted sharply with his condescension toward the latter. These sentiments were communicated to his readers, who saw in the modern Greeks the phantoms of their former selves steeped in hopeless ignorance and lethargy. One of the contemporary reviewers of the *Itinéraire* expressed this feeling very aptly. "The spectacle of this lost illustriousness and the degradation of Greece, formerly so flourishing, so free, so polished, today humiliated, debased, almost as barbarous as its barbarous dominators, makes him utter eloquent regrets."[24] Unlike most romantic Hellenists from Guys to Fauriel, "Chateaubriand almost never reintegrates the life of the past into that of the present; he opens a fissure between the two Greeces."[25]

This dichotomy, this distressing absence and ever widening distance were especially marked in the Greek landscape. A society that had pulsated with life and vigor was but a distant echo in the mind of Chateaubriand, while the places that had nurtured it were strewn with its ruins. Furthermore, the integrity of the ruined monuments had been violated by the intrusion of contemporary structures, which, like the Greek language, betrayed foreign influences. Byzantine, or "gothic" churches, as he called them, displeased him because he found their cupolas, arches, and protrusions bizarre, incoherent, and incongruous with the lines of the Greek landscape, whose serenity, limpidity, and radiance invited uniformity, harmony, and conformity with nature. "In Greece . . . everything is gentle and smooth, full of calmness in nature as it was in the writings of the ancients. One can almost imagine how the architecture of the Parthenon has such felicitous proportions, how ancient sculpture is so little contorted, so peaceful, and so simple when one has seen the pure sky and the peaceful landscape of Athens."[26] His Greece was in many respects the Greece of calm nobility envisioned by Winckelmann and the eighteenth century. He believed that cloistered buildings and dark interiors were ill-suited to Greece and were another sign of its decadence. The mysterious, the subterranean, and the arcane belonged to a more mystical and transcendental world symbolized by the Holy Sepulcher in Jerusalem.

Chateaubriand was a purist who had no tolerance for the disparate and heterogeneous. Natural surroundings and human creations, such as art and architecture, ought to harmonize, complement, and enrich one another. In his view certain lines and styles were most fitting and authentic in a particular setting. Their transposition and mixture would give rise to awkward and discordant structures. He considered the transportation of the sculptures of the Parthenon to England by Elgin not only a sacrilege against a hallowed monument but an artistic travesty as well. Away from the luminescent atmosphere of Greece, severed from the temple that supported them, and encased in the somber walls of a museum in an alien country, their beauty was petrified and lifeless. In Greece ignorance compounded by irreverence for classical ruins had produced, in Chateaubriand's eyes, hybrid structures composed of the debris of ancient monuments and other nondescript materials.

Confronted with disharmony and discontinuity in space and time, Chateaubriand sought a partial restitution of the past in his own consciousness and memory. His *Itinéraire* was in one sense a search for a personal communion with Hellenism and Christianity. It was a pilgrimage to the places that had bequeathed to Europe its two formative spiritual forces. No longer regarding them as hostile or mutually exclusive, Chateaubriand saw himself as the heir to this dual legacy. "I was going to visit the Parthenon and Jerusalem as an offspring of Pindus and a crusader of Jerusalem."[27]

For him the physical world provided the necessary medium for self-expansion. He moved between a nature free from contingency and mutability and a transitory humanity unable to arrest the constant flow of time. His incessant movement and restlessness were an attempt to explore and absorb as much of this world as possible. However, he did not seek to be absorbed by it. Instead of a blissful effacement of his separate identity, he strove to heighten his consciousness and to dominate the external world. He placed himself "in a Napoleonic manner at the center of the universe."[28] When he was young, the New World, with its vast horizons, unburdened as yet by a past, signified a reaching outward and a liberation. As he aged, the Old World, deeply impressed by human deeds measuring the passing of time, drew his attention:

> All this [America] delights when one is twenty years old because life is self-contained, so to speak, and because youth has an element of restlessness and indefiniteness which propels one incessantly to seek chimeras . . . ; but at a more mature age, the mind returns to more solid tastes: it desires especially to be nourished by the memories and examples of history . . . ; what I need now . . . are fields whose furrows instruct me, and where I rediscover man that I am, the blood, the tears and the sweat of man."[29]

His first voyage reflected his desire to embrace the spatial world, whereas the second was an endeavor to recapture the historical experience of Europe. In a symbolic way it was a dialogue *avec les morts*. Responding to a question from a Turk who wanted to know the reason for his journey, Chateaubriand astounded him by explaining that he traveled in order to see people and "especially the Greeks who were dead" (*I*, 121).

In all his travels, Chateaubriand sought the expansion of the self through the interiorization of the physical cosmos. At times this was accomplished not by an abstract mental projection but by a concrete physical gesture: "I always feel pleasure in drinking from the water of the famous rivers that I crossed in my life" (*I*, 192). He was aware, however, that this communion was a self-induced act. In Greece the gods of old no longer animated nature, and the ancient poets were forever silent. His own voyage was but a reenactment of humanity's race with time and its efforts to bridge the fissure separating it from the past and from the rest of the world. "And I, obscure voyager, retracing the obliterated paths of vessels carrying the great men of Greece and Italy, I was going to look for the muses in their country; but I am not Virgil, and the gods no longer inhabit Olympus" (*I, 73*).

Display of Erudition:
The *Itinéraire* and Its Critics

Contemporary reaction to the *Itinéraire* was overwhelmingly favorable.[30] Critics were almost unanimous in their encomium of Chateaubriand's exceptional descriptive powers, his ability to trace the delicate lines and capture the nuances of light and color of the Greek landscape, and, finally, his melancholy lyricism. In spite of this, there were some dissenting voices. Their criticism—faint, to be sure, in the midst of the general enthusiasm—was directed against the topographical and archeological accuracy of the work. The critic Millin, editor of the *Magasin encyclopédique*, while expressing praise and admiration in his review of the *Itinéraire*, thought it his duty to point out its inaccuracies. His critique is a valuable record not so much because it is an incisive analysis of the work as because it communicates the reaction the *Itinéraire* generated.

> The works of M. DE CHATEAUBRIAND inspire a great interest; the magic of his style, the choice of his subjects, justify fully the ardor with which his creations are sought after. The one we are announcing was awaited with impatience. . . . We have expressed the admiration that we profess for his writings; his knowledge reveals a profound writer . . . despite some slight inaccuracies, which, however, cannot blemish a beautiful work; and if we have pointed them out, it is because we wanted to show the care with which we have read his work.[31]

Chateaubriand was piqued by the adverse criticism and felt impelled to defend the exactitude of his descriptions because he valued the traveler's role as an objective reporter. "A traveler is a kind of historian: his duty is to relate faithfully what he has seen and heard. He must invent nothing but also he must omit nothing."[32] In addition to his claims of objectivity, he placed particular emphasis on his extensive knowledge of the literature and history of the people whose countries he visited. This was particularly true, he insisted, of the ancients. He read Virgil, Horace, Hesiod, and Homer, among others. He knew most of the classicists of his time; Delille, the poet and the translator of the *Georgics*, and Fontanes, the author of *La Grèce sauvée*, were well known to him. In his preface to the *Itinéraire*, he informed the reader that his voyage was not a distraction but a serious undertaking that necessitated long preparation and painstaking research.

Still, he wanted to quell unfavorable comments, and in 1812 he published a second, revised edition of the *Itinéraire*. He was especially sensitive to criticism arising from his exaggerated sense of self-importance, and he subdued expressions of self-indulgence and egotism. But he never ceased to consider the *Itinéraire* a reliable guide based on solid research and scrupulous accuracy. In 1826, in the preface of his *Oeuvres Complètes* published by Ladvocat, he wrote:

> I have had the very small merit of opening the way and the great pleasure of seeing it followed after me. In fact, my *Itinéraire* had only just been published, and it began to serve as a guide to a host of travelers. Nothing recommends it more to the public than its exactitude; it is the guidebook to the ancient sites; in it I mark most scrupulously the routes, the habitations, and the places of glory.[33]

Immodest and boastful though this assertion may appear, it was not entirely unfounded. In 1816 the comte de Marcellus, an ardent admirer and later a friend of Chateaubriand, visited Greece with Homer in one hand and Chateaubriand in the other, so to speak. Chateaubriand's fame reached as far as America: Edward Everret, an important American philhellene during the Greek War of Independence, decided to visit Greece after having read the *Itinéraire*. "Your *Itinéraire*," he wrote to the author on 11 September 1825, "gave me the idea several years ago of traveling to this country; and I will always have a pleasant association of the names of Greece and of Chateaubriand."[34] However, it was not so much the exactitude of his historical and archeological observations that inspired his American admirer to come to Greece. What fascinated him and the rest of

Chateaubriand's readers was the brilliance of his imagery and his cadenced prose.

It was precisely Chateaubriand's qualities as a *paysagiste* that drew the eulogies of his admirers. They dismissed his inaccuracies as minor defects in no way affecting the essence of the work. One of them, the poet Fontanes, saw the *Itinéraire* as the quintessence of travel accounts. He commended Chateaubriand for uplifting and enriching a genre that had become very popular by the beginning of the nineteenth century. When a place as rich in legends and natural beauty as Greece is described by a writer equally rich in artistic talent, then a travelogue ceases to be a mere curiosity and becomes an aesthetic and psychological experience.

Malte-Brun, another contemporary critic, expressed the opinion that a writer of Chateaubriand's sweeping vision and vivid imagination should not be held accountable for minute observations fit for academically inclined and pedestrian minds. "But these minds, which are devoted to the study of vast details, do not fail to appreciate others that grasp incisively the general forms . . . [and] throw new light on objects patiently examined by a large number of detached investigators."[35] Thus, for most contemporary critics the significance of the historical and archeological narrative of the work was minimized. No attempt was made to elucidate it in terms of the author's historical vision. Struck by the splendor of his imagery and moved by his lyricism, they excused his inaccuracies as negligible offenses and interpreted his claims to veracity as pardonable idiosyncrasies.

It was a Greek, Dionysios Avramiotti, who exposed the errors and inexactitudes of the *Itinéraire*. His work, *Les notes critiques d'Avramiotti sur le voyage en Grèce de Chateaubriand*, written in Italian, was published in Padua in 1816.[36] In 1817, Millin published excerpts from it in the *Annales encyclopédiques*. It was not translated in its entirety into French until 1929. Born on the island of Zante in 1770, Avramiotti studied medicine in Padua and then returned to Argos, where he practiced his profession. His avocation was the archeological exploration of ancient sites. He knew the French consul Fauvel and admired his extensive knowledge of antiquity and his erudition. In 1813 he became a member of the Athens Society of the Philomusoi. He came to live in Athens shortly before the Revolution and died there in 1835. Avramiotti exemplified the growing national consciousness among Greeks at that time. Proud of his nation, he derived particular gratification when he saw the veneration European visitors had for his ancestors.

He would undoubtedly have remained an obscure figure had he not hosted Chateaubriand when the latter visited Argos. Elated to offer hospitality to such a renowned visitor, he took it upon himself to act as his guide to the surrounding antiquities. Since they shared an admiration for classical Greece, Avramotti expected Chateaubriand to examine the ruined monuments patiently and meticulously. He believed that Chateaubriand, as an enlightened European well versed in the classics, would carefully examine the defaced antiquities to determine their nature and origin by sifting through the debris. Avramiotti's own erudition and the methods of others such as Fauvel had prepared him to appreciate this academic approach to antiquity. Therefore, when he confronted a new kind of traveler in Chateaubriand, he was bewildered and disillusioned. Instead of scrutinizing broken columns and fragmented inscriptions, Chateaubriand preferred to stand on elevated places from where he could embrace the surrounding space. He had to perceive the contours of the Greek landscape in order to understand the world of the ancient poets. Avramiotti interpreted this as idle fantasizing at best and as a presumptuous superficiality utterly disregarding truth and accuracy at worst.

These antithetical attitudes reveal the difference between the two men: the French author cast a sweeping glance around him, gleaning images for his literary compositions, while the Greek doctor scrutinized the ruined monuments, trying to decipher their signs. For Chateaubriand ancient Greece was a vision to be recaptured in moments of intense concentration whereas for Avramiotti it was a reality to be comprehended by the painstaking examination of its ruins.

These individual divergences exemplify the divergent meaning of the Hellenic past for the Europeans as opposed to the modern Greeks. For the former it was a field of archeological and scholarly study and a source of artistic and poetic themes. André Chénier and Chateaubriand, among others, explored the second aspect. For the educated Greeks, their Hellenic heritage was a relatively new discovery from which they derived pride and dignity. They believed that with great effort on their part its greatness could be theirs again. The examination of the ruined monuments and the knowledge of Hellenic history were not merely a scholarly enterprise but a way of

bringing their classical heritage closer to them. The appeal was emotional and patriotic, but it reached them through intellectual and
didactic channels. The literary and artistic appreciation of the past
requires a certain distance and tension between past and present. At
a time of a growing sense of national identity, the recognition of
such a distance conflicted with the political and cultural aspirations
of the Greeks. They wanted to experience classical Greece directly,
and, paradoxically, they felt its existence in its ruins.

Seen in this light, Avramiotti's response to Chateaubriand acquires
a broader significance. His work, though a biased examination of
minutiae revealing nothing but contempt for Chateaubriand's literary talent, is valuable because it exemplified the reaction of the
Greeks to Western European visitors. Taught by them to value their
ruins as their most prized possessions, they could not tolerate hasty
and impatient visitors such as Chateaubriand. Seeing themselves as
the rightful heirs of the ancients, they expected to be treated with
the same respect that was shown to the ancient monuments. Failure
to see them as an integral part of the Hellenic world was an affront
and gave rise to indignation. Thus motivated, the doctor from Argos
wrote his diatribe against Chateaubriand. In a disdainful tone he set
out to disprove Chateaubriand's claims to objectivity and expose his
fallacies. He wanted to enlighten his readers who, according to
Avramiotti, beguiled by Chateaubriand's style, failed to perceive his
disregard for truth.

> Even though his book was amply applauded just as soon as it ap-
> peared—current taste, the ornaments of a vivid imagination and
> the prestige of an elegant style deceived the superficial reader—in
> spite of all this . . . one can quickly see this: the author going
> swiftly across the Peloponnesus and Attica, without definite ob-
> ject and plan, accomplishes nothing else but the travesty of the his-
> torical reality of places and facts. . . . It is, therefore, my intention
> to examine how in this work reality and the public have been lit-
> tle respected.[37]

The polarity between the two men appeared early in their brief
acquaintance. Chateaubriand, hasty and restless as always, intended
to leave Argos the day following his arrival. Avramiotti, somewhat
displeased and puzzled at such impatience, persuaded him to post-
pone his departure for one more day. Together they visited the cita-

del of Argos. For Chateaubriand the magnificent view unfolding before them conjured up scenes of splendor and majesty. Avramiotti, however, found such flights of imagination improper for a savant.

> And I added that from this elevation only captains found satisfaction reviewing their troops or painters in drawing their landscapes, and that the learned man searched every stone and every inscription and found his joy comparing the authors with his personal observations. He answered me that nature had not created him at all for these servile studies, that for him a peak was enough to awaken in his memory the smiling images of fable and history. (39)

Chateaubriand became somewhat annoyed, as he preferred to be left alone to contemplate the scenery in the privacy of his own imagination. A few verses from Homer, some broken columns gleaming in the morning sun, were enough to stir the shadows of the dead and make them come alive for a brief moment. His host, however, was intent on giving him a detailed account of Argos, Mycenae, and Tiryns. The memory of this well-intentioned but prosaic antiquarian stayed with Chateaubriand for a long time. Almost two decades later he confided to Marcellus his vexation at being followed by this self-appointed guide. "This captious and spiteful doctor spared me nothing. He hounded my dreams one by one; when I was in the ruins with the shadow of Agamemnon, he wanted me to measure stones. He followed all my steps as an irksome companion; and in my recollection I compare him to the leeches he obtained from the swamp of Lerna to treat his patients."[38] The disappointment was mutual, and Chateaubriand's departure came as a relief to both of them.

Avramiotti's critique was not a calm and detached refutation of Chateaubriand's claims to historical veracity. His tone was mocking and scornful. He was especially piqued by Chateaubriand's claims of having discovered important sites and monuments. He considered such pretensions false and presumptuous. Though Avramiotti's critical insight was far from profound, he did possess a talent for irony and parody. In his attacks he purposely chose passages where Chateaubriand portrayed himself in a dramatic and even theatrical manner. By reducing these passages to their concrete details and isolating them from their psychological and artistic associations, he showed a man feverishly moving from place to place, now lamenting the destruction of the ancient world and now exclaiming with pride at the discovery of a new monument.

> Crown him with laurels, applaud, quiver with joy. We are not endowed with an imagination vivid enough to follow him in the ruins of Magoula when he glides here and there flitting about like a magpie, when he cries and laughs over the vicissitudes of man, when he recites verses and picks lilies in honor of Helen, when he eats dry figs and drinks the water of Evrotas, when he complains bitterly of not having found a single swan. Let's rather follow him when he imposes on each place its real name and when he measures the hill with his own feet, a new and very exact method.[39]

Avramiotti was referring to one of the best-known passages of the *Itinéraire,* in which Chateaubriand, after having consulted ancient historical accounts, concluded that he was one of the discoverers of the ruins of ancient Sparta. He conceded that this was a personal discovery because other travelers such as Spon, Fourmont, and Le Roy had been there before him. But he absolved himself by insisting that at the time of his visit their works were unknown to him and that he had accepted the current view, which placed Sparta in the location of the modern city of Mistras. Therefore, he maintained, his determination of the site of ancient Sparta was a personal feat and the exhilaration he felt from such a discovery was sincere and justifiable.[40] Avramiotti did not find this argument convincing and interpreted it as another pretext for the display of self-importance at the expense of truth. He did not neglect to expose several other instances of exaggeration and inaccuracy in the same sarcastic vein.[41]

Of all the errors, conscious or unconscious, committed by Chateaubriand, none infuriated Avramiotti more than his own portrait in the *Itinéraire.* Describing his visit to Argos, Chateaubriand mentioned briefly his acquaintance with the doctor. While respecting his erudition and knowledge of antiquity, he referred to him as "the Italian doctor . . . [who] was beginning to yearn for Italy." (*I,* 161–62). Avramiotti, highly conscious and proud of his origin, took this as an unforgivable offense. Is this, he asked, how civilized Europeans express their gratitude for the hospitality they receive? "I desire Venice, Venice my birthplace? I am Greek in religion and national-ity and I live in Greece."[42] What distressed him even more was Chateaubriand's failure to appreciate the modern Greeks and to perceive their strides toward progress and enlightenment. At least he should have refrained from passing any judgment since his contact with them was so brief and superficial. "M. de Chateaubriand," Avramiotti admonished him, "after having run through the villages of Peloponnesus and Attica and completed your voyage between 10 August . . . and the last days of the month, . . . do not think that in such a short time you could know the Greek nation and so do not have the temerity to judge it" (58).

Avramiotti's caustic and acrimonious criticism, therefore, reveals issues deeper than an infraction of intellectual integrity. As an individual, he felt slighted by a guest who mistook his identity and could not even remember the basic facts of his existence. As a Greek educated in the West, desiring to see his nation more closely associated with Europe through the emulation of classical antiquity, he was disappointed to find his countrymen treated only as victims and separated from their ancient heritage. He resented Chateaubriand for placing himself in the foreground and for treating the Greeks as shadows in their own land.

Avramiotti's critique did not alter the overwhelmingly favorable view of French critics. The few who read it accepted the validity of some of his points but dismissed them readily because, in their estimation, Chateaubriand had not made a historical and archeological exploration and thus any errors in that area were forgivable. Millin accepted this view because "the purpose [of Chateaubriand] was not to do . . . research on antiquity and architecture; thus the inexactitudes to which Avramiotti seems to attach so much importance are in essence very insignificant."[43] Likewise, Sainte-Beuve minimized the significance of Avramiotti's exposé because Chateaubriand was not a pedant but an artist.[44]

At the beginning of the twentieth century, Avramiotti's work received more critical consideration. This was mainly due to a more careful examination of Chateaubriand's geographical and archeological observations and use or misuse of sources. The enthusiasm over his lyricism and plastic imagination had subsided, and critics began to analyze the composition of the work more rigorously. One critic found Avramiotti's remarks not totally irrelevant. "This doctor, whose guest Chateaubriand was, although quite ironic, was not at all capable of lying, and if he corrected Chateaubriand it was because of pure love of truth."[45] Another, Aulard, after a long search, was able to locate a copy of this "rarissime libelle," as he called Avramiotti's work. In his article he quoted extensively from it so as to show that there was some justification for its criticism. His conclusion, however, favored Chateaubriand in much the same way as others in the previous century had. He attributed Chateaubriand's misrepresentations to the transformation immediate reality underwent during the creation of his compositions. For this reason, "Avramiotti's mordant satire is a document on Chateaubriand's method of working: one sees in it how the poet combines his fantasies with reality, and perhaps this is seen more clearly here than anywhere else."[46] In the final analysis, Chateaubriand inevitably emerged victorious, and Avramiotti was almost invariably characterized as a narrow-minded and unimaginative pedant. Curiously, none of these critics perceived Avramiotti's work as a patriotic outburst against an unjust treatment of his country and countrymen.

The whole question of Chateaubriand's historical veracity and its relation to the composition of the *Itinéraire* was thoroughly examined by the critic Garabed Der-Sahaghian in his study *Chateaubriand en Orient*, a systematic and minute examination of the *Itinéraire's* sources and the manner in which they were used. Der-Sahaghian endeavored to establish the chronology of the voyage by scrutinizing all the given dates. He put topographical descriptions to the test by comparing them to those of previous travelers and found striking similarities, which led him to conclude that "in a certain sense there are few works that belong less to their author and contain less truth."[47] By "truth" he meant the details of the external world, which Chateaubriand did not always convey unaltered. Arbitrary placement of monuments and their imaginary reconstruction were common in his narrative. Moreover, important sources from which he borrowed freely often remained unacknowledged, whereas others, less important, were given undue attention. Chateaubriand often took liberties with his sources and confused names and geographical locations.

Der-Sahaghian pointed out certain similarities between Barthélemy and Chateaubriand in their description of the Peloponnesus. Undoubtedly, the *Voyage du jeune Anacharsis* was one of the literary sources of both the *Martyrs* and the *Itinéraire*, though Chateaubriand neglected to acknowledge it. However, the method and the vision of the two authors were diametrically opposed: Barthélemy's depiction of the ancient world, though vivid and picturesque, was a linear presentation encompassing all aspects of Greek life. Furthermore, in his work Greece appeared in its full glory, prosperous and unblemished by any signs of decay. Chateaubriand, on the other hand, condensed and transposed material from other sources, interwove it with personal experience, and suppressed superfluous details. In Barthélemy everything moved forward in a horizontal fashion; chronological time and human progress were in perfect consonance. To the horizontality of spatial movement, Chateaubriand added the verticality of time, which meant negation, absence, and destruction.

To compose the *Itinéraire*, Chateaubriand had consulted works by historians, naturalists, missionaries, and especially travelogue writers. It was customary for the travelers of that time to borrow from one another. Chateaubriand followed their example and in a way "made his voyage with other voyages."[48] In his preface he stated that in preparing his work he had recourse to other books. Also, he admitted that personal inspiration had to be supplemented by literary sources. "Others have their resources in themselves; I need to supplement what I lack with all sorts of works."[49] While Chateaubriand was not always scrupulous in his use of other works, he did not conceal the importance they had in the writing of his own book.

Seen in this light, the *Itinéraire* was a work of synthesis springing from the combination of the subjective and the objective, of the personal and the collective. In their interpenetration these elements underwent a transformation, and the resulting order did not mirror the external world but revealed the hidden correspondences among myth, history, and nature. Spatial relationships were determined not so much by the arrangement of things in their physical setting as by the rapport between their forms and colors. The direct perception of the external world was enriched and amplified by the memory of human events recorded by literature and history. This may explain and to some extent excuse the obvious misrepresentations and factual errors committed by Chateaubriand. In his *Itinéraire* the depiction of Greece is neither a spontaneous and direct recollection of a voyage nor a painstaking and detached description of archeological sites. Rather, it is the artistic recreation of a world whose past he had absorbed through the channels of classical learning and whose present he experienced personally. This poetic vision of Greece expresses essentially "the reign of aesthetic harmony in the world restructured by thought."[50]

Chateaubriand's use of historical narrative, its inaccuracies notwithstanding, was applied successfully as an artistic and structural device in the composition of the *Itinéraire*. Its development is an integral part of the dual structure of the book. There is the progressive unfolding of his voyage conveying information on places, their history, and their people. This horizontal exposition is essentially of a learned nature. At regular intervals the expository narrative is interrupted; the progress of time is momentarily suspended, and the author-character steps forth and begins to sketch the scene around him, recalling its literary and mythological associations. If this binary structure were graphically represented, there would be a horizontal line indicating the onward movement of the author in time and space. This linear progression would be arrested at points represented by circles symbolizing the author's quest for a fusion with the external world of nature and history. The tension created between these two levels functions admirably as a literary device. His images, instead of succeeding one another in a monotonous and repetitive pattern, stand out as self-contained units with an inner movement of their own. Yet they are not isolated visions. The author's experience, their correspondences, their association with legend and history, and the repetition of certain motifs unify and integrate them into the whole structure.

Chateaubriand's display of erudition in the *Itinéraire* has an artistic as well as a psychological function. On the one hand, he emphasized the personal nature of his work while, on the other, he insisted on the objectivity of his observations, the accuracy of his historical narrative, and his unbiased use of other sources. In this work he wanted to combine the impartiality of a reliable and learned observer and the artistic expression of his inner vision. By quoting liberally from previous travelers, he intended not to copy them but to verify their remarks by comparing them with his own. Furthermore, their works served not only as sources of information but also as signs of the endurance of human memory. They gave him a sense of belonging to and participating in a literary tradition beginning with the ancient Pausanias and moving forward to the modern Choiseul-Gouffier. It was gratifying and comforting to know that one belonged to a line of famous travelers. Thus personal vanity and a search for continuity and stability in the face of change and mutability were at once satisfied by resorting to authoritative sources.

His quest for stability was counterbalanced by a more powerful drive for the exploration and discovery of new things. These two seemingly antithetical forces stemmed from the same underlying desire to make a permanent impression of one's existence and leave a lasting mark of one's accomplishments. Chateaubriand wanted to link his name with that of famous men of antiquity by retracing their steps and anticipating those of future visitors. Moreover, he liked to think of himself as a pioneer and discoverer of long-forgotten sites restoring them to the memory of present and future generations. "Even if I had only determined the site of Lacedemon, discovered a new tomb of Mycenae, ... I would still deserve the goodwill of travelers."[51] When he arrived in Sparta, he tells us, he was overwhelmed by exhilarating emotions. The ruins of the ancient city, undisturbed by human presence and overgrown with vegetation, were revealed to him from an elevation. Alone, without a guide and relying only on his personal knowledge and intuition, he began to measure distances, identify monuments, and reconstruct an imaginary picture of the city. When he could not recognize a structure, he named it according to his fancy as if the act of naming conferred upon it a new existence.

How much of this was genuine emotion and how much literary artifice is difficult to distinguish, especially since there was a four-year period of gestation between the actual voyage and the writing of the *Itinéraire*. Suffice it to say that Chateaubriand's display of learning and insistence on accuracy and objectivity, though often a travesty of immediate reality, reflected a search for structure and order both in the inner world of thought and imagination and in the outer world of nature and history. That this order was the result of a dynamic interaction between sensory stimuli and inner structural patterns is characteristic of every creative process. In the case of Chateaubriand it was indicative of his desire to dominate the external world by reshaping its forms in his writings. "He went to the Orient in order to add the memory of his name to that of classical locales, in order to place his figure among those of the Greek heroes and the prophets of Israel. When he went to look for 'images' there, he wanted to leave his own forever."[52]

Broken Harmony:
The Distasteful Heterogeneity

Chateaubriand's desire to envision antiquity and to experience the beauty of its art and poetry led him more and more to the realization of the impossibility of its restitution. Nowhere else did he feel this fissure more intensely than in Greece. For him successive foreign invasions, beginning with the Romans and ending with the Turks, had violated both the physical integrity of Greece and the purity of its civilization. He considered the movement and mingling of different peoples on its soil a contamination and distortion of the Hellenic spirit. Moreover, his conviction that the past cannot be recreated in the present prevented him from entertaining the palliative expectation of seeing ancient Greece revived. Though he expressed some sympathy for the modern Greeks, he denied them any affinity with their classical progenitors. In his *Itinéraire* the significance of their presence was minimized and they were dispossessed of their ancient inheritance. In this respect he did not follow the path of nascent philhellenism.

Chateaubriand's understanding and appreciation of the ancients combined elements of romantic Hellenism and modernism. As a modern, he understood that humanity's incessant spiritual quest seeks new sources of inspiration and new forms of expression. Therefore he viewed the rise of Christianity as the most potent force filling the void left by the eclipse of the ancient pantheon. His *Génie du christianisme* and *Martyrs* are a vindication of the spiritual superiority of Christianity over paganism. Yet his attachment to the ancients was equally powerful. He admired their simplicity, their closeness to nature, and the inner harmony and symmetry of their literary and artistic creations. He felt that there was a plenitude and self-sufficiency in their world which modern people, no matter how much they tried, could never attain. "Although modern people present . . . some interesting epochs, . . . one must agree that they do not provide the historian with this comprehensive totality, these lofty lessons, which make ancient history a complete whole, a perfect picture."[53]

When he went to Greece and saw the ancient monuments, he marveled at their symmetrical proportions, the purity and simplicity of their lines, and their harmony with their surroundings. It was then that he realized how important it was to see and feel the beauty of the Greek landscape so as to appreciate the ancient poets. "When I examined this mountain, I was convinced how difficult it is to understand ancient authors without having seen the places of which they speak."[54] Ancient literature was not an abstract source of poetic formulas and mythical figures. For Chateaubriand it was the expression of an experienced reality recreated through the plastic imagination of the ancient poets, whose texts pulsated with the sounds and sights of the Greek land.

In the *Martyrs* we see antiquity in its waning stages. The priest Demodocus and his daughter Cymodocée are its last representatives dedicated to the worship of the ancient gods. They symbolize an era that is gradually fading away before their very eyes. Demodocus, still paying homage to the gods of a fascinating but fictitious mythology, is an august and majestic figure reminiscent of his Homeric prototype, who was a bard at the court of Alcinous in Phaeacia. Cymodocée is young and full of charm and grace. She lives in an atmosphere of quiet sumptuousness and discreet voluptuousness. Thus a certain simplicity and innocence coexist with glittering luxury and delicate sensuousness. Paganism in its declining years "combines virtue with voluptuousness so that the two major motifs of Hellenism will be for Chateaubriand, without any internal conflict, primitive innocence (Rousseauist) and sensuality (pagan)."[55]

If Demodocus is the personification of patriarchal simplicity and dignity, Cymodocée, the priestess of the Muses and the future Christian martyr, is revealed through her physical charms. Chateaubriand presented her during some of her most intimate moments, when her innocence and naïveté make her appear even more voluptuous and desirable. She, however, is utterly unconscious of her attractiveness and acts with disarming artlessness. Her purity combined with her loveliness envelop her in a tantalizing mystery. Here is her portrait in her intimate surroundings:

> Cymodocée retires to her apartment, and after having enjoyed the pleasures of a bath, she lies on Lydian rugs overlaid with fine Egyptian wool. . . . [In the morning,] in a chaste sanctuary, she lets her garment, mysterious work of modesty, glide down to her feet. She clothes herself in a robe resembling the *fleur de lis*, which the discreet Graces themselves fasten around her bosom. She laces light

sandals upon her bare feet and gathers the perfumed tresses of her
hair on her head with a golden pin. Her nurse brings her the
white veil of the Muses, which shines in the sun and which was
kept under all the others in a perfumed box.[56]

This intriguing combination of naïveté and sensuality in Cymodocée's countenance, heightened by the author's emphasis on physical details, is similar to Chénier's poetic treatment of ancient myths.
In Chénier's poetry, eroticism and sensuality were expressed more
directly and were bound intimately with love and maturation. In
Chateaubriand they become less direct and more concealed; their
intensity stems from the tension imposed by Christianity between
the spiritual and the physical worlds. Chateaubriand sensed this dual-
ity, and in Cymodocée he delineated an exquisite maiden born pagan
but ready to accept the purifying revelations of Christianity. Nevertheless, both Chénier and Chateaubriand describe pagan antiquity
in its twilight, when it gave forth a shimmering glow before its final
eclipse. They portrayed it not in its vigorous youth and robust creativity but at a time when its energy and vitality were ebbing away.
Unlike Barthélemy, whose Greece was active, industrious, and progressive, Chénier and especially Chateaubriand captured the last rays
of a vanishing era. In the *Martyrs* as well as the *Itinéraire*, one becomes aware that for Greek antiquity "its youth belongs only to
memory."[57]

The *Martyrs* was described by its author as an epic in prose. Sainte-
Beuve, however, characterized it as "une épopée obligée" because its
original intention was not so much to recreate the cultural fabric and
social patterns of that era as to prove the superiority of Christianity
over paganism. It was a work with a preconceived thesis that directed
its development and shaped its characters, thus depriving them of
any real depth and individuality. The author wanted to endow them
with an epic grandeur and archetypal simplicity. Instead, with the
exception of Cymodocée, he created types conforming to predetermined notions and lacking an inner life and movement of their own.

Demodocus is a solitary figure who in the end has to accept the
decline of his gods and the ascendancy of the new religion. His own
daughter eventually renounces her role as a priestess of the Muses
and wears the robe of a Christian martyr. Lasthenes, the Christian
patriarch, is the new protagonist. His simplicity, kindness, and be-

nevolent authority recall the virtues of olden times. Finally, Eudore and Cymodocée are the young converts to the new faith who sacrifice their lives for its cause. The first stages of the epic take place in Greece, notably in Arcadia, in an atmosphere of idyllic beauty and simplicity. Some of the scenes are magnificent, and Chateaubriand once more proves to be a master *paysagiste*.

Yet there is something forced and artificial in the treatment and contrast of the two religions. In his preface to the first edition of the *Martyrs*, Chateaubriand stated that Christianity was an appropriate subject for an epic work; sublime in spirit, having its roots in biblical antiquity, it offered more possibilities for the development of character and human passions. Moreover, the Christian *merveilleux* could compete and even surpass that of classical mythology. In his understanding of the two religions we see at least two basic fallacies. First, he failed to perceive the significance of mythology as a key to comprehending the universe in paganism. As Richard observed, "for an ancient imagination, there is in effect no difference between the text—the universe—and the meaning—the presence of the Gods—which is exuded from its flesh and which illuminates it. Mythology is the immediate key of the perceptible world" (36). Chateaubriand, like most of his contemporaries, saw mythology as a collection of charming, picturesque, and even brilliant stories devoid of any metaphysical meaning. Second, he had the two religions compete on the same level without a differentiation in their spiritual and metaphysical dimensions. He substituted one mythology for another; he made the Christian *merveilleux*, with a majestic procession of angels and a host of scenes of celestial splendor, too visual and immediate instead of being transcendental and figurative. This is one case where Chateaubriand's descriptive powers did not enhance his work because they obfuscated the differences between Christianity and the pagan ethos.

Like the *Itinéraire*, but in a more pronounced way, the *Martyrs* was the product of extensive reading transformed and enriched by the author's imagination. He confided to Marcellus that it took him seven years to complete the *Martyrs* because he wanted to produce a stylistically polished and soundly researched work.[58] To make his descriptions more vivid and concrete, he undertook his voyage to the East, where the imaginary drama of the *Martyrs* would be enacted. The impressions he derived were conveyed more or less directly

in the *Itinéraire* and were indirectly interwoven into the texture of
the *Martyrs*. The images of the first work, however, are truer and
more animated because they reflect a direct rapport between subject
and object. There is a personal tone in it free of the didacticism of
the *Martyrs*.

The *Martyrs* was neither a work of pure imagination nor a scholarly treatise but a combination of both, and therefore it failed to recreate a distant era. "If I were to give a general assessment of the
Martyrs," observed Sainte-Beuve, "I would say that it is a *composite*
poem where all the pagan and Christian beauties are artificially clus-
tered in a narrow space."[59] Louis Bertrand, a more severe critic of the
Hellenism of the neoclassical era, placed the *Martyrs* within its literary context and criticized it for its lack of inner unity and the
absence of historical and human truth. He reproached its author for
having misunderstood the idea of pantheism and having a very narrow concept of paganism. Though he admired his flowing style and
lofty lyricism, he detected a certain pomposity and theatricality,
which made the *Martyrs* an even more heterogeneous and disparate
work.[60]

Chateaubriand certainly had a limited understanding of mythology and paganism, but he was portraying an era when these forces
were no longer viable and had lost their supremacy. In the *Martyrs*
we see that the emergence of Christianity, at least in Greece, was preceded by an erosion and decline of pagan polytheism. The Olympians were still worshiped and festivals were still held in their honor.
But how different they were from the ones celebrated at the time of
Anacharsis's visit. No longer were they panhellenic events bringing
together exhilarated crowds in an atmosphere of feverish excitement
and ceremonial festivity. In the *Martyrs* we have only a furtive and
oblique glimpse of such events. The narrator is not a participant, as
Anacharsis was, but a detached and distant observer. Symbolically
removed from the scene of the celebration, he describes the outer
forms and ritual gestures of a few participants as if they were actors
in a shadow theater performing their pantomime. As in times past,
brilliant deputations left Athens for Delos; but they appeared as a
bright apparition that for a brief moment shone in the horizon and
then vanished like a mirage.

It was not only the ancient gods who were being displaced by the
rise of a new religion. Greece itself already bore marks of deteriora-

tion and decay. The ruins of the once superb temples had already become a feature of its landscape. The void left by the passing of glorious events and great men, so eloquently evoked in the *Itinéraire*, was foreshadowed in the *Martyrs*. The Greece of the golden era had already vanished, and the memory of past greatness had begun to weigh on it. "We sailed through this Archipelago of Greece," says Eudore, "where the enchantment of its shores, the brilliance of the light, the sweetness and fragrance of the air compete with names and memories. We saw all these promontories capped with temples or tombs."[61]

For Chateaubriand the advent of Christianity had no regenerating effect on Greece because its most dramatic events took place elsewhere. Eudore and Cymodocée, the two young protagonists of the *Martyrs*, were conveniently removed, to meet their martyrdom in Rome. Christianity, after its initial stages fictitiously enacted in the *Martyrs*, had little influence on the shaping of postclassical Greece in Chateaubriand's eyes. This is much more evident in the *Itinéraire*, where religion was represented as a poor consolation for the unrelieved misery of the Greeks and their Byzantine heritage was treated off-handedly.

Time was not the only culprit in the decay that had befallen Hellas. Rome had brought destruction and tyranny to some of the most renowned Greek cities. It was the first foreign and disruptive influence that speeded Greece's downfall. Rome also portended the successive waves of assaults that overran it. Chateaubriand, however, viewed the decline of the ancient Greek city-states as something not entirely due to external factors. Civilizations, like people, have their youth and their old age with all its attendant infirmities. How else can one explain the bloody spectacle of gladiatorial games in the theater where the masterpieces of Greek drama had been performed? How could the Athenians enjoy such demoralizing games? They did, said Chateaubriand, because "nations, like individuals, are cruel in their decrepitude, as they are in their childhood; perhaps the genius of nations exhausts itself; and when it has produced everything, gone through everything, tasted everything, satiated with its own masterpieces and incapable of producing new ones, it becomes dazed and returns to purely physical sensations."[62]

In Chateaubriand's judgment the Greek world had suffered a combination of the principle of "rise and fall" with a series of disastrous invasions that brought about its disintegration. His personal impressions during his brief visit confirmed this conviction. Instead of renewal and regeneration he saw the signs of ceaseless destruction repeating itself with increased frequency. Turks and Albanians alike, especially after the 1770 uprising, ravaged the countryside in the Peloponnesus and decimated its inhabitants. Churches lay in ruins and peasants were exploited and terrorized. "Destructions in Greece multiply with such rapidity that often a traveler does not see even a trace of a monument another traveler had admired a few months before him." (*I*, 124–25).

One of Chateaubriand's recurrent themes was silence, which in his work operated on several levels. The most important in the *Itinéraire* were the psychological, the historical, and the aesthetic. To him silence meant the absence of human presence and human activity. Many were the times when he sought isolation. In the peace of his solitude he could give free rein to his imagination, contemplating and exploring the surrounding world, trying to penetrate its mystery and capture its essence. When he visited Sparta, he tells us, he left his janissary alone tending the horses while he probed its ruins in an effort to envision its past. Silence acted as a psychological shield excluding all undesirable intrusions. It focused attention on the author, and his surroundings for a time became his world. Silence was a positive force because it heightened his consciousness. But on the historical level silence was a negative force. It signified the disappearance and obliteration of past generations and reminded one of one's own transitoriness. Seen in this way, silence meant absence, emptiness, and death. Finally, silence played an important role in the structural and aesthetic organization of the *Itinéraire*. It acted as a leitmotif around which the author constructed a series of images of isolated temples, a deserted countryside, and desecrated tombs.

By surrounding both the author-character and the ancient monuments, silence conferred upon them for a brief moment a certain dignity and inviolability. These were in a sense privileged moments during which the observer could recall at will the past grandeur and then contrast it with the present forlornness. The tone that dominated Chateaubriand's account of his visit to Greece was set in the opening scene. Upon arriving at Modon, the Peloponnesian port, he saw everything enshrouded in a veil of stillness. "Not a boat in the port; not a man on the shore; everywhere silence, abandonment, and oblivion" (*I,* 1:81). As his exploration of the mainland continued, this mood was amplified and intensified. First there was the perfect, almost somnolescent stillness of Sparta and then the foreboding and sinister silence of Mycenae. Everywhere he went he dispensed with the living as soon as he had seen them. Then, immersing himself in silence, he began to look around in order to establish his field of vision, arranging its features in contrasting patterns.

Absence presupposes a lost presence, and silence implies a hiatus and the interruption of speech. Here, the missing voice was that of the ancients. Chateaubriand did not find their echo in either the customs of the modern Greeks or their language. He was not fond of parallels between ancients and moderns. Few European visitors before him had avoided facile comparisons between past and present. Chateaubriand found no reasons for such comparisons, only for contrasts. Fragments of statuary, columns, and inscriptions were important to him not as threads leading to the reconstruction of the past but as the last tangible vestiges of a lost civilization.

In Chateaubriand silence elicited two seemingly contradictory responses: pleasure and sadness. He derived a certain joy from the freedom to contemplate the world around him with its beauty and mystery; it was precisely this feeling of solitary exaltation which impelled him to undertake so many journeys. If he liked the voyage, he tells us, it was only "because of the independence it gives me, as I incline toward the countryside not for the countryside but for the solitude."[63] At the same time, sadness and melancholy arose, like a counterpoint, out of the realization of the transience of such independence. He conveyed this dual aspect of peaceful, solitary contemplation and painful awareness in the superb scene of the revelation of Sparta.

> As I was arriving at its summit, the sun was rising behind the Menelaion mountains. What a magnificent spectacle! but how melancholy! Eurotas was flowing solitary under the debris of the bridge Babyx; ruins on every side and not a single man to be seen among them. I stood motionless, in a kind of stupor, contemplating this scene. A mixture of admiration and sadness arrested my steps and my thoughts; profound silence reigned around me. Determined, at least, to bring forth an echo in these places where the human voice was no longer heard, I called out with all my might, "Leonidas!" Not one ruin repeated this great name, and Sparta herself seemed to have forgotten him.[64]

Monuments, although they are the creation of individual artists, form the collective legacy of past generations. Graves, on the other hand, are the last resting places of individuals. Chateaubriand's preoccupation with the themes of death and destruction led him naturally to the exploration of ancient tombs and modern cemeteries. The treatment of the tomb as a psychological, religious, and metaphysical symbol was akin to the pre-Romantic and Romantic imagination.[65] For Chateaubriand, who excelled in the use of chiaroscuro, the impression of a Turkish cemetery, with its gleaming white tombstones and its lugubrious cypress trees, remained indelible. Its beauty and solitude made it a place of peaceful repose for the conquerors of Greece. Nearby there were some Christian graves. Their physical proximity suggested to him that only after death could these two people lie side by side. Furthermore, the cemetery was the only place where the presence of the East in Greece did not offend him. Ironically, "one would gladly stop at a cemetery where the laurel of Greece, dominated by the cypress of the Orient, seems to recall the memory of the two people whose dust rests in this place."[66] Death in the case of these two embattled peoples had a positive value because it put an end to a wretched existence. It returned them to the secure and serene enclosure of the earth. Yet not all graves appeared to him as shelters. The empty tombs of Mycenae, violated by human hands and exposed to public view, had lost their solitude and mystery. With their contents dispersed, they had the appearance of a gaping void epitomizing absence and total annihilation.

The stillness of death which reigned over cemeteries and ancient graves disappeared as soon as our traveler approached an inhabited place. The sight that awaited him, however, was scarcely less distressing. In his eyes, an atmosphere of gloom hovered over people and buildings. Greeks and Turks seemed to share a common life based on the relation of master and subject. To Chateaubriand this uneasy coexistence lacked the inner unity and common purpose that must characterize a viable community of people. In spite of their long cohabitation, he thought that their customs and manners did not fuse into an organic and harmonious whole. He perceived an amorphous incongruity that seemed to have penetrated all the forms of their life. Their abodes, their dress, their gestures, and their language bespoke a disparate combination of two heterogeneous styles and characters.

Nowhere did Chateaubriand perceive a synthesis and an interpenetration of modes and values, mainly because he did not think that anything positive could rise out of what he considered two basically unhealthy civilizations. The barbarity of the Turks and the hopeless decline of the Greeks reinforced their mutual corruption and deterioration in his view. A long period of successive subjugations had taken all the vigor and vitality out of Greek culture. He believed that a period of stagnation and aimless existence had brought the Greeks to the level of almost simple physical subsistence. Would they ever find the strength to regain their freedom and reinvigorate their civilization? Chateaubriand was doubtful.

> Even if they were to rid themselves of the tyranny that oppresses them, they would not lose the marks of their fetters in one instant. Not only have they been crushed under the weight of despotism, but they have been existing as an aged and degraded people for two thousand years. They have not been renewed, like the rest of Europe, by barbarous nations: the very nation that conquered them has contributed to their corruption. This nation has not brought to them the primitive and robust mores of the people of the north but the pleasure-seeking customs of the people of the south. (*I*, 1:266–67)

What he saw of the life of the modern Greeks offended his aesthetic sensibilities and cultural values. He found the view of small towns and poor houses jarring and unprepossessing. Ancient ruins possessed the dignity of a glorious past and stimulated his imagination, whereas these unembellished habitations repelled him. He attributed their unkempt exteriors, with their irregular lines and heterogeneous styles, to a lack of taste and refinement almost shocking when compared with the standards of the ancients.

His reaction to Mistras—Misithra, as he called it—typifies his views on postclassical architecture in Greece. Located near the site of ancient Sparta, it became the seat of a flourishing province during the waning years of Byzantium. Here members of the imperial family established their residence and embellished the city with beautiful churches. But in 1460 Mistras, along with the rest of the Morea, fell to the Ottoman Turks. Its artistic development was suddenly arrested, but not before it left to posterity works worthy of admiration. The mosaics and iconography of its churches are among the best examples of the last revival of Byzantine art. These churches, which exist to this day, appeared so uncomely and graceless to Chateaubriand that he had no desire to explore their interior. While he was there, his one and only concern was the determination of the site of Sparta, and he made passing denigrating remarks on the Byzantine edifices, which he characterized as "a chaotic mixture of the Oriental and Gothic styles, Greek and Italian: not a single ancient ruin, which would give some consolation in the middle of all this" (*I*, 1:132).

The Turks fared even worse in Chateaubriand's pages than the modern Greeks. He denounced them on several counts: servile with their superiors, they vented their wrath on their inferiors in explosive outbursts of violence. Above all, he bemoaned the effects of absolute power, whose signs he claimed to have witnessed in the Ottoman dominions. "Eh! Madame," he wrote to the marquise de Pastoret in 1807, "what a subject for reflection the frightful Tyranny and dreadful misery I have witnessed provide! I advise those who preach an absolute government to make a tour of Turkey: deserted provinces, dazed people stupefied by slavery, brutality of power, these are the admirable results of absolute power."[67]

In evaluating the Turks' collective character, he saw it as a combination of disparate traits: lethargic in nature, they shook off their torpor occasionally by performing acts of fitful violence; tyrannical with their subjects, they were often obsequious to foreigners, especially to the French, as Chateaubriand's egotism would have him believe; untouched by feelings of patriotism and an awareness of a common culture and civilization, they looked to their religion as the only link of common identity. Chateaubriand thought that once religion began to decline among them, the Ottoman Empire would collapse.

The total disappearance of harmony and order in the Greek lands took various forms, as far as Chateaubriand could see. They varied from the deeply distressing to the farcical and caricaturesque. Instead of the proud and invincible Spartans marching to victory, he saw two Greeks obediently following a Turk, who was mounted on his horse; instead of the sonorous and mellifluous language of the ancients, he witnessed and participated in some of the most preposterous attempts at verbal communication. The heterogeneity and discordance that to him characterized all outer forms of life had permeated the very process of linguistic expression and had made human communication almost impossible.

Chateaubriand had a very keen sense of the ridiculous, and, with a few swift strokes, he could reduce a person or a situation to a caricature. His vaunted lyricism overshadowed his talent for parody and mockery. "There was a comical and jesting Chateaubriand whom the other, solemn one overshadowed but who reappeared in travel."[68] In the *Itinéraire* he exhibited this talent many times, always with the intention of exposing what he thought was pretentious, odd, and incongruous. At times his irony was benign and amusing, as in the portrait of his Milanese servant Joseph, whose superficial knowledge of Greek qualified him as an interpreter for Chateaubriand. "This Milanese was a short, fair man, with a large belly, a ruddy complexion and an affable look; he was dressed all in blue velvet; two long horse-pistols stuck under a tight belt made his waistcoat bulge in such a grotesque way that the janissary could never look at him without laughing."[69]

Most times, however, Chateaubriand's mockery had a more serious intention, seeking to reveal an underlying dissonance and incoherence between persons and events that somehow came into contact but failed to establish a rapport. It seemed to him that everyone in Greece, including himself, was there as if by a strange coincidence. Personal encounters failed to promote mutual understanding. Instead, they accentuated and dramatized the irreconcilable differences between the indigenous population, their conquerors, and the foreign visitors. Not only was it impossible to see a continuity and an affinity with the past, but attempts to create channels of communication with the local inhabitants oftentimes ended in a bewildering confusion. Chateaubriand describes a scene in which he tried to reach an understanding with his Greek guide. When he failed, Joseph intervened, and then the janissary. The result was a veritable pandemonium.

> My cicerone knew scarcely more than a few words of Italian and English. To make myself better understood by him, I attempted some clumsy phrases in modern Greek; I scribbled with my pencil some words of ancient Greek, I talked Italian and English, mixing French with all this. Joseph wanted to help us communicate, but instead he increased the confusion. . . . We were all speaking at the same time; we were shouting and gesticulating; with our

different dress and our diverse languages and physiognomy, we looked like an assembly of demons, perched at sunset on the summit of these ruins. (*I*, 1:132–33)

Thus the alienation was complete and all-pervasive. Like marionettes in a shadow play, the members of this motley company engaged in a meaningless and absurd dialogue. To the silence of the dead the living had nothing to offer but dissonant cries.

Above this ill-matched assortment of human beings loomed the eery sight of towns and cities. Athens and Constantinople, the two main urban centers in the *Itinéraire* that could claim a Greek past, struck Chateaubriand by their composite character. At that time, Athens was only a small town of ten thousand people, with little political and commercial significance. Constantinople, on the other hand, once the fabulous capital of Eastern Christendom, was now the seat of the sultan. Active and populous, it was the great center where people of all nationalities in the Ottoman Empire gravitated. While the classical past of Athens brought it closer to the West, Constantinople was a mysterious and exotic city of the East.

The physical charm and beauty of Athens and the memories it awakened redeemed and transfigured it in the eyes of every visitor and especially of Chateaubriand. Still, from the distance it seemed to him an oriental town, with its pointed minarets and domed mosques.

> Between these two hills, and at the foot of the Acropolis, Athens was emerging before me: its flat roofs interspersed with minarets, cypresses, ruins, isolated columns, the domes of its mosques crowned by large stork nests, created an agreeable effect under the rays of the sun. But if Athens might still be recognized by its ruins, one could also see in the general appearance of its architecture and the state of its monuments that the city of Minerva was no longer inhabited by her people. (*I*, 1:189).

As he approached the city, his agitated emotions, the unfolding countryside strewn with ruined monuments, and a benign, smiling sky, made these alien features disappear. But suddenly, at night, his sleep was interrupted by the strident voice of the muezzin. As it pierced the air, it made him aware of a foreign, unfamiliar presence. That voice alone, reverberating in the stillness of the night, encapsulated for him all the invasions and intrusions in the city of Athena. Though calling the faithful to prayer, for Chateaubriand its sound was dissonant and cacophonous, part of a nightly ritual renewing the powers of negation and dissolution over those of affirmation and creation.

> Overcome with fatigue, I had been fast asleep for some time when I was suddenly awakened by the tambourine and the Turkish bagpipe, whose discordant tones were coming from the top of the Propylaea. At the same time a Turkish priest began to sing in Arabic the late hour to the Christians of the city of Minerva. I cannot describe what I felt. There was no need for this imam to mark in this manner the flight of time; his voice alone, in these places, announced all too clearly that the centuries had slipped away. (*I*, 1:204–5)

However, the morning sun dispelled his nocturnal fears, and Athens could still enchant and transport him.

Constantinople, on the other hand, was totally alien to him. He felt no attraction either for its Byzantine past or for its Ottoman present. He saw its history and successive rulers as a progression of tyranny, enslavement, and decadence. Yet from a distance the city seemed enveloped in an aura of mystery full of hidden magic. Being very receptive to natural beauty, he could not but admire the astonishingly magnificent view that unfolded before him. As he approached the Bosphorus, the city emerged through a thin veil of mist pierced by its towering cypress trees, its soaring minarets, and the masts of ships swaying in the breeze of the harbor. If he could have contemplated it only from afar, he would have always kept the vision of this enthralling spectacle.

But his enchantment disappeared once he found himself in the streets of the city. What he saw there was not a bustling, colorful crowd of people going about their daily activities but a heterogeneous and incongruous multitude moving like an amorphous mass of phantoms. "You see around you a mute crowd seemingly desiring to pass unnoticed, with the constant appearance of wanting to slip away from the master's gaze. You invariably go from a bazaar to a cemetery, as if the Turks were there only in order to buy, sell, and die" (*I*, 1:318).

Constantinople appeared to him the embodiment of decay and corruption where people moved as if spurred by an evil, poisonous force that robbed them of their human dignity and freedom. This corrupting power, which he felt defiled the atmosphere, was the same one he had sensed in Greece. But here, being closer to its source, it was more oppressive and pervasive. Here, he remarked, blind despotism and depraved sensuality had perverted both rulers and subjects and led them into a path of mutual degradation. "No sign of joy and no appearance of happiness meet your eye: what you see is not a people but a herd driven by an imam and slaughtered by a janissary. . . . The despot's eyes draw the slaves as the gaze of a snake hypnotizes the birds on which it preys" (*I*, 1:319). When it came time for him to depart, he tells us, he was more than happy to leave such an infernal place.

If Constantinople's human element appeared offensive to Chateaubriand, its art and architecture were no less distasteful. He had an equal aversion for both Byzantine and Muslim monuments. Their grandeur and elaborate decorations, ranging from the exquisite and subtle to the sumptuous, did not move him. Their unfamiliar outer forms, the unseemly appearance of the crowds that surrounded them, confirmed his prejudices and gave no incentive for further exploration. The few classical antiquities that still remained had no rapport either with the modern inhabitants or with their edifices. The very diversity of these people in dress, language, and demeanor showed their contrasting backgrounds and, in Chateaubriand's view, alienated them from the city and from one another. Constantinople was not a place where East and West met but a hybrid where nothing coalesced and harmonized. He emphasized the antithesis of his world and that which he came to visit. "It was two months, to the very day and almost to the very hour, since I had left the capital of the civilized people, and I was going to enter the capital of barbarism" (*I*, 1:318). His visit left no fond memories and no regrets. "I like to visit only places embellished by virtues or by the arts, and in this birthplace of the Phocas and the Bayazids I found neither the first nor the second (*I*, 1:323).

Arts, or rather the remains of arts, he found aplenty in Greece itself; but its people appeared to him as shadowy and lifeless as those of Constantinople. The sketchiness of his views of them derived from his classical prejudices, his exceedingly brief stay in their country, and an essential lack of interest in them as a people whose individual and collective existence had value and needed probing. This would have meant a temporary abandonment of his self-absorption and a shift in focus from contemplation to observation, from thoughts of grandeur to material reality. His most revealing and profound experiences took place not within a closed space in the company of other men but in the open air, under a starry sky, alone in direct communion with the universe. It is for this reason that "man is absent from his most sumptuous paintings."[70]

Accordingly, the people of Greece are but pale figures in his tableaux. They appear and disappear gliding softly and unobtrusively like silhouettes. Seldom do we hear them speak in the pages of the *Itinéraire*. We only have glimpses of them as they withdraw and hide from foreign and unfamiliar faces. The author does not allow us to meet them face to face because then he would have to make them appear alive. Instead, he wanted them to remind us of the dead, with their pallor and remoteness but none of their greatness. In every direction,

> at each moment living ruins turn your eyes away from those of marble and stone. In Greece, in vain one would indulge in illusions: sad reality haunts you. Huts made of dried mud, more fit for animals than for man; women and children in rags, taking to flight at the approach of a stranger or a janissary; even frightened goats scampering off to the mountains; only the dogs stay to receive you with their howlings; this is the scene that dispells the magic of memories.[71]

Fear of sudden and unexpected violence made them flee and shun every unknown presence. Chateaubriand related an incident that he claimed he witnessed: a Turkish officer shot at a Greek peasant without any provocation and without any apparent emotion. It was as if he was performing a routine task that did not in the least disturb his apathetic expression.

Such oppression, Chateaubriand noted, could not but have unfortunate effects on the character of the Greeks. Dispirited and debilitated, as he believed them to be, many resorted to servility to appease their rulers. Others, like the Maniots, became brigands and robbers. Chateaubriand did not share the view that they were brave mountaineers defending their freedom and refusing to subordinate themselves to arbitrary rule. Instead, he spoke of them with contempt and suspicion and dismissed them as "de grands voleurs" to be feared and avoided.

Chateaubriand was convinced that physical deprivations were accompanied by spiritual impoverishment. For him, the silence and desolation that surrounded the ruined monuments and the ravaged countryside penetrated the very consciousness of the people, making them apathetic and lethargic. "This indifference of the Greeks in regard to their fatherland is as deplorable as it is shameful: not only do they not know their history, but they ignore, almost all of them, the language that is their glory" (*I*, 1:185). Modern Greek architecture struck him as a disordered mixture of heterogeneous styles. Spoken Greek, although he did not know it, seemed full of barbarisms and foreign locutions that had contaminated the purity of the classical idiom and vitiated its beauty and subtlety.

He conceded that there were a few important exceptions to this general ignorance, Korais being the most notable among them. Of the Greeks he met, not one impressed him with his knowledge of the ancients. On the contrary, intentionally or unintentionally, he misrepresented those who appeared knowledgeable and scoffed at others who seemed half-learned and confused. Doctor Avramiotti, whose erudition he could not deny, was presented as an Italian. Tselebi Titlicara, a merchant whom he met in the environs of Eleusis, was painted as a comical figure, greeting him by placing his hand on his heart "à la façon des Turcs." Though he was a friend of Fauvel, he was not able to explain the significance of the surrounding antiquities to Chateaubriand's satisfaction and kept repeating in a rambling and incoherent manner information he had allegedly derived from "M. Fauvel." He humbly avowed complete ignorance of the importance of such places as Salamis and Eleusis. His deferential manner, his simple-mindedness, and his muddled monologue amused and at the same time saddened Chateaubriand.

And yet this man was not as ignorant as Chateaubriand's caricaturesque depiction would have us believe. Educated in Italy, he taught classical Greek in Athens, where he had amicable relations with Fauvel.[72] Why these distortions? Were they merely errors due to hastiness and unfamiliarity with modern Greece or were they intentional misrepresentations? It is perhaps unwarranted to impute deliberate falsification to Chateaubriand, but at the same time it is difficult to refute a certain unwillingness on his part to see any redeeming qualities in the character and demeanor of the modern Greeks.

Such a recognition would have upset his general scheme of a culture blemished by foreign influences and uprooted and hopelessly separated from its classical past. Seen in this context, it appeared to Chateaubriand as a forlorn world closed in on itself, with no channels of communication with outsiders which could revitalize and awaken it. This isolation was symbolized by the inarticulateness of the Greeks whom Chateaubriand described. Their impassiveness was typified by the Greek sailors who accompanied him to Sounion. While he remained awake, contemplating the serene beauty of the landscape, they fell asleep. "Around me there were tombs, silence, destruction, and death, and a few Greek sailors sleeping, without cares and without dreams, on the ruins of Greece. I was going to leave forever this sacred land: my mind filled with its past grandeur and present debasement, I contemplated the picture that had just afflicted my eyes."[73]

If one can detect sentiments of philhellenism in the *Itinéraire*, they are manifested only in expressions of commiseration with the subjugated Greeks and condemnation of their rulers. Chateaubriand's expectations for a free and regenerated Greece, however, were indeed very dim. Even when he envisioned a liberated Greece, he populated it with an aggregation of various nationalities, among whom the Greeks did not hold a prominent place. In a moment of self-indulgence he saw himself as the leader of a European gathering.

> I founded a university where the youth of all Europe came to learn ancient and vulgar Greek. I invited the Hydriots to settle at Pireaus, and I had a navy. The bare mountains were clothed with pines to replenish the waters of my rivers; I encouraged agriculture; numbers of Swiss and Germans mingled with my Albanians; every day brought to light new discoveries, and Athens arose from the tomb. (*I*, 1:247)

Not unexpectedly, Chateaubriand subscribed to the notion that the legacy of ancient Greece had passed to the West. For this reason the establishment of Europeans in Greece and the Near East was to him the only comforting presence. He was especially proud to find traces of his countrymen as crusaders, merchants, and missionaries. Even the crusaders, whose ravages had precipitated the fall of Byzantium, were for Chateaubriand champions of Christianity and put "a French nobleman on the throne of Constantinople" (*I*, 1:77). He thought of his own voyage as a reenactment of the pilgrimages and missions of his compatriots and relived mentally their fervor and faith. Although fully conscious that the past cannot be resurrected, he often liked to appear in the guise of historical figures; these impersonations—staged roles, as he knew all too well—nonetheless established his identity as a Westerner and a Catholic in places where the lights of civilization had gone out. "I was going to touch these shores," he wrote, speaking of his visit to the Holy Land, "which the Godefrois, the Richards, the Joinvilles, and the Coucis had visited like me. Obscure pilgrim that I am, will I dare to trample a soil consecrated by so many illustrious pilgrims? At least I too have faith and honor: and by virtue of these qualities I would still be recognized by the ancient crusaders."[74]

Chateaubriand, however, was not a religious pilgrim but a literary one. His voyage to the Orient was above all a personal exploration of "a locale sympathetic to [his] private myths, obsessions, and requirements."[75] For this reason, monuments and historical sites etched with the aura of past events were the focal points of his interest. Contemporary life was important insofar as it illuminated the rise and fall of ancient civilizations. In his picture of Greece its modern inhabitants represented its decline, and thus they were presented as the human counterparts of ruined monuments.

During the Greek War of Independence, however, he liked to think of his *Itinéraire* as a work imbued with philhellenic sentiments and good wishes for the Greeks. By that time he had become a supporter of the Greek Revolution and wanted to point out that the roots of his philhellenism were deep. "As for us," he wrote in the preface of his *Note sur la Grèce* (1825), "if we dare count ourself for something, our opinion was formed a long time ago; we expressed it at a time when scarcely anyone thought of the emancipation of the country of Leonidas."[76]

Chateaubriand's *Note sur la Grèce* was addressed to the European heads of state urging them to use their influence to ensure the liberation of the Greeks. To make his appeal more convincing, he presented it in a dispassionate tone and free from emotional and sentimental pleas. Europe should come to Greece's succor, he contended, in the name of Hellenism, Christianity, and the natural rights of man, which the Turks had violated, thus discrediting any claims to legitimacy they might have had over their Christian subjects. Written at a critical moment of the Greek struggle for independence when philhellenic sentiments were very high, and because of the fame of its author, the *Note* had a strong impact. It was immediately translated into modern Greek under the auspices of the publishing house of Firmin-Didot, which undertook its publication and dissemination among the French and the Greeks.[77]

There was one dissenting voice, however, which took Chateaubriand to task: that of Linny-Babagor, a Turk reared and educated in Europe, who espoused Western modes of political thought while keeping his Muslim faith and identity. He declared that he professed enlightened humanitarian ideas and opposed oppression of any kind. He, therefore, did not condemn the uprising of the Greeks; on the contrary, "if they triumph, it will be to their eternal glory, by the right of the stronger: they will owe their liberty to no one but themselves and to force, which this time, by exception, will be on the side of justice."[78]

If Linny-Babagor took exception to Chateaubriand's philhellenic views, it was because they exemplified, in his estimation, the hypocrisy and the double standard practiced by Europeans in their relations with non-Western peoples. How could they support so vociferously the cause of the Greeks while they themselves tolerated and even practiced slave trade? How could they champion the liberation of the Greeks as a fellow Christian people when these same Europeans were guilty of cruelty and intolerance against Jews, Indians, and even other Christians, in the name of religion? "By what right did all Europe come armed, under your Louis IX, to put the Orient to fire and sword in order to conquer a tomb?" (22). When it came to cruelty and inhumanity, he remarked, East and West were equally guilty, but the West even more so because it boasted high moral standards. Linny-Babagor's criticism questioned the perceptual schema of Europeans, who saw the world as made up of two irreconcilable halves, West and East, civilized and uncivilized.

After Chateaubriand's eloquent defense of the rights of the rebellious Greeks, his reputation as a great philhellene was firmly established. The Greeks were ever grateful and bestowed on him, after the establishment of the independent Greek kingdom, official honors. In 1843, King Othon conferred on him the Grande Croix de l'Ordre Royal du Sauveur de Grèce. In 1848, the year of Chateaubriand's death, a Greek poet paid homage to his memory by likening him to the great literary figures of antiquity.

O you dead, still all too alive, who were our ancestors,
Happy inhabitants of shady Elysium,
You, Socrates and Plato, and most of all you, Homer,
This is what your mother, Greece, bids you:
This august and noble shadow who comes to your portals
Who was called François Chateaubriand among mortals—
He too was my son whom I rightfully claim;
He bore my seal and breathed my spirit.
Take him among you so that he may always live
In love, contemplation, and fragrant scents.[79]

[O vous morts trop vivans qui fûtes nos aieux,
De l'ombreux Elysée habitans bienheureux,
Vous Socrate et Platon, et vous surtout Homère,
Voilà ce que vous dit la Grèce votre mère:
Cette ombre qui vous vient à l'air noble, au front grant,
Que la terre a nommé François Chateaubriand,
Elle est aussi mon fils qu'à bon droit je réclame;
Il portait mon cachet et respirait mon âme.
Prenez le dans vos rangs, et qu'il vive à toujours
De contemplation, de parfums et d'amours!

Yet Chateaubriand seemed unaware of the great esteem his name enjoyed among the Greeks. Once Greece became independent and the new state had to grapple with the problems of a war-devastated country, the dream of many classically inspired philhellenes of seeing ancient Hellas resurrected appeared ever more elusive. The fervor of the revolutionary era was succeeded by disenchantment. Chateaubriand expressed this disappointment:

Greece has become free from the yoke of Islam, but, instead of a federated republic, as I desired, a Bavarian monarchy was established in Athens. Well, as kings have no memory,[80] I who had been of some service to the cause of the Argives, no longer heard of them except in Homer. Delivered Greece did not tell me: "I thank you." She ignores my name as much as and even more than on the day when I cried on her ruins crossing her deserts.[81]

This last pronouncement on the modern Greeks was closer to the reproving and aloof spirit of the *Itinéraire* than to the brief enthusiasm of the *Note sur la Grèce*.

In Search of an Enduring Vision

The *Itinéraire* was constructed thematically around a series of contrasts: between past and present, between East and West, between
Islam and Christianity, and, above all, between the immutability of
nature and the mutability of human affairs. Greece was the summa-
tion of these antinomies for Chateaubriand.

> This mobility of human affairs is all the more striking for the trav-
> eler because it contrasts with the immobility of the rest of nature.
> . . . The day after our arrival at Athens, they showed us some
> storks flying up in the air. . . . From the reign of Cecrops down to
> our days, these birds have made the same pilgrimage every year
> and have often returned to the same place. But how many times
> they have found in tears the host whom they had left in joy.[82]

Whereas the world of nature follows a regular and predictable
rhythm, the destiny of man is subject to sudden changes. The Greek
landscape contained both of these elements, the natural and the
human. The ubiquitous presence of ruined monuments transformed
it by their power of suggestiveness and made the contrast between
nature and man all the more striking. For Greece to be fully understood and appreciated, then, it had to be experienced in its physical
as well as its ideational dimensions. This was the experience of
Greece that Chateaubriand communicated in the *Itinéraire*.

His image of Hellas was neither an objective and comprehensive
presentation of the country and its people nor a literary creation di-
vorced from perceptible reality. Barthélemy's ancient Greece and
Pouqueville's modern Greece were both intended to be all-embracing portrayals of the Greek world. On the other hand, the majority
of literary works since the time of the Renaissance had invoked an
ideal Greece that existed in the realm of the intellect and imagination. Chateaubriand belonged to neither of these categories. For him
the essence of Greece lay in the harmonious contours and shimmering colors of its landscape, where Mnemosyne was the only divinity
that had survived the eclipse of the Olympians. It was during moments of contemplation and self-absorption that he captured the
uniqueness of the Greek landscape, the Greek light, and the Greek
night and revealed "their magic and metaphysical depth."[83] In the
Itinéraire he established the correspondences and interplay between

nature and human existence, between past and present, and showed that "geography is a resurrection."[84]

Historical consciousness and the remembrance of things past have a peculiar power that can effect a veritable metamorphosis of an otherwise unimpressive site. As a name rich in legend and history is enunciated, an aura of enchantment descends on that place. How many times Chateaubriand felt the exultation of such a transfiguration.

> What is then the magic of glory? A traveler is going to cross a river that offers nothing remarkable: he is told that this river is called Sousonghirli; he passes and continues his way; but if someone exclaims to him, "This is Granicus!" he steps back, opens his astonished eyes, and fixes his gaze on the current of the water, as if this water had a magic power.[85]

Civilizations come and go, monuments disintegrate slowly, but names survive and immortalize certain epochs and places. They are perpetuated through song and myth, poetry and legend. True, the stones of Greece still spoke, but they could always be defaced by new barbarians. Only the word of the poet was indestructible. Like Chénier in *L'Aveugle*, Chateaubriand viewed the poet as a seer who recreated the world with his imagination and then surrendered it to posterity. His voice is the only echo that traverses the centuries. The thoughts he expresses, the fables he invents, and the images he weaves immortalize a people and transmit a reflection of its achievements. "If the ruins that are impressed with illustrious memories show quite clearly the vanity of everything down here, one must, however, agree that the names that survive the eclipse of Empires and immortalize epochs and places count for something" (*I*, 1:141–42). Corinth, despite its ancient renown and splendor, would have been but slightly interesting had it not been for "Jason, Medea, . . . Pegasus, the Isthmus games instituted by Theseus and sung by Pindar; that is to say, as usual, fable and poetry" (*I*, 1:170).

Memory is the awareness of the constant flux in human affairs. At the same time it is humankind's only means of recapturing some of its vanished moments and interweaving them into a meaningful and coherent pattern. Some, like Proust, sought this integration in the privacy of their rooms, attentive only to their inner voice. Chateaubriand's inspiration, on the other hand, needed open horizons in order to be kindled. If time signifies negation, division, and eventual death, space means the affirmation of life and the expansion of the self. "The space of intimacy and the space of the world become consonant. When man's solitude deepens, the two immensities touch each other and merge."[86] To achieve this union, Chateaubriand preferred to stand on elevated places, alone, with the starry firmament above him and the silence of nature around him.

The presentation of the Greek space in the *Itinéraire* followed a triadic pattern: heights crowned with ancient temples, the omniscient eye of the author trying to seize the lines of the unfolding scenery, and the cyclical repetition of sunrise and nightfall. In constructing his images, Chateaubriand, posing as the central character, placed himself in a prominent position from which he could take in everything with a sweeping glance. His art was in a sense a means of conquering the world by finding hidden correspondences, grouping its objects according to their aesthetic and mythological associations, and composing a scene while at the same time remaining faithful to the essence of external reality.[87]

Chateaubriand's delineation of the Greek landscape unfolds in an ascending plane. Upon approaching a famous site, such as Sparta, Athens, or Mycenae, he presents a panoramic view of the surrounding area. The perspective is broad but its lines and features are etched clearly. Then we follow the author's progress toward the focal site. Its outline, already visible from a distance, emerges more vivid as we come closer. Mentally we can picture the author moving onward and upward until he reaches the most elevated point. There we stop. Chronological time is momentarily arrested as we contemplate through the author's eyes the sweeping view. Everything is resplendent under the radiant Mediterranean sun. Inert figures engraved on marble begin to stir as if infused with a life and movement of their own. Forms and colors are outlined brilliantly against an iridescent background. At that climactic moment the division between past and present and between the external and internal ceases to exist. Instead, harmony and unison reign everywhere. Then, gradually, the magic is dispelled, and reality with all its discordances and incongruities reaffirms itself.

The structure of Chateaubriand's sentences closely followed the dramatic composition of his tableaux. His was a clear style, rhythmic and delicately orchestrated, now brisk and swift, now ample and stately, always following the movement of his feeling and the sugges-

tive modulations of the unfolding scenery. His sentences followed
the tempo of his steps and the tenor of his emotions: a swift, ascending trajectory, followed by a sustained and slower development contained in symmetrically arranged independent clauses; this even
movement, which seized his moments of contemplation, was brought
to a quick denouement, an expression of the affirmation and intrusion of external reality.

The depiction of Athens, with the Acropolis and the Parthenon,
is the most representative case of this schema. After having spent a
sleepless night, he awakened his two guides at three o'clock in the
morning to prepare for his long-anticipated entrance into the city of
Athens. In his usual dramatic manner he tells how all three of them
put on their best clothes and groomed their horses so as to be suit-
ably attired for this festive occasion.[88] In the distance the Parthenon
emerged noble and indomitable in the morning sun. As Athens rose
before his eyes more and more distinct, its profile began to be
marked by irregularities. Isolated columns and ruined edifices were
interspersed among the modest abodes, minarets, cypress trees, and
domes of mosques. In spite of their incongruity, they composed a
pleasant ensemble, immersed as they were in the sunlight. After a
brief pause at the river Cephisus, where Chateaubriand stopped to
have a taste of its water—a ritual that amused many of his critics, especially Avramiotti—Chateaubriand directed his steps to the residence
of the French consul Fauvel, who offered him hospitality and respite.

After almost two weeks of self-imposed solitude, Chateaubriand
was delighted to find a distinguished fellow countryman with whom
he could communicate. In the afternoon they visited the environs of
the Acropolis. Fauvel, in his eyes, unlike the inept and ignorant
native cicerones he had been exposed to, was a most invaluable and
knowledgeable classicist admirably suited for the role of guide.
While they were passing through the narrow streets leading to the
Acropolis, people gathered around them paying their respects to
their "M. Fauvel" and welcoming the foreign visitor in a vociferous
and cheerful manner. This is one of the few instances in the *Itinéraire* where the mood of a crowd was mentioned. The two Frenchmen were accompanied for some distance by a procession of gesticu-
lating Greeks, who eventually dispersed and left them to their
solemn and profound conversation.

Early the next morning, Chateaubriand commenced his ascent to the Acropolis and its noble temples. From its height he commanded a view of the surroundings. Everything that seemed ill-proportioned and disparate from close up was hardly visible from this elevation. A glorious sunrise revealed a landscape of graceful modulations and glistening colors. The flood of sunlight brought about harmony and consonance, which unified the variegated forms and groupings. For an instant it seemed as though the city of Athens was reborn. Life began to stir anew in the cultivated vineyards, olive groves, and small huts dotting the countryside. The scattered ruins no longer awakened feelings of distress. Instead, the memories they evoked enhanced the beauty and the magic of the Attic land.

At that moment the author invites us to behold with him the splendid panorama of these legendary hills and mountains, these sacred monuments and scintillating islands, all enveloped in an aura of dazzling light. After this arresting contemplation of the Athenian space, we lift our eyes to the Parthenon. From its commanding height it dominates this superb view, resplendent in bright tones and delicate hues. Its grandeur, Chateaubriand notes, has none of the forbidding and awesome massiveness of the Egyptian pyramids. Instead, its nobility is an eternal testimonial to man's creative intelligence and nature's beauty, both of them interwoven into an integrated whole. In a frequently quoted passage, Chateaubriand recreates the majesty of the Parthenon beheld in a moment of exultation.

> From the summit of the Acropolis, I beheld the sun rise between the twin peaks of Mount Hymettus: the crows that build their nests around the citadel but never soar above its summit hovered below us; their black, lustrous wings were tinged with roseate hues by the first beams of dawn; columns of light, blue smoke rose in the shade, along the side of Hymettus, and heralded the presence of beehives; Athens, the Acropolis, and the ruins of the Parthenon were colored with the most beautiful tints of peach blossom; the sculptures of Phidias, struck horizontally by a ray of gold, came to life and seemed to move on the marble, animated by the moving shadows of the relief. (*I*, 1:217–18)

Chateaubriand's imagery in the *Itinéraire* is dominated by colors, with their vibrant tones and subtle hues. The Greek landscape, barren and uncultivated in many places, is transfigured into a phosphorescent kaleidoscope by its brilliant coloration. As the day goes on and the dazzling light loses its intensity, a glorious sunset with a new array of colors appears in the horizon. It was during such a sunset that Greece began to emerge before Chateaubriand as he entered its waters.

> The colors of the sunset were not brilliant: the sun descended between the clouds, which it tinted with a roseate hue; it sank below the horizon, and twilight took its place for half an hour. During this short interval, the sky was white in the west, pale blue at the zenith, and pearl-gray in the east. . . . The horizon of the sea, fringed with a light vapor, blended with that of the sky. (*I*, 1:75)

If the diurnal movement of the sun symbolized the rebirth of nature and awakened one's consciousness of one's surrounding world, the coming of night brought a temporary respite, inner peace, and cosmic harmony. Chateaubriand experienced the blissful serenity of such nights in Greece. Two of them stand out: they are the famous nights of Eurotas and Sounion. In both instances he was alone. His guides, he tells us, indifferent to their surroundings, enjoyed their lethargic sleep. Only our traveler remained awake. Removed from the agitation of human affairs, he felt absorbed by the universe, which enveloped him like a protective mantle. At Sounion, "the most beautiful sunset was succeeded by the most lovely night. The firmament, reflected in the water, seemed to rest on the bottom of the sea. . . . Now and then, a passing breeze ruffled the image of the sky in the sea, stirred the constellations, and then died away with a gentle murmur among the columns of the temple" (*I*, 1:256–57).

Sounion was the last stage of Chateaubriand's visit to mainland Greece. It was one of the highlights of his voyage because it stirred in him feelings of elation accompanied by a pervasive sadness. Immersed in the nocturnal solitude, he experienced once more the eternal magic of the Greek space. The legends and fables of antiquity mingled with personal memories of similar nights spent in the vast expanses of America. For a moment past and present were fused into a perfect union. But this equilibrium did not last long. Scattered stones, mutilated columns, some still erect and others lying helplessly on the ground, broken pediments with only fragments of their sculpted figures showing, were strewn all around him. The awareness that his own presence there and his own experiences would become memories in just a few hours filled him with melancholy. Once more the irreversible flow of time, which robs one of one's intimate joys, swept him away and sent him in quest of new feats of memory. The exquisite *plaisir de tristesse* that he felt so intensely in Greece would be repeated, but less vividly, during his travels in the Orient.

Chateaubriand approached Greece not entirely unlike previous French travelers. For him as for them, the true Greece was that of the ancients. The destruction of their physical world, however, did not obliterate their civilization. Fortunately, its legacy was passed on to Europe, whose people preserved it. An idealized vision of Greece, which excluded the developments of the postclassical period, combined with a sense of superiority to make most of these travelers adopt a condescending stance toward the modern Greeks. Chateaubriand typified these attitudes in many respects. He thought of himself as a European and above all as a Frenchman possessing the keen intelligence and refined sensibilities of his race. His encounters with the natives, be they Greeks, Turks, or Albanians, confirmed his feelings of self-confidence and arrogance. Like many of his predecessors, he expressed compassion mixed with ironic disdain for the fallen Greeks. Also, like them, he condemned the Turks for their oppressive rule and "uncivilized" character in a manner reminiscent of Voltaire's most biting remarks.

This is where the similarity ends. Others, like Guys and Choiseul-Gouffier in his youthful years, had hoped to see some of the ancient nobility revived by the regeneration and liberation of the modern Greeks. Still others, like Choiseul-Gouffier, Lord Elgin, and Fauvel, to mention but a few, expected to come closer to possessing ancient Greece by excavating and carrying off its monuments. Chateaubriand shared none of these feelings. The people of modern Greece were only on the periphery of his interests when he undertook his voyage, and therefore their liberation, an issue that was to win his ardent support by 1824, was at that time of no concern to him. Besides, he thought of the past as something that cannot be repeated in the present, and hence expectations of seeing the moderns recapture and recreate it seemed a mere illusion.

Chateaubriand severely criticized those who pillaged the antiquities of Greece to enrich European museums and private collections, but he did so mainly on aesthetic grounds and not because of any moral considerations. Being a faithful patriot, he found only

Lord Elgin guilty of such irreverent greed and rapacity. He held Choiseul-Gouffier and Fauvel, who did not abstain from similar activities, in too high an esteem as representatives of the French nation to reprehend them. He himself had no desire to take from the Greek soil anything more precious than a few stones. The memories and images he carried with him were far more enduring and valuable. It was they, not perishable objects, that embodied his vision of Hellas and gave birth to a literary monument, the *Itinéraire*, which made Chateaubriand's passage to Greece a memorable event and enriched French literature by offering it its first truly literary travel account.

He, too, wanted to possess Greece and capture its appeal. But he did not seek it among its people. Instead, he saw it shining in its luminous countryside and marble monuments, and he recreated it through his imagination and poetic intuition. He envisioned ancient Greece, for him the only pure and enduring Greece, as the culmination of "justice, harmony, and simplicity of proportions" (*I*, 1:207) achieved through a perfect equilibrium of nature and the human intellect. Chateaubriand believed that this harmony was destroyed centuries before and that modern people could no longer partake of it. Nevertheless he tried to transcend this dissipation by a heightened consciousness of space and time—not chronometric time but time experienced as an inner dimension.

Chateaubriand's subjective response to Greece and the other places he visited gave a new direction to travel literature. The all-inclusive and expository approach inaugurated by sixteenth-century travelers, which remained essentially unaltered through the eighteenth century, gave way to a more selective treatment of foreign locales. The author's aim now was the stimulation and nourishment of the individual imagination and the discovery of new aesthetic motifs and literary themes. The voyage took on a metaphorical significance revealing more the structures of the creative impulse and conveying less the realities of the external world.

During the course of the nineteenth century, especially among the symbolist poets, the voyage became a pure metaphor, a source of images and symbols whose association depended more on their inner correspondences of sound, color, and feeling and less on their direct relation with the outside world. Oftentimes authors did not even feel the need to visit the places pictured in their poems. Their mythological, literary, and historical connotations or their exotic aura were all that was needed to construct the images and express one's feelings.

Thus, in Baudelaire's "Un Voyage à Cythère," a place he never visited, the Greek island linked in myth with the pagan goddess of love and beauty was for the French poet the scene of punishment and retribution visited upon its last resident. On his savagely torn body mercilessly attacked by hideous birds, Baudelaire saw mirrored his own destiny riven by guilt and a search for atonement. There is, of course, a great distance separating *Les Fleurs du Mal* from the *Itinéraire*. Chateaubriand's literary recreations of his voyages were firmly anchored in his direct contact with the outside world, but his works contain the seeds of a process whereby the voyage became a metaphor for humanity's incessant movement through space and time and whereby a site with its multiple associations became the stage where the author saw his own destiny reenacted.

When the voyage began to be treated more as a source of literary themes and less as a relation of witnessed events and conditions, then the native people with their customs and traditions were seldom the focus of attention. If they were mentioned at all, it was only to fit the decor and add local color. Whether the Greeks were treated with sympathy or derision in the *Itinéraire*, they were presented as either caricatures or abstractions illustrating in Chateaubriand's eyes the law of historical decline. Therefore philhellenic attitudes defending the modern Greeks' rights, and making them the main object of observation, were outside Chateaubriand's perceptual order. It was his own fate that he saw impressed on its landscape and not that of the modern Greeks. It was the first time that Greek nature was so graphically and amply depicted, while those who peopled it were presented as fleeting shadows. There was only one presence that dominated this world, and that was Chateaubriand himself.

6

TOWARD A BROADER IMAGE OF MODERN GREECE

Hellenism and Philhellenism Reunited

The *Itinéraire*, though devoid of philhellenic sentiments seeking to establish parallels between the ancient and the modern Greeks, was in a sense the apogee of romantic Hellenism. It raised nostalgia for a nobler past to lofty heights and stirring lyricism. Chateaubriand's contemporaries saw in its pages a land strewn with ruins and transfigured by the magic of its legends. Above all, they envisioned a land mirrored in the delicately modulated images and the cadenced style of a consummate *paysagiste*. His inaccuracies, exaggerations, and arrogant stance toward the native people notwithstanding, Chateaubriand fused admirably the idealized concept of classical Greece with his personal experiences in that country. "A book, or rather a poem on the Orient," Lamartine commented, "M. de Chateaubriand created it in the *Itinéraire*; this great writer and poet passed only briefly through this land of wonders, but he imprinted forever the trace of genius on this dust that so many centuries have stirred."[1]

Chateaubriand's depiction of Greece and the Orient cast a spell on contemporary and later visitors to that part of the world. French travelers especially tried to imitate his style, melancholy musings, and dramatic gestures. This imitation was particularly transparent in minor writers, whose lack of imagination and personal vision made their mimicry all the more obvious. Such was the case of Auguste de Forbin, who dabbled in art and literature and whose wit and affability endeared him to the Parisian beau monde. In 1817 he visited Greece, Asia Minor, Syria, Palestine, and Egypt. Athens was an early stop. His description of his visit to the Acropolis is unmistakably Chateaubriandesque in expression, tone, and composition: the same agitation, the same trepidation in stepping on hallowed ground, the same self-absorption and momentary resuscitation of the past, and, finally, the same abrupt return to the dislocating realities of the present.

> Our first steps were directed toward the temple of Minerva and the Propylaea; we ascended there with eagerness: I was agitated, I wanted to admire everything at once. . . . We advanced slowly amid a pile of overturned columns, broken friezes, until we reached the place where the statue of Minerva used to be; it had been replaced by a small mosque. . . . From there I surveyed this immense theater of pomp, dissension, and combat of the people of Attica; I recalled their memories: everything became animated; the sea was covered with victorious fleets; triumphant songs echoed along the shores of Phaleron and Munichia . . . and proud Corinth tried to shake off the dust from its brow formerly covered with gold. Man's awakening is sad: when I came out of my long reveries, I saw nothing around me except endless ruins, barren plains, a deserted sea.[2]

Marcellus, Forbin's son-in-law, admitted to being influenced by the *Itinéraire*; his only regret was that he was unable to rise to its height. Even Pouqueville, a critic of the *Itinéraire*, injected scenes of romantic effusion in an otherwise factual and discursive work.

Nineteenth-century travelers viewed Greece through not only the writings of Homer and Pausanias, but also those of Chateaubriand, Byron, and other literary figures who made the grand tour. The influence of the latter, however, began to weigh on some travelers by the end of the century because they wanted to arrive at a more personal and authentic appreciation of Greece. Barrès, for example, who visited Greece in 1900, realized that his perception was refracted by that of previous voyagers, especially the most celebrated ones, and tried to extricate himself from their hold. "My own judgment had no part in my enthusiasm because this first aspect of Athens, precisely, disconcerted me by its appearance of a bizarre ornament; but the Chateaubriands, the Byrons, the Renans, the Lecontes de Lisle stirred and clamored in the subconscious parts of my being."[3]

Although Chateaubriand felt the general desire of his time to relive the past, he did not expect to see it resuscitated in Greece. For this reason the *Itinéraire* represents a hiatus in the development of French philhellenism exemplified in the works of Guys and Choiseul-Gouffier and based almost exclusively on the establishment of affinities between the ancient and the modern Greeks.

But the condition and fate of the modern Greeks did not cease to attract the interest of other travelers. To a certain extent they underwent the influence of the *enchanteur*, but unlike him they were elated to discover "in the present the miraculous survival of ancient charms."[4] Marcellus, Ambroise Firmin-Didot, and Pouqueville exemplify the development of French philhellenism in the two decades preceding the outbreak of the Greek Revolution. Their impressions are valuable both for their sympathetic treatment of the Greeks and for the presentation of facets of contemporary Greek life which had eluded previous French travelers.

Their accounts vary in scope and depth of observation. But they are all permeated with a desire and willingness to approach the Greeks directly and to look at their activities with a more genuine interest. Undoubtedly their reactions were circumscribed by their personal tastes, cultural preconceptions, and the nature of the Greek communities they visited. But their fairly long acquaintance with the Greeks and favorable disposition toward them led them to discern some progress in certain strata of Greek society. Moreover, since the places they visited and described did not coincide, their accounts reveal a varied and more complete picture of the modern Greek world.

The comte de Marcellus and Ambroise Firmin-Didot embarked on their voyages in 1816. Although they did not travel together, they followed approximately the same route. They sailed around the southern tip of the Peloponnesus and then traversed the Aegean, before disembarking on the coast of Asia Minor near Troy. Continental Greece was not part of their itinerary, and consequently the Greeks they came to know best were those of the thriving communities of Constantinople, Asia Minor, and the more prosperous Aegean Islands. Pouqueville's voyage, on the other hand, took him to northern Greece, a region virtually unknown to most travelers of that time. His long sojourn there, which spanned the better part of the two decades preceding the Revolution, brought him into close contact with the people of the area and revealed to him the variety of their character, customs, and activities. Marcellus and Firmin-Didot, young and incurably enamored with classical antiquity, left us accounts that are impressionistic and interspersed with sentimental passages. Pouqueville, though not wanting in literary aspirations and descriptive talent, was a man of insatiable curiosity, painstaking observation, and encyclopedic inclusiveness. His account, therefore, is the most extensive, detailed, and informative of the three.

The Last of the Romantic Hellenists:
Marcellus

"I am assuredly a Hellenist. . . . Yes, I love the Greek language with a passion," declared Marcellus in the opening page of his *Episodes littéraires en Orient*.[5] During his voyage to the Near East, everything he saw reminded him of a gentle and charming past. On the island of Chios he thought he recognized the ruins of the school of Homer, a legend that was still believed by early nineteenth-century travelers. In Troy, thinking that he was standing on Hector's tomb, he cried out, "Hector, ubi es?" as if his voice could break the silence of the centuries.[6] All this may seem naïve and melodramatic, but, being young and enthusiastic and intoxicated with the joy of discovery, he was experiencing antiquity in the immediacy of its ruined monuments. "In my schoolboy's enthusiasm," he wrote twenty years later, "I noted everything: I tried to say everything, to paint everything: I would have believed my voyage incomplete and failed if a classical name had escaped my memory. It seemed to me that no one had traversed these seas and lands before me; especially that no one had described them sufficiently before me" (*S*, iv).

Marie-Louis-Jean-André-Charles Demartier du Tyrac, comte de Marcellus, was born in Agenais in 1795. While he was still an infant, his paternal and maternal grandfathers were put to death during the Terror. The memory of this event, his family background, and his personal views placed him decidedly on the side of the monarchists. At the very beginning of the Restoration, in 1815, he was appointed secretary to the French embassy at Constantinople at the age of twenty. Thus he began his diplomatic career, following the trail of many *diplomates lettrés*, who served their country at various posts in the Ottoman Empire, pursuing at the same time their antiquarian interests. Marcellus received a sound classical education and at a very young age developed a taste for Greek art and literature, a passion he shared with his father. He could read ancient Greek authors in the original, a pleasure he frequently indulged in when he visited the lands they had once inhabited (*S, 4*).[7]

In 1816 and 1817 he toured the coast of Asia Minor and in 1820 the Aegean Islands, Attica, and the Peloponnesus. In April 1820, while he was preparing for his Aegean tour, Dumond d'Urville, an officer on the warship *La Chevrette*, informed the French ambassador de Rivière that an ancient statue of incomparable beauty had been unearthed on the island of Melos by a peasant while he was plough-ing his field. D'Urville had seen the statue and sketched it while *La Chevrette* was anchored in the harbor of Melos. The French consul on the island, Brest, had tried unsuccessfully to buy it. De Rivière decided to send Marcellus with instructions to use his influence and authority to obtain the purported masterpiece. Marcellus was all too willing, although he did not yet know that he was about to enrich his country with one of the most beautiful sculptures of antiquity, the Venus de Milo.

On 23 May 1820 he boarded the *Estafette*, sailing directly to Melos. As soon as he arrived, he found out, much to his discomfiture, that the coveted treasure had already been taken by the Greek monk Oikonomos and placed aboard a Greek brig for transportation to Constantinople. There Oikonomos was going to present it to Nik-olaos Mourouzis, the dragoman of the sultan's navy and an avid col-lector of antiquities. The hapless caloyer, however, was not able to conclude his mission successfully because Marcellus was determined to wrest the statue from him.

The French emissary requested an assembly of the elders of the island, and by cajolery and intimidation he was finally able to per-suade them that the statue should rightfully be sold to the French, whose consul Brest was the first to express the desire to buy it. The Venus de Milo was brought aboard the *Estafette* in five pieces, and

Marcellus sailed off feeling much like a victor who had triumphed over his rivals. For four months the *Estafette* paraded its precious cargo, taking it to Cyprus, Alexandria, Rhodes, and Piraeus, where Fauvel had a glimpse of it. The *Estafette* finally reached Smyrna, where the Venus de Milo was transferred to another warship, the *Lionne*. It arrived in Paris in February 1821 and was placed in the Louvre. The inscription on its pedestal perpetuates the memory of the two diplomats who saw to it that France possessed it: "Acquired by M. de Marcellus for the marquis de Rivière, ambassador of France, who gave it to King Louis XVIII, in 1821" (18). By obtaining this artistic masterpiece, Marcellus felt that he had performed a patriotic act, making his country and his compatriots all the richer for its acquisition.[8]

Years later, Marcellus's account of his feat was contradicted by eyewitnesses, some of whom maintained that when the statue changed hands, force was used and there was an armed confrontation between the Greeks and the crew of the *Estafette*, who won in the end.[9] The evidence surrounding this episode is conflicting. But the conduct of the whole affair shows clearly that in European eyes the modern Greeks had no right to the monuments of antiquity because they could be of no use to a people who had neither enough culture nor sufficient means to appreciate and safeguard them. So pervasive was this patronizing and arrogant attitude that even philhellenes such as Marcellus subscribed to it implicitly.[10]

His mission on Melos successfully completed, Marcellus set out on his tour of the Aegean Islands, Attica, and the Peloponnesus. Highlights of his itinerary were Rhodes, Paros, Naxos, Syra, Chios, and Athens. During his stop in Athens, Fauvel offered him hospitality. While spending the night in the famous museum-room that housed Fauvel's collection of antiquities, Marcellus felt a hard, cold hand grazing his forehead. He grasped it, only to find that it belonged to a statue suspended from the ceiling in a net, swaying back and forth.[11] This curious little episode, as well as Marcellus's involvement in the purchase-"abduction" of the Venus de Milo illustrate the direct way that European antiquarians at that time experienced the classical past, surrounded as they were by its relics.

Marcellus left the Near East in 1820. In 1822 he was appointed secretary to the French embassy in London while Chateaubriand was the French ambassador there. Marcellus was elated to serve under a man whose books he had read and admired since his early youth. This acquaintance, Marcellus tells us in his *Chateaubriand et son temps* (1859), developed into a strong friendship based on their mutual literary interests and the reminiscences of their experiences in the eastern Mediterranean. In reality, the relationship was more that of a mentor-disciple, the master needing an audience and the secretary a model to emulate. Being a confidant to such a renowned man flattered Marcellus. His diplomatic career ended in 1829 because he felt that he could not give his loyalty to the new king, Louis Philippe. Writing about his experience and activities in the Levant was to absorb his efforts and interests from that time on.

The first account of his recollections of Greece and Asia Minor appeared in 1839 under the title *Souvenirs de l'Orient*. A second, *Episodes littéraires en Orient*, followed in 1851. In both of these the Greek world, both ancient and modern, concerned him the most. He stated that his impressions and observations, despite the late appearance of his books, possessed an enduring value because they treated not the temporary and the ephemeral but the permanent characteristics of the people of that area. He believed that, the turbulent history of the region notwithstanding—especially in the decade after his departure—there were certain traits that persisted, "and Homer, after three thousand years, is true in all these accounts" (*S*, iii).

Seen through the tradition of philhellenic literature, these works are a belated manifestation of the spirit of romantic Hellenism with all its yearning and nostalgia for a nobler past and its facile and sentimental comparisons of the ancient and the modern Greeks. Removed from the theater of revolutionary activities where Greece's destiny was being decided, Marcellus did not feel impelled to reexamine and reevaluate his first impressions in the light of these events. Therefore, despite his literary pretensions, pompous tone, and rhetorical style, he recreated scenes from the prerevolutionary Greek world, guided only by the memory of his experiences and by his philhellenic sentiments.

Whereas his first two books were mainly informed by recollections of subjective feelings and reactions, the subsequent two, *Chants du peuple en Grèce* (1851) and *Les Grecs anciens et les Grecs modernes* (1861), explored the history, customs, and traditions of the modern Greeks and dwelled on the familiar parallels with their progenitors. Greek folk songs had attracted the attention of others before him.

Guys was one of the first French travelers to comment extensively on them. Pouqueville emphasized their significance for a better understanding of the Greeks. Claude Fauriel collected, examined, and classified them systematically in his *Chants populaires de la Grèce moderne* (1824).

Marcellus's work added very little that was new and significant on this subject. It is of interest, nevertheless, because, like the rest of his works, it reveals his abiding interest in the continuity of Greek civilization and in the recurrence of themes and images from antiquity down to the present. This of course excluded everything that in his eyes did not bear a resemblance to a largely idealized classical past. His image of ancient Greece was that of a graceful, noble, and pristine civilization, a sort of mixture of Hellenistic refinement and Homeric nobility. Nevertheless, he enriched his *Chants du peuple en Grèce* with lengthy commentaries and lists cataloguing and classifying songs. Although erudite, he was never pedantic or ponderous. If he failed to be original and profound, he succeeded in delighting his reader with his disarming grace.

In undertaking to write the recollections of his voyage, Marcellus had a twofold intention: to describe the places and the people he had seen and to relive the experiences and emotions they had elicited in him. Now a mature man, he looked at his youthful enthusiasm and tried to recapture some of the joyous moments of his past. Not once did he express any misgivings for having spent four years in a place of so many contrasts and incongruities. Thanks to his classical fervor and his optimism, he was able to avoid any unpleasant or distressing sensations or experiences.

Though he was aware of the profound changes that had taken place in the life of the modern inhabitants, he did not let them distort his harmonious image of a still viable Hellenic world. The nineteen-year interval separating his voyage from his recording of it heightened his ardor rather than subduing and minimizing it. Unlike Choiseul-Gouffier, whose sobering experiences during the latter part of his ambassadorship in Constantinople had made him look at his youthful infatuation with Greece with scepticism, Marcellus contemplated his past with nostalgia and cherished the memories of his Greek experience.

I try to recall the joys of my youth and the impressions I sought
so avidly; I feel overwhelmed by so many memories. I stop them
at each step of my memory; my pen falls, and I begin to dream end-
lessly of these immense delights, of these nights so serene and so
pure, of this azure sky, of these seas so brilliant, of the lustrous
marvels of the most beautiful country in the world; and when
this magical image of these vanished times besieges my thought,
I do not know whether my heart beats faster under the charm of
the happiness these illusions still give me, or under the weight of
the regrets that bygone days, which never return, leave behind
them. (*S, 4*)

If he were to have omitted his personal reactions, his lyrical musings, and the exaltation he felt as he visited various famous sites, he
tells us, he would have falsified the authentic and original character
of his work. One might also add that he would have deprived himself of the opportunity to fulfill his literary aspirations. His works
are interspersed with long descriptive passages in which he tries to
reconstruct the lines and contours of a particularly memorable place
in an obviously Chateaubriandesque manner. Recreating it objectively was not enough; he also wanted to convey the emotions he
had experienced and to make his presence felt. "In my poetic imagination of twenty years, I repopulated these solitudes; I leaped with
joy seeing myself in the direction of the Cyclades; recalling all my
memories of poets, I gave ancient epithets to each reef" (*S, 18*).

Marcellus's acquaintance with the classics was surprisingly extensive considering his youth at the time of his journey. His was a literary voyage par excellence. Whenever he set out on a tour, he was
equipped with a whole array of books both ancient and modern.
Among the classical authors, he had Thucydides, Xenophon, Strabo,
Pausanias, and, above all, Homer. From the moderns he chose
Racine, Byron, and, most of all, Chateaubriand. Homer and Chateaubriand were undoubtedly his best companions. Not only did
they guide his way to certain places and told him what to see, but,
more importantly, they showed him how to see. A small *Odyssey*, he
tells us, never left his pocket except when he held it in his hands.

When he visited Chios, he and his fellow travelers began to look
for what they believed to be the school of Homer. After having
located some unrecognizable ruins and sat on a rock—"Homer's
rock"—he took out his *Odyssey* and began to read some of its beau-

tiful verses, stopping now and then to translate them for his uniniti-
ated friends. The people and the landscape around them made
Homer's images come to life. "This passion for Homer, which my
first studies had impressed on me, had increased during my stay in
the Orient by my observations on the primitive manners, which I
compared to present-day customs . . . ; finally, this passion—I should
perhaps say this frenzy—had become for me a sort of a cult" (*S*, 184).

Marcellus was highly conscious of the plastic and artistic qualities
of language and tried to use it as a medium for recreating a lived experience and not simply for transmitting information. By describing
Greece he sought to present a personal vision of it and reconstruct
his subjective perceptions and reactions. He saw himself not as a
mechanical recorder of external reality but as a unique and receptive
viewer acting upon his environment through the power of his memory and imagination. Walking around the completely deserted and
arid island of Delos, he felt—at least this is what he tells us—the exquisite sensation derived from the imaginary presence of a resplendent
past: "These enormous masses, today lying ignobly in some wild
thickets, recaptured in my thought the place once assigned to them
by an accomplished architecture; I repopulated the temples of the
gods, and I prostrated myself before their grandeur" (*S*, 216).

The importance of visual imagination in literature, and especially
in travel literature, had become a significant aspect of this genre, especially after Chateaubriand. Marcellus, with an inclination and at
times even a talent for descriptive and evocative writing, painted the
landscape of several Greek islands and Asia Minor, especially Troy.
Contrasting colors, delicate, undulating lines, and the ubiquitous
ruins are the main features of his descriptive passages. But in spite of
his graceful style, the purity of his diction, and his harmoniously
constructed sentences, he is nowhere near the *paysagiste* that Chateaubriand was. Marcellus's images tend to be rather abstract and nebulous. They seek to impress by rhetorical figures of speech, erudition, and a tone of forced grandeur rather than by the inner cohesion
of the image and its correspondence to an actual landscape. He
lacked Chateaubriand's sweeping grasp of the external world and his
ability to recreate it by well-integrated and artistically composed
scenes still bearing a resemblance to the original objects and at the
same time exuding a lyrical and aesthetic beauty of their own.

But Marcellus emphasized another aspect of Greek reality, one that Chateaubriand had largely neglected or ignored. He was genuinely interested in contemporary life and recorded several episodes that affirmed the existence of intellectual activity and progress among certain groups of Greeks. He took just as much time to get acquainted with the modern Greeks as he did to inspect the ruined monuments of the ancients. What impressed him the most was their zealous effort to understand and identify with their classical past and spread the benefits of education among the young. Constantinople and Chios provided ample opportunities to observe this.

His visit to Chios was one of the more memorable events of his voyage. After an outpouring of emotions over the discovery of what he mistook for the school of Homer, he visited the educational institution of the island, which was one of the best in Greece at that time. He was greatly impressed by the facilities, the product of private donations, and by the program, which the director of the school, Neophytos Vambas, explained to him. Its library contained three thousand volumes in Greek, Latin, and French, Korais's works being among its most prized possessions. Its students, numbering five hundred and coming from all parts of the Greek world, were pursuing their studies with zeal and dedication.

Marcellus formed a most favorable impression of the director of the college. A man of enlightened and progressive ideas, Neophytos Vambas was the author of works on rhetoric, grammar, and ethics. An ecclesiastic, he was also a capable mathematician and man of letters. As a young man he had visited France and lived in Paris.[12] He was a fervent admirer of Korais and like him considered the French to be closer to the ancient Greeks than any other Europeans. While in Paris, Vambas was invited by his compatriots to return to his native island, Chios, to teach mathematics and physics. He accepted, though it was not without regret that he left the capital of the arts and sciences, as he called Paris.

Vambas was very proud and eager to explain to Marcellus his ideas on education and his system of instruction. He viewed the dissemination of education as the most important contribution to the progress of the Greek people. He considered the young to be its direct beneficiaries because it was incumbent upon them to fulfill their national duties through enlightened patriotism. "The most sacred duty of every man," he exhorted them, "is to contribute to the best of his ability to the common good of his fellow men; but the most important contribution is that which furthers education. This truth, which was proven centuries ago, is even more evident today when we witness the astonishing progress that the *genos* [the Greek people] has made within a short time."[13]

What did education signify, according to Vambas? As he explained to Marcellus, the teaching of foreign languages was of primary importance as the best means of acquiring and absorbing Western ideas. French of course was one of the main languages taught in the school. History, philosophy, mathematics, and physics were equally emphasized. The study of literature was mainly a grammatical and rhetorical exegesis of classical texts, often accompanied by a comparison between ancient and modern Greek locutions. Last but not least, as an ecclesiastic he considered theology the cornerstone of his institution. "True knowledge is the knowledge of God."[14] However, he believed in a religion that brought people closer to God not by fear and superstition but by the cultivation of reason and the exercise of virtue and ethical conduct. He wished to see the study of theology and the instilling of religious principles taken out of the hands of stubborn and narrow-minded priests and entrusted to enlightened and rational clergymen and laymen. Apparently his ideas had drawn the official disapprobation of the church, which caused him to denounce the hostility and the prejudices of the official clergy as a threat even more serious to the regeneration of Greece than Turkish rule.

Marcellus was delighted to hear of the educational advances of the Greeks and found his interlocutor a most charming and engaging host. His description of him is indeed most complimentary. "I found myself with a learned man, a profound observer of politics, consumed with a zeal for letters and sciences, an ardent propagator of the institutions he believed useful for his country" (*S*, 193). Vambas, for his part, was extremely pleased and flattered to see Marcellus's interest and affection for Greece. In spite of his youth, Marcellus was respected not only as a dignitary, since he was a member of the French embassy, but also as a representative of a superior and highly esteemed culture.

After his visit to the college of Chios, Marcellus strolled through the town. The obvious prosperity of the people, reflected in their apparel and demeanor, made a favorable impression on him. In the environs of the town, he visited the house of a wealthy Chiote merchant, Rodocanaki, set in the midst of orchards and enjoying a superb view of the sea.

Rodocanaki's residence and family life were a felicitous blending of traditional manners and new acquisitions derived from the West. A life of comfort and ease surrounded by an idyllic environment was enhanced by objects of learning and intellectual stimulation. Marcellus considered the library of two thousand volumes and a telescope signs of enlightenment and educational progress. His description of the Rodocanaki residence gives a rare glimpse by a foreigner of a wealthy Greek household of that time. Many travelers had commented on the prosperity and affluence of the island, but rare was the case of a visitor who presented a concrete example of a well-to-do family:

> The wife of Tchelebi Rodocanaki, Coccona Tharsitza, herself brought me preserves and coffee, while her husband, lying on the divans next to me, filled a long pipe for me with his own hands and lit it. After this first ceremony, Tharsitza conducted us into a gallery, where she showed me some paintings of the Venetian school: from there we went up on the terrace located on the top of the house. A telescope had already been placed there under a tent.
>
> Tchelebi Rodocanaki then led me leisurely and without affectation to his beautiful gardens. We took a long walk along the pools filled with limpid water under the shade of orange trees.
>
> When I reentered the house, some of the rooms on the ground floor were open; I found there billiards and a library of approximately two thousand volumes; the works had been chosen by Neophytos Vambas during his voyage to France; I noticed that here, as in the public college, he had placed next to the great writers of Greece the masterpieces of Italy and of the century of Louis XIV. (*S,* 196–99)[15]

Marcellus perceived similar manifestations of intellectual stirrings among the Greeks of Constantinople. As a secretary of the French embassy in that city, he knew and appreciated its unique and varied character, with its tall minarets and gilded domes and its mixed population. Unlike Chateaubriand, he was not repulsed by the heterogeneity of the city. Instead he was stimulated and excited by its diversity and fascinated by the discovery of so many novel things. Furthermore, its location overlooking two continents and linking the West with the East increased its appeal in his eyes.

Then the sun gilded the dome of Saint Sophia with its first rays and showed me in all its splendor the city where I had come to live. Europe and its elegant minarets, Asia and its rich shades, a thousand sounds reverberating in the midst of a populous city and an immense port . . . and the great name of Constantinople dominating this resplendent spectacle; everything immersed me in a profound ecstasy; then one no longer describes—one meditates. (*S, 59*)

The Greeks were an important element of the city's life and Marcellus took an early interest in them. He was favorably impressed by their zealous study of the ancients, whose literature and language seemed to enjoy a high esteem in ecclesiastical circles. Despite its traditionalism and its suspicious attitude toward ideas of Western provenance, the church had always considered itself the repository of classical learning. With the rising prestige of ancient Greek civilization, classical letters were considered even by many clerics to be the most potent force for the regeneration of Greece. During his stay in Constantinople Marcellus came to know some of these ecclesiastics. They impressed upon him that they were actively engaged in the spiritual revival of their people and the propagation of Hellenism.

Among the various episodes he relates, two are of particular interest. Once, while walking in the environs of Constantinople, he encountered a Greek priest. The Orthodox clergyman, desiring to impress his foreign interlocutor, expressed his admiration for the ancients. He himself was involved in the intellectual resurgence of his compatriots and talked about a treatise he was writing on ancient Greek literature. The ancients, though pagans, received his unreserved praise. He appreciated the beauty and eloquence of their literature and the wisdom of their philosophers. To instruct his countrymen, the cleric chose the Hellenic tradition, along with the Christian ethos, as a guide and source of inspiration. He exhorted the young to study their ancestors carefully and to imitate their noble actions so that, when the day of their national liberation came, they would be worthy of them.

When he visited the Phanar, the site of the Greek Orthodox patriarchate and a section of Constantinople inhabited by Greeks, Marcellus witnessed once more the vivid interest of several ecclesiastics in Hellenic letters. One of them, Bishop Constancios, was an "archéologue passioné" and was compiling a historical description of

the Greek monuments of Constantinople, which he was planning
to have published in Venice. The monk Hilarion, who showed Marcellus the printing establishment of the patriarchate, commented on
the preparation of a new dictionary entitled *Kivotos*.[16] Those who
conceived such an ambitious project did so with the hope of preserving the "masterpieces of our first authors," dispelling ignorance, and
purifying the Greek language. Hilarion pointed out that they had
used as a model Henri Estienne's *Thesauraus Graecae Linguae* and
that,

> ashamed of the darkness that seemed to enshroud their genera-
> tion, our worthy leaders had seen to it in advance that everywhere
> in Greece . . . the love of true knowledge is aroused; and when
> they saw young people impassioned for knowledge, mature and
> even old men become animated with equal ardor, and everyone,
> so to speak, rejected the blemishes of an idiom altered by the mix-
> ture of peoples in order to return to the pure and elegant language
> of our ancestors, they thought that the time had come to extend
> a liberating hand to all these young men eager to came out of the
> abyss of ignorance.[17]

Hilarion's statement reveals both the admiration antiquity enjoyed among the members of the upper hierarchy of the church and
their didactic use of it as well as their stand on the language question
through their support of the ancient idiom instead of the modern
spoken one.

During the four years of his stay in the Near East, or the Orient,
as he called it, Marcellus became acquainted with enough prominent
Greeks to be convinced of their progress. Had he written his works
soon after his visit, the cause of philhellenism would have been
strengthened by his favorable depiction of the Greeks. As it was, he
published his works at a time when philhellenism, as considered
here, had run its course. Its main objective, the liberation of Greece,
had been largely realized, but not to the satisfaction of many philhellenes, whose expectation of seeing the ancients rise was not fulfilled.
Marcellus's books belong to an earlier era when it was still possible
to combine idealism with the vision of a nobler past.

Although Marcellus described but a small part of early nineteenth-century Greek life, his portrayal takes on an added significance because he witnessed it on the eve of the Revolution and, also,

because he gives glimpses of communities whose life came to an end in the course of the struggle for independence. To be sure, the usual contrasts between past and present, the dolorous musings on the irreversible flow of time, the desire to evoke the world of classical antiquity, themes all too familiar in the writings of his precursors, take up a large part of his work. But at the same time he was interested in the immediate world and therefore was less given to despondency over the eclipse of the ancients. Thus his claim that his observations retained their intrinsic interest, even though they appeared after Greece had gained its independence, is not entirely unfounded. "Besides," he noted, "I was traveling on the eve of the Greek insurrection, and I imagine that there will be some interest to know the point from which this revolution started."[18]

The Educational Voyage:
Firmin-Didot

By coincidence, Ambroise Firmin-Didot began his voyage to the Near East at the same time as Marcellus. They met on their way from Troy to Constantinople. "I was accompanied," wrote Marcellus, recalling their first encounter, "by the doctor of the embassy and by M. Ambroise Didot, son and nephew of the famous printers of this name. He was as young as I was and equally devoted to the investigation of the ancients" (S, 42). As Marcellus's statement implies, the two young travelers had several things in common: they were both descendants of distinguished families and had been trained in the classics; the focal point of their itinerary was not Attica and the Peloponnesus but the coast of Asia Minor and the Aegean Islands; and finally, they had all the fervor, enthusiasm, and curiosity that youth and energy gave them.

Didot was twenty-five when he left Paris on 14 March 1816. By 15 May he was in Cythera, off the southern coast of the Peloponnesus. He departed the next day, and, after sailing through the islands of the Aegean, he landed on the coast near Troy on 25 May. It was here that he met Marcellus. Traveling together, they arrived at Constantinople on 2 June. Didot remained there for some time and then left for a tour of the islands and the coast of Asia Minor.

Before leaving Paris, Didot saw Choiseul-Gouffier for the last time. The venerable Hellenist and diplomat remembered with affection the many years he had spent in the Near East. He was especially fond of his memories of Greece. In spite of his advanced age, Didot recalled later, "he still envied me . . . for having the fortune to visit Greece."[19] Didot was particularly attached to another Hellenist, Adamantios Korais, who was well known to his family and who had taught him Greek. He had instilled in the young Didot a love and admiration for the ancients and a genuine interest and sympathy for the modern Greeks. It was mainly due to Korais's influence that Didot decided to visit Greece. When he published his book, he paid homage to his mentor by dedicating it to him: "Kindly accept this homage, since it is to the interest that you inspired in me in the unfortunate nation you so worthily represent that I owe the undertaking of a Voyage whose memories are so precious to me." He went on to praise Korais's inestimable contribution to his compatriots' awakening and considered himself fortunate to have been his student.

Although Didot visited the Levant before the outbreak of the Greek Revolution, his book, *Notes d'un voyage fait dans le Levant*, did not appear until 1826, a time most crucial for the struggle for independence. This may in part explain the strong and direct expression of philhellenic sentiments, the agitated tone of his narrative, his animosity toward the Turks, and his impatience with the Europeans. By publishing his account he believed that he paid tribute to the Greeks and was furthering the cause of philhellenism. There was certainly enough travel literature on them, Didot conceded, but he felt that insufficient recognition had been accorded their advancement before the Revolution. To redress this wrong, he decided to publish his own work showing that considerable progress had already been achieved in spite of adverse conditions.

Pleading for the liberation of the Greeks, he called on the Europeans to support their struggle. For too long, he told them, for centuries, they had watched idly as the Turks overran Greece and conquered its people. Sharing the feelings of other philhellenes, he saw the struggle for independence as a conflict not simply between two hostile peoples but between the forces of good and evil.

Greece, which by her noble efforts has proved worthy of recovering her rank among civilized nations, appears before the eyes of

Europe with her brilliant memories, her religion, her harmonious language, her heroic courage, and her long misfortunes. For three centuries, Greece has been seeking the gratitude owed to her by the world civilized by her. The Turks, on the contrary, have always offered nothing but ignorance, fanaticism, and stupid ferocity . . . ; the recollections of their history conjure up nothing but massacres whose cruelty revolts us, and an inveterate hatred against the Christians must render them even more odious. To sum up, Greece asks for her civil and religious liberty; the Turks want nothing but blood and slavery. (2)

Still under the influence of his classical education and an intellectual milieu imbued with the ideas of romantic Hellenism, Didot approached Greece with joyous anticipation. His vision of ancient Greece had already been formed through reading Barthélemy and Homer. He was prepared to find smiling shores, verdant mountains, and sparkling islands. Conversations with Choiseul-Gouffier and Korais, on the other hand, informed him about the state of the modern Greeks, and he was disabused of any unrealistic hopes he might have entertained. Didot's response to Greece reveals a young man imbued with the ideas of his era concerning ancient Greece but also open to new and unfamiliar experiences. Preconceived notions had not yet congealed into hardened prejudices. His directness, the absence of the censorious tone so common in most visitors of that time, and the occasional display of wonderment and even fascination with the new and unexpected invest his narrative with a refreshing and invigorating candor. His was an educational voyage par excellence not because he discovered the Greece of his imagination but because he took the opportunity to acquaint himself with people around him and to attend a Greek school with young men of his age.

Though Didot did not expect to witness scenes of classical splendor, he anticipated with excitement the moment when he would see the Greek lands and the Greek sea. The first view from the distance did not equal his expectations. Arid mountains and desolate shores were exposed to the rarefying heat of the dazzling Mediterranean sun. The islands of the Aegean, immortalized by the ancient poets, bore no resemblance to their literary prototypes in the eyes of Didot. Sailing past them and gazing at them from the deck of the ship, he found them uninviting and barren. "Arid rocks preserving only the skeleton of these islands present on all sides forbidding and inhospitable reefs" (27). Obviously the starkness of the islands was too austere to be pleasing. Moreover, the transition from imagination to reality was a dislocating experience because he had envisioned "Greece still shining with some remnants of its antique brilliance" (22).

Didot found Troy more gratifying and more evocative of the legends with which it was associated. For French travelers of the eighteenth and the early nineteenth century, the authority of Homer was undisputed and the heroes he portrayed had the presence of real beings and not the remoteness of abstract literary figures. Most of all, they admired the nobility, grandeur, and valor surrounded by pomp and ceremony of the Homeric world.

Hector and Andromache were two of the most frequently invoked characters. The scene of their last parting represented the quintessence of familial love and tenderness. Romantic Hellenists attributed to the Homeric characters a certain sentimentality and affection that reflected their own yearnings. By emphasizing these qualities, they failed to perceive the driving force, the primeval energy, and the tragic fate of the Homeric heroes falling in the fury of battle. For them Troy was not so much the city that was destroyed by the Greeks as the one immortalized by their greatest poet. Its existence was seen as an integral part of the Hellenic world or, more precisely, of the literature this civilization had bequeathed to the West. As such, the figures that populated it had all the immediacy of characters that are part of one's educational experience.

In the realm of the imagination, the distance separating the ancients' world from the present was often obliterated by the vividness of their invoked presence. Paradoxically, it was the desolation and the barrenness of the Trojan landscape that helped preserve the integrity and the inviolability of the Homeric world in the eyes of its classically inspired visitors. The intrusion of ancient ruins or contemporary habitations would have struck a discordant note because it would have injected contingency and change where they preferred to see none. Didot's impressions of Troy were in consonance with this idealized and romanticized vision.

While the presence of heterogeneous elements was deemed offensive in places associated with antiquity, their occurrence elsewhere was stimulating and picturesque. Constantinople was such a place.

Its relation to antiquity was very remote, and its Christian-Byzantine past had no appeal to Western visitors. Therefore they expressed no regrets for its conquest by the Ottomans, and their impression of it was not conditioned by preconceived notions. To them it was an imperial center with all the splendor and squalor of an oriental city. While they found the presence of the Turks in mainland Greece and on the islands distressing, they saw no reason to remonstrate against their predominance in Constantinople.

Yet most French visitors at that time had a mixed reaction to the city. Their initial enchantment was succeeded by a feeling of discontent and even alienation. Their refined tastes and classical predilections were stronger than their sense of wonder at the strange and the exotic. Though the city of the sultans, with its impenetrable mysteries, secret intrigues, eunuchs, odalisques, and multifarious crowds, excited their curiosity, at times it defied their comprehension and offended their sensibilities. The romantic spirit searching for local color and passionate adventures had not yet manifested itself fully. Of these visitors, Guys concentrated mainly on the Greeks; Choiseul-Gouffier, although he presented some magnificent sketches of sites and people, avoided the expression of personal feelings; Chateaubriand had no such reservations, but what he had to say was scarcely complimentary. It is only in Marcellus and Didot that the sense of fascination and enchantment with the city begins to emerge.

Unlike Chateaubriand, who portrayed Constantinople as a city haunted by lifeless figures moving about stealthily, Didot discerned beauty, alien to the European eye, to be sure, but beauty nevertheless. "London and Paris can give no idea of the exterior beauty of this city, the most admirable in the universe by its position and the picturesque image it presents. . . . Its gilded minarets soaring in the air, its cypress-shaded cupolas display its vast expanse" (60).

Didot's lengthy description of the city is informative and engaging at the same time. The interior was full of contrasts: narrow, tortuous streets, where dogs jostled with people, were malodorous; while walking through this maze, one would suddenly come upon exquisite fountains decorated with brilliant floral patterns and intricately executed passages from the Koran; one could see imposing mosques standing beside humble abodes, since grandeur and squalor were never far apart.

In touring Constantinople, one was remiss if one did not pause to contemplate the unique beauty of a Turkish cemetery. There, eternal repose was never disturbed. The dark cypress trees soaring majestically above the dazzling marble of inscribed tombstones reminded one of the ultimate peace and conciliation that comes with death. Chateaubriand had been deeply moved by the sight of Turkish cemeteries. Ten years later, Didot, in spite of his youth, was also impressed by their peaceful atmosphere and contrasting hues.

Didot tried to convey some of the visual splendor of this oriental city and the variety of its monuments and the human types that made up its population. There was the Turk "smoking his pipe on the balcony in front of his house . . . with his customary indifference" (98). There was the black eunuch zealously guarding the entrance to the harem and discouraging potential intruders by his menacing look. There were the Greek, the Armenian, and the Jew, all enterprising merchants, pursuing their activities and displaying their wares. It is a pity that Didot did not dwell more on delineating this human mosaic. But his youth, education, and sensibilities, attuned to the beauties of the classical world, had not prepared him to appreciate such a quixotic combination. The city stimulated his interest and at times captivated his attention, but in the end its world remained alien to him. He was glad to have gazed at its surface and not to have partaken of its life.

Didot came to know the Greeks most intimately of all the peoples who lived in the capital. While in Constantinople he frequented their section, the Phanar, where he attended lectures at the public college. He was most impressed by the emphasis on the study of classical authors and the facility with which the Greek students learned ancient Greek. On several occasions he also visited the printing establishment of the patriarchate and was able to give some useful advice.

His most memorable educational experience was at the school of Kydonies, a town on the coast of Asia Minor. Together with Smyrna and Chios, Kydonies was one of the seedbeds of the modern Greek revival in the eastern Aegean. Didot was favorably impressed with the prosperity and progressive spirit of this predominantly Greek center and eagerly followed Korais's advice to attend its academy. Kydonies enjoyed a privileged position within the Ottoman Empire because of a firman issued by the sultan in 1773, according to which the town was to be inhabited only by Greeks, who were given the right to exercise a limited autonomy over their local affairs in exchange for a rather heavy tax. Only three Turkish officials, the governor, the judge, or kadi, and a customs officer, resided there.

The town was a thriving commercial center with a population of 15,000 at the time of Didot's visit in 1816.[20] A local militia of 250–300 men, in Didot's estimation, protected property and ensured personal safety. Another public service was the two hospitals.[21] The administration of local affairs was in the hands of a council of 15 elders, 12 of whom served for life and 3 who were elected. This was a mixture, though not a balanced one, of oligarchy and democracy.

But the most prized institution, the one that spread the fame of Kydonies beyond Asia Minor, was its celebrated school or academy. The size and curriculum were similar to those of the school of Chios. Its three hundred students were housed in a large rectangular building with a spacious central court. The structure itself and the equipment in it were fairly new, dating from 1803. The school was well endowed and gave financial assistance to poor students in the form of free room and board. Because of this and its high academic standards, it attracted students from distant Greek communities, including mainland Greece. The Lancastrian system was used; that is, the older students taught the younger ones, presenting to them the professors' lectures in a simplified form. In addition to training them as future teachers, this method gave the less prosperous ones an extra source of income. Didot observed that a sense of responsibility and decorum reigned and that, although class attendance was not obligatory, the lecture halls were always full.

Didot attended classes in that school for two months. He fraternized easily with the students, most of whom were not much younger than he. He had little difficulty in adjusting to his environment as his own educational background was consonant with the classical orientation of the school. Even the language barrier was overcome because, at the time of Didot's visit, the student body passed a resolution decreeing that only ancient Greek, a language Didot could speak, be used in their conversations. Those who did not conform had to recite a page from Homer in the presence of their fellow students. In signing this resolution the students used ancient Greek names alongside their Christian ones. Didot, not surprisingly, was named Anacharsis.[22]

The adoption of ancient Greek names by modern Greeks during

that time, recalling a similar phenomenon among the French revolutionaries, was one sign of the spirit of renascence in Hellenic *paedeia*. First names and family names were changed, and the names of ships as well. Their Christian patron saints were replaced with ancient heroes and mythological figures: Leonidas, Diomedes, Pylades, Ares, and Achilles, among others, became familiar appellations. Underlying this practice was the conviction that in order to recapture and recreate the spirit of the ancients, one had to imitate them outwardly. "Imitation was the base of the literary teachings of classicism; through imitation one could reach the exemplary prototypes. Imitation would begin from the outer forms, dress, names, language, so as to come closer to the substance."[23]

The emulation of ancient Greek ideals and the strong emphasis on classical studies among the faculty and students of the school of Kydonies made a lasting impression on the young Didot. So pervasive was the influence of classical learning that it also became a source of diversion and entertainment. During their free hours the students rehearsed and performed ancient Greek plays, such as Euripides' *Hecuba*, and organized readings of ancient Greek poetry. Didot participated in these activities and felt his love for the classics grow stronger because of them.

Didot was ever grateful to the town and the academy of Kydonies for giving him the opportunity to study ancient Greek, and, when the occasion arose for him to contribute to its betterment, he responded enthusiastically. The leaders of the community and the teachers of the school expressed the desire to have a printing press. But they needed technical assistance and trained people. At Didot's suggestion a student, Konstantinos Tobras, was sent to Paris, where he was trained at the Firmin-Didot publishing establishment. He returned to his native town in 1819, bringing with him a printing press, which functioned under his direction until the destruction of the town by the Turks in 1822. Tobras was able to escape to the Morea, where he offered his services to the Greek revolutionaries. The printing equipment that he used there was also supplied by Didot.[24]

Didot's unwavering support for the fighting Greeks, expressed in both deeds and words, received some of its impetus from his fond memories of his Greek experience. Not everything he had seen was positive and gratifying; but the awakening of Greek nationalism

based on the emulation of the ancients and the embracing of Western models of education received his full and enthusiastic approbation. That the Greeks took up arms against their rulers proved to
him their determination to shake off centuries-old rule and join the
family of European nations.

Didot's and Marcellus's observations on Greek society in general
and Greek schools in particular, though fragmentary and impressionistic, reveal certain tendencies that permeated the Greek intellectual world at that time. Foremost among them was the cultivation
of the classics. The purpose was mainly to provide models for the formation of an individual and national ethos promulgating ethical conduct and patriotism. Clearly, the past was studied not simply for its
own sake but in order to serve the needs of awakening Greek nationalism. Its appeal was didactic and instructional, not artistic and creative. Didot and Marcellus did not comment on this use of the past
as a means of fulfilling present aspirations because they were more
interested in praising the Greeks than in evaluating them critically.
The very fact that they emulated the ancients was sufficient to gain
the favor of these two Frenchmen. Didot had the added advantage
of experiencing personally this educational venture into the classics.

Greece Revisited: Pouqueville

The year 1805 was an important one in Pouqueville's life and in the
development of French philhellenism as well. It marked the publication of his first work on Greece, *Voyage en Morée, à Constantinople,
en Albanie, et dans plusieurs autres parties de l'empire Ottoman*, and
the beginning of his second stay there. The circumstances of his second voyage, however, differed substantially from those of his first.
This time he was going as a consul general of the French government
to the court of Ali Pasha of Jannina. He was appointed to this post
by Napoleon, who discerned in him an exceptional adaptability and
perceptiveness. Pouqueville himself had indirectly sought the emper-
or's favor by dedicating his work to him:

Sire, the honor to publish my voyage under the auspices of YOUR
MAJESTY, and to associate the most illustrious name of ancient and

modern times, that of NAPOLEON, with the immortal memories of Greece; such an honor, Sire, overwhelms me with a favor I was far from deserving! It makes me forget my captivity and my three years of suffering among the Muslims.[25]

François-Charles-Hugues-Laurent Pouqueville was born in Normandy in 1770. He studied theology at the university of Caen and was ordained in 1791. Then he went to Paris, where he studied medicine. In 1798 he was offered the position of physician to the Commission des arts et sciences, which accompanied Napoleon on his Egyptian campaign. Soon after his arrival in Egypt, however, Pouqueville fell ill and was forced to return to France. He did not reach his destination, for he was captured by pirates near the coast of Calabria. From there he was taken to Navarino and then to Tripolitsa (Tripolis), where he was delivered to the local pasha. Though a prisoner, he was not guarded strictly and enjoyed relative freedom of movement because he was a doctor, a profession highly regarded by the Ottomans. He was held in Tripolitsa for only two months. Then he was transferred to Constantinople, where he was imprisoned in the fortress of the Seven Towers, where he remained for two years. In 1801 he was finally set free and allowed to return to France.

Soon after his return Pouqueville began work on his medical thesis, which he defended with distinction. However, he decided not to pursue a medical career. Instead he concentrated his efforts on completing his book, *Voyage en Morée, à Constantinople, en Albanie, et dans plusieurs autres parties de l'Empire Ottoman*, in which he chronicled his experiences in the Ottoman Empire. Its publication earned him immediate acclaim and established his reputation as an authority on the Greek lands of the empire, a circumstance that led to his appointment as consul general at Jannina.

He arrived at the capital of Epirus on 2 February 1806. He was received with great honors by Ali Pasha, the redoubtable governor of the area, whom he met for the first time in March 1806. The Albanian ruler was most eager to please Pouqueville as an expression of his approval of the French policies that affected his dominions. He provided the French consul with armed guards to protect him from brigands as he explored northern Greece. This harmony and good will, however, soon came to an end when Britain replaced France in Ali Pasha's favor after the Treaty of Tilsit (1807). Pouqueville was hence-

forth viewed with suspicion and was under the constant surveillance
of Ali Pasha's spies. Despite the restrictions and inconveniences
imposed on him, Pouqueville stayed on at his post until February
1815, when he was transferred to the consulate of Patras. He served
his country in his new position for two years. In 1817 he departed for
France following the appointment of his brother Hugues as the new
French consul at Patras.

His eleven-year stay in Greece—the best period of his life, as he
characterized it—proved to be most fruitful not because of his distinguished diplomatic activities (his was a minor post at best) but
because of the wealth of information he was able to gather on Greece
and its people. He used this vast amount of material in his most
important work on Greece, *Voyage dans la Grèce* (1820). A second,
expanded and revised edition, *Voyage de la Grèce,* followed in 1826.
Pouqueville was now considered incontestably an authority on modern Greek affairs. When the Firmin-Didot firm decided to publish
a history of the developments that led to the Greek Revolution, they
entrusted this task to Pouqueville. He accepted, and in 1826 he
presented a four-volume work, *Histoire de la régénération de la Grèce,*
in which he examined the course of events from 1740 until 1824. The
rise and fall of Ali Pasha occupied a prominent part in it because of
Pouqueville's personal knowledge of his spectacular career. A decade
later, Firmin-Didot once again invited Pouqueville to contribute to
the series L'Univers: Histoire et description de tous les peuples (1835)
by writing the volume on Greece. Thus for forty years, from 1798,
the year of his captivity, to 1838, the year of his death, Pouqueville
was directly or indirectly involved with Greece as an observer, com-
mentator, and philhellene.

Pouqueville's reputation grew as his books were translated into
other European languages. A heightened interest in Greece partially
explains the popularity enjoyed by accounts such as his. However,
Pouqueville's work was seen not as a mere travelogue, but rather as
a history of Greece. The views of the editor of the English periodical
New Voyages and Travels typify this perception. He published excerpts of the *Voyage dans la Grèce* in his periodical even before the
book appeared in France. To inform his readers and to stimulate
their interest, he commented extensively on the author and the
nature of his account.

The French original is not yet completely published; but the editor is desirous to gratify the eagerness of public curiosity, with regard to the important work of Dr. Pouqueville by producing, in the first instance, what relates to the greater portion of the north of Greece. . . . It will serve as the TRAVELLING COMPANION, the VA-DEMECUM of the traveller for information whenever he shall visit the venerable source of science and art. It will call back to his remembrance many an event, many an operation, recorded in voluminous works, ancient and modern, which he cannot be expected to carry with him.[26]

Pouqueville's first work on Greece, *Voyage en Morée, à Constantinople, en Albanie*, was justly criticized for its inaccuracies and unreliability.[27] It was a compendium of information garnered from secondary sources, because his imprisonment prevented him from conducting personal observations. Yet one can already see in it the delineation of his approach to the Greek world, both ancient and modern. That the two were intimately and directly connected Pouqueville never doubted. At the outset of his investigation, he declared that his purpose was to seek Greece within Greece. Moreover, an emphasis on the complexity and diversity of the modern Greek world was already apparent in his first work.

This comparative approach found ampler development and a more eloquent treatment in the *Voyage dans la Grèce*. In his introduction, Pouqueville stated that he valued the accurate recording of observable reality both because it led to a better grasp of the present and because it illuminated the past. He worked back in time, from the present state—from what he could see and verify—to the reconstruction of the past.

To achieve this he supplemented his personal observations with erudition. He had recourse to a variety of sources, such as ancient texts, Byzantine chronicles, ecclesiastical records, and folk traditions. Pouqueville's detailed examination, covering every aspect of the Greek world from the exploration and identification of ancient sites to the investigation of present political, social, and economic conditions, was dictated not only by his own inclination but also by the French Ministry of Foreign Affairs.

My instructions directed that I execute, independently of the functions I was called upon to fulfill, the voyage to classical lands not in the manner of those who approach a country only in order to honor it with their presence but by identifying with it. They expected from me not notes or designs sketched in the midst of languages and ruins but exact descriptions of the country without conjecturing anything; a thorough study of the institutions and the mores of the inhabitants, free from maxims or metaphors which serve to mask allusions or ulterior motives.[28]

Pouqueville followed enthusiastically and indefatigably his government's directives. His work on modern Greece was similar in its all-embracing scope to Barthélemy's fictionalized history of ancient Greece. It also suffered from some of the same weaknesses, namely, a plethora of details often cumbersome and undigested, erroneous conclusions based on insufficient evidence, and a lack of cohesiveness and overall structure. The archeological sections were the least successful from the scholarly as well as the aesthetic point of view.

Other travelers, particularly the Englishmen Chandler, Dodwell, Stuart, and Leake, made a more judicious and discreet use of their erudition to elucidate the difficulties they encountered. As a result, their works were more reliable guides to the antiquities of Greece for the nineteenth-century traveler. Letronne, a critic and contemporary of Pouqueville, remarked rather severely that:

M. Pouqueville's book . . . is certainly more *complete* than any of those I have just cited; however, they are, at least in my view, more *significant* books, because their authors possessed in a higher degree qualities indispensable for all travelers to Greece, namely, a precise knowledge of the texts and monuments and the skill to apply it to the elucidation of the difficulties that puzzle the traveler before each monument in this country, where every step awakens a memory. This is, in my opinion, the weakest part of M. Pouqueville and his work . . . and his *Voyage en Grèce*, if it is the *most complete*, is perhaps at the same time, with regard to erudition, one of the least *exact* that exist.[29]

Pouqueville's work was rooted in the travel literature of his time, but it also branched out into new directions. The use of ancient texts, constant references to the accounts of other visitors, a display of erudition, an incessant quest for parallels between ancients and moderns, and a painstaking examination of antiquities—these were some of the most common devices used by most travelers. He heralded a new attitude, however, by shifting the focus from the ancients to the moderns. Prominent in his work are the popular elements, a description of brigands, known as *klepht*s, and their heroic songs and a broad depiction of the inhabitants of northwestern Greece. He did not choose to spend ten years in this rather forbidding region, but his thorough exploration of it reflects his fascination with and abiding interest in its people. Attica, the Peloponnesus, and the Aegean Islands were no longer the focal points. Instead, Pouqueville revealed to his readers other sites rich in natural beauty and human resources. Thus in his writings, Greece is presented in a wider context, including people and places that had been overshadowed by those with more direct classical associations.

Because of his determination to show contemporary life as faithfully as possible, a more complex picture emerged which was closer to reality than the oversimplified contrasts propagated by previous travelers. Pouqueville witnessed scenes of destruction and oppression as well as instances of relative peace and prosperity. He observed the activities of prosperous merchants, who acquired their wealth in the Balkans and Europe and who spent part of it for the betterment of their compatriots. He admired the free spirit of the *klepht*s and felt compassion for the more timid and submissive peasants. His humanistic principles and feelings were outraged by the cunning and ferocity of the feared Ali Pasha.

During his travels through Epirus he was often confronted with scenes of destruction and desolation. "One can still see in the burnt houses of the village of Examili the recent passage of barbarity in this desolate land, where there are no longer any hamlets or inhabitants, and where the noxious air . . . would chase away any settlers who would attempt to settle there."[30] On the other hand, he was gratified to see signs of progress and education and the stirring of nationalist sentiment among the Greeks of Jannina. Ali Pasha's oppressiveness and acts of fitful violence notwithstanding, there were signs of prosperity among some of its inhabitants.

Pouqueville was particularly impressed by their civic consciousness and generous support of the college, which was reputed to be one of the best Greek schools of that time. "In the state of barbarity that afflicts Greece, Jannina is proud to have cultivated in silence the letters banished from the territory that was their cradle and sanctuary" (*G,* 1:154). He saw Albanians, Jews, and Vlachs living side by side with the Greeks and sharing some of their experiences. This was not necessarily a sign of decadence and the adulteration of Greek culture, as Chateaubriand believed, but an interesting amalgamation of peoples and traditions.

The only presence he could not tolerate was that of the Turks. Philhellenism, from its inception until the liberation of Greece, contained implicitly or explicitly a hostile attitude toward them, because they were viewed as the main perpetrators of the evils that had befallen the Greek people and the menace that threatened their existence. Pouqueville shared these feelings and portrayed the Turks as representatives of oppression and intolerance.

> The look of the Orientals, in general, has something sinister, and that of the Turk combines with this expression that of ferocity. Stare at his features, and you will see his eye roll, and in the dark fire that animates it, in the convulsive movement of his eyebrows, you will recognize the old and irreconcilable enemy of everything Christian. If sometimes a smile tempers the terrible action of his eyes, his haughty tone, the imperious sound of his voice, quickly reveal that he is addressing what he calls a giaour [unbeliever]. (*G,* 6:94)

In Pouqueville's view the effects of Ottoman rule were as nefarious for the Turkish masses as they were injurious for the conquered non-Muslim peoples. Mistreated by their own government, he remarked, the Turks gave free rein to their passions by tyrannizing the subject Christians. Like Chateaubriand, Pouqueville perceived the Turkish character as a mixture of irreconcilable traits. He believed that under a surface of lethargy and inertia seethed a violent and cruel temperament, which threatened to erupt when it encountered resistance from the subject peoples.

Pouqueville subscribed to the idea that the anomalous symbiosis between the Greeks and the Turks was based on an unequal relationship. It could end only with the emancipation of the former, because he saw the Ottoman government as an autocratic system incapable of reforming itself. This view had been voiced before by eighteenth century philhellenes. But they had had little faith in the modern Greeks' ability to rise against their conquerors. Pouqueville, on the other hand, was much more optimistic. What was previously merely a wish to see the Greeks free became a conviction for Pouqueville. The signs of prosperity and the stirrings of nationalism which he dis-

cerned among the more affluent and educated Greeks assured him
that the spirit of freedom had not been entirely extinguished. It had
survived because, in his opinion, it permeated the very soil of Greece.

Being physically and morally superior to their rulers, he continued, the Greeks should be able to overthrow them. Once free, they
would join the family of progressive nations. These were familiar
arguments and echoed the sentiments of other philhellenes. But Pouqueville expressed them with more forcefulness and conviction.
Time and time again he proclaimed his partiality for the Greeks and
his commitment to them because "such is our pronounced love for
the Hellenes that we would like to see their names, their images,
those of their tyrants and the historical maps of their country,
spread, occupy and attract the attention and the thoughts of all the
people of the universe" (*G,* 1:lxv).

Pouqueville, like all the philhellenes of that time, believed that for
the Greeks to rise they needed the support and understanding of the
Europeans. It was not so much Europe's pity and nostalgia for a
nobler past that would benefit the Greeks as their genuine interest,
encouragement, and an appreciation of their strides. A willingness
to probe below the surface, sift through the debris, both literally and
figuratively, a knowledge of ancient and modern Greek, and an itinerary that covered more than just Athens ought to be the guiding
principles for anyone seriously interested in Greece. Only then
would the European be able to understand its past and present and
to do justice to its people. Few travelers, in Pouqueville's view, mer-
ited that distinction. Some were too hasty and others, disappointed
in their expectations, denigrated the Greeks.[31] Their basic error was
that they started with the past and proceeded to judge the present
according to it. He followed a reverse method. He began by observing the present, which he could examine with his own eyes, and used
this as a thread leading him to the reconstitution of the past.

His claims to the contrary notwithstanding, this comparative
approach was not entirely new. Almost half a century earlier, Guys
had maintained that the past had survived in the culture of the people. Although Pouqueville's concept of continuity was more complex than that of Guys and although he realized that this cultural
heritage could not have come down through the centuries unaltered,
he still saw the modern Greeks as the reflection of the ancients
refracted through the distance of time. "Just like in the august ruins

of their ancestors' monuments, where one notices substructures and restorations of different epochs, I observed in their customs . . . traces of ancient mores, mythological ideas, and several scenes of the domestic life of their ancestors" (*G*, 1:liv–lv).

His perception of affinities between the ancient and modern Greeks, however, was the outcome of his long sojourn among the latter and not an instant revelation. When he assumed his diplomatic duties in Epirus, he was uneasy and apprehensive. Its stern and rugged landscape with its towering mountains and rushing streams, impressed him at first as an inhospitable and menacing place.[32] Epirus appeared to him as "a chaos of mountains, torrents, and precipices."[33] Its mythological associations were no less dark and haunting. This was the place where Theseus and his friend Peirithous came in order to enter the underworld, where the river Acheron and its tributary Cocytus were traversed by Charon ferrying the souls of the dead to Hades, and where Andromache was carried after she was captured by the Greeks. The present was equally foreboding for the new consul. "I saw myself abandoned on this barbarous land, because at that time very few Europeans had visited Jannina; I found myself almost at the mercy of a man who, despite his visible flattery, gave us ample cause to complain. Should I say it? The appearance of the land I had glimpsed frightened me" (*G*, 1:122).

The feared man Pouqueville alluded to was the Albanian Ali Pasha, a redoubtable figure of extraordinary powers. Born in 1744 in the Albanian village Tepelen, he was brought up by his mother, Chamko. At the age of fourteen he became a bandit, leading bands of marauders and amassing a great deal of wealth. He increased his power rapidly through treachery, deception, and the indiscriminate murder of relatives and enemies. A skillful manipulator, he convinced the Sultan that these murders were necessary to ensure imperial authority. He was rewarded by being appointed governor of Thessaly in 1786. Two years later, Jannina was added to his pashalik. His rapid rise to power and the expansion of the territories he ruled were helped considerably by an ingeniously planned system of alliances, murders, and extortions.

The major threat to his hegemony at the time were the Souliots, the unsubmissive warrior clans who inhabited the mountain ranges above Jannina. After a series of confrontations, the defiant Souliots proved superior to the Albanian bands Ali sent against them. To subdue them he employed his more successful methods of bribery and trickery. By 1820, however, his insatiable thirst for power and ever increasing grasping of possessions made him suspect in the eyes of the higher Ottoman authorities. They began viewing his schemes and machinations with distrust. War was the only way to curtail his personal power. Finally he was killed by Ottoman imperial soldiers on the island in the lake of Jannina on 22 February 1822.[34]

Pouqueville was familiar with this fierce man's reputation from his first stay in Greece. At that time he had met several French officers who had been prisoners of Ali and had many stories to tell. The French occupation of the Ionian Islands had given rise to a series of negotiations with him during which the French discovered both his duplicity and his admirable perspicacity. Knowing that he would have to deal with him directly made Pouqueville approach his new post with trepidation. Yet there was a certain sense of fascination at the prospect of meeting such an extraordinary man.

In his *Voyage en Morée* he had already given a description of Ali.[35] But since it was based on accounts of others, it lacked the convincing power and the living presence of the second portrait, in the *Voyage dans la Grèce*. This time he had the opportunity to meet the fearsome and wily satrap in person, an event that he recorded dramatically. He describes Ali in his private domain surrounded by boisterous Albanians and meek Greeks. It was a motley gathering of obsequious servants moving about furtively, cunning emissaries and conniving spies, fearsome guards, and obstreperous and unruly warriors. The harem was of course invisible to the foreign visitor, but its presence was nonetheless felt. Oriental opulence and a certain rustic coarseness reflected the love of luxury, the sensuality, and the physical strength of the man who was the master there. No common creature of nature was he. Pouqueville's personal acquaintance with him revealed to him the complex nature and sinister qualities of the powerful pasha.[36]

> My curiosity was keenly piqued: finally I was going to see a very famous man, a new Theseus, an old warrior covered with scars, a satrap grown white in the craft of war, the modern Pyrrhus of Epirus; I had been told all this. We arrive at the gates of the seraglio, which groan as they swing on their hinges; we traverse a silent courtyard, we ascend a dark staircase; a trapdoor is lifted, a curtain is raised, and we find ourselves in the audience chamber of Ali Pasha, who was standing waiting for us.[37]

The meeting took place at night. The room was partially lit by candles emitting a yellowish light. Ali Pasha was the dominant figure and everyone was magnetized by his presence.

> He neared his sixtieth year; his figure, which was scarcely five feet three inches tall, was deformed by excessive corpulence. His features, furrowed by wrinkles, had not been entirely effaced; the playful mobility of his expression, the sparks of his small blue eyes, gave him a terrible mask of cunning combined with ferocity. Among the bursts of guttural laughter, he knew how to say things tinged with a certain grace. (*G*, 1:120)

His entourage consisted mostly of villains and blackguards ready to perform any act no matter how heinous. Thoroughly unscrupulous and otherwise afraid for their own lives, they readily fulfilled their master's dictates and their own violent impulses. Even his seraglios (at Jannina and Tepelen) were imbued with the wickedness of their owner. Within their glittering wealth and sumptuousness—products of Ali's legendary avariciousness—intrigue, suspicion, and fear pervaded every aspect of life. Pouqueville conveys this lugubriousness in his picture of Ali's residence in his native Tepelen. Located in the midst of bare mountains and desolate valleys,

> The seraglio was a prison no less frightening. At the end of the day, its gates were carefully barricaded; armed guards went to their assigned posts; and the echo of the barking of molossian dogs, which were let loose in the courtyards, resounded in the distance. I myself was confined with my domestics to a windowless room. . . . Everything signaled suspicion and surveillance in that abode of tyranny. Several times during the long night I spent there, I heard the noise of the chains of the wretches who groaned in the depths of the subterranean dungeons, as well as the vaults where the treasures of the satrap were deposited, below the sumptuously furnished salons. This luxury, wealth, misery, and wretchedness coexisted in this Tartar, image of sterile opulence and infernal despair. (*G*, 1:286:87)[38]

Pouqueville emphasized the dark nature and oppressive character of Ali Pasha's rule. Though these elements were certainly true, at the same time they lent themselves to dramatic treatment that impresses and startles the reader. Pouqueville sought to produce these effects time and time again. But he was also a writer with a realistic pen-

chant and penetrating insight. He therefore perceived that Ali
Pasha's rule had a few redeeming aspects and that there was more to
the life of this region than terror and destruction. Ali had imposed
a certain order and security, which made the countryside safe from
brigands preying on travelers. Merchants benefited from this and
prospered by making certain concessions to their lord, who exacted
from them a part of their wealth. Jannina, his capital, was a thriving
city of thirty-five thousand people.

Pouqueville was particularly impressed by its commerce, the patriotism and generosity of its more affluent inhabitants, and its educational institutions, which made Jannina a vital center of learning and
culture. He noted that in its schools, Greek, Latin, French, physics,
chemistry, and logic were taught and that some of the most prominent Greek scholars had served there as teachers. Its library possessed
fifteen hundred volumes, not a negligible number for that time and
place. In the *Voyage dans la Grèce* and to some extent in his previous
work, the *Voyage en Morée*, Jannina figures as one of the first cities to
feel the stirrings of educational and cultural resurgence.[39]

Once settled in his post, Pouqueville's curiosity prevailed over his
fears and anxiety. No sooner was he established in Jannina than he
began to explore the adjacent area. His diplomatic status facilitated
his movements in places never before explored by a foreigner. His
enthusiasm and resilience remained undaunted, and his probing
knew no boundaries. A resident of Kastoria, a town in western Macedonia, left us a revealing description of the French visitor.

> During the year 1814, if I am not mistaken, a European traveler vis-
> ited my city, and, as I was informed later, he was the French con-
> sul at Jannina, Mr. Pouqueville. Because his attire was unfamiliar
> in Kastoria, it attracted attention, especially that of children, who
> ran after him wherever they met him. This man indiscriminately
> visited churches, mosques, synagogues, and everything else that
> was worthy of attention in my hometown.[40]

In this brief account three points of interest can be noted: first, the
presence of Europeans was unknown in this area until Pouqueville's
visit, a claim that he made several times; second, it shows the variety
of people who inhabited it, a fact emphasized in the *Voyage dans la
Grèce*; and third, it attests to Pouqueville's inquisitiveness and eagerness to learn and see everything.

His description of modern Greece and its inhabitants followed a twofold scheme. A plethora of numbers and statistics pertaining to the agricultural and maritime life of the country alternated with evocative passages extolling the beauty of the Greek and especially the Epirot landscape and the antique dignity of its mountaineers. Guided by his extensive knowledge of history and geography, he revealed for the first time the life of people hitherto unknown, mainly because few if any foreigners had penetrated their inaccessible abodes. Prominent among them were the inhabitants of the mountain ranges of northwestern Greece and the peasants of the plains. The former impressed him as a vigorous, independent, and intrepid group, whereas the latter, though more industrious, appeared to him more timid and submissive.

Extremely fond of contrasts, Pouqueville offset the violent, aggressive, and fiercely independent *klepht* with the more docile cultivator of the plain who asked for nothing more than peace so as to enjoy the meager fruits of his labor and avoid the wrath of his master. Extending this contrast a little further, he likened the fearless seaman of the Aegean, often given to piracy, to the brigand of the mountains and the comfort-seeking artisan of the towns to the peasant of the lowlands. As was customary with him, he traced these two distinct types back to antiquity. As proof he chose Thessaly, whose towering mountains, picturesque valleys, and fertile plains harbored people of contrasting moral qualities that, according to Pouqueville, had undergone little change through the centuries. "Brave and timid, audacious and effeminate, active and apathetic, forming as of old two different people depending on the locality, they have preserved the qualities that used to be attributed to them and the vices blamed on their indolence."[41]

The categorization of human types according to the places they inhabit is by no means original with Pouqueville. Rather, it is a manifestation of the idea of the influence of climate and physical environment on the character of a people, a theory that was developed and propagated during the eighteenth century. Almost half a century before Pouqueville, Choiseul-Gouffier in his *Discours préliminaire* had applied it in his evaluation of the Greek people. He believed that liberty and independence descended from the mountains, so to speak. Pouqueville expressed the same conviction and with unconcealed admiration depicted the robust men who roamed the highlands. He

felt the same attraction for them as did Childe Harold, who was fascinated by their untamed and fearless character. Pouqueville was one
of the few French travelers of that time to have experienced the invigorating beauty of Greece's precipitous mountains. To Chateaubriand's masterful evocation of graceful lines, delicate contours, and
iridescent light, Pouqueville added a new dimension, more somber
perhaps but equally poignant. For contemporary readers this image
of a rugged and wild Greece added a new feature to its landscape.

Although Pouqueville professed to examine objectively and im-
partially the people whose life he studied, his enthusiasm was more
aroused by what he perceived as the free spirit and individualism of
the mountaineers than by the meekness of the peasants. Like many
city dwellers who envy the hardiness and the simplicity of people
who live closer to nature, Pouqueville idealized the nomads and the
*klepht*s he met and placed them in an idyllic environment. Their
character and milieu lent themselves to romantic treatment and ima-
ginative writing. Pouqueville said that he wrote his descriptive passages not in order to be original, but to express inner feelings elicited
by the places he visited. A lively imagination and his desire to display his literary talent made for a vivid style rich in imagery and
striking details. The mountains of Epirus and Thessaly provided a
fitting background. Moreover, the demeanor and customs of their
people reflected the survival of a more primitive and at the same
time more virile and pristine world. By linking them to the ancient
people who populated the area, Pouqueville unveiled an antiquity
untamed, heroic, and even barbarous existing on the fringes of the
civilized and cultured ancient Greek communities.

Thus Barthélemy's image of a refined and enlightened Greece,
while not renounced, was expanded to include a primordial and unspoiled Greece. Unlike the fragile poleis that disappeared under the
blows of powerful invaders, the resilient mountaineers lived on,
largely unchanged. At least this is how Pouqueville saw them. In
their way of life he discerned a timeless quality that enabled them to
transmit from generation to generation rituals and patterns long ago
established. The shepherds of the Pindus range, who depended on
their flocks of sheep and goats for their livelihood, were able to maintain their essential way of life largely because they were beyond the
reach of their rulers and were not affected by foreign elements. In
their yearly migrations, patriarchal family organization, daily work,
and seasonal festivities, Pouqueville saw the enactment of ancient

traditions and the perpetuation of a long-shaped attitude toward life and the world. Their religious festivals provided diversion and respite from their daily labor. Their tasks, however simple, satisfied their material needs. Above all, their closeness to nature gave them an enviable spiritual calmness and imperturbability.

Undoubtedly Pouqueville romanticized and idealized these people without necessarily distorting their character. Furthermore, the admiration he felt for them was a reflection of the desire inherent in every "civilized" person to shed the strictures of society and enjoy the simple pleasures of nature. Manifold expressions of this attitude are found in French literature, from the *bergers* and *bergères* of pastoral and idyllic poetry and the *romans d'antiquité* patterned after *Daphnis and Chloe,* to the more serious contemplation of a pure and vigorous world by such thinkers as Rousseau.

In presenting these nomads, Pouqueville avoided numbers and statistics, an approach he applied to other groups. Instead he adopted an evocative and graphic mode of expression. Throughout his treks in the mountains of Epirus he witnessed scenes of bucolic charm, which he later presented in portraits of groups and individuals. His intent was to add variety to an otherwise factual narrative and inject a note of subjectivity. Furthermore, the alternation of these two modes, the objective and the evocative, reflected a dualism in Pouqueville's temperament. An insistence on facts, on a systematic description of observable events and minute details, reveals a desire— almost a compulsion—to be true, thorough, and all-inclusive. His emotional outbursts, on the other hand, attest to his ability to be moved by natural beauty and human suffering and to appreciate heroism, courage, and individualism. Thus in his own limited way, Pouqueville mirrored the intellectual and literary transition from the eighteenth to the nineteenth century, from rationalism to romanticism. In his evaluation of Greece he admired order, progress, and signs of enlightenment, and at the same time he sublimated the fierceness, daring, and prowess of the intrepid mountaineer.

One of Pouqueville's recurrent devices was the use of representative types encapsulating the essential physical traits and moral qualities of the various inhabitants of Greece. Thus we have a series of composite sketches of the Turk, the Albanian, the *klepht,* the artisan, and many others. It is evident that these portraits were intended to embody the characteristics of a group.

One such group, whose warlike ethos and defiant character Pouqueville admired and extolled, were the *klepht*s, or brigands. Armed outlaws, who from the earliest days of Turkish occupation had found their natural abode in the steep mountain ranges of Greece, their numbers were continually increased by fugitives from central authority, poverty or social forces imposing discipline and obedience. Once they became members of a band, they owed allegiance to their chiefs, known as *kapetanioi*. Regardless of their geographic distribution and varied origins, the *klepht*s shared a way of life and inner organization. Living outside the established social order, they were a law unto themselves. They enjoyed military feats, exalted warlike skills and virtues, and despised menial work. They lived by plundering and robbing wealthy landowners and merchants, attacking affluent Greeks and Turks indiscriminately. The latter, however, were raided more often because they were a more lucrative source of plunder and because they were of a different race, religion, and social class. Often these brigands exercised control over entire villages at the foothills of the mountains by exacting tribute in exchange for protection.

To defend themselves against the predatory *klepht*s, the Ottoman authorities employed mercenary bands known as *armatoloi*. The *armatoloi* were used to curb brigandage, secure open communications, guard key passes, and maintain order. Many Greek landowners resorted to this system of defense. The *armatoloi* differed from the *klepht*s in that they had the right to bear arms and thus were lawful warriors. They operated and lived in communities whereas the *klepht*s roamed the mountains in bands. The similarities between the two groups, however, were greater than their differences. Often the line between them was not very clear. The distinction was blurred even more by the practice of the Turks of recruiting *armatoloi* from the ranks of the *klepht*s. In other words, they legalized brigands so as to subdue other brigands for the simple reason that they employed the same tactics and had the same skills. Thus a *klepht* could change status overnight by enlisting in the service of a local pasha or a wealthy landowner. When his duties became too restrictive and unprofitable, he could return to the mountains and join his former companions.

The *klepht*s, with their martial qualities and redoubtable courage, became the objects of admiration of the simple folk, who saw in them the protagonists of defiant opposition to established but often

repressive authority. In the *klepht*'s uncompromising pride and independence, his physical endurance and intrepidity, and above all his
cult of personal freedom—qualities that overshadowed his violence
and cruelty—the common people saw the realization of desires that
they could not fulfill. An entire body of oral folk poetry that
revolved around the character and the feats of the *klepht*s testified to
the appeal they had enjoyed among the people. What the folk poet
wanted to capture and convey was not so much the heroic deeds performed by extraordinary beings as the human will to harness adversity and the refusal to surrender one's personal freedom. In other
words, it was the manner in which the *klepht* confronted life and
death that moved the creator or creators of these folk songs, or *klephtika*. His deeds, insofar as they were important, were the vehicles for
these attitudes.

As expressed in the original folk songs, the concept of freedom
was a pursuit of personal independence and not a commitment to
national liberation.[42] Later the contribution of the *klepht*s and the
armatoloi to the Greek Revolution led many commentators of the
folk songs to attribute patriotism and national consciousness to
these brigands. They erroneously identified a highly individualistic
ethos with nationalism at a time when the latter hardly existed
among the common people.

Pouqueville came to know the *klepht*s when their reputation as
protagonists of national independence was spreading. He not only
accepted this image, but he also elaborated and embellished it in his
own manner. Since he knew their language, he listened to their
songs and described and commented on them extensively. He interpreted them as a poetic recreation and exaltation of their feats, allegiance to their chief, sufferings, and above all lifelong dedication to
arms and war. Antedating Fauriel by a few years, he saw in these
songs the preservation and commitment to collective memory of historically significant deeds and events.

Pouqueville contributed enthusiastically to the romanticizing of
the *klepht*s that had already begun. Their brigandage and violence
were, in his view, mitigated by their love for their country. He
argued that a national consciousness had already taken root among
them and that he was able to verify this by personal observation.
Once, for example, while he was traversing the southern Peloponnesus, he chanced to meet a band of *klepht*s whose chief was Kolokotro-

nis, the famous revolutionary hero. "Fear nothing, they told me
. . . we are all robbers, but brave robbers who respect the consuls of
the Christian kings."[43] They ate roasted kid, then they drank to the
liberty of Greece, and finally they finished their feast by singing
songs.

Pouqueville attributed their harsh character and actions to the
tyranny and oppression that had forced them to go to the mountains, not to any self-serving motives. These men were accustomed
"to scorning life, braving torture, countering violence with violence,
fanaticism with fanaticism. . . . Accustomed to privations, inured to
fatigue, without a country in the middle of their country, exiled in
the midst of their native land . . . they embark on a career of brigandage with an audaciousness worthy of a better cause" (G, 4:37–39). He
drew their character as a mixture of fierceness and loyalty. They
moved swiftly from one mountain to another, appeared and disappeared at will, and suffered physical privations with astounding
endurance. Though they were cruel to their enemies, they treated
priests and women with the utmost respect. Their temperament was
violent and explosive, their pride inordinate, but their morals puri-
tanical. Obviously, the saga of the *klepht* had found a sympathetic
audience in Pouqueville.

In his view, brigands were not a modern phenomenon but an
ancient occupation characteristic of certain Greek groups. First,
some slaves of the ancients, victims of an unjust institution, escaped
to the mountains and became robbers, avenging themselves by
attacking travelers from their hideouts. In mythology, Theseus subdued these ancient brigands and murderers. Later, Pouqueville
remarked, when Greece succumbed to one foreign conqueror after
another, it was they who preserved the spirit of freedom. The Turkish conquest strengthened their ranks by forcing more and more
young men to join them, and it intensified their belligerence. Thus,
if the time ever came for the Greeks to overthrow Ottoman rule,
they would be an invaluable fighting force.

Pouqueville described the life of the *klepht* using instances he had
witnessed. His testimony makes his narrative both more vivid and
picturesque and more personal and concrete. However, his habit of
injecting a melodramatic note and distilling moral qualities that
ennobled the *klepht* has been characterized as an unwarranted exaggeration that detracts from the credibility of his account. Yet the

character and the life style of the *klepht* could easily arouse the emotions of a passionate man such as Pouqueville.

Pouqueville's familiarity with the court of Ali Pasha afforded him the opportunity to witness instances of undisputed courage. He once saw a *klepht* tied to the stake, his body bearing the disfiguring marks of torture. But his glance, according to Pouqueville, was clear and direct and his expression calm with the assurance that he had not betrayed himself. Pouqueville remembered having seen him when he was the leader of a band. Now a captive, he was still proud and uncompromising. Such steadfastness under the most adverse conditions made a strong impression on the French consul and confirmed his admiration for the *klephts*.[44]

Another warlike people known for their independent and defiant character was the Souliots, who inhabited the craggy ranges overlooking the course of the Acheron. Pouqueville visited their rugged homeland and described it in a striking manner.

> The path of the traveler soon becomes as constricted as that of the river, which can be heard roaring in the abyss and whose course appears as a blackish line lost in the depths of the abyss. He walks on a narrow path rising six or seven hundred feet above the precipices, brushing against frightful rocks and the debris of schists, which leads him to chasms whose openings are the receptacle of torrents and avalanches. . . . In the middle of this labyrinth, among these crags, one walks more than a league skirting. . . . Selleis, whose depth the eye does not dare fix nor look at without feeling dizziness at the view of mountains rising like gigantic ramparts in the higher regions of the air.[45]

The social organization of the Souliots was centered on certain prominent family clans that exercised authority over the other members of the community. They despised menial labor and prized martial excellence. They made their livelihood by exacting tribute from the peasants of the richer parts of their territory and by occasional raids on the villages of the lowlands. Their strength stemmed from their military prowess and the geography of the area, which made their strongholds inaccessible. This enabled them to remain largely unfettered by Ottoman authority. Of all those who tried to subdue them, none was as persistent and relentless as Ali Pasha. Their resistance spread their fame as valiant warriors and stirred feelings of admiration among Greeks and foreign travelers alike.

Pouqueville was aware of their reputation even before he came to Jannina. Their fearlessness, stubborn resistance, and self-sacrifice in the face of inevitable doom impressed him. He was one of the first foreign travelers to record an episode that became a legend in modern Greek folklore: the famous dance of the Souliot women. When Ali Pasha's forces finally blockaded the Souliots and penetrated their mountain fastness, their women congregated with their children on an elevation overlooking a precipice. Forming a circle, they began to dance. As they approached the cliff they threw themselves off one by one, preferring death to certain slavery. This story acquired mythical dimensions and was used to instill pride in future generations. Pouqueville saw in it an expression of the free spirit of the Greeks.

However, Pouqueville's attitude toward the Souliots was ambivalent. While he admired their warlike qualities, he criticized their lack of industriousness and progress. This ambivalence is mirrored in his portrait of the typical Souliot:

> His medium height, his booming voice like that of an eagle, his gestures, his brusque and agile movements announce a mountain warrior. His irascibility and outbursts reveal his ancient origin. . . . Avid for fighting and loot, proud in prosperity and intrepid in adversity, he scorns fatigue, dangers, and death in order to attain his goal. . . . Uncaring about the future, living entirely for the present, his feasts are a delirium, and he seeks repose only when he is overcome with wine and pleasure. (G, 2:230–31)[46]

This lack of providence and temperance offended Pouqueville. Furthermore, the Souliots' contribution to Greece's advancement was minimal since they had no use for commerce, the "foundation of all civilization, and expected everything from the violence of their sword, preferring the life of a *klepht* or a highwayman to improve their lot to the honorable occupation of agriculture and the crafts."[47]

Pouqueville, however, found nothing objectionable in the behavior of the *klepht*s who had the same ethos. This contradiction was reflected in Pouqueville's own temperament. A proponent of progress and enlightenment, he nonetheless was attracted by the freer way of life that valued pride and independence. But he could accept this way of life only to the extent that it served the aspirations and the ideals of the rest of society. Thus the *klepht*s epitomized the desire of the Greeks to be free. They took to the mountains, Pouqueville thought, to flee from oppression and not because they found violence and brigandage intrinsically attractive. In a just and equitable society, he would argue, such behavior would not be acceptable. In the case of the Souliots, who, unlike the *klepht*s, lived in settled communities and were not fugitives from the authorities, the practice of brigandage and pillage seemed unsavory.

If the heroic character of the people of northwestern Greece stirred Pouqueville's emotions, the beauty of its land kindled his imagination. The progressive emergence of the Greek landscape from Guys to Pouqueville is interesting because it reveals both the temperament of individual writers and the gradual affirmation of external nature. Guys paid little attention to it because he sought the survival of antiquity in people, not in nature. It must be remembered that Guys was a classical humanist writing in the 1760s for whom human activities were more important than their physical setting. When Choiseul-Gouffier visited the Greek lands, he was captivated by the charm and grace of the Attic and the Aegean scenery. In the superb drawings that illustrated his *Voyage pittoresque de la Grèce,* the landscape was interwoven with the ruined monuments that were embedded in it. When Chateaubriand came, he brought with him a descriptive talent far superior to that of any of his compatriots who visited Greece at that time. In his *Itinéraire* the suggestiveness of the landscape and its external features and contours attained a perfect balance. Still, nature was not entirely free from his own quest for historical and personal meaning. His landscape bore the imprint of his inner vision of the world.

It was mainly the Attic and the Aegean scenery that figured prominently in the writings of these travelers. Farther north, however, there lay a Greece unspoiled, untamed, and largely free from antique associations. Lord Byron was captivated by its pristine and wild beauty. Likewise, Pouqueville felt its exhilarating and sweeping power and set about capturing it. He compensated for his lack of stylistic originality and immoderate effusiveness by a sincere appreciation of his surroundings and a sensitivity to natural beauty. He felt its impact even more intensely because he believed that nature influences the character and the life of the people it harbors. Thus the portrayal of the Greek landscape from Guys to Pouqueville acquired expanding dimensions. It progressed from the celebration of the Greek sea and the Greek sun to the delineation of the more somber and harsh northern regions of the country. Inherent in this movement was a partial disengagement of the physical setting from its history. Lingering memories of a vanished past always persisted, but now nature revealed itself in its full glory:

> And yet how lovely in thine age of woe,
> Land of lost gods and godlike men! art
> thou!
> Thy vales of evergreen, thy hills of snow,
> Proclaim thee Nature's varied favorite now.[48]

Pouqueville was particularly fond of the Epirot landscape. During his explorations of the countryside, he tells us, he often found repose in a valley or on a hilltop and gazed at the unfolding view. In his contemplation of natural scenery, he rarely indulged in recollections of antiquity. Here is a typical scene that recreates the lines, sounds, and colors of an idyllic view:

> There began to unfold before my eyes the horizon of Drynopolis on the morning of one of the most beautiful days of the year, which seemed as a creation all the more beautiful because I was coming out of the lugubrious vale of Tepelen. The perfumed breeze, which announced the return of the sun, the concerts of the birds, the bleatings of innumerable flocks, which were lined in long columns on the mountains, recalled the charms of rural life and the innocent happiness of shepherds. I admired the reborn view of hamlets that were illuminated imperceptibly, the swift streams rushing from the mountains, the silvery brooks coming out of dark forests . . . as I walked amid a succession of enchanting scenes.[49]

Pouqueville's descriptive powers lost their freshness and élan when he was surrounded by classical locales. Nowhere else is this more evident than in his picture of Athens and its monuments, which he visited in 1815 on his way to Patras.[50] He felt impelled to pay homage to the city of Athena because he believed that, had he failed to do so, his knowledge of Greece would have been incomplete. He speaks of his excitement upon approaching the hallowed places of the city and of his eagerness to set eyes on the Parthenon.

> I was burning with impatience; finally the stars began to pale and the dawning day revealed the acropolis of Athens. The temple of Minerva, which appeared before me, seemed to rest on the clouds

because of a dense fog accumulated between its hills. This mist created a ravishing optical illusion. I was in a state of ecstasy; but when the sun dissipated it, the Parthenon remained isolated on the rock, which rises like an altar, and I saw nothing but a sad barrenness, a soil stripped of verdure and rocks calcified by time. (*G*, 5:20)

By reading this description carefully one realizes that he is not expressing his own feelings. His words echo sentiments and attitudes voiced by so many others before him. His visits to sites associated with the classical world were rituals accompanied by all the appropriate clichés, but displaying little of the prodigious energy and enthusiasm that he lavished on northwestern Greece. Instinctively he felt that he entered a domain explored by others, and he was neither ready nor willing to compete with them. Still, he felt obliged to utter a few expressions of regret and nostalgia for the glories of the past. He even sketched a few scenes of ancient monuments in a grand, Chateaubriandesque manner. But his vigor and exultation seem to ebb away when he entered classical terrain.

His extolling of the antiquities notwithstanding, Pouqueville was not attracted either to the Athenian landscape or to its inhabitants. Physical barrenness was accompanied by human stagnation, which, by means of contrast, recalled all the more vividly the eclipsed glory of the ancients. Once more the ideal Athens dwarfed the modern one and made its infirmities appear even more disfiguring. "Modern Athens has undergone so many misfortunes that one would recognize none of its ancient physiognomy if one looked only at its inhabitants in order to judge the centuries of Themistocles and Pericles. Genius, the letters, and the fine arts have fled from this desolate province" (*G*, 5:90–91).

And yet Pouqueville was aware that not all learning was defunct and not all cultural life was tenebrous. He knew about the activities of the Athens Society of the Philomousoi, which was founded in 1813 and whose aim was to disseminate knowledge based on classical ideals and European models of education. But, contrary to one's expectations, the Athenian society failed to gain Pouqueville's approbation. He berated its teachers, all young and inexperienced in his estimation, for their superficial acquaintance with the classical past and hollow infatuation with it. He derided them for promoting the use of ancient Greek names instead of teaching their students the rudiments of learning and sound moral principles.

Why this mockery and deprecation of the Athenian educational society when Pouqueville lauded signs of learning and enlightenment elsewhere in Greece? Did Fauvel, who made no secret of his disdain and derision for the modern Athenians, transmit these negative attitudes to his fellow consul, as some critics have suggested? Although Pouqueville's scathing pronouncements were in consonance with Fauvel's views, their source can be located in the contrastive approach that informed his own treatment of the Greek world. To the ubiquitous diachronic contrast between the ancients and the moderns, Pouqueville added the synchronic antithesis among the various strata of modern Greek society. There were the indomitable mountaineers and the docile plain dwellers, the pretentious and affected *nouveaux riches* and the simple and unalloyed common people. Pouqueville's sympathy and admiration lay with the last group because it was in them that he detected the survival of ancient traits and an unadulterated Christian faith; it was they who embodied the true national character of the Greeks.

> These virtues of hospitality, as I have said, are no longer practiced, outside the cloisters, anywhere except under the nomads' tents or in the huts of the poor of Greece. It is also among the people where the type of national virtues that distinguished the Greeks before they became, as Aristotle remarked, corrupted by luxury, were preserved. . . . It is in those classed respectable by their steady forebearance of misfortune that one finds the songs intended to cheer the toils and hardship of the men who earn their bread with the sweat of their brow under the burden of the day. (G, 5:436)

One may conjecture, then, that Pouqueville's castigation of the modern Athenians derived from his view that they exhibited none of the virtues of the simple folk. Their educational society, therefore, appeared to him as a fatuous mimicry of high culture.

Yet it would be misleading to think of Pouqueville as an opponent of progress and the advancement of learning. He advocated their propagation under certain conditions: they had to be intertwined with those time-honored traditions that bound Greek society since antiquity; also, they had to be in consonance with the Christian faith of the people. Unlike the other philhellenes of his time, Pouqueville saw no inherent contradiction between progress and adherence to established cultural and religious practices. On the contrary, he maintained that only their successful merging would ensure the viability and advancement of the Greek communities. In Kastoria he witnessed the activities of such a community in which cosmopolitanism and traditionalism existed side by side.

> Some spoke German, others Slavic, a small number knew Italian, and almost all of them possessed in a high degree of perfection literary Greek, which is now the basis of public education in the schools of Greece. I observed that these merchants, in spite of the habits they had contracted abroad, conformed, when they appeared before their metropolitan, to the ancient etiquette of worship, which they performed by prostrating themselves and by advancing respectfully to this feet, from where they rose only after having received his benediction and kissed his hand. . . . When they were all assembled, they informed me that they were going to attend to the affairs of the eparchy, an ordinary object of deliberations of this religious and civil assembly, in which a suffragan bishop and the deacons were admitted to participate under the direction of the notables. (G, 3:2)

The community at large abided by the decisions of the mixed council, a practice that Pouqueville found "prudent and wise."

The participation of ecclesiastics in the management of community affairs would undoubtedly have been decried by any other European visitor as a sign of the church's stifling influence on the social and cultural life of the Greeks. Not only did Pouqueville refrain from such accusations, but he perceived the role of the church as an integral and vital force in the communal existence of the Greeks. The absence of a censorious tone in his treatment of the Orthodox church was a departure from previous and contemporary philhellenic thought and sentiments. This novel element was due as much to Pouqueville's open and direct approach to the modern Greek world as to the waning anticlericalism in early nineteenth century France.

Kastoria was a prosperous community whose leading citizens made their fortunes as merchants in the Balkans and Western Europe. This was not, however, the lot of all the Greeks, particularly those who cultivated the land. Even when nature rewarded their toil, the tax collector and the purchasing agents of the monopolies saw to it that their harvest was depleted while their compensation was minimal. The effects of this economic repression and exploitation, com-

pounded by the indifference of a distant and ineffectual central government, were debilitating for the peasants and injurious to the general welfare of the state as well.

Unlike the oppressive and restricted world of the Greek peasant,
who was bound to the land, the merchant and especially the mariner
enjoyed relative freedom of movement, which allowed them to exercise their ingenuity and their business acumen. Pouqueville espoused
the commonly held view that commerce had been the trademark of
the Greeks since the dawn of their civilization.

The Greeks penetrated the trade routes to the Near East during the
second half of the eighteenth century. Before the 1770 insurrection,
Pouqueville tells us, Marseilles imported large quantities of silk from
Kalamata. The commercial link between Marseilles and Kalamata
was strong. Ships sailed from the ports of the southern Peloponnesus
loaded with leather goods, silk, cotton, and grain. After the suppression of the 1770 uprising, the economy of the Morea was severely
affected. But the maritime power of some of the Aegean Islands began
to grow. This development was abetted considerably by Russia's offer
to let Greek ships sail under its flag, a measure that protected them
from Ottoman restrictions. Pouqueville used the island of Hydra as
an example of the organization, management, and operation of the
Greek merchant marine. He observed that although the Greek sea-
men had little technical training in navigation, their experience, skill-
fulness, and hardiness made them incomparable mariners.

The turmoil created by the French Revolution was a boon for the
Greek-owned merchant ships because they filled the gap left by the
disarray that incapacitated the French commercial fleet. The Morea
benefited indirectly from the activities of the shipowners of Hydra
and Spetsai. By 1798 its population had risen to 240,000 Christians
and 40,000 Turks.

This momentum abated somewhat at the beginning of the nineteenth century, but the wars of Spain and the Continental blockade
gave a further impetus to the commercial activities of the Greeks.
The dramatic rise in the fortunes of the Greek marine merchants
was exemplified by the inhabitants of Galaxidion, a small town on
the littoral to the south of Delphi.

The personal holdings of the Galaxidiotes, consisting of ships of
all sizes, are estimated to be fifteen thousand Turkish piasters, and

their capital amounts to an equal sum. Without a doubt, never did the public fortune of the Ozoles Locreans rise to such a degree; one is surprised to find in present-day Greece such a wealth as in this gulf region that was scarcely known a few years ago. (*G*, 4:46)

Pouqueville's depiction of the modern Greek world was a kaleidoscope of people and places. Although the old stereotypes of the Greek character as a mélange of duplicity, mendacity, and shiftiness persisted,[51] the Greeks in Pouqueville's narrative are a multifaceted society, not merely the shadowy reflections of their ancestors. Pouqueville noted that a substantial number of them were no longer the passive victims of oppression languishing under the Turkish yoke but were actively engaged in bettering their lot through commerce and education. The relative complexity of early nineteenth-century Greek society described in the *Voyage dans la Grèce* was at variance with previous and contemporary travel accounts, most of which focused on a particular geographic location, primarily the islands, Attica, and the Peloponnesus, and on a specific segment of the population.

Pouqueville differed from the majority of French observers of the modern Greek scene in that he presented a wider and more varied picture of it. But he shared their views on the historical development of Greece. In the speculative and theoretical parts of his text, he voiced the commonly held concept of a descending line from the zenith of classical Hellas to the nadir of Ottoman occupation. Like other philhellenes of his time, he viewed the Byzantine era of Greek history as an epoch of ignorance and superstition. (*G*, 1:liv).[52]

However injurious the legacy of the Byzantines was to the modern Greeks, fortunately it did not make as lasting an imprint on them as their classical heritage had. This belief led Pouqueville to trace the roots of the religious practices of the Greek Orthodox Christians to pagan antiquity. It is indicative of the persistence of the basic premises of philhellenism that almost fifty years after Guys we find the same arguments and the same parallelisms in the *Voyage dans la Grèce* as in the *Voyage littéraire de la Grèce*.

In the eyes of these two French writers, Eastern Orthodoxy had little in common with Western Christianity. For Pouqueville as well as for Guys, ancient rituals and patterns of worship had survived under the guise of Christian practices. The veneration of saints appeared to them as the continuation of the cult of gods and demi-gods. Religious festivities were compared to the celebrations of the ancients, and the superstitious beliefs of the people were traced back to antiquity. The myths and fables of a pagan religion had found new forms of expression in the lives and miracles of the saints.

The two religions shared modes of worship and were practiced in the same physical setting; Christian churches and chapels were erected on the very precincts of ancient temples. The advent of Christianity, then, if it signified any change at all in the religious out-look of the Greeks, affected only the outer forms of its expression, not its spirit.

> Always scintillating with enthusiasm, those [the beliefs] of the Greeks, although they became Christians, have remained full of idolatrous ideas. The saints, stripped of the thyrsus and the lyre, replaced the demigods; and the Panagia, who has been substituted everywhere for the good goddess, just like the icons for the legend-ary heroes, received the homage that is due only to the creator. (*G*, 4:406)

Pouqueville interpreted the religious beliefs of the Greeks, both ancient and modern, as the manifestations of a lively imagination that animated the universe with divine and semidivine beings. He was ambivalent toward this pantheistic mentality. On the one hand, he lauded the continuity of age-old beliefs that bound the Greek peo-ple through the millennia. On the other, he considered the myths of the ancients and their subsequent transmutations as fictions gratify-ing the emotions and stimulating the imagination but not condu-cive to higher spiritual truths. The same penchant for embellish-ment that had survived in the rituals and ceremonies of the people had also permeated the writings of the early fathers of the church. "The first church fathers, instead of announcing the divine word in its simplicity, entered the field by taking the colors of their adversar-ies. The graces of speech and the charms of style were therefore presented during the first period, because the new doctors, by model-ing themselves on the classics, wanted to prove the principles of the Gospel in Demosthenes' style." (*G*, 6:135)

Pouqueville's amphibolic attitude toward the religious precepts and traditions of the Greeks from antiquity to the present is indica-tive of the dualism of his own temperament: his romantic sensibilities disposed him favorably toward the spontaneous and emotional character of the Greeks, while his rational and analytical turn of mind objected to the figurative and symbolic ways of apprehending the world.

Although Pouqueville was negative in his assessment of Byzantium and although he was sceptical about the spiritual values of Eastern Orthodoxy, he viewed the role of the church in Ottoman Greece in a positive light. In the absence of a sovereign state directing the affairs of the people, the church was the only institution to which they could turn for guidance and leadership. "Since the time of the conquest, the Orthodox church has remained the repository of a very extensive power over the faithful of the Greek community. It is to this mother that they addressed their sighs, and they have never ceased to find in her inexhaustible consolation."[53]

In the long line of French travelers to Greece who commented on the Orthodox church, beginning with the sixteenth century naturalist Belon, Pouqueville was among the first not to denounce it as a body of ignorant, fanatic, and schismatic priests. Instead, he saw it as a powerful and complex institution whose authority and influence reached the people through a tiered network of episcopal sees and local churches. Not only had the church been the focal point of the Greeks' communal life during the centuries of Ottoman rule, but it would, in Pouqueville's judgment, play an equally important role in the struggle for independence if and when the Greeks rose against their rulers. To the potent stimulus of Hellenism, Pouqueville joined Christianity as a force propelling them toward the path of liberation. Pleading for the liberation of the Greeks in the name of their Hellenic lineage had become a commonplace by that time. But to see them as adherents of one faith subjugated by those of another was a novel attitude, and Pouqueville was one of its first exponents.

His treatment of the Greek caloyer, a figure so often maligned by foreign visitors, was also novel. Whereas other travelers, Choiseul-Gouffier among them, had pictured an ignoble and benighted figure whose ignorance was surpassed only by his cunning and greed, Pouqueville portrayed a venerable personage of dignified demeanor and simple, genuine faith.

The illuminated face of the good prior, his cheerfulness, his turn of mind reminded me of what the chroniclers say of the superiors of our abbeys at a time when France boasted its gallant knights, its mitred abbés, and its troubadours. The Superior Gregory had all this; he drank, he sang improvised songs, and, in his youth, more than one Turk had felt the force of his arm; but, as with all drinkers, he was an honest man. . . . His white beard, agitated by the wind, reflected a gentle light in his face; thick waves of hair fell on the broad folds of his vestments, and his smile, reflection of the inner peace of his conscience, animated all his features.[54]

This romanticized image of an Orthodox monk was but one example in a series of composite portraits that animated Pouqueville's narrative. Whether they depicted a shepherd, a *klepht*, or a caloyer, they all had certain common features: a proud dignity, an almost primal simplicity, and a free and fearless spirit. These were the attributes that were best preserved among the inhabitants of the remote mountain areas, Pouqueville maintained, that linked the modern Greeks with their ancient progenitors. By identifying certain individual and social traits as Hellenic, Pouqueville, like Guys, posited the existence of a Hellenic ethos little subject to historical change. Also, by associating the modern Greek mountaineer with his ancient prototype, he revealed "by certain details that have survived . . . a wild, mysterious, and consequently an even new antiquity."[55] In this instance philhellenism modified, expanded, and even enriched Hellenism by projecting a more primeval and robust Hellenic world.

If Pouqueville extolled the virtues of the free-spirited mountain dweller, he was no less generous in his praise of the industrious and progressive merchant. Greece needed both of them in order to gain its freedom and establish a viable state: the former's courage and intrepidity would serve its cause on the battlefield and the latter's education and entrepreneurial skills would direct its political and economic affairs. Clearly, Pouqueville perceived the different strata of modern Greek society and delineated their role in the shaping of this society. But he attributed their strength and momentum not so much to the dynamics of their own activities and to their own initiative as to the regenerative influence of their ancient heritage.

One recognizes the Greek, as well as the monuments of his country, by his classical type, by the grace of the brilliant ideas that he preserves; and just as in those mutilated horses of the school of Phidias, where one finds the imprint of the *beau idéal*, one discerns in the traits of the people, who were subjugated twice, the noble origin from which they were descended. . . . One is astonished how, after all these vicissitudes, the descendants of the Hellenes, deprived of the glorious name of their ancestors, have lasted as a nation. (*G,* 6:122)[56]

In tracing the development of French philhellenism from Voltaire to Pouqueville, one can discern two salient characteristics that marked its course: an attachment to the classical past bound up with an unwavering faith in its rejuvenating influence on the present, and the advocacy of the political emancipation of the modern Greeks as a means of bringing about the revival of this past.

Within this broad spectrum, however, there were shifting perspectives and differences among individual observers as well as between the two more or less distinct generations of philhellenes who spanned this era. Voltaire and Choiseul-Gouffier supported liberation, but their vision of a free Greece existed more in the realm of the ideal and less in the world of attainable reality. Even Guys, although more optimistic and confident in the ability of the Greeks to shape their destiny, did not see their independence as forthcoming. What was a vague wish, stemming more from a sentimental contemplation of the classical past than from a firm commitment to the present in these eighteenth century philhellenes, became a strong conviction in Firmin-Didot, Pouqueville, and Marcellus.

These three differed from the philhellenes of the previous century by presenting a broader and more complex Greek world and perceiving progress and the first vibrations of national consciousness among the Greeks of their day. They believed that liberation was both realizable and imminent. The outbreak of the Greek Revolution shortly after their departure from Greece justified their expectations. Of the three, Pouqueville and Firmin-Didot lent their active support to the insurgents, the first through his writings and the second by making his publishing establishment available to the promoters of philhellenism. They, along with a host of other philhellenes, wielded their prestige and influence to mobilize public opinion in favor of the Greeks and persuade the French government to intervene on their behalf.

EPILOGUE: REBIRTH
AMID THE RUINS

The year 1821 was a turning point in the progress of philhellenism because at last it seemed possible that one of its expectations, the liberation of the Greeks, might be fulfilled. This historical milestone changed the character of philhellenism from a theoretical concern for the condition of the modern Greeks to a concrete commitment to their fate, which was being decided both on the battlefield and in European political and diplomatic circles. Between 1821 and the creation of the independent Greek state in 1830, the diffuse philhellenic strands of the preceding fifty years crystallized. Those philhellenes who fought alongside the Greek insurgents and the more numerous ones who galvanized public opinion at home acted on the liberal, humanistic, and philanthropic principles that had already been voiced by such figures as Voltaire, the young Choiseul-Gouffier, and Pouqueville.

The French public was all the more receptive to the cause of the Greeks because it had been made aware of their plight through the long series of travel accounts going back to the sixteenth century. The rediscovery of the Greek lands and the modern Greeks was by and large due to Western travelers who began to visit the Near East in the early modern era. Until then, Greece as a physical entity had fallen into a state of oblivion, and medieval Europe identified its existence with faint images of its classical past which reached it from Roman sources. It was the explorers of the Renaissance and post-Renaissance periods who bridged the fissure between the geography of Greece and its cultural heritage in the West. Their descriptions encompassed three aspects: monuments, landscape, and the people. The development of these themes followed an uneven pace because they reflected the literary and cultural trends of the travelers' own time and milieu.

Although sixteenth-century French and European visitors in general expressed admiration for the ancients, their knowledge of Greek antiquity was nebulous and their remarks on classical monuments, if they made them at all, were at best passing. There are three main reasons for this seeming neglect. First, the legacy of the Greeks, as distinct from that of the Romans, was just beginning to assert itself in European thought. The first creations to be examined, however, were not the monuments but Greek texts. Second, most sixteenth-century French travelers to the Near East were naturalists, whose main interest was the observation of natural phenomena and social customs. Third, their itinerary followed the already established trade routes to the Near East, which did not include Attica and the Peloponnesus, the two pivotal centers of classical Greek antiquity.

It was not until the second half of the seventeenth century that ancient monuments became the focus of attention. Not unexpectedly, it was Athens that drew the first French systematic observer of Greek monuments, Jacob Spon. He recorded meticulously their current state and ventured to make some perspicacious, though not always accurate, conjectures about their origin. Also during this time, the activities of antiquarians and procurers of antiquities increased in the Greek lands and the Near East. Employed by wealthy patrons, including the French monarch, these agents scoured monastic libraries, classical sites, and markets in search of coins, ancient texts, and any art objects they could find. Unlike Spon and other serious students of antiquity, these emissaries were primarily merchants, who looked at the monuments as sources of gain and favor from highly placed personages. Nevertheless, the antiquities they brought back intensified the already strong interest in the ancients and spurred more travelers to journey to those lands.

By the end of the eighteenth century, the profile of those monuments that stood above ground had been carefully delineated. Alongside this objective approach, there arose at that time a new attitude toward the relics of antiquity. The classicists of the preceding two centuries had looked at them as the isolated signposts of a bygone era. They measured and described them painstakingly, but they rarely tried to place them in their natural setting or capture the spirit that had created them. The romantic Hellenists, on the other hand, added a sentimental and aesthetic dimension to the hitherto historical one. In their eyes, a ruin glimmered with the radiance, faint though it might be, of the life that had nurtured it.

The revelation of the Greek landscape in the pages of travel narratives followed a trajectory similar to that of the monuments. It proceeded from the impersonal and objective descriptions of the sixteenth-century naturalists to the emotionally charged and evocative depictions of the travelers of the pre-Romantic and Romantic eras. Its progressive unfolding was a gradual unveiling of contours where colors and lines fused with legends and fables. Choiseul-Gouffier, one of the first French travelers to place ancient monuments in their natural surroundings, was captivated by the delicacy and limpidity of the Greek shores and islands. Chateaubriand's magnificent tableaux were the creations of an intense lyricism and a sweeping imagination, which blended the external world with the inner quest of his own destiny. Pouqueville, the last important French observer before the Greek Revolution, revealed a robust and untamed Greece by focusing his attention on the rugged northern regions of the land and their indomitable inhabitants. In his pages we witness the emergence of a more vigorous, primal past and a more dynamic present.

Monuments and natural scenes were the physical setting that encased the life of the modern Greeks. Their collective character and their social and religious practices were treated and recorded extensively by all travelers. Certain criteria remained unchanged during the centuries studied in this work. Invariably, the assessment of their material and cultural life was predicated on the achievements of the ancients. Contrasting the preclassical and postclassical eras of Hellenism was a ubiquitous theme in all travel accounts. The modern Greeks were found lacking in those qualities that had distinguished their ancestors. From the universal point of view, their fate illustrated the law of rise and fall.

Yet not all continuity had been severed. Similarities still existed, some of them in a latent state, others more apparent. But of the traits that survived, not all were edifying. In fact, many travelers pointed out that the modern Greeks delighted in exhibiting some of the less commendable propensities of their ancestors, such as frivolity, craftiness, and contentiousness. In a more positive vein, some of the practices and creative impulses of the ancients had survived in the religious and social observances of the people.

The antithesis between the ancients and the moderns led inevitably to the examination of the decline of the latter. It is here that one can see the evolution of attitudes during the centuries considered in this study. Sixteenth- and seventeenth-century accounts abound in comments on the abasement of the modern Greeks. However, when they examined its etiology, which was infrequent, they attributed it more to inner forces of decay and to the stray ways of the Greeks and less to Ottoman rule. Expressions of sympathy were rare, and the wish to see the Greeks liberated was nonexistent. Just as the landscape elicited no emotional response in these detached observers, the lot of the subjugated Greeks drew from them no cries of protest against their rulers. This would have been untimely given the unquestionable authority and unquestioned legitimacy of monarchical rule.

It was during the eighteenth century when the power and the prerogatives of monarchs and noblemen were attacked and the natural and civil rights of man were defended that the decline of the modern Greeks began to be viewed as the consequence of the loss of their political freedom first under the Byzantines and then under the Ottomans. The linking of politics and culture put the condition of the modern Greeks in a new light. Their rebirth and renascence was now deemed not only desirable, but also feasible if they were emancipated and guided on the path to political freedom.

Thus the treatment of the modern Greeks in French travel literature was first expressed as a neutral stance interspersed with berating and castigating remarks. Negative views on their national and individual character continued unabated, but during the closing decades of the eighteenth century there arose a chorus of voices advocating their revival. This chorus of philhellenes became more resonant and reached a crescendo during the Greek War of Independence. The Romantic spirit of the time found a cause worthy of its exuberant energy.

For the Romantic visitor, Greece reverberated with the myths and fables of the ancients and the folk songs of the modern Greeks. It is no mere coincidence that descriptions of nature and a serious and systematic look at Greek folk songs appeared concurrently at the beginning of the nineteenth century. They both appealed to the emerging Romantic spirit, the former with its idyllic beauty full of hidden correspondences, and the latter with their celebration of a defiant and individualistic ethos.

Pouqueville devoted a considerable portion of his multifaceted study of Greece to the historical significance of folk songs. A few years later, Fauriel published his collection of Greek folk songs, commenting on their artistic and historical evolution and geographical distribution. The underlying theme in his introduction to the *Chants populaires de la Grèce moderne* (1824) was the tracing of the continuity of the same spirit from antiquity down to the modern times. The origins of this theme went back to the first French work of pronounced philhellenic sentiments, Guys's *Voyage littéraire de la Grèce*, and remained the most persistent preoccupation of all subsequent philhellenes. But for most of them, the affinity modern Greeks exhibited with their progenitors was mainly due to their ability to preserve some of their traits. For Fauriel and for other philhellenes of the Romantic era, however, affinity meant both preservation and active contribution.

The people's songs were seen as the repository of the experiences of the Greeks during their long and tumultuous history. At the same time, they were a manifestation of their creative intellectual energies during the centuries of Ottoman rule. In Fauriel's view, the folk songs represented a fusion of the primitive and the classical, of the spontaneous and the artistic elements. Following this interpretation, folk songs gave expression to the primal human urge to recreate through poetry and music one's emotions, perceptions of the surrounding world, and group experiences. Thus the anonymous bards had created a record of the collective existence of their race which ensured the perpetuation of its traditions. However, they did not faithfully chronicle objective historical facts; rather, their ballads recreated and transmitted the folk heroes' attitude toward life and death.

The serious observation and cataloguing of folk traditions was undertaken by a number of travelers to Greece. In examining them, they sought a key to understanding the present in terms of the past and vice versa. In addition, those favorably disposed to the modern Greeks based their philhellenic arguments on the Hellenic character of these traditions. Conversely, those less sympathetically inclined viewed these same customs as the superstitious practices of an ignorant people and used them to prove the deviation of the modern Greeks from their ancestors. Thus, paradoxical though it may seem, both the philhellenes and the detractors of modern Greece shared a characteristic: an unwillingness to understand and evaluate the present in terms other than those of the classical past. Both invoked the spirit of antiquity and superimposed it on contemporary reality.

The idealized and largely mythologized image of Greece projected by the Europeans had a lasting impact on the modern Greek intellectuals, who accepted it and tried to shape their own national identity in accordance with it. For them philhellenism was both a challenge and a sign of approval by the culturally superior Westerners. By spurring them to emulate classical antiquity, it strengthened their aspirations to extricate their countrymen from foreign rule. Seen in this light, the ancients were invested with a dual role by their modern descendants: first, they became a potent force uniting them in their search for national consciousness and identity, and second, they were seen as a link with Europe's secular civilization.

The process of cultural regeneration advocated by the philhellenes and undertaken by modern Greek intellectuals implied a clash between the high culture of classical Greece and modern Europe, on the one hand, and the traditional world of the Greeks in the Ottoman Empire, on the other. In order to raise the latter to the level of the former, the proponents of philhellenism believed that the present had to be cleansed of the intrusions that had permeated and, in their view, disfigured postclassical Greece. Three distinct areas that bore the marks of this unfortunate legacy were thought to be the Greek language, education, and religion. Both the philhellenes and Greek intellectuals predicated the reform of these three domains on ancient Greek *paideia* and enlightened European principles, which would bring about the reintegration and unification of Greek culture. In their optimistic zeal, however, they failed to realize that efforts to integrate two distant epochs by suppressing the intervening developments of almost two millennia were tantamount to cultural alienation and even deracination. By severing its links with its Christian-Byzantine legacy, an era unanimously condemned by

Europeans, modern Greek culture ran the risk of becoming artificial and devitalized. But, in the framework of the secular and rationalistic spirit of that time, the holistic concept of Greek civilization encompassing its Hellenic, Byzantine, and post-Byzantine strands was perhaps impossible.

French philhellenism, while being a facet of a European complex of attitudes and feelings toward Greece, held a unique appeal for the modern Greeks. A belief that the French, more than any other Europeans, resembled the ancient Athenians led modern Greek intellectuals such as Korais to admire and emulate French culture. Intellectual subtlety, clarity, and refinement—qualities attributed to both the ancient Greeks and the French—made the latter a mirror in which the Greeks would have liked to see their own image. This affinity, real or imagined, strengthened the preeminence of French literary influences in Greece. Furthermore, for the Greeks of the pre-revolutionary and revolutionary eras, the French Revolution kindled their desire for independence and fortified their hopes for victory.

In the end victory and independence did come to them. During the long struggle, European philhellenes played an active role. What had begun as a literary pilgrimage undertaken by travelers with a common faith, romantic Hellenism, turned into an active and even militant commitment when at last it seemed possible that Hellas was going to be reborn.

In France as well as in the rest of Europe, the government, part of the press, and conservative politicians greeted the outbreak of the Greek Revolution with suspicion and even hostility. The philhellenes, on the contrary, applauded its initial successes and wielded their influence in the hope of changing the official stance of their country. Their support for the insurrectionists was manifested in various ways: there were a social charitable philhellenism; a religious philhellenism espousing the cause of the Christians against their Muslim rulers; a liberal philhellenism proclaiming human rights; and above all, a Romantic artistic and literary philhellenism, which inspired painters and poets—Delacroix and Hugo among others—and which sought to assimilate the exploits of the *palikars* (young warriors) with those of the ancient heroes.

The granting of independence and the creation of the Greek kingdom signaled the end of the second and higher phase of philhellenism. After 1830 travelers continued to visit Greece. But philhellenism had lost its grip on them. With the war concluded, there were no more heroics to be sung. What was left was a ravaged country whose war-devastated people bore little or no resemblance to the celebrated ancients. Now it was up to the Greeks themselves to fashion their Hellenic image.

NOTES

CHAPTER 1. The Uses of Hellenism from the Renaissance to the Romantic Era

1. Voltaire, *Essai sur la poésie épique,* in *Oeuvres complètes,* ed. Beaumarchais et al. (Kehl, 1785–89), 10:351.

2. Frank E. Manuel, *The Eighteenth Century Confronts the Gods* (Cambridge, Mass., 1959), 3.

3. Paul Oskar Kristeller, *Renaissance Thought and Its Sources* (New York, 1979), 182.

4. For a distinction between *scientia* and *sapientia* in Renaissance and medieval philosophy, see Ernst Cassirer, *The Individual and the Cosmos in Renaissance Philosophy* (Philadelphia, 1963), 52.

5. Ibid.

6. Cited by Pietro Redondi, *Galileo: Heretic* (Princeton, 1987), 11.

7. Cassirer, *Individual and Cosmos,* 54.

8. For a cogent interpretation of the relation between the corporeal and incorporeal in the medieval vision of the world, see Carolly Erickson, *The Medieval Vision: Essays in History and Perception* (New York, 1976), chap. 1.

9. Kristeller, *Renaissance Thought,* 183.

10. Michel de Montaigne, "Du Repentir," *Oeuvres complètes,* ed. Albert Thibaudet and Maurice Rat (Paris, 1962), 782, 785.

11. Cassirer, *Individual and Cosmos,* 54.

12. A. C. Dionisotti, "On the Greek Studies of Robert Grosseteste," in *The Uses of Greek and Latin,* ed. A. C. Dionisotti, Anthony Grafton, and Jill Kraye (London, 1988), 20–28. For a further examination of European centers where Greek learning still survived in the Middle Ages, see Roberto Weiss, "Greek in Western Europe at the End of the Middle Ages," *Medieval*

and Humanist Greek (Padua, 1977), 3–12. For an account and interpretation of the relations and cross-influences between the Latin Catholic West and the Greek Orthodox East, see Deno J. Geanakoplos, *Byzantine East and Latin West* (New York, 1966), 11–54; Geanakoplos, *Interaction of the "Sibling" Byzantine and Western Cultures in the Middle Ages and Italian Renaissance* (New Haven, 1976). Furthermore, beginning with the mid-eleventh century and mainly because of Arabic influences that stimulated the growing interest in philosophy and the sciences, the works of Greek thinkers such as Aristotle, Euclid, and Ptolemy became accessible for the first time in Latin translations from Arabic renditions.

13. Paul Oscar Kristeller, "The Place of Classical Humanism in Renaissance Thought," *Journal of the History of Ideas* 4, no. 1 (1943): 59.

14. Kristeller, *Renaissance Thought*, 21.

15. Ibid., 59–60, 26–27.

16. For a romanticized and idealized portrait of Byzantine scholars who arrived in Italy after the fall of Constantinople, see A. F. Villemain, *Lascaris, ou les Grecs au XVe siècle* (Paris, 1825). Also, Egger emphasized their importance for the revival of classical studies by presenting an image full of emotional overtones: "Europe received them, few in number, in a humble position, with sadness and uneasiness. They arrived with their hands full of books, their minds graced with a literature that began to attract Europe's curiosity." Emile Egger, *L'Hellénisme en France* (Paris, 1869), 1:108.

17. Deno John Geanakoplos, *Greek Scholars in Venice* (Cambridge, Mass., 1962), 285. For an enthusiastic appraisal of the contribution of Byzantine Hellenists and their scholarly tradition to the revival of Greek learning in the West, see Kristeller, *Renaissance Thought*, 138–50.

18. Geanakoplos, *Sibling*, 175. Some of the scholars of the Greek diaspora expressed feelings of patriotic affinities with the ancients going well beyond the bonds of intellectual kinship. They even used their connections with European heads of state to induce them to deliver the Greeks from bondage in the name of Hellenism and Christianity. One of the most eloquent pleas for the liberation of the subjugated Greeks was addressed in 1525 by Janus Lascaris to Charles V, at whose court he had arrived as an ambassador of Pope Clement VII: "From the time, your holy Majesty, that I became aware of the affairs of this world, seeing myself chased away from my country by the tyranny of the Infidel Mohametans, I have never ceased to try to discover the means of recovering that same liberty I once enjoyed. . . . In short, in view of these considerations . . . , I have never ceased to pursue peace among the Christian Princes so that they might undertake a general expedition against the Infidels. . . . [It] is ancient Greece and the relics of modern Greece that bid me to come to you to implore you to take pity on their misery and abasement." Börje Knös, *Un Ambassadeur de l'hellénisme:*

Janus Lascaris et la tradition gréco-byzantine dans l'humanisme français (Paris, 1945), 189–91. Such pleas were short-lived, however, and the dawning Hellenic identity of the Byzantines was eclipsed in the ensuing centuries of Ottoman rule. Their appeal, however, would be sounded again, only stronger and more impassioned, by the philhellenes and the modern Greek nationalists of the neoclassical era. For individual cases of Byzantine exiles who invoked ancient Hellas in order to move European potentates to action against the Turks, see Geanakoplos, *Greek Scholars*, 150–53; Geanakoplos, *Sibling*, 172–82.

19. Cyriac of Ancona, cited by Richard Stoneman, *Land of Lost Gods: The Search for Classical Greece* (Norman, Okla., 1987), 31.

20. Knös, 81. For the relatively late appearance of Greek studies in France, see also Giuseppe di Stefano, "L'Hellénisme en France à l'orée de la Renaissance," in A. H. T. Levi, ed., *Humanism in France at the End of the Middle Ages and the Early Renaissance* (Manchester, 1970), 31; Arthur Tilley, *The Dawn of the French Reanaissance*, (New York, 1968), 257ff.; Roberto Weiss, "Learning and Education in Western Europe from 1470 to 1520," in *The New Cambridge Modern History*, vol. 1, *The Renaissance 1493–1520* (Cambridge, 1967), 102.

21. Tilley, 258–59.

22. Ibid., 262–65.

23. For a detailed examination of Budé's works, see Louis Delaruelle, *Guillaume Budé: Les Origines, les débuts, les idées maîtresses* (Paris, 1907), 91–116 (*Annotationes in Pandectas*), 131–38 (*de Asse*), 202–14 (*Institution du Prince*).

24. "Formerly I amused myself with Greek literature" wrote Erasmus in 1501, "but only in a superficial fashion. Now that I have gone rather deeper into it I realize the truth of what I have often read and written of authority, that a knowledge of Latin, however extensive, loses half its value without a knowledge of Greek." Cited in Tilley, 259. For an account of Erasmus's presence in Paris at different times and his influence on French humanists, see ibid., 291–302.

25. Montaigne, "A Demain les affaires," 344.

26. Jean Seznec, *The Survival of the Pagan Gods* (New York, 1953), 306–9.

27. Paul Hazard, *The European Mind 1680–1715* (New York, 1963), 445.

28. Ernst Cassirer, *The Philosphy of the Enlightenment* (Princeton, 1951), 290.

29. Kirsti Simonsuuri, *Homer's Original Genius: Eighteenth-Century Notions of the Early Greek Epic (1688–1798)*, (Cambridge, 1979), 23.

30. Peter Gay, *The Enlightenment: An Interpretation* (New York, 1966), 31.

31. Louis Bertrand, *La Fin du classicisme et le retour à l'antique dans la seconde moitié du XVIIIe siècle et les premières années du XIXe en France* (Paris, 1897), 26.

32. Gay, *Enlightenment*, 38–44.

33. Arnaldo Momigliano, *Studies in Historiography* (London, 1966), 1–3.

34. Lionel Gossman, *Medievalism and the Ideologies of the Enlightenment* (Baltimore, 1968), 154.

35. Condorcet, *Esquisse*, in *Oeuvres complètes* (Paris, 1847), 6:59.

36. Bertrand, 3–5.

37. Edmond and Jules de Goncourt, *L'Art du XVIIIe siècle*, 3d ser. (Paris, 1859–75), 267.

38. Jean Starobinski, *The Invention of Liberty 1700–1789* (Geneva, 1964), 58.

39. Manuel, 40.

40. Letter quoted in Bertrand, 286.

41. Bertrand, 6–7.

42. Jean-Jacques Rousseau, *Les Confessions* (Paris, 1964), 8–9.

43. Jean-Jacques Rousseau, *Les Rêveries du promeneur solitaire* (New York, 1961), 76.

44. Jean-Jacques Rousseau, *Discours sur les sciences et les arts,* in *Oeuvres complètes* (Paris, 1959), 3:12.

45. For a thorough examination and incisive analysis of the history of laconism, see Elizabeth Rawson, *The Spartan Tradition in European Thought* (Oxford, 1969).

46. Chantal Grell and Christian Michel, eds. *Primitivisme et mythes des origines dans la France des Lumières 1680–1820* (Paris, 1989), 14.

47. Momigliano, *Studies*, 21.

48. Some critics have seen an analogy between the moral zeal of the Revolutionaries and religious fanaticism. See Julien Tiersot, *Les Fêtes et les chants de la révolution française* (Paris, 1908), 92–93; James A. Leith, *The Idea of Art as Propaganda in France 1750–1799* (Toronto, 1965), 106.

49. Mona Ouzouf, *Festivals and the French Revolution* (Cambridge, Mass., 1988), 276.

50. Ducos, quoted in M. Badolle, *L'Abbé Jean-Jacques Barthélemy et l'hellénisme en France dans la seconde moitiè du XVIIIe siècle* (Paris, 1926), 359.

51. On the educational reforms proposed by the revolutionaries, see Harold Parker, *The Cult of Antiquity and the French Revolutionaries* (New York, 1965), 127–28.

52. Rawson, 268, 281.

53. Starobinski, 101.

54. Robespierre, quoted in Parker, 162.

55. Delecluse, *Louis David, son école et son temps,* quoted in Bertrand, 318. For a description of revolutionary festivals, see George Renard, "Notes sur la littérature thermidorienne," *Revolution française; Revue d'histoire moderne et contemporaine,* 12 (1887): 770–71.

56. Parker, 134–35.

57. Excerpt from a speech delivered by Billaud Varennes in 1794, quoted in Badolle, 352–53.

58. The abbé Grégoire, quoted in Badolle, 363. Some other critics were even more caustic in their reactions against the imitation of the ancients. For a sample of their opinions, see Renard, 779–81.

59. Bertrand, 83–84.

60. Claude-Philippe, comte de Caylus, *Receuil d'antiquités égyptiennes, étrusques, grecques et romaines* (Paris, 1761), 1:ii. For a study of Caylus's life and work, see S. Rocheblave, *Essai sur le comte de Caylus* (Paris, 1889).

61. Caylus, 119.

62. Julien David Leroy, *Les Ruines des plus beaux monuments de la Grèce, considerées du côté de l'histoire et du côté de l'architecture* (Paris, 1770), 1:xvi.

63. Johann Joachim Winckelmann, *Histoire de l'art chez les anciens* (Paris, 1793), 2:427–28.

64. René Canat, *L'Hellénisme des romantiques* (Paris, 1951), 1:207–12; René Canat, *La Renaissance de la Grèce antique 1820–1850* (Paris, 1911), 6–7.

65. André Chénier, "Elégies," *Oeuvres complètes*, ed. Gérard Walter (Paris, 1958), 71–72.

66. Stephen Rogers, *Classical Greece and the Poetry of Chénier, Shelley and Leopardi* (Notre Dame, 1974), 15.

67. Chénier, "L'Invention," *Oeuvres Complètes*, 125.

68. Ibid., 127. Chénier's use of the pointed contrast between new thoughts and antique verses is a statement of faith in their interdependability. In Dimoff's words, "there is in *L'Invention* a sense of measure, a respect for tradition, and an effort to reach an equitable balance between the past and the present." Paul Dimoff, ed. in André Chénier, *L'Invention* (Paris, 1966), 22.

69. Chénier, "Mnazile et Chloé," *Oeuvres complètes*, 15.

70. Ibid.; Chénier, "Elégies," 72.

71. Ibid., "L'Aveugle," *Oeuvres complètes*, 46.

72. Rogers, 48.

73. Léonce Pingaud, *Choiseul-Gouffier: La France en Orient sous Louis XVI* (Paris, 1887), 144.

74. Badolle, 190.

75. For a fuller treatment, see ibid., 180–83.

76. He remarked of the Greek writers: "They had less wit than the Roman authors. . . . It seems to me that the Greeks were daring in style but timid in thought." Montesquieu, *Mes Pensées*, in *Oeuvres complètes* (Paris, 1949), 1:1232.

77. Egger, 1:277.

78. Voltaire, *Essai sur les moeurs et l'esprit des nations*, in *Oeuvres complètes*, 16:116.

79. Voltaire, *Les Lois de Minos*, in *Oeuvres complètes*, 6:76. This ambiva-

lent attitude toward Homer is best exemplified in Voltaire's *Essai sur la poésie épique* (1735). The essay first appeared in English in 1727 because Voltaire wrote it during his eighteen-month stay in England at a time when Homer, thanks to Pope's translation, was in vogue. The essay was part of a larger work entitled *An Essay upon the Civil Wars of France, Extracted from Curious Manuscripts and also upon the Epick Poetry of the European Nations, from Homer down to Milton*, by Mr. de Voltaire. In it, Voltaire's opinion of Homer was scarcely favorable. In trying to explain the Greek poet's appeal, Voltaire observed that his readers were more "aw'd with the Fame of Homer, rather than struck with his Beauties." Furthermore, he surmised that the readers must be offended by the manners of the Homeric heroes, bored and little amused with the "Uniformity" of his style, and repelled by the absurdities of the gods. "The best reason for that Languor which creeps upon the Mind of so many Readers, in Spight of the Flashes which rouse her now and then, is that *Homer* interresses us for none of his Heroes." Florence Donnell White, ed. *Voltaire's Essay on Epic Poetry: A Study and an Edition* (New York, 1970), 90. The same feeling of ennui is expressed by Pococurante in *Candide*: "I was led to believe in the past that I derived pleasure in reading him; but this endless repetition of identical combats, these gods who are always active without doing anything decisive, this Helen who is the object of the war and who scarcely qualifies to be an actress; this Troy ceaselessly besieged and never captured; all this gave me the most mortal ennui." Voltaire, *Candide and Other Philosophical Tales*, ed. Morris Bishop (New York, 1957), 113. But in his *Essai sur le poésie épique*, Voltaire, instead of criticizing Homer, came to his defense. "However, twelve beautiful verses from the *Iliad* are above the perfection of these trifles in the same way a big diamond, a raw product of nature, is superior to iron or brass trinkets, regardless of the skill of the industrious hands that produce them. The great merit of Homer is that he was a sublime painter." Voltaire, *Essai sur le poésie épique*, 10:351.

80. Homer seen in this light was treated by Chabanon, *Dissertation sur Homère comme poète tragique* (Paris, 1764); Jean-Jacques Barthélemy, *Voyage de jeune Anacharsis en Grèce* (1788).

81. Simonsurri, 14.

82. Voltaire, *Discours sur la tragédie ancienne et moderne*, in *Oeuvres complètes*, 3:333–34.

83. Henry Vyverberg, *Human Nature, Cultural Diversity, and the French Enlightenment* (New York, 1989), 157–58, 155.

84. Voltaire, "Athéisme," *Dictionnaire philosophique* (Paris, 1967), 36.

85. Marmontel, "Comédie," *Encyclopédie méthodique*, quoted in Badolle, 318.

86. Mme de Staël, *De la littérature* (Paris, 1959), 47.

87. Canat, *La Renaissance de la Grèce antique*, 72–76. Schlegel's *Cours de la littérature dramatique* appeared in French in 1813 and contributed to a better understanding of the properties of the Greek stage and the significance of Greek drama.

88. Mme de Staël, quoted in Canat, *L'Hellénisme des romantiques*, 1:72.

89. "It is safe to say that a full understanding of the Greeks owes something to the new spirit of relativism brought by the Romantic revolution." Henri Peyre, *Bibliographie critique de l'hellénisme en France de 1843 à 1870* (New Haven, 1932), 20.

90. Bertrand, 67.

91. Canat, *L'Hellénisme des romantiques*, 1:19.

92. Badolle, 124. The atlas was prepared by the cartographer Barbié du Bocage.

93. For more information on the editions of *Anacharsis* and the extent of its popularity, see Badolle, 227–31.

94. Chrysovergis Kouropalatis, trans., *Periegesis tou Neou Anacharsidos eis ten Ellada para tou Abbé Barthélemy* (The Voyage of Young Anacharsis to Greece by the Abbé Barthélemy), (Vienna, 1829), xx.

95. Canat, *La Renaissance de la Grèce antique*, 99–101.

96. Dacier, "Choiseul-Gouffier," in Marie-Gabriel-Florent-Auguste, comte de Choiseul-Gouffier, *Voyage pittoresque de la Grèce* (Paris, 1782–1822), vol. 2, pt. 1, ii.

97. Jean-Jacques Barthélemy, *Voyage du jeune Anacharsis en Grèce vers le milieu du quatrième siècle avant l'ère vulgaire* (Paris, 1822), 3:386–87.

98. The distinction between history and fiction was not as clear in the eighteenth century as it is today. This is why novelists could tresspass on the domain of historians and use their techniques. See Vivienne Mylne, *The Eighteenth Century Novel: Techniques of Illusion* (Manchester, 1965), 20–22.

99. Badolle, 105.

100. Fontanes, cited in Badolle, 268. Choiseul-Gouffier's praise for Barthélemy, his former teacher, was in the same vein. "The beautiful work that was going to present the treasures of a vast erudition in the most seductive forms and, thanks to the noble and pure style of the author, was going to revive the ancient glory of the country that I had just visited, was already announced to the literary world of Europe." Choiseul-Gouffier, vol. 2, pt. 1, 1.

101. Stendhal, *La Peinture en Italie*, quoted in Canat, *L'Hellénisme des romantiques*, 1:115–16.

102. Peyre, *Bibliographie critique*, 5.

CHAPTER 2. First Contacts:
French Travelers to Greece, 1550–1750

1. In 1663 the Capuchin mission, headed by Simon de Compiegne, acquired the Monument of Lysikrates, then called the Lantern of Diogenes. Père Simon bought it from a Greek, who shortly thereafter changed his mind, claiming that it was the custom of the Greeks not to sell their antiquities to strangers for fear they would be destroyed. The Capuchin missionary pleaded his case with the Council of Elders, which decided against him. As a last resort, he sought a judgment from the *kadi*, the Turkish judge, who granted him the monument on the condition that it be made accessible to visitors. See André Guillet (La Guilletière), *Athènes ancienne et nouvelle* (Paris, 1675), 222–25.

2. In England, Thomas Howard, Earl of Arundel (1586–1646), a knowledgeable lover of art, developed antiquarian interests when he visited Rome in 1612. Not unexpectedly, his taste embraced Greek antiquities, over 150 of which adorned his gardens and sculpture gallery. So sizable and varied was his collection that the sight of it made Peacham exclaim with wonderment, "To his liberal charges and magnifiscence, this angle of the world oweth its first sight of Greek and Roman statues, with whose admired presence he began to honour the gardens and galleries of Arundel House about twenty years ago, and hath ever since continued to transplant old Greece into England." Henry Peacham, *The Compleat Gentleman*, 1634, cited in Richard Stoneman, *Land of Lost Gods: The Search for Classical Greece* (Norman, Okla., 1987), 42–43.

3. For the geographical span and wide ethnographic scope of Herodotus's work, see Margaret T. Hodgen, *Early Anthropology in the Sixteenth and Seventeenth Centuries* (Philadelphia, 1964), 21–29.

4. Stephen Greenblatt, *Marvelous Possessions: The Wonder of the New World* (Chicago, 1991), 124–27.

5. For the development of Herodotus's influence in Western historical thought, see Arnaldo Momigliano, "The Place of Herodotus in the History of Historiography," in his *Studies in Historiography* (London, 1966), 127–42.

6. The relations between the corporeal and the incorporeal elements in the perceptual constructs of medieval travelers and the differences between their sense of reality and ours are examined by Carolly Erickson, *The Medieval Vision* (New York, 1976), 3–28.

7. Greenblatt, 39–40.

8. Marco Polo's work *Liber diversorum* is a factual account of his experiences in the Far East in the years 1271–75. Its adherence to objective reality was uncommonly innovative for its time, but its impact was negligible in the following two centuries. See Hodgen, 94–103.

9. Erickson, 30.

10. John B. Friedman, *The Monstrous Races in Medieval Art and Thought* (Cambridge, Mass., 1981), 38.

11. Ibid., 2.

12. When Columbus met the natives of Guyana in 1492, he was surprised to see that, far from being monstrous, they were physically attractive. "In these islands I have so far found no human monstrosities, as many expected, on the contrary, among all these people good looks are esteemed." Columbus cited in Friedman, 199.

13. Greenblatt, 20.

14. Bernal Diaz, *The Conquest of New Spain,* cited in Greenblatt, 133. Geoffrey de Villehardouin described similar feelings experienced by the soldiers of the Fourth Crusade at the sight of Constantinople in June 1203. "All those who had never seen Constantinople before gazed with astonishment at the city. They had never imagined that anywhere in the world there could be a city like this. . . . As they gazed at the length and breadth of that superb city there was not a man, however brave and daring, who did not feel a shudder down his spine." Geoffrey de Villehardouin, *The Conquest of Constantinople,* cited in Ernle Bradford, *The Great Betrayal: Constantinople 1204* (London, 1967), 29.

15. Greenblatt, 2.

16. Pierre Belon, *Les Observations de plusieurs singularitez et choses memorables trouvées en Grece, Asie, Indée, Egypte, Arabie, et autres pays estranges . . .* (Paris, 1553), ey.

17. André Thevet, *Cosmographie de Levant* (Lyon, 1554), 13–14. It was not a mere coincidence that Cortés, upon undertaking his voyage, also invoked Aristotle's authority by using the same quotation, with a slight variation: it is "a universal condition of men to want to know." Cortés, cited in John Huxtable Elliott, *The Old World and the New* (Cambridge, 1970), 30.

18. Belon, ey.

19. Henry Bordeaux, *Voyageurs d'Orient: Dès pèlerins aux méharistes de Palmyre* (Paris, 1926), 1:30.

20. Samuel Purchas, "A Discourse of the diversity of Letters used by the divers Nations of the World . . . ," cited in Greenblatt, 10.

21. One hundred years earlier, Montaigne, commenting on his voyage to Italy, upon which he embarked on 22 June 1580, expressed essentially the same idea. "The voyage is in my view a beneficial experience . . . and I know of no better school for the forming of life than its constant exposure to the diversity of forms of our nature." Michel de Montaigne, *Journal de Voyage en Italie par la Suisse et l'Allemagne* (Paris, 1955), ii.

22. Baudelot de Dairval, *De l'utilité des voyages et de l'avantage que la recherche des antiquitez procure aux sçavans* (Paris, 1686), 1:8.

23. Ibid., 18.

24. Hodgen, 167.

25. Edward W. Said, *Orientalism* (New York, 1978), 21.

26. Buondelmonti, cited in Stoneman, 23.

27. For more details on the activities of Buondelmonti and Cyriac of Ancona, see Stoneman, 23–36; Roberto Weiss, *The Renaissance Discovery of Classical Antiquity* (Oxford, 1969), 131–141.

28. Paul Lucas, *Voyage du sieur Paul Lucas fait par l'ordre du Roy dans la Grèce, l'Asie Mineure, la Macédoine et l'Afrique* . . . (Paris, 1712), 1:av.

29. Greenblatt, 9.

30. Hodgen, 196.

31. On Eurocentrism see Elliott, 41–53; Hodgen, 197, 483.

32. Montaigne perceived clearly the attitude of Eurocentrism vis-à-vis the inhabitants of the New World and criticzed it as self-centered and even hypocritical. "There is nothing barbarous and savage in this nation . . . unless we call barbarousness that which is not part of our usage; it is true, it seems, that we have no other norm of truth and reason than the examples, ideas, opinions, and usages of the country where we are." Then he remarks that we may then call the people of the New World "barbarians in regard to the rules of reason but not when compared to us, who surpass them in every sort of barbarity." Michel de Montaigne, "Des Cannibales," in *Oeuvres complètes*, eds. Albert Thibaudet et Maurice Rat (Paris, 1962), 203, 208.

33. Iaques Gassot, *Le Discours du voyage de Venise à Constantinople* (Paris, 1550), 20.

34. Although folklore and legends contained elements of antiquity, such as the figure of Alexander the Great, they existed in a latent state in the collective memory of the people, who acted as the transmitters of ancient practices and beliefs. See C. Th. Dimaras, *La Grèce au temps des lumières* (Geneva, 1969), 110–11. The focus of the collective identity of the Greeks was not Hellenism but Christianity because "with the passing of time, the national consciousness of the enslaved Christian peoples of the Ottoman Empire is weakened and finally numbed. In its place there appears, grows, and prevails the consciousness of the Christian, which rises against the consciousness of the Muslim." Apostolos E. Vakalopoulos, *E poreia tou genous* (The Course of the Nation), (Athens, 1966), 70.

35. The French merchant and philhellene Pierre-Augustin Guys was one of the first to treat this subject exhaustively and systematically. See his *Voyage littéraire de la Grèce ou Lettres sur les Grecs anciens et modernes, avec un parallèle de leurs moeurs* (Paris, 1783), 3 vols.

36. Belon, 5, 6.

37. Lionel Gossman, *Medievalism and the Ideologies of the Enlightenment* (Baltimore, 1968), 159.

38. R. P. Robert de Dreux, *Voyage en Turquie et en Grèce* (Paris, 1925), 103. De Dreux wrote his account at the behest of a fellow Jesuit and completed it in 1672, three years after his return from the Levant. For this reason it remained unknown until Henri Omont discovered the manuscript and brought it to the attention of the public in "Athènes au XVIIe siècle: Relation du P. Robert de Dreux, lettres de J. Spon et de P. Babin," *Revue des études grecques* 14 (1901): 270–82. It was finally published in its entirety by Hubert Pernot in 1925.

39. Joseph Pitton de Tournefort, *Relation d'un voyage du Levant fait par l'ordre du Roy . . .* (Paris, 1717), 1:53–54.

40. Jacob Spon, *Voyage d'Italie, de Dalmatie, de Grèce et du Levant, fait aux années 1675 et 1676* (Lyon, 1678), vol. 1, Preface.

41. Tournefort, 1:19.

42. De Dreux, 71–72, 35.

43. George Guillet [Sr. de la Guilletière], *Athènes ancienne et nouvelle* (Paris, 1675), 96.

44. Sieur du Loir, *Les voyages du Sieur du Loir* (Paris, 1654), 166.

45. L.S.D.V. (Le Sieur de Villamont), *Les Voyages de la Terre Saincte, et autres lieux remarquables et signalez d'icelle, ensemble de l'Italie, Sclavonie, Grèce, Turquie . . .* (Paris, 1627), 31.

46. Tournefort, 1:185.

47. Du Loir, 166.

48. Albert Vandal, *L'Odyssée d'un ambasadeur: Les Voyages du marquis de Nointel 1670–1680* (Paris, 1900), 301–2. The allusion to a "secret union" refers to the efforts of the Catholic church to exercise its influence over the Orthodox Christians of the Levant through the activities of its missionaries. See P. Bruno, "Ambassadeurs de France et capucins français à Constantinople au XVIIe siècle d'après le Journal du P. Thomas de Paris," *Etudes franciscaines* 29:232–59; 30:401–14; 31:388–402.

49. Belon, 4.

50. Spon, *Voyage d'Italie*, 2:253–54. Similar elements of decay in modern Greek were pointed out by the Englishman Brerewood, who noted them "not onely as touching the largenesse and vulgarnesse of it, but also in the purenesse and elegancy." Edward Brerewood, *Enquiries touching the diversity of languages and religions through the cheife parts of the world* (London, 1614), 8, cited in Hodgen, 265.

51. Belon, 37–38. Belon was one of the earliest French travelers to mention the Greek word *caloyer* (monk), a term that became established in all subsequent travel literature related to Greece. He gave the following exact translation: "caloiere: bon vieillard" and "calogria: bonne vieille" (34).

52. De Dreux, 97–98. The Jesuit Père Babin, who gave the first reliable and comprehensive account of modern Athens, was no more generous in

his treatment of the Greek church. "But what seems more deplorable to me," he wrote about the nuns of a convent near Athens, "is the ignorance of these poor women, which is so great that one can be quite assured that none of them is formally heretic or schismatic, although Athens, as well as Mount Athos and Constantinople, are the Throne and the fortress of the Greek schism." Jacques Paul Babin, *Relation de l'état présent de la ville d'Athènes, ancienne capitale de la Grèce, bâtie depuis 3400 ans* (Lyon, 1674), 21–22.

53. Timothy Ware, *The Orthodox Church* (Baltimore, 1963), 99.

54. Tournefort, 1:137.

55. Thevet, 37. Thevet's denunciation of the Cretans recalls Polybius's criticism of their ancient predecessors. The Greek historian, writing in Rome about 150 B.C., remarked, "Greed and avarice are so native to the soil in Crete . . . that the Cretans . . . are engaged in countless public and private seditions, murders and civil wars, [and] you could find no habits prevailing in private life more steeped in treachery than those in Crete and no public policy more inequitable." Polybius, *The Histories of Polybius*, trans. Everyn S. Shuckburgh (London, 1889), 1:497–98.

56. Suleiman Mustapha Aga's arrival caused a stir in Paris. Molière used him as a model for the character of the Grand Turk in *Le Bourgeois gentilhomme*. He is also known to have introduced coffee to the court of Louis XIV.

57. Tournefort, 1:39.

58. Belon, 85.

59. Spon, *Voyage d'Italie*, 2:152.

60. De Dreux, 105.

61. Thevet, 85.

62. M. L. F. De Bausset, *The Life of Fénelon, Archbishop of Cambrai* (London, 1810), 1:16.

63. Charles Perrault, in (L. E. S. T.) Comte de Laborde, *Athènes aux XVe, XVIe et XVIIe siècles* (Paris, 1854), 1:87–88.

64. Nointel to Colbert, 9 February 1672, in Laborde, 1:99–100.

65. Colbert to French consuls in the Levant, November 1672, in Henri Omont, *Missions archéologiques françaises en Orient aux XVIIe et XVIIIe siècles* (Paris, 1902), 1:222–23.

66. Colbert to Nointel, 10 November 1674, in Laborde, 1:115–16, n. 1.

67. Spon was overwhelmed by Nointel's sizable and varied collection. Nointel "showed us several interesting things in his place which we would not have been able to see in all of Constantinople. We saw there about thirty marbles or ancient inscriptions that he brought from Athens or the Archipelago. Being exceedingly kind, he allowed us to copy whatever we wanted. He has a great number of coins, some quite rare, and four hundred

drawings of bas-reliefs, edifices, and landscapes, which he had made during all his travels in Greece and Turkey. There are few persons in the world who deserve this credit in a country so hostile to paintings." Spon, *Voyage d'Italie*, 1:263.

68. Nointel to Pomponne, 17 December 1674, in Laborde, 1:124–25.

69. Lucas, *Voyage dans la Grèce*, 1:aij–aiij.

70. After each voyage, Lucas brought back, in addition to antiquities, copious notes on his experiences. They appeared in three books: *Voyage du sieur Paul Lucas en Levant . . .* , 2 vols. (La Haye: Guillaume de Voys, 1705); *Voyage du sieur Paul Lucas fait par l'ordre du Roy dans la Grèce, l'Asie Mineure, la Macédoine et l'Afrique . . .* , 2 vols. (Paris: Nicolas Simart, 1712); *Troisième voyage du sieur Paul Lucas, fait en MDCCXIV par ordre de Louis XIV dans la Turquie, l'Asie, Sourie, Palestine, Haute et Basse Egypte . . .* , 3 vols. (Rouen: Roberty Machuel, 1719). Lucas emphasized his observations of contemporary life in the dedication of his second book to the king. "But, SIRE, there are rarities that only the mind can seize and which can be communicated only through discourse; and as they are no less precious than the others, I have taken great care to collect them in order to offer them to YOUR MAJESTY. This Book, SIRE, which I take the liberty to present to you, encloses them." See Lucas, *Voyage dans la Grèce*, 1:aiij.

71. Dom Vincent Thuillet, "Mémoire pour un voiage littéraire de la Grèce et du Levant," (1708), in Omont, *Missions archéologiques*, 1:423.

72. Dom Bernard de Montfaucon, "Mémoire pour servir d'instruction à ceux qui cherchent d'anciens monumens dans la Grèce et dans le Levant" (1720), in Omont, *Missions archéologiques*, 1:414.

73. Maurepas to Sevin and Fourmont, 28 August 1728, in Omont, *Missions archéologiques*, 1:427.

74. These directives were issued by the king himself. "Mémoire du Roy pour servir d'instruction aux sieurs Sevin et Fourmont" in Omont, *Missions archéologiques*, 1:436–38.

75. Abbé Bignon to Sevin and Fourmont, in Omont, *Missions archéologiques*, 1:443.

76. The view that the Greeks were the unworthy possessors of ancient monuments persisted for a long time. On 22 August 1798 a musical play was performed in Paris entitled *Palma ou le voyage en Grèce*. The action unfolds among the ruins of Athens, and the protagonists—or rather, antagonists— are Mabouc, an ignorant Greek bent on destroying ancient monuments, and Paul, a French painter paying homage to them. The latter, overcome by indignation, upbraids this unworthy descendant:

> What fury devours you!
> Barbarians, your unjust scorn renounce,

And respect these beautiful ruins
That even time has spared!

[Quelle fureur vous dévore!
Barbares, renoncez à d'injustes mépris,
Et respectez ces beaux débris
Que le temps épargnait encore!]

The Greek responds insolently,

He is truly losing his head
With his respect for stones;
But his pleas let us ignore,
And with joy let us destroy.

[Il perd la tête en vérité
Avec son respect pour les pierres;
Mais n'écoutons pas ses prières,
Et détruisons avec gaîté.]

Aikaterine Koumarianou, "To taxidi tou Choiseul-Gouffier" (Choiseul-Gouffier's Voyage), in *Periegeseis ston elleniko choro* (Travels in the Greek Space), ed. C. Th. Dimaras (Athens, 1968), 44. Korais's comments on the same subject are quite revealing since they express the views of a Western-oriented Greek intellectual.

Until now the question, even though the cause of great sadness and shame for the Greeks, bore some consolation, and, instead of envying the foreigners, who became enriched because of our ignorance, we must in a way be grateful to them because they saved the proofs of our ancestral glory, which probably would have disappeared completely had they stayed here. Yes, we owe them gratitude for all they have taken not by force but as wise men buying the works of other wise men from the hands of people unworthy of holding them. . . . But we should be grateful only until now. Henceforth, even if they have an excuse to entice us still with money because they persist obstinately in their view of us as barbarians, it will be to our great shame if we do not try to convince them that the time of our barbarousness has passed, never to return again. . . . We must inform them that we no longer give away or sell our ancestral possessions.

Ioannis Gennadios, "Ta Ioannitika cheirographa" (Manuscripts from Ioannina), *Epeirotika chronika*, 1927, 234.

77. Sevin to Maurepas, 2 April 1729, in Omont, *Missions archéologiques*, 1:463.

78. The Phanariots were wealthy Greeks from the Phanar (Fener) district in Constantinople. Some of them entered the service of the Ottoman sultan and occupied high positions in the government. The Phanariot prince mentioned by Sevin was Nikolaos Mavrokordatos, who had served as a doctor and dragoman to the Ottoman government before becoming prince (*hospodar*) of Wallachia. He not only collected literary works but also was an author in his own right. Among other things, he wrote the first modern Greek novel, *Ta Philotheous parerga* (Philtheos's Diversions) (1718). He was instrumental both in promotiong and spreading education in the Danubian principalities through the establishment of Greek schools and in creating an intellectual atmosphere by attracting men of letters, many of them Europeans, to his court. See Apostolos Vakalopoulos, *Istoria tou neou ellenismou* (History of Modern Hellenism), (Thessalonike, 1973), 4:257–58.

79. Fourmont to Maurepas, in Omont, *Missions archéologiques,* 1:603.

80. Fourmont to Villeneuve, 20 April 1730, in Omont, *Missions archéologiques,* 1:625–26.

81. Edward Dodwell, cited in Stoneman, 106.

82. Villeneuve to Fourmont, 27 July 1730, in Omont, *Missions archéologiques,* 1:628.

83. Fourmont to Bignon, 20 April 1730, in Omont, *Missions archéologiques,* 1:617.

84. Ibid.

CHAPTER 3. Athens and Its Monuments: The Seventeenth Century

1. For more information on these two visitors to Athens, see Roberto Weiss, *The Renaissance Discovery of Classical Antiquity,* (Oxford, 1969), 133–35.

2. The full title of this pioneer work is: Louis des Hayes, baron de Courmerin. *Voiage de Levant fait par le commandement du Roy en l'année 1621 par le Sr. DC.* Seconde édition, à Paris: Chez Adrian Taupinart, Rue St. Jacques à la Sphère, 1632. The book went through three editions: the first in 1624, following his first voyage, the second in 1632, after his second journey to the Levant—most probably it was then that he passed through Athens since the first edition does not mention Greece; and the third edition, in 1643. See Morton James Paton, *Chapters on Mediaeval and Renaissance Visitors to Greek Lands* (Princeton, 1951), 56–58.

3. Laborde, comte de. *Athènes aux XVe, XVIe et XVIIe siècles* (Paris, 1854), 1:64.

4. This small book became so rare by the nineteenth century that

Laborde had to search inside and outside France in order to locate a copy. He judged it valuable enough to merit a second edition bearing the same title as the original one: Jacques Paul Babin, *Relation de l'état présent de la ville d'Athènes, ancienne capitale de la Grèce, bâtie depuis 3400 ans.* Paris: Jules Renouard et Cie, 1854. Annotée et publiée par Cte de Laborde.

5. When referring to the Acropolis and the Parthenon, French travelers in the seventeenth century used the terms *la citadelle* or *le chateau* and *le temple*.

6. Babin, 25–26.

7. Jacob Spon, *Voyage d'Italie, de Dalmatie, de Grèce, et du Levant, fait aux années 1675 et 1676 par Jacob Spon . . . et George Wheler* (Lyon, 1678), 1:273. Hereafter cited in text as *V.*

8. For an analysis of the new techniques of historical investigation used by seventeenth- and eighteenth-century historians, see Lionel Gossman, *Medievalism and the Ideologies of the Enlightenment* (Baltimore, 1968), 153; and Arnaldo Momigliano, "Ancient History and the Antiquarian," in his *Studies in Historiography* (London, 1966), 1–5.

9. Spon, *Voyage d'Italie*, 1:324–25.

10. Laborde, 2:19, 20.

11. Spon, *Voyage d'Italie*, 1:190.

12. The same information, although more extensive and detailed, is given by Giraud in "Relation de l'Attique," an essay he wrote in 1674–75. Maxime Collignon, "Le Consul Jean Giraud et sa relation de l'Attique au XVIIe siècle," *Mémoires de l'Académie des Inscriptions et Belles-Lettres* 39 (1913): 28–37. Spon's facts on modern Athens were largely based on Giraud.

13. Spon, *Voyage d'Italie*, 2:238.

14. Albert Vandal, *L'Odyssée d'un ambassadeur: les voyages du Marquis de Nointel (1670–1680)*, (Paris, 1900), 3.

15. Sensitive to his declining success as a doctor, Spon insisted that he did not compromise his profession. "Thus, however beneficial this [antiquity] may have been abroad, there is no doubt that the books I have published have caused me harm here at home because it is deemed that I was no longer attached to my practice and that the antiquities, which in fact are only a card game for me, were my greatest occupation." Jacob Spon, *Nouvelles de la république des lettres*, quoted in Laborde, 2:40, n. 1.

16. Spon, *Voyage d'Italie*, 1:120.

17. The full title of the French translation of Wheler's work was *Voyage de Dalmatie, de Grèce, du Levant, par M. George Wheler, enrichy de médailles et de figures des principales antiquités qui se trouvent dans ces lieux, avec la description des villes, rivières, ports de mer et de ce qui s'y trouve de plus remarquable.* Traduit de l'anglais. Amsterdam: Jean Wolters, 1689.

18. Spon, *Voyage d'Italie*, 2:100.

19. The quarrel between the two writers unfolded rapidly: Guillet's answer to Spon's critical remarks was contained in his *Lettres écrites sur une dissertation d'un voyage de Grèce, publié par M. Spon* (Paris: Estienne Michallet, 1679). Spon's counterattack followed shortly thereafter under the title *Réponse à la critique publiée par M. Guillet, sur le "Voyage de Grèce" de Jacob Spon* (Lyon: Antoine Celier fils, 1679). For a succinct presentation of the sequence of events, see Henri Omont, "Athènes au XVIIe siècle: Relation du P. Robert de Dreux, lettres de J. Spon et de P. Babin," *Revue des études grecques* 14 (1901): 282–83.

20. André Guillet, *Lettres écrites sur une dissertation*, 10.

21. Laborde, 1:214–15.

22. Subsequent travelers and critics sided with Spon and rejected Guillet's claims. Chateaubriand accepted Spon's arguments unquestioningly and remarked that "Guillet, or la Guilletière, deserves no confidence as a traveler; but his work at the time when he published it did not lack a certain merit. Guillet made use of information he obtained from fathers Simon and Barnabé, both missionaries in Athens." François-René de Chateaubriand, *Itinéraire de Paris à Jérusalem et de Jérusalem à Paris* (Paris, 1812), 1:31. Similar views were expressed by Laborde, 1:214–17; Eugène Lovinesco, *Les Voyageurs français en Grèce au XIXe siècle* (1800–1900), (Paris, 1909), 7; Nicholas Jorga, *Les Voyageurs français dans l'Orient européen* (Paris, 1928), 79.

23. André Guillet, *Lacédémone ancienne et nouvelle* (Paris, 1676), 19. Hereafter cited in the text as *L*.

24. André Guillet, *Athènes ancienne et nouvelle* (Paris, 1675), 4.

25. Maxime Collignon discovered among the papers of the marquis de Nointel deposited with the Bibliothèque nationale three manuscripts, which he attributed to Giraud: "Relation des antiquités d'Athènes"; "Relation de l'Attique"; "Description des lieux maritimes." See Maxime Collignon, "Le Consul Jean Giraud et sa relation de l'Attique au XVIIe siècle," *Mémoires de l'Académie des Inscriptions et Belles-Lettres* 39 (Paris, 1913).

26. Although Spon relied on Giraud for information on contemporary Athens, his conjectures about the history of its monuments often diverged from those of the consul: he gave 1656 as the date of the explosion of the Propylaea, whereas Giraud placed it more accurately, in 1640; Spon was also in error when he attributed the bas-reliefs of the Parthenon to Hadrian, whereas Giraud, who accompanied him on the Acropolis, named Phidias as their creator.

27. For detailed information and an analysis of the causes of the destruction of the Parthenon, see T. E. Mommsen, "The Venetians in Athens and the Destruction of the Parthenon in 1687," *Medieval and Renaissance Studies* (Ithaca, 1959), 50–70.

28. Laborde, 2:277.

29. Vandal, *L'Odyssée,* ix.

30. Laborde, 1:122. In August of the same year, he had visited Aleppo, Syria, which he had entered in the same grandiose style. "I have been at Aleppo for eight days after having made an honorable entrance preceded by my trumpets, my eight janissaries, an equal number of dragomans, ten liveried servants, my lead horses, and about eight men dressed in the Greek style." Ibid., 1:120.

31. Nointel, cited in Laborde, 1:138.

32. When Tournefort visited the Aegean island of Antiparos in 1700, he found that Nointel's visit there twenty-seven years earlier was still remembered by the islanders. He was told a story that, even though most certainly exaggerated, reveals Nointel's penchant for the fantastic and the eccentric. "M. le Marquis de Nointel, French Ambassador to the Porte, spent the three feast days of Christmas in this cave accompanied by more than five hundred persons, some of them members of his household, and others, merchants, corsairs, or natives who had followed him. One hundred thick yellow wax candles, and four hundred lamps, which were burning day and night, were placed so well that it was as bright as in the best lit church." Joseph Pitton de Tournefort, *Relation d'un voyage du Levant fait par ordre du Roy* (Paris, 1717), 1:193.

33. Nointel, cited in Laborde, 1:123.

34. There is some disagreement as to the identity of the painter. Vandal, 166–67, n. 1, maintains that it was the Flemish Rombault Faidherbe, whereas Laborde, 1:125, states that it was the Frenchman Jacques Carrey. The latter view seems to be correct. Henri Omont, *Missions archéologiques françaises en Orient au XVIIe et XVIIIe siècles* (Paris, 1902), 1:191, notes that Faidherbe died on Naxos before Nointel's arrival in Athens. Since Galland had parted company with Nointel shortly after the beginning of the latter's tour, Carrey was the only artist who stayed with him until its conclusion.

35. Vandal, 170. The painting is housed in the museum of Chartres.

CHAPTER 4. The Rise of Philhellenism

1. Voltaire, *Pensées sur l'administration publique,* in *Oeuvres complètes,* ed. Beaumarchais et al. (Kehl, 1785–89), 29:30.

2. Peter Gay, *Voltaire's Politics: The Poet as Realist* (New York, 1965), 180.

3. Margaret T. Hodgen, *Early Anthropology in the Sixteenth and Seventeenth Centuries* (Philadelphia, 1964), 257–58.

4. Pierre Martino, *L'Orient dans la littérature française aux XVIIe et XVIIIe siècles* (Paris, 1906), 15.

5. For a caustic commentary on the desire of the Europeans to Hellenize

the modern Greeks, see Joseph-Arthur, comte de Gobineau, "Le Royaume des Hellènes," in *Deux études sur la Grèce moderne* (Paris, 1905), 93ff. "It was therefore agreed that it was necessary to find the Greeks, to liberate the Greeks, because the Greeks were the most tenderly heroic and the most elegantly patriotic people that one could imagine. But did the Greeks exist? Assuredly."

6. Voltaire, *Essai sur les moeurs et l'esprit des nations*, in *Oeuvres complètes*, 16:120. Hereafter cited in text as *E*. At the end of the eighteenth century, Mme de Staël expressed the same attitude toward Greek mythology in *De la littérature*.

7. Helvétius voiced essentially the same view when he remarked that pagan religion, in spite of its absurdities, "was nevertheless the best suited for men. . . . Through it, the imagination, always kept active, put all of nature under the empire of poetry, vivified all the parts of the universe, animated everything." Helvétius, *De l'homme, de ses facultés intellectuelles, et de son éducation*, in *Oeuvres complètes* (Paris, 1818), 2:65.

8. Voltaire, *Essai sur les moeurs*, 110.

9. Voltaire, *D'Hérodote*, in *Oeuvres complètes*, 27:30.

10. Voltaire, *Essai sur les moeurs*, 114.

11. Helvétius, *De l'homme*, 64.

12. Montesquieu, *Considérations sur les causes de la grandeur des Romains et de leur décadence*, in *Oeuvres complètes* (Paris, 1951), 2:203.

13. Ibid., 196.

14. Eyewitness accounts by Westerners, themselves crusaders, attest to the amazement of the invaders at the sight of so many riches. "You can know that they looked a lot at Constantinople, those who had never seen it; because they could not believe that there could be in the whole world such a rich city, when they saw these high walls and these rich towers that enclosed it all around, and these rich palaces and these high churches, of which there were so many that no one would have believed it if he had not seen them with his own eyes." Geoffrey de Villehardouin, *La Conquête de Constantinople*, trans. into modern French by Natalie de Wailly (Paris, 1882), 73.

15. Montesquieu, *Considérations*, 207. Yet the Western knights and soldiers did more than ridicule the people of Constantinople. In the words of a historian, "the treasured monuments of antiquity which Constantinople had sheltered for nine centuries, were overthrown, carried off, or melted down. Private houses, monasteries and churches were emptied of their wealth. Chalices, stripped of their jewels, became drinking cups; icons became game-boards and tables; and nuns in their convents were raped and robbed. In St. Sophia the soldiers tore down the veil of the sanctuary and smashed the gold and silver carvings of the altar and the amvon [pulpit].

They piled their trophies on to mules and horses which slipped and fell on the marble pavement, leaving it running with their blood; and a prostitute sat on the Patriarch's throne singing bawdy French songs." J. M. Hussey, ed., *Byzantium and Its Neighbours*, in *The Cambridge Medieval History: The Byzantine Empire* (Cambridge, 1966), vol. 4, pt. 1, p. 286.

16. Voltaire, *Essai sur les moeurs*, 145.

17. Gay, 171–72.

18. Montesquieu, *Considérations*, 469–70.

19. Voltaire, *Essai sur les moeurs*, 448.

20. Helvétius, *De l'esprit*, in *Oeuvres complètes*, 1:420.

21. For a broader analysis of European reaction to the 1770 insurrection, see David Constantine, *Early Greek Travellers and the Hellenic Ideal* (Cambridge, 1984), 168–87.

22. Voltaire, *Correspondence*, ed. Theodore Besterman (Geneva, 1953–65), 77:82. Hereafter cited in text as *C*.

23. Gay, 180.

24. Voltaire, *Correspondence*, 77:52–53.

25. Voltaire, *Epitre à l'impératrice de Russie, Catherine II*, in *Oeuvres complètes*, 13:230.

26. Voltaire, *Correspondence*, 71:23.

27. Voltaire, *Ode pindarique*, 407.

28. Gay, 180.

29. Voltaire, *Correspondence*, 77:122.

30. Pierre-Augustin Guys, *Voyage littéraire de la Grèce ou lettres sur les Grecs anciens et modernes, avec un parallèle de leurs moeurs*, 3d ed. (Paris, 1783), 1:76.

31. Nikolai Iorga, *Les Voyageurs français dans l'Orient européen* (Paris, 1929), 104.

32. Guys, 1:471, 473.

33. For favorable comments on Guys's appreciation of Greece and its folk traditions, see Iorga, 103; E. Egger, *L'Hellénisme en France* (Paris, 1869), 1:287. Iorga characterized Guys as "the premier folklorist who directs his eyes to the Orient."

34. Guys, 1:20.

35. For a lengthy and detailed description of Greek folk dances, see ibid., 160–79.

36. Elizabeth Chénier, "Lettre de Mme Chénier à l'Auteur sur les danses grecques," in Guys, *Voyage littéraire de la Grèce*, 1:188.

37. Guys, 2:280.

38. A detailed account of the return voyage is given in an unpublished journal kept by one of Choiseul-Gouffier's companions—probably his secretary, Kauffer—on deposit at the Gennadius Library. See Barbié du Bocage

papers. Catalogue of Manuscripts in the Gennadius Library. File 127, 17–30.

39. The relation between the two men and Barbié du Bocage's contribution to the *Voyage pittoresque* is shown in detail in letters and memoires contained in the papers of Barbié du Bocage on deposit at the Gennadius Library. See Catalogue of Manuscripts. File 127.

40. Jacques Delille, *L'Imagination* (Paris, 1806), 1:223–24.

41. Léonce Pingaud, *Choiseul-Gouffier: La France en Orient sous Louis XVI* (Paris, 1887), preface.

42. For Choiseul-Gouffier and his assistants, Homer was not only the prince of poets but also an invaluable source of information and a reliable guide. In Choiseul-Gouffier's words, Homer was "a primary web of truths, which make his songs the most valuable as well as the most ancient annals of Greece." Marie-Gabriel-Florent-Auguste, comte de Choiseul-Gouffier, *Voyage pittoresque de la Grèce* (Paris, 1809), vol. 2, pt. 1, p. 4.

43. Barbié du Bocage followed the progress of the *Voyage pittoresque* from its inception to its completion. His genuine interest notwithstanding, he was to be remunerated for his services by receiving an annual stipend designated by Choiseul-Gouffier himself in a letter he sent to him from St. Petersburg in 1801. However, he received only part of that amount and brought suit against Choiseul-Gouffier's heirs, who by that time had recovered part of the family fortune. In defending his claims, he listed the services he had rendered to the author of the *Voyage pittoresque*: "I saw his plans. I wrote some notes about them, and M. de Choiseul took them and made them part of his *Voyage pittoresque de la Grèce*, which he began to publish soon afterwards. I made several other notes and designs of maps for him without any reward other than a copy of the first volume when it was completed. M. de Choiseul-Gouffier was named ambassador at Constantinople in 1784. I did not stop corresponding with him, and I sent him an even greater number of memoranda than before. In 1793 he emigrated to Russia and a long time passed without any news of him. I saved for him, either in a portfolio or in my published works, the ownership of many works that they had tried to take away from him. Finally, in 1801, I received a letter from him, from Vilno, on 30 January, in which he expressed his gratitude and begged me to take on the task of continuing his work. I did not accept his offer entirely, but I promised to help him and to give him notes and all the materials I would assemble for the continuation of his *Voyage pittoresque*." Barbié du Bocage papers. Catalogue of Manuscripts in the Gennadius Library. File 127, p. 148.

44. Choiseul-Gouffier, "Discours préliminaire du Voyage pittoresque de la Grèce," *Voyage pittoresque de la Grèce* (Paris, 1782), 1:i.

45. Choiseul-Gouffier, *Voyage pittoresque,* vol.2, pt.1, p.1.

46. Ibid., 1:97.

47. Dacier, "Notice sur la vie et les ouvrages de M. le comte de Choiseul-Gouffier," in Choiseul-Gouffier, *Voyage pittoresque*, vol. 2, pt. 1, pp. i–iv.

48. Choiseul-Gouffier, *Voyage pittoresque*, 1:14.

49. Ibid., 1:44.

50. For an examination of Choiseul-Gouffier's relation of this event seen in the light of more recent historical studies, see Kyriakos Simopoulos, *Xenoi taxidiotes sten Ellada 1700–1800* (Foreign Travelers to Greece 1700–1800) (Athens, 1973), 2:364–70.

51. Choiseul-Gouffier, *Voyage pittoresque*, 1:165.

52. For an analysis of the penetration and influence of the ideas of the Enlightenment on eighteenth-century Greece, see C. Th. Dimaras, *La Grèce au temps des Lumières* (Geneva, 1969).

53. Choiseul-Gouffier, *Voyage pittoresque*, frontispiece.

54. Choiseul-Gouffier, "Discours préliminaire," *Voyage pittoresque*, 1:vii.

55. Choiseul-Gouffier expressed his emotions in an impassioned plea to his readers: "If any one of my Readers has traveled to Greece, if living among the Greeks under this beautiful sky and on this favored land he experienced the charm attached to their amiable qualities; if he received from them this ancient and touching hospitality that was offered to me daily; finally, if he carried for a long time the heavy burden of this distressing contrast between their ancient glory and present humiliation, he will cry out with them, with me, '*Exoriare aliquis*'" Ibid., xv.

56. Choiseul-Gouffier, quoted in Pingaud, 211.

57. Delille, 1:224.

58. Dacier, ii.

CHAPTER 5. Chateaubriand's Greece: The Romantic Pilgrimage

1. René Canat, *L'Hellénisme des romantiques* (Paris, 1951–55), 1:146–47.

2. François-René de Chateaubriand, *Correspondence générale de Chateaubriand*, ed. Louis Thomas (Paris, 1912–14), 1:36.

3. Georges Poulet, *Etudes sur le temps humain* (Paris, 1949), xxxii.

4. Chauteubriand, *Mémoires d'outre-tombe*, ed. Maurice Levaillant (Paris, 1964), 1:49–50.

5. Poulet, xxiv.

6. Konstantinos Tsatsos, "O Romantismos, o Chateaubriand, kai e Ellas" (Romanticism, Chateaubriand, and Greece), *Nea Estia*, 74 (Christmas 1968): 177.

7. Chateaubriand, *Correspondence*, 1:37.

8. Chateaubriand, *Itinéraire de Paris à Jérusalem et de Jérusalem à Paris*, 2d ed. (Paris, 1812), 1:iii. Hereafter cited in text as *I*.

9. Chateaubriand, *Correspondence*, 1:37.

10. Edward Said, *Orientalism* (New York, 1978), 170.

11. Chateaubriand, *Mémoires d'outre-tombe*, 1:231–32.

12. Jean-Pierre Richard, *Paysage de Chateaubriand* (Paris, 1967), 34.

13. The maturation of his plan to visit Greece and the Orient from its inception in 1803 to its realisation in 1806 is delineated in a series of letters. See Chateaubriand, *Correspondence*, 1:121, 124, 220–21, 226, 231.

14. Poulet, xl.

15. Chateaubriand, *Correspondence*, 1:226.

16. The accuracy of these dates was disputed by Fauvel, his host in Athens, who stated that Chateaubriand arrived in Athens on 19 August by sea and not by land, as the author claimed, and that he left on the twenty-third. For more details on this chronological controversy, see Louis Hogu, "Documents sur le séjour à Athènes de Chateaubriand," *Revue d'histoire littéraire de la France*, 19 (1912): 631–34.

17. Chateaubriand, *Mémoires d'outre-tombe*, 2:261–62.

18. G. Pailhès, *Chateaubriand, sa femme et ses amis* (Paris, 1896), 473.

19. Alice Poirier, *Les Idées artistiques de Chateaubriand* (Paris, 1930), 235.

20. Ibid., xiv–xv. Chateaubriand expressed his subjective response to Greece and to the Mediterranean in general very succinctly: "I beg the reader to look at this Itinerary . . . as the Memoires of a year of my life." Chateaubriand, *Itinéraire*, 1:iii. The same idea was conveyed in a letter written to the duchesse de Duras on 27 September 1812: "It is the story of my thoughts and of the movements of my heart during a year." Chateaubriand, *Correspondence*, 1:269.

21. Garabed Der-Sahaghian, *Chateaubriand en Orient* (Venice, 1914), 30.

22. Pierre Jourda, *L'Exotisme dans la littérature française depuis Chateaubriand* (Paris, 1938), 1:24.

23. Said, 173.

24. Louis de Fontanes, "*Itinéraire de Paris à Jérusalem et de Jérusalem à Paris*, . . . par F. A. de Chateaubriand," *Mercure de France* 47 (April 1811): 60.

25. Canat, 1:171.

26. Chateaubriand, *Itinéraire*, 1:75–76.

27. Chateaubriand, quoted in M. L. J. A., comte de Marcellus, *Chateaubriand et son temps* (Paris, 1859), 171.

28. Manuel de Diéguez, *Chateaubriand ou le poète face à l'histoire* (Paris, 1963), 129.

29. Chateaubriand, *Itinéraire*, 1:154.

30. See reviews of the *Itinéraire* in the following periodicals: *Mercure de France* 17 (April 1811); *Le Moniteur universel*, 15 April 1811; *Journal de l'empire*, 13 March 1811; *Annales encyclopédiques* 2 (March 1817); 3 (May 1817).

31. Aubin-Louis Millin, "Itinéraire de Paris à Jérusalem," *Magazin encyclopédique*, 2 (April 1811): 22.

32. Chateaubriand, *Itinéraire*, 1:iv.

33. Chateaubriand, *Itinéraire de Paris à Jérusalem*, ed. Emile Malakis (Baltimore, 1946), 1:2.

34. This letter was first published by George Soulis, "O Chateaubriand kai e Ellenike Epanastasis" (Chateaubriand and the Greek Revolution), *Nea Estia* 44 (September 1948): 1103–4.

35. See review of the *Itinéraire* by Malte-Brun, *Journal de l'empire*, 13 March 1811, reprinted in Chateaubriand, *Itinéraire*, ed. Malakis, 2:452–53.

36. Its full title was: *Alcuni cenni critici del dottore Gian-Dionisio Avramiotti sul viaggio in Grechia che compone la prima parte dell' "Itinerario de Parigi a Jerusalemme" del signor F. A. de Chateaubriand, con varie osservazioni sulle anticheta greche* (Padua, 1816).

37. Dionysios Avramiotti, *Les Notes critiques d'Avramiotti sur le Voyage en Grèce de Chateaubriand*, trans. Alice Poirier (Paris, 1929), 2.

38. Marcellus, 438.

39. Avramiotti, 26–27.

40. Chateaubriand, *Itinéraire*, 1:130–55.

41. Two such instances were the discovery of a tomb in the vicinity of Mycenae, which Chateaubriand promptly identified as that of Clytaemnestra and Egisthus, and the misnaming of a metropolitan as a *"patriarche de la Morée"* when he should have known that there was only one patriarch in Constantinople. See Chateaubriand, *Itinéraire*, 1:166, 109.

42. Avramiotti, 41–42.

43. See Millin's introductory remarks in Avramiotti, "Quelques traits critiques sur le voyage en Grèce qui compose la première partie de l'*Itinéraire de Paris à Jérusalem*," *Annales encyclopédiques*, 3 (May 1817): 373.

44. "M. Avramiotti can say whatever he wishes . . . ; this does not prevent Chateaubriand from being the greatest and most faithful painter when he sits on top of the hill and describes with his words full of light everything he sees at his feet under the sun." See Charles-Augustin Sainte-Beuve, *Chateaubriand et son groupe littéraire sous l'Empire* (Paris, 1872), 2:83.

45. Champion, quoted in Alice Poirier, *Les Notes critiques d'Avramiotti*, xviii.

46. A. Aulard, "Les Illusions grecques de Chateaubriand," *La Revue* (ancienne *Revue des revues*), 88 (1910): 32, 40.

47. Der-Sahaghian, 415.

48. Malakis, in Chateaubriand, *Itinéraire*, ed. Malakis, 1:xiii.

49. Chateaubriand, *Itinéraire*, 1:65. In a letter written soon after his return from the Levant, Chateaubriand stated: "Before leaving for the Levant, I had done considerable work on ancient and modern authors who treat Greece and Judea." Chateaubriand, "Quelques détails sur les moeurs des Grecs, des Arabes et des Turcs," *Mercure de France*, August 1807, 197.

50. Der-Sahaghian, 350.

51. Chateaubriand, *Itinéraire*, ed. Malakis, 1:81.

52. Der-Sahaghian, 421.

53. Chateaubriand, *Le Génie du christianisme* (Paris, n.d.), 2:4.

54. Chateaubriand, *Itinéraire*, 1:98.

55. Richard, 34.

56. Chateaubriand, *Les Martyrs* (Paris, 1809), 1:106–7.

57. Richard, 36.

58. Marcellus, 67–68.

59. Sainte-Beuve, 2:57.

60. "In vain he journeyed and leafed through big books; his mind had already been made up. He saw only scenery, countries, and ruins, and he thought only of the effects he would derive." Louis Bertrand, *La Fin du classicisme et le retour à l'antique dans la seconde moitié du XVIIIe siècle et les premières années du XXIXe en France* (Paris, 1897), 356–57.

61. Chateaubriand, *Les Martyrs*, 1:173.

62. Chateaubriand, *Itinéraire*, 1:233.

63. Chateaubriand, *Mémoires d'outre-tombe*, 1:621–22.

64. Chateaubriand, *Itinéraire*, 1:141.

65. "One of the most intimate elements of pre-Romanticism, one of those that were to reappear in certain aspects of the Romanticism of the nineteenth century, is the nocturnal and sepulchral poetry, which from the middle of the eighteenth century flows copiously through the most diverse countries of Europe." Paul Van Tieghem, *Le Préromantisme* (Paris, 1930), 2:3.

66. Chateaubriand, *Itinéraire*, 1:92.

67. Chateaubriand, *Correspondence*, 1:229.

68. Henry Bordeaux, *Voyageurs d'Orient: Dès pèlerins aux méharistes de Palmyre* (Paris, 1926), 37.

69. Chateaubriand, *Itinéraire*, 1:88.

70. Poirier, *Les Idées artistiques de Chateaubriand*, 234.

71. Chateaubriand, *Itinéraire*, 1:258.

72. For more information on this Greek, see C. Th. Dimaras, "O Chateaubriand sten Ellada" (Chateaubriand in Greece), *Nea Estia* 74 (Christmas 1968): 270–71.

73. Chateaubriand, *Itinéraire*, 1:257.

74. Chateaubriand, "Quelques détails sur les moeurs des Grecs, des Arabes et des Turcs," *Mercure de France*, August 1807, 201.

75. Said, 170.

76. Chateaubriand, "'Avant-Propos' to 'Note sur la Grèce,'" *Itinéraire*, ed. Malakis, 1:24.

77. The full title of the Greek translation of the *Note* was: *Ypomnema peri tes Ellados, tou K. Antikometos Satomvriandou, Melous mias apo tas yper*

ton Ellenon Etaireias, metaphrasmenon eis ten Elleniken glossan. Paris: Firmin-Didot, 1825.

78. Linny-Babagor, *Réponse d'un Turc à la "Note sur la Grèce" de M. le Vte de Chateaubriand* (Bruxelles, 1825), 32.

79. Ioannes Karasoutsas, *Poème sur la mort de Chateaubriand* (Athens, 1848), 4.

80. Chateaubriand's memory seems to be faulty in this instance, because he was not previously opposed to a constitutional monarchy as the best form of government for an independent Greece. "Be that as it may, it is very conceivable that a form of monarchy, adopted by the Greeks, would dissipate all the fears, unless of course constitutional monarchies themselves become suspect." Chateaubriand, *Note sur la Grèce,* 49.

81. Chateaubriand, *Mémoires d'outre-tombe,* 2:124.

82. Chateaubriand, "Voyage pittoresque et historique de l'Espagne par M. de Laborde," *Mercure de France,* July 1807, 12.

83. Tsatsos, 18.

84. Canat, 1:40.

85. Chateaubriand, *Itinéraire,* 1:307.

86. Gaston Bachelard, *Poétique de l'espace* (Paris, 1957), 154.

87. Sainte-Beuve underscored Chateaubriand's desire to dominate through his art. "He is a painter as others are conquerors: *Veni, vidi, vici.* He paints from above and with authority, from a birds-eye view, from eagle heights." Sainte-Beuve, 2:81.

88. Chateaubriand, *Itinéraire,* 1:87. In writing this, he forgot that on p. 88 he would mention that his apparel consisted of what he had on "and some shawls to cover my head at night."

CHAPTER 6. Toward a Broader Image of Modern Greece

1. Alphonse de Lamartine, *Voyage en Orient,* vol. 3 of *Oeuvres complètes* (Paris, 1829), 3.

2. Louis-Nicolas-Philippe-Auguste, comte de Forbin, *Voyage dans le Levant en 1817 et 1818* (Paris, 1819), 7–8.

3. Maurice Barrès, *Le Voyage de Sparte,* nouvelle édition (Paris, n.d.), 31. Louis Bertrand was even more critical of the literary tradition of eighteenth- and nineteenth-century Hellenism and philhellenism because it had created an idealized and factitious image of Greece. "People who are aroused only by books are tempted to forget the elementary necessities of the life of a people. These books provide them a generally idealized image. Moreover, they retain from them only what flatters their literary dream. The entire positive side and historical and social background elude them. It is a reflection that

feeds on itself when one reads our modern fictions on Greece." Louis Bertrand, *La Grèce du soleil et des paysages* (Paris, 1908), xx.

4. René Canat, *L'Hellénisme des romantiques* (Paris, 1951–55), 1:51.

5. M.-L.-J. comte de Marcellus, *Episodes littéraires en Orient* (Paris, 1851), 1:iii.

6. Marcellus, *Souvenirs de l'Orient* (Paris, 1839), 30. Hereafter cited in text as *S*.

7. For a more complete biographical profile of Marcellus, see Alfred Dumaine, *Quelques oubliés de l'autre siècle* (Paris, 1928).

8. For Marcellus's version of the discovery and acquisition of the Venus de Milo, see Marcellus, *Souvenirs*, 234–50.

9. For a fuller exposition of the circumstances surrounding the removal of the Venus de Milo, see Kyriakos Simopoulos, *Xenoi taxidiotes sten Ellada 1810–1821* (Foreign Travelers to Greece 1810–1821), (Athens, 1975), vol. 3, pt. 2, pp. 239–50.

10. The young philhellene Ambroise Firmin-Didot, who visited the Levant at the same time as Marcellus, envied the latter's good fortune. "I also aspired to have the happiness to offer to my country a similar present, but when I stopped at Rhodes, the season did not permit me to realize the hopes I had conceived." Ambroise Firmin-Didot, *Notes d'un voyage fait dans le Levant en 1816 et 1817* (Paris, 1826), 25, n. 1.

11. Marcellus, *Souvenirs*, 352–53.

12. It was there that he published his work on rhetoric, *Retorike*, in 1813. It was reviewed enthusiastically by Constantine Nikolopoulos in the *Mercure étranger* 3 (1814): 87–89.

13. Neophytos Vambas, *Retorike* (Rhetoric), in *O Korais kai e epoche tou* (Korais and his Era), Vasike Vivliotheke, no. 9 (Athens, 1958), 325. Vambas was highly valued by Korais, who extolled the school of Chios as one of the best educational institutions in Greece. "It is in Homer's own birthplace, on the island of Chios, that modern Greece has had the satisfaction of seeing for some years now the first establishment of a kind of university or polytechnic school. This establishment is a landmark in the modern history of this country; and, although it is still incomplete, the advantages it promises are all the greater and more imminent because, scarcely conceived and formed, it attracted from all parts of Greece students avid to learn." Adamantios Korais [Coray], "Mémoire sur l'état actuel de la civilisation dans la Grèce," in *Lettres inédites de Coray à Chardon de la Rochette (1770–1796)*, (Paris, 1877), 471.

14. Marcellus, *Souvenirs*, 191.

15. The appelations *tchelebi* and *coccona*, for men and women respectively, are of Turkish provenance and were used when addressing persons of distinction.

16. *Kivotos tes ellenikes glosses* (Ark of the Greek Language), (Constantinople, 1819). Of the four projected volumes only the first appeared. See D. Gines and V. Mexas, *Ellenike vivliografia 1800–1863* (Greek Bibliography 1800–1863), (Athens, 1939), 1:186.

17. Marcellus, *Épisodes littéraires*, 1:329–30.

18. Marcellus, *Souvenirs*, iii.

19. Didot, 9.

20. Simopoulos, 418.

21. Didot, 393ff.

22. For a more detailed description of the school of Kydonies, see ibid., 382–86.

23. C. Th. Dimaras, *Istoria tes neoellenikes logotechnias* (History of Modern Greek Literature), (Athens, 1968), 161. See also C. Th. Dimaras, *Neoellenikos diafotismos* (Modern Greek Enlightenment), (Athens, 1977), 58–60.

24. Simopoulos, 423.

25. Emile Malakis, "French Travellers in Greece (1770–1820): An Early Phase of French Philhellenism" (Diss., University of Pennsylvania, 1925), 55.

26. F.-C.-H.-L. Pouqueville, "Travels in Epirus, Albania, Macedonia and Thessaly," *New Voyages and Travels* 4 (1820): iv.

27. Byron and Chateaubriand, among other critics, attacked Pouqueville for being inaccurate and misleading. The former said that "Pouqueville is always out." Byron, *Childe Harold's Pilgrimage* in *The Poems and Dramas of Lord Byron* (New York, n.d.), canto 2, stanza 47, n. 3, p. 283. Chateaubriand noted ironically that "the best guide for the Morea would certainly be M. Pouqueville, if he had been able to see all the places he described. Unfortunately, he was a prisoner in Tripolitsa." Chateaubriand, *Itinéraire de Paris à Jérusalem* (Paris, 1812), 1:39. Even Korais, who welcomed all expressions of philhellenism, had reservations about Pouqueville's accuracy. "The truth is," he wrote to Barbié du Bocage, "although I may very well be mistaken, that the reading of this work produced in me the same impression that a novel would have made." Adamantios Korais [Coray], *Lettres inédites de Coray à Chardon de la Rochette (1790–1796)* (Paris, 1877), 391.

28. Pouqueville, *Voyage de la Grèce* (Paris, 1826), 1:viii–ix.

29. M. Letronne, "Analyse critique du *Voyage de la Grèce*," *Projet de diviser en sections l'Académie des Inscriptions et Belles-Lettres* (Paris, 1834), 3.

30. Pouqueville, *Voyage de la Grèce*, 2:45.

31. Pouqueville most probably had Chateaubriand in mind when he condemned haste. In another passage he commented: "No one pays more homage to the beautiful talent of M. de Chateaubriand than I: he would have restored the Peloponnesus giving it a new luster if time had allowed him to describe it." Ibid., 1:xlvi.

32. Unlike him, Byron, who visited Albania and Epirus in 1809, was

immediately captivated by the wild beauty of the area. In *Childe Harold's Pilgrimage* many verses evoke its natural splendor.

> Dark Suli's rocks, and Pindus' inland peak,
> Robed half in mist, bedewed with snowy rills,
> Arrayed in many a dun and purple streak,
> Arise; and, as the clouds among them break,
> Disclose the dwelling of the mountaineer.
>
> (Canto 2, stanza 42, ll. 2–6)

Or:

> Yet in famed Attica such lovely dales
> Are rarely seen; nor can fair Tempe boast
> a charm they know not; loved Parnassus fails,
> Though classic ground and consecrated most,
> To match some spots that lurk within this lowering cast.
>
> (Canto 2, stanza 46, ll. 5–9)

33. Pouqueville, *Voyage de la Grèce*, 2:381.

34. Douglas Dakin, *The Greek Struggle for Independence 1821–1833* (London, 1973), 30–34, 67–70.

35. "Now forty-eight years old, he does not show traces of premature old age; his noble, open countenance, characterized by sharply defined features, expresses powerfully the passions that agitate him. Master, however, when he wishes, of the play of his physiognomy, his look charms, and his cadenced laughter masks a sentiment opposite to the one he expresses; but he cannot contain his anger when he punishes, and it is manifested by a terrible convulsion of his features which betrays the violence of his character." Pouqueville, *Voyage en Morée, à Constnatinople, en Albanie, et dans plusieurs autres parties de l'Empire Ottoman pendant les années 1798, 1799, 1800 et 1801* (Paris, 1805), 3:24.

36. Byron, who visited Ali Pasha at Tepelen four years after Pouqueville, was equally struck, though somewhat less repulsed, by his heinous crimes, the agility of his mind, and the affability of his manners when he wanted to please. In a letter written to his mother from Preveza on 12 November 1809, he characterizes Ali Pasha thus: "His Highness is 60 years old, very fat and not tall, but with a fine face, light blue eyes & a white beard, his manner is very kind & at the same time he possesses that dignity which I find universal among the Turks. He has the appearance of anything but his real character, for he is a remorseless tyrant, guilty of the most horrible cruelties, very brave and so good a general, that they call him the Mohametan Buonaparte." Byron, *Selected Letters and Journals*, ed. Leslie A. Marchand (Cambridge, 1982), 31. Ali Pasha's reputation as the Napoleon of the East

captured the imagination of yet another romantic writer. 'We must recall that it is it [Asia]," wrote Victor Hugo in the preface of *Les Orientales*, "that has produced the only colossus who can match Bonaparte in this century, if indeed Bonaparte can have a match . . . ; this man of genius, Turk and Tartar in fact, this Ali-pasha, who is to Napoleon as the tiger is to the lion, as the vulture is to the eagle." Victor Hugo, *Les Orientales*, ed. Elizabeth Barineau (Paris, 1952), 1:12.

37. Pouqueville, *Voyage de la Grèce*, 1:115.

38. Byron found Ali Pasha's "court" colorful and intriguing and not quite as menacing and sinister as Pouqueville did. "I shall never forget the singular scene on entering Tepalen at five in the afternoon as the Sun was going down, it brought to my recollection . . . Scott's description of Branksome Castle. . . . The Albanians in their dresses (the most magnificent in the world, consisting of a long *white kilt*, gold worked cloak, crimson velvet gold laced jacket & waistcoat, silver mounted pistols & daggers,) the Tartars with their high caps, the Turks in their vast pelisses & turbans, the soldiers and black slaves with the horses, the former stretched in groups in an immense open gallery in front of the palace, the latter placed in a kind of cloister below it, two hundred steeds ready caparisoned to move in a moment . . . the kettle drums beating, boys calling the hour from the minarets of the mosques, altogether, with the singular appearance of the building itself, formed a new and delightful spectacle for a stranger." Byron, *Selected Letters and Journals*, 30.

39. Pouqueville spoke of the people of Jannina as "the most industrious in Greece" and of the city itself as a place that, "in addition to its privilege of cultural rebirth, is also the center of considerable commerce, which extends to all parts of the empire." *Voyage en Morée*, 3:42.

40. Quoted in Alkes Aggelos, "O Pouqueville kai e Ellada tou" (Pouqueville and His Greece), in *Periegeseis ston Elleniko Choro* (Travels in the Greek Lands), (Athens, 1968), 115.

41. Pouqueville, *Voyage de la Grèce*, 1:vii.

42. For a penetrating analysis of the historical development and of the social, psychological, and aesthetic value of the *klephtika*, see the introduction by Alexes Polites in *To Demotiko tragoudi: Klephtika* (The Folk Song: *Klephtika*), ed. Alexes Polites (Athens, 1973), xi–lxii.

43. Pouqueville, *Voyage de la Grèce*, 6:35.

44. The man whose tragic end Pouqueville witnessed was the *armatole* Thymios Vlahavas, who was taken captive after an abortive uprising in 1808. See Simopoulos, 360.

45. Pouqueville, *Voyage de la Grèce*, 2:218.

46. Pouqueville, insisting on tracing everything back to antiquity, identified Souli with the ancient Selleis and the Souliots as the descendants of

its inhabitants. The historian George Finlay considered them to be Christians of Albanian origin. See George Finlay, *History of the Greek Revolution* (London, 1971), 1:42–43.

47. Pouqueville, *Voyage de la Grèce*, 2:229.

48. Byron, *Childe Harold's Pilgrimage*, Canto 2, stanza 85, p. 290.

49. Pouqueville, *Voyage de la Grèce*, 2:3.

50. While at Athens, Pouqueville was a guest of Louis François Sebastian Fauvel. Of all the Europeans received by the French consul, it was Pouqueville who gave the fullest description of his house, a veritable mosaic of antiquities pilfered from the surrounding area. "The house of the simple and modest philosopher, who serves the king in the capacity of consul and enriches the belles-lettres with his researches, is built with the remnants of the palaces of Pericles and Aspasia and of the edifices that used to embellish Athens. The walls of his courtyard are decorated with pillars and marbles filled with inscriptions dedicated to the heroes and citizens who had served their fatherland. At the entrance of this humble sanctuary, full of the relics of venerable antiquity, one sees a white marble sarcophagus; by the gate there is a bench onto which one steps to mount a horse and which is inscribed with the contract of an Athenian setting out the distribution of wine. . . . Nearby, one can see a column of Pendelic marble, which supports an Ionic capital so perfect that one would believe that it was made by mechanical means." Pouqueville, *Voyage de la Grèce*, 5:46–47.

51. "A long experience has taught me," noted Pouqueville sceptically, "that the Greeks in this respect [good faith], with some exceptions, are very open to the temptation of deceiving a Christian who is not a member of their church." Ibid., 4:45.

52. Pouqueville saw the Byzantine era as an artistic wasteland. "But how can one explain its [the Parthenon's] preservation under the reign of Constantine and Theodosius—tyrants unworthy of the name great—who have destroyed more artistic masterpieces than the barbarians and the Turks." Ibid., 5:77–78.

53. Pouqueville, *Histoire de la régénération de la Grèce* (Paris, 1824), 1:6–7.

54. Ibid., 1:118–19.

55. Canat, *L'Hellénisme des romantiques* (Paris, 1951–55), 106.

56. Pouqueville gave a similar description of the modern Greeks in his *Régénération*. "Their national physiognomy was like an inscription where one could recognize the past and read into the future: one discovered in it the traits of the Hellenes, and it was sufficient to look at the mountaineers, who are never dominated in any country of the world, in order to conclude that the destiny of Greece would change one day." *Régénération*, 1:4.

BIBLIOGRAPHY

Aggelos, Alkes. "O Pouqueville kai e Ellada tou." In *Periegeseis ston elleniko choro*, edited by C. Th. Dimaras. Athens: O.M.E.D., 1968.

Amelinckx, Frans C. "Les Structures artistiques et les structures de l'imaginarie dans l'*Itinéraire de Paris à Jérusalem* de François-René de Chateaubriand." Diss., University of Iowa, 1970.

Andleau, Béatrix de. *Chateaubriand et "Les Martyrs."* Paris: Corti, 1952.

Atkinson, Geoffrey. *Les Relations de voyage du XVIIe siècle et l'évolution des idées; contribution à l'étude de la formation de l'esprit du XVIIIe siècle.* Paris: Champion, 1924.

Aulard, A. "Les Illusions grecques de Chateaubriand." *La Revue* (ancienne *Revue des revues*) 88 (1910): 31–40.

Avramiotti, D. "Alcuni cenni critici del dottore Gian-Dionysio Avramiotti: Quelques traits critiques sur . . . l'*Itinéraire de Paris à Jérusalem* de M. de Chateaubriand." *Annales encyclopédiques* 2 (1817): 159–66; 3 (1817): 372–76.

———. *Les Notes critiques d'Avramiotti sur le Voyage en Grèce de Chateaubriand.* Translated by Alice Poirier. Paris: PUF, 1929.

Babeau, Albert. "Le Mouvement philhellène sous la Restauration." *Le Monde moderne* 5 (1897): 593–99.

Babin, J. P. *Relation de l'état présent de la ville d'Athènes, ancienne capitale de la Grèce, bâtie depuis 3400 ans.* Lyon: Louis Pascal, 1674. Reprint edited by the comte de Laborde. Paris: Jules Renouard, 1854.

Bachelard, Gaston. *La Poétique de d'espace.* Paris: PUF, 1957.

Badolle, M. *L'Abbé Jean-Jacques Barthélemy et l'hellénisme en France dans la seconde moiteé du XVIIIe siècle.* Paris: PUF, 1926.

Barbié du Bocage papers. Athens. Gennadius Library Catalogue of Manuscripts. Files 124–47.

Barrès, Maurice, *Le Voyage de Sparte*. Paris: Juven, 1906.

Barthélemy, Jean-Jacques. *Voyage du jeune Anacharsis en Grèce vers le milieu du quatrième siècle avant l'ère vulgaire*. 7 vols. Paris: Mme Veuve DABO, 1822.

Bartholdy, Jakob Ludwig Salomon. *Voyage en Grèce fait dans les années 1803 et 1804*. Translated by A. du C. [Auguste de Coudray]. Paris: Dentu, 1807.

Beaujour, Louis Auguste Félix de. *Tableau du commerce de la Grèce, formé d'après une année moyenne, depuis 1787 jusqu'en 1797*. Paris: Ant.-Aug. Renouard, 1800.

Belloc, Louise S. W. *Bonaparte et les Grecs, suivi d'un "Tableau de la Grèce" par le comte Pecchio*. Paris: Urbain Conel, 1826.

Belon, Pierre. *Les Observations de plusieurs singularitez et choses mémorables trouvées en Grèce, Asie, Iudée, Egypte, Arabie, et autres pays estranges*. Paris: Guillaume Cavellat, 1553.

Bertrand, L. *La Fin du classicisme et le retour à l'antique dans la seconde moitié du XVIIIe siècle et les premières années du XIXe en France*. Paris: Arthème Fayard, 1897.

Bikelas, Demetrios. *La Grèce byzantine et moderne; Essais historiques*. Paris: Librairie Firmin-Didot, 1893.

Boppe, A. *L'Albanie et Napoléon (1797–1814)*. Paris: Hachette, 1914.

Bordeaux, Henry. *Voyageurs d'Orient: Dès pèlerins aux méharistes de Palmyre*. 2 vols. Paris: Librairie Plon, 1926.

Borst, William A. *Lord Byron's First Pilgrimage*. N.p.: Archon Books, 1969.

Boulvé, Léon. *De l'hellénisme chez Fénelon*. Paris: Ancienne Librairie Thorin et Fils, A. Fontemoing, 1897.

Bradford, Ernle. *The Great Betrayal: Constaninople 1204*. London: Hodder & Stoughton, 1967.

Bruno, P. "Ambassadeurs de France et capucins français à Constantinople au XVIIe siècle d'après le Journal du P. Thomas de Paris." *Etudes franciscaines* 29 (March 1913): 232–59; 30 (October 1913): 401–14; 31 (April 1914): 388–402.

Bulgari, Stamati. "Extraits de quelques lettres de M. Stamati Bulgari, de Corfu sur les Grecs modernes." *Annales des voyages, de la géographie et de l'histoire* 9 (1809): 368–71.

Butor, Michel. "Travel and Writing." *Mosaic* 7 (Fall 1974): 1–16.

Byron, George Gordon [Lord Byron]. "Childe Harold's Pilgrimage," *Poems and Dramas of Lord Byron*. New York: Thomas Y. Crowell & Co., n.d.

――――. *Selected Letters and Journals*. Edited by Leslie A. Marchand. Cambridge: Harvard University Press, Belknap Press, 1982.

Campbell, John, and Philip Sherrard. *Modern Greece*. London: Ernest Benn, 1968.

Canat, René. *L'Hellénisme des romantiques*. 3 vols. Paris: Marcel Didier, 1951–55.

——. *La Renaissance de la Grèce antique (1820–1850)*. Paris: Hachette, 1911.

Cassirer, Ernst. *The Individual and the Cosmos in Renaissance Philosophy*. Philadelphia: University of Pennsylvania Press, 1963.

——. *The Philosophy of the Enlightenment*. Princeton: Princeton University Press, 1951.

——. "Some Remarks on the Question of the Renaissance." *Journal of the History of Ideas* 4, no. 1 (1943): 49–56.

Castellan, Antoine Laurent. *Lettres sur la Morée, et les îles de Cérigo, Hydra et Zante*. Paris: H. Agasse, 1808.

Caylus, A. C., comte de. *Recueil d'antiquités égyptiennes, étrusques, grecques et romaines*. New ed. 7 vols. Paris: Deraint et Saillant,1761.

Chassang, A. "Du Génie grec et de ses affinités avec le génie français." *Revue contemporaine*, 1869, 5–20.

Chateaubriand, François-René, vicomte de. *Atala e oi erotes dyo agrion egchorion tes Voreiou Amerikes: poiema tou Frantseskou Avgoustou Satovrian; metafrasthen ek tes gallikes eis ten mixovarvaron elleneken fonen*. N.p.: Panos Theodosiou from Ioannina, 1805.

——. *Correspondence générale de Chateaubriand*. Edited by Louis Thomas. 5 vols. Paris, 1912–24.

——. *Itinéraire de Paris à Jérusalem et de Jérusalem à Paris*. 2d ed. 2 vols. Paris: Le Normant, 1812.

——. *Itinéraire de Paris à Jérusalem*. Edited by Emile Malakis. 2 vols. Baltimore: Johns Hopkins Press, 1946.

——. *Les Martyrs*. 2 vols. Paris: Flammarion, n.d.

——. *Mémoires d'outre-tombe*. Edited by Maurice Levaillant. 4 vols. Paris: Flammarion, 1964.

——. *Note sur la Grèce*. Paris: Le Normant, 1825.

——. "Quelques détails sur les moeurs des Grecs, des Arabes et des Turcs." *Mercure de France* 29 (1 August 1807): 197–213.

——. "Voyage pittoresque et historique de l'Espagne par M. de Laborde." *Mercure de France* 28 (1 July 1807): 7–21.

——. *Ypomnema peri tes Ellados tou K. antikometos Satovriandou, melous mias apo tas yper ton Ellenon etairias; metafrasmenon apo ten galliken glossan*. Paris: Firmin-Didot, 1825.

Chénier, André. *L'Invention*. Edited by Paul Dimoff. Paris: Nizet, 1966.

———. *Oeuvres complètes*. Edited by Gérard Walter. Paris: Gallimard, Bibliothèque de la Pléiade, 1958.

Chénier, Elizabeth. *Lettres grecques de Madame Chénier précédées d'une étude sur sa vie par Robert de Bonnières*. Paris: Charavay Frères, 1879.

Choiseul-Gouffier, Marie-Gabriel-Florent-Auguste, comte de. *Voyage pittoresque de la Grèce*. 2 vols. Paris: J. J. Blaise, 1782–1822.

———. *Discours préliminaire du Voyage pittoresque de la Grèce*. Paris: Ph.-D. Pierres, 1783.

Collas, George, ed. *Chateaubriand: Le livre du centenaire*. Paris: Flammarion, 1949.

Collignon, Maxime. "Le Consul Jean Giraud et sa relation de l'Attique au XVIIe siècle." *Mémoires de l'Académie des inscriptions et belles-lettres*, vol. 39. Paris: Imprimerie Nationale, 1913.

Condorcet, Antoine-Nicolas de. *Esquisse d'un tableau historique du progrès de l'esprit humain*. In *Oeuvres complètes*, vol. 6. Stuttgard: Frommann, 1847–49.

Constantine, David. *Early Greek Travellers and the Hellenic Ideal*. Cambridge: Cambridge University Press, 1984.

Constantinidou-Bibicou, Hellène. "Les Origines du philhellénisme français." *Hellénisme contemporain*, 2d ser., 7 (1953): 248–65.

Dacier. "Notice sur la vie et les ouvrages de M. le comte de Choiseul-Gouffier." In Choiseul-Gouffier, *Voyage pittoresque de la Grèce*, vol. 2, pt. 1. Paris: J. J. Blaise, 1809.

Dairval, Baudelot de. *De l'utilité des voyages et de l'avantage que la recherche des antiquitez procure aux sçavans*. 2 vols. Paris: chez Pierre Aubouin et Pierre Emery, 1686.

Dakin, Douglas. *The Greek Struggle for Independence 1821–1833*. London: B. T. Batsford, 1973.

Daulphinoys, Nicolas de. *Les navigations, peregrinations et voyages, faicts en la Turquie*. Anvers: Guillaume Silvius, 1577.

Daux, Georges. *Les Étapes de l'archéologie*. Paris: PUF, 1948.

De Bausset, M. L. F. *The Life of Fénelon, Archbishop of Cambray*. Translated by William Mumford. 2 vols. London: Sherwood, Neely & Jones, 1810.

De Benazé. "Révolutionnaires et classiques." *Révolution française* 4 (1883): 900–914; 1073–90.

Dehérain, Henri. "Une Correspondance inédite de François Poqueville, consul de France à Jannina et à Patras sous le premier Empire et la Restauration." *Revue de l'histoire des colonies françaises*. 9th year, 2d semester (1921): 61–100.

Delaruelle, Louis. *Guillaume Budé: Les Origines, les débuts, les idées maîtresses.* Paris: Librairie Honoré Champion, 1907.

Delille, Jacques. *L'Imagination.* 2 vols. Paris: Giguet et Michaud, 1806.

Der-Sahaghian, Garabed P. *Chateaubriand en Orient.* Venice: Saint-Lazare, 1914.

Diderot, Denis. "De la Poésie dramatique." *Oeuvres esthétiques.* Paris: Garnier Frères, 1965.

Diéguez, Manuel de. *Chateaubriand ou le poète face à l'histoire.* Paris: Plon, 1963.

Dimaras, C. Th. "O Chateaubriand sten Ellada." *Nea Estia* 84 (Christmas 1968): 267–80.

———. *La Grèce au temps des Lumières.* Genève: Librairie Droz, 1969.

———. *Istoria tes neoellenikes logotechnias.* 4th ed. Athens: Ikaros, 1968.

———. "Notes sur l'évolution des idées du XVIe au XIXe siècle dans le domaine grec et sur les doctrines qui l'ont enregistrée." *Sonderdruck, Zeitschrift für Balkanologie,* 2d ser. (1967): 160–66.

———. "O periegetismos ston elleniko choro." In *Periegeseis ston elleniko choro,* edited by C. Th. Dimaras. Athens: O.M.E.D., 1968.

Dionisotti, A. C. "On the Greek Studies of Robert Grosseteste." In *The Uses of Greek and Latin: Historical Essays,* edited by A. C. Dionisotti, Anthony Grafton, and Jill Kraye. London: Warburg Institute, 1988.

Dreux, Robert de. *Voyage en Turquie et en Grèce.* Edited by Hubert Pernot. Paris: Société d'Edition "Les Belles-Lettres," 1925.

Driault, Edouard, et Michel Lhéritier. *Histoire diplomatique de la Grèce.* 5 vols. Paris: PUF, 1925.

Droulia, Loukia. "O Spon kai alloi xenoi sten Ellada." In *Periegeseis ston elleniko choro,* edited by C. Th. Dimaras. Athens: O.M.E.D., 1968.

Dumaine, Alfred. *Quelques Oubliés de l'autre siècle.* Paris: Librairie de Vélin d'Or, 1928.

Egger, E. *L'Hellénisme en France.* 2 vols. Paris: Didier, 1869.

Elliott, John Huxtable. *The Old World and the New 1492–1650.* Cambridge: Cambridge University Press, 1970.

Erickson, Carolly. *The Medieval Vision: Essays in History and Perception.* New York: Oxford University Press, 1976.

Esménard, J. "Rapport de M. Esménard sur le *Voyage pittoresque de la Grèce* par M. de Choiseul-Gouffier." *Mercure de France* 36 (1809): 641.

Espérandieu, M. "Renseignements inédits sur la collection du comte de Choiseul-Gouffier." *Bulletin de la Sociéte Nationale des Antiquaires de France* 58 (1897): 161–211.

Feletz, M. de. "Article nécrologique sur M. le comte de Choiseul-Gouffier." *Journal des Débats,* 2 July 1817, v–vi.

Félix-Beaujour, [Félix Auguste]. *Tableau du commerce de la Grèce, formé d'après une année moyenne, depuis 1789 jusqu'en 1797.* 2 vols. Paris: De l'Imprimerie de Crapelet, 1800.

Finlay, George. *History of the Greek Revolution.* 2 vols. London: Zeno, 1971. (Reprint of George Finlay, *A History of Greece from Its Conquest by the Romans . . . ,* vols. 6, 7. Edited by H. F. Tozer. Oxford: Clarendon Press, 1877).

Firmin-Didot, Ambroise. *Notes d'un voyage fait dans le Levant en 1816 et 1817.* Paris: Firmin-Didot, [1826].

F[ontanes], Louis de. *"Itinéraire de Paris à Jérusalem et de Jérusalem à Paris par F. A. de Chateaubriand." Mercure de France* 47 (April 1811), 55–67.

Forbin, L. M. P. A., comte de. *Voyage dans le Levant en 1817–1818.* Paris: Imprimerie Royale, 1819.

Fougères, G. "La Mythologie classique chez les poètes modernes [Chénier, Lamartine, Hugo, Leconte de Lisle]." *Revue universitaire,* 15 July 1903, 128–45.

Friedman, John Block. *The Monstrous Races in Medieval Art and Thought.* Cambridge: Harvard University Press, 1981.

Gassot, Iaques. *Le Discours du voyage de Venise à Constantinople, contenant la querele du Grand Seigneur contre le Sophi, avec élégante description de plusieurs lieux, villes et citez de la Grèce et choses admirables en icelle.* Paris: Antoine le Clerc, 1550.

Gay, Peter. *The Enlightenment: An Interpretation.* New York: Alfred Knopf, 1966.

———. *Voltaire's Politics: The Poet as Realist.* New York: Random House, 1965.

Geanakoplos, Deno John. *Byzantine East and Latin West: Two Worlds of Christendom in the Middle Ages and Renaissance.* New York: Harper & Row, Harper Torchbooks, 1966.

———. *Greek Scholars in Venice.* Cambridge: Harvard University Press, 1962.

———. *Interaction of the "Sibling" Byzantine and Western Cultures in the Middle Ages and Italian Renaissance.* New Haven: Yale University Press, 1976.

Gennadios, Ioannis. "Ta Ioannitika cheirografa." *Epeirotika Chronika,* 1927, 234.

Gines, D., and V. Mexas. *Ellenike bibliographia 1800–1863.* 3 vols. Athens: Academy of Athens, 1939.

Gobineau, Joseph-Arthur, comte de. "Le Royaume des Hellènes." *Deux études sur la Grèce moderne*. Paris: Nourrit, 1905.

Goncourt, Edmond and Jules. *L'Art du dix-huitième siècle*. 3d ser. Paris, 1859–75.

Gossman, Lionel. *Medievalism and the Ideologies of the Enlightenment*. Baltimore: Johns Hopkins Press, 1968.

Greenblatt, Stephen. *Marvelous Possessions: The Wonder of the New World*. Chicago: University of Chicago Press, 1991.

Grell, Chantal. "Histoire ancienne et érudition. La Grèce et Rome dans les travaux des érudits en France au XVIIIe siècle." Diss., Paris-Sorbonne, 1986.

Grell, Chantal, and Christian Michel, eds. *Primitivisme et mythes des origines dans la France des Lumières 1680–1820*. Paris: Presses de l'Université de Paris-Sorbonne, 1989.

Guillet, André [Sr. de la Guilletière]. *Athènes ancienne et nouvelle et l'estat present de l'empire des Turcs, contenant la vie du Sultan Mahomet IV. . . .* Paris: Estienne Michallet, 1675.

———. *Lacédémone ancienne et nouvelle où l'on voit les moeurs, et les coûtumes des Grecs Modernes, des Mahometans et des Juifs du pays*. Paris: Jean Ribou, 1676.

———. *Lettres écrites sur une dissertation d'un voyage de Grèce, publié par M. Spon*. Paris: Estienne Michallet, 1679.

Guys, Pierre-Augustin. *Voyage littéraire de la Grèce ou lettres sur les Grecs anciens et modernes, avec un parallèle de leurs moeurs*. 3d ed., rev. and corrected. 3 vols. Paris: Chez la Veuve Duchesne, 1783.

Hazard, Paul. *The European Mind 1680–1715*. New York: World Publishing, 1963.

Helvétius, Claude Adrien. *De l'Esprit*. In *Oeuvres complètes*, vol. 1. Paris: chez Mme Veuve Lepetit. 1818.

———. *De l'Homme, de ses facultés intellectuelles, et de son éducation*. In *Oeuvres complètes*, vol. 2. Paris: chez Mme Veuve Lepetit, 1818.

Hodgen, Margaret T. *Early Anthropology in the Sixteenth and Seventeenth Centuries*. Philadelphia: University of Pennsylvania Press, 1964.

Hogu, M. L. "Documents sur le séjour à Athènes de Chateaubriand." *Revue d'histoire littétaire de la France* 19 (1912): 631–34.

Howard, Martha Walling. *The Influence of Plutarch in the Major European Literatures of the Eighteenth Century*. Chapel Hill: University of North Carolina Press, 1970.

Hugo, Victor. *Les Orientales*. Edited by Elizabeth Barineau. 2 vols. Paris: Librairie Marcel Didier, 1952.

Ibrovac, Miodrag. *Claude Fauriel et la Fortune européenne des poésies populaires grecque et serbe.* . . . Paris: Marcel Didier, 1966.

Isambert, Gaston. *L'Indépendance grecque et l'Europe.* Paris, 1900.

Joret, C. *D'Ansse de Villoison et l'hellénisme en France pendant le dernier tiers du XVIIIe siècle.* Paris: Champion, 1910.

Jorga, Nicholas. *Les Voyageurs français dans l'Orient européen.* Conférences faites en Sorbonne. Paris: 1928.

——. *Une Vingtaine de voyageurs dans l'Orient européen pour faire suite aux "Voyageurs français dans l'Orient européen."* Paris: J. Gamber, 1928.

Jourda. Pierre. *L'Exotisme dans la littérature française depuis Chateaubriand.* Paris: Boivin, 1938.

Karasoutsas, Ioannes D. *Poème sur la mort de Chateaubriand.* Athens: Angelides, 1848.

Kerviler, [R]. *Essai d'une bio-bibliographie de Chateaubriand et de sa famille.* Vannes, 1895.

Knös, Börje. *Un Ambassadeur de l'hellénisme: Janus Lascaris et la tradition gréco-byzantine dans l'humanisme français.* Paris: Les Belles Lettres, 1945.

——. *L'Histoire de la littérature néo-grecque.* Stockholm: Almougvist & Wiksell, 1962.

——. "Voltaire et la Grèce." *Hellénisme contemporain,* 2d ser., 9 (1955): 6–31.

Korais, Adamantios [Coray]. *Mémoire sur l'état actuel de la civilisation dans la Grèce.* In *Lettres inédites de Coray à Chardon de la Rochette (1770–1796).* Paris: Firmin-Didot, 1877.

Koumarianou, Aikaterine. "To taxidi tou Choiseul-Gouffier." In *Periegeseis ston elleniko choro,* edited by C. Th. Dimaras. Athens: O.M.E.D., 1968.

Kouropalates, Chrysoverges, trans. *Periegesis tou Neou Anacharsidos eis ten Ellada, para tou ava Vartholomaiou, metenechtheisa d' ek tes gallikes eis ten kath'emas dialekton.* . . . 7 vols. Vienna: Ionnes Sneireros, 1819.

Kristeller, Paul Oscar. "The Place of Classical Humanism in Renaissance Thought." *Journal of the History of Ideas* 4, no. 1 (1943): 59–63.

——. *Renaissance Thought and Its Sources.* New York: Columbia University Press, 1979.

Laborde, comte de. *Athènes aux XVe, XVIe et XVIIe siècles.* 2 vols. Paris: Jules Renouard, 1854.

Lamartine, Alphonse de. *Voyage en Orient.* Vol. 3 of *Oeuvres Complètes.* Paris, 1829.

Legrand, Ph.-E. "Biographie de Louis-François-Sébastien Fauvel antiquaire et consul (1753–1838)." *Revue archéologique* 30 (1897): 41–46, 181–201, 385–404; 31 (1897): 94–103, 185–223.

Leith, James. *The Idea of Art as Propaganda in France 1750–1799*. Toronto: University of Tornoto Press, 1965.

Leroy, Julien David. *Les Ruines des plus beaux monuments de la Grèce, considerées du côté de l'histoire et du côté de l'architecture*. 2d ed. 2 vols. Paris: Louis-François Delatour, 1770.

Letessier, Fernand. "Une Source de Chateaubriand: Le voyage du jeune Anacharsis." *Revue d'histoire littéraire de la France* 59 (1959), 180–203.

Letronne, M. "Analyse critique du *Voyage de la Grèce*." *Projet de diviser en sections l'Académie des Instriptions et Belles-Lettres*. Paris, 1836.

Leval, André. *Voyages en Levant pendant les XVIe, XVIIe et XVIIIe siècles. Essai de bibliographie*. Budapest: Singer & Wolfner, 1897.

Linny-Babagor. *Réponse d'un Turc à la "Note sur la Grèce" de M. le Vte. de Chateaubriand*. Brussels: Baudouin, 1825.

Loménie, Louis de. "Chateaubriand et ses *Mémoires*." *Revue des deux mondes* 23 (1848): 133–67, 674–707.

Loir, Sieur du. *Les Voyages du Sieur du Loir*. Paris: Gervais Clouzier, 1654.

Longi, Olga. *La Terre et les morts dans l'oeuvre de Chateaubriand*. Baltimore: Johns Hopkins Press, 1934.

Longnon, Jean. "Quatre Siècles de philhellénisme français." *Revue de France* 1, no. 6. (1921): 512–42.

Lovinesco, Eugène. *Les Voyageurs français en Grèce au XIXe siècle (1800–1900)*. Paris: Champion, 1909.

Lowe, C. G. "Fauvel's First Trip through Greece." *Hesperia* 5 (1936): 206–24.

L.S.D.V. [Le Sieur de Villamont]. *Les Voyages de la Terre Saincte, et autres lieux remarquables et signalez d'icelle, ensemble de l'Italie, Sclavonie, Grèce. . . .* Paris: Guillaume Loyson, 1627.

Lucas, Paul. *Voyage du sieur Paul Lucas en Levant. . . .* 2 vols. The Hague: Guillaume de Voys, 1705.

——. *Voyage du sieur Paul Lucas fait par l'ordre du roy dans la Grèce, l'Asie Mineure. . . .* 2 vols. Paris: Nicolas Simart, 1712.

——. *Troisième Voyage du sieur Paul Lucas, fait en 1714. . . .* 3 vols. Rouen: Robert Machouel, 1719.

Malakis, Emile. "Chateaubriand's Contribution to French Philhellenism." *Modern Philology* 25 (1928): 91–105.

——. "French Travellers in Greece (1700–1820)." Diss., Univ. of Pennsylvania, 1925.

Mango, Cyril. "Byzantinism and Romantic Hellenism." *Journal of the Warburg and Courtauld Institute* 28 (1965): 29–43.

Manuel, Frank L. *The Eighteenth Century Confronts the Gods.* Cambridge: Harvard University Press, 1959.

Marcellus, Marie Louis Jean André Charles Demartier du Tyrac, comte de. *Chants du peuple en Grèce....* 2 vols. Paris: Jacques Lecoffre, 1851.

——. *Chants populaires de la Grèce moderne réunis, classés et traduits par le Cte de Marcellus....* Paris: Michel Lévy Frères, 1860.

——. *Chateaubriand et son temps.* Paris: Michel Lévy, 1859.

——. *Episodes littéraires en Orient.* 2 vols. Paris: Jacques Lecoffre, 1851.

——. *Les Grecs anciens et les Grecs modernes....* Paris: Michel Lévy Frères, 1861.

——. *Souvenirs de l'Orient.* Paris: Debécourt, 1839.

——. "La Vénus de Milo." *Revue contemporaine,* 1 April 1852, 129–33.

Martino, Pierre. *L'Orient dans la littérature française au XVIIe et XVIIIe siècle.* Paris: Hachette, 1906.

Masson, P. M. "Chateaubriand en Orient." *Revue des deux mondes,* 6th ser., 24 (1914): 94–123.

Milliex, Roger. *Ellenogallika: Adamantios Korais, Victor Hugo.* Athens: Collection de l'Institut Français d'Athènes, 1953.

Millin, Aubin-Louis. "*Itinéraire de Paris à Jérusalem* par F. A. Chateaubriand." *Magazin encyclopédique* 2 (April 1811): 1–23.

Momigliano, Arnaldo. *Studies in Historiography.* London: Weidenfeld & Nicolson, 1966.

Mommsen, T. E. "The Venetians in Athens and the Destruction of the Parthenon in 1687." *Medieval and Renaissance Studies.* Ithaca, N.Y.: Cornell University Press, 1959.

Montaigne, Michel de. *Journal de Voyage en Italie par la Suisse et l'Allemagne en 1580 et 1581.* Paris: Editions Garnier Frères, 1955.

——. *Oeuvres complètes.* Edited by Albert Thibaudet and Maurice Rat. Paris: Gallimard, Bibliothèque de la Pléiade, 1962.

Montesquieu, Charles de Secondat, baron de. *Considérations sur les causes de la grandeur des Romains et de leur décadence.* In *Oeuvres complètes,* vol. 2. Paris: Gallimard, Bibliothèque de la Pléiade, 1951.

——. *De l'Esprit de lois.* In *Oeuvres complètes,* vol. 2. Paris: Gallimard, Bibliothèque de la Pléiade, 1951.

——. *Mes Pensées.* In *Oeuvres complètes,* vol. 1. Paris: Gallimard, Bibliothèque de la Pléiade, 1949.

Moore, Thomas, ed. *Letters and Journals of Lord Byron with Notices of his Life.* 3d ed. 2 vols. London: John Murray, 1833.

Mylne, Vivienne. *The Eighteenth Century Novel: Techniques of Illusion.* Manchester: Manchester University Press, 1965.

Olivier, G. A. *Voyage dans l'Empire Ottoman, l'Egypte et la Perse.* 4 vol. Paris: Agasse, 1801–4.

Omont, Henri. "Athènes au XVIIe siècle: Relation du P. Robert de Dreux, lettres de J. Spon et de P. Babin." *Revue des études grecques* 14 (1901): 270–94.

——. *Missions archéologiques françaises en Orient aux XVIIe et XVIIIe siècles.* 2 vols. Paris: Imprimerie Nationale, 1902.

Osborn, J. M. "Travel literature and the Rise of Neo-Hellenism in England." *Bulletin of the New York Public Library* 67 (1963): 279–300.

Outrey, Amédée. "Note sur la maison habitée par Chateaubriand pendant son séjour à Athènes au mois d'août 1806." *Bulletin de la Société Chateaubriand* 6 (1936).

Ozouf, Mona. *Festivals and the French Revolution.* Cambridge: Harvard University Press, 1988.

Pailhès, G. *Chateaubriand, sa femme et ses amis.* Bordeaux: Feret et Fils; and Paris: Libraires Associés, 1896.

Parker, Harold T. *The Cult of Antiquity and the French Revolutionaries.* New York: Octagon Books, 1965.

Paton, Morton James. *Chapters on Mediaeval and Renaissance Visitors to Greek Lands.* Princeton: Princeton University Press, 1951.

Penn, Virginia. "Philhellenism in Europa." *Slavonic Review* 16 (1937–38): 638–53.

Pertussier, Charles. *Promenades pittoresques dans Constantinople et sur les rives du Bosphore. . . .* 3 vols. Paris: H. Nicole, 1815.

Peyre, Henri. *Bibliographie critique de l'hellénisme en France de 1843 à 1870.* New Haven: Yale University Press, 1932.

——. *Historical and Critical Essays.* Lincoln: University of Nebraska Press, 1968.

——. *L'Influence des littératures antiques sur la littérature française moderne.* New Haven: Yale University Press, 1941.

——. *Qu'es-ce que le classicisme?* Paris: Nizet, 1965.

——. *The Persistent Voice; Essays on Hellenism in French Literature since the Eighteenth Century.* Edited by Walter G. Langlois. New York: New York University Press, 1971.

Pingaud, Léonce. *Choiseul-Gouffier: La France en Orient sous Louis XVI.* Paris: Alphonse Picard, 1887.

Poirier, Alice. *Les Idées artistiques de Chateaubriand.* Paris: PUF, 1930.

Polites, Alexes, ed. *To demotiko tragoudi: Klephtika.* Athens: Nea Ellenike Bibliotheke, 1973.

Polybius. *The Histories of Polybius.* Translated by Evelyn S. Shuckburgh. 2 vols. London: Macmillan & Co., 1889.

Poulet, Georges. *Etudes sur le temps humain.* Paris: Librairie Plon, 1949.

Pouqueville, F.-C.-H.-L. *Histoire de la régénération de la Grèce.* 2 vols. Paris: Firmin-Didot, 1824.

————. "Travels in Epirus, Albania, Macedonia and Thessaly." Translated from the French. *New Voyages and Travels* 4 (1920): 1–120.

————. *Voyage de la Grèce.* 2d ed. 6 vols. Paris: Firmin-Didot, 1826–27.

————. *Voyage en Morée, à Constantinople, en Albanie, et dans plusieurs autres parties de l'Empire Ottoman pendant les années 1798, 1799, 1800, et 1801.* 3 vols. Paris: Gabon et Cie., 1805.

Quemeneur, Pierre. *O Chateaubriand kai e Ellas.* Thessalonike: IMHA, 1962.

Queux de Saint-Hilaire, marquis de. "Notice sur les services rendus à la Grèce et aux études grecques par M. Ambroise Firmin-Didot." *Association pour l'encouragement des études grecques en France,* 10e année. Paris, 1876: 226–59.

Rangabé, A. R. *Histoire littéraire de la Grèce moderne.* 2 vols. Paris: Calmann-Lévy, 1877.

Rawson, Elizabeth. *The Spartan Tradition in European Thought.* Oxford: Clarendon Press, 1969.

Redondi, Pietro. *Galileo: Heretic.* Princeton: Princeton University Press, 1987.

Renan, Ernest. "Prière sur l'Acropole." *Souvenirs d'enfance et de jeunesse.* Paris: Calmann-Lévy, 1956.

Renard, Georges. "Notes sur la littérature thermidorienne." *Révolution française; Revue d'histoire moderne et contemporaine* 12 (1887): 769–91.

Richard, Jean-Pierre. *Paysage de Chateaubriand.* Paris: Editions du Seuil, 1967.

Rocheblave, Samuel. *Essai sur le comte de Caylus, l'homme, l'artiste, l'antiquaire.* Paris: Hachette, 1889.

Rogers, Stephen. *Classical Greece and the Poetry of Chénier, Shelley, and Leopardi.* Notre Dame, Ind.: University of Notre Dame Press, 1974.

Rousseau, Jean-Jacques. *Les Confessions.* Paris: Garnier Frères, 1964.

————. *Considérations sur le gouvernement de Pologne et sur la réformation projettée.* In *Oeuvres complètes,* vol. 3. Paris: Gallimard, Bibliothèque de la Pléiade, 1959.

———. *Discours sur les sciences et les arts.* In *Oeuvres complètes,* vol. 3. Paris: Gallimard, Bibliothèque de la Pléiade, 1959.

———. *Emile ou De l'Education.* In *Oeuvres complètes,* vol. 4. Paris: Gallimard, Bibliothèque de la Pléiade, 1959.

———. *Les Rêveries du promeneur solitaire.* New York: Doubleday & Company, Collection Internationale, 1961.

Said, Edward W. *Orientalism.* New York: Pantheon Books, 1978.

Saint-Sauveur, André Grasset. *Voyage historique, littéraire et pittoresque dans les isles et possessions ci-devant vénitiennes du Levant.* 3 vols. Paris: Tavernier, an VII [1799–1800].

Sainte-Beuve, Charles Augustin. *Chateaubriand et son groupe littéraire sous l'Empire.* 2 vols. Paris: Calmann-Lévy, 1872.

Seznec, Jean. *The Survival of the Pagan Gods.* New York: Pantheon Books, 1953.

Sherrard, Philip. *The Greek East and the Latin West: A Study in the Christian Tradition.* London: Oxford University Press, 1959.

Simonsuuri, Kirsti. *Homer's Original Genius: Eighteenth-Century Notions of the Early Greek Epic (1688–1798).* Cambridge: Cambridge University Press, 1979.

Simopoulos, Kyriakos. *Xenoi taxidiotes sten Ellada.* 3 vols. Athens, 1970–75.

Sonnini, C. S. *Voyage en Grèce et en Turquie, fait par l'ordre de Louis XVI, et avec l'autorisation de la cour ottomane.* 2 vols. Paris: Buisson, 1801.

Sorel, Albert. *The Eastern Question in the Eighteenth Century.* New York: Howard Fertig, 1969.

Soulis, George. "O Chateaubriand kai e Ellenike Epanastasis." *Nea Estia* 44 (1 September 1948): 1102–5.

Spon, Jacob. *Réponse à la critique publiée par M. Guillet, sur le "Voyage de Grèce" de Jacob Spon.* Lyon: Antoine Celier Fils, 1679.

———. *Voyage d'Italie, de Dalamtie, de Grèce, et du Levant, fait aux années 1675 et 1676. . . .* 3 vols. Lyon: Antoine Cellier Fils, 1678.

Staël, Mme de. *De la Littérature.* Paris: M. J. Minard, 1959.

Starobinski, Jean. *The Invention of Liberty 1700–1789.* Translated by Bernard C. Swift. Geneva: Skira, 1964.

Stefano, Giuseppe di. "L'Hellénisme en France à l'orée de la Renaissance." In *Humanism in France at the End of the Middle Ages and the Early Renaissance,* ed. by A. H. T. Levi. Manchester: Manchester University Press, 1970.

Stephanopoli, Dimo, and Nicolo Stephanopoli. *Voyage de Dimo et Nicolo Stephanopoli en Grèce, pendant les années V et VI, (1797 et 1798) . . . ,* rédigé par un des professeurs du Prytanée. Paris: De l'Imprimerie de Guilleminet, 1800.

Stoneman, Richard. *Land of Lost Gods: The Search for Classical Greece.* Norman: University of Oklahoma Press, 1987.

Thevenot, Monsieur de. *Relation d'un voyage fait au Levant.* Paris: Thomas Iolly, 1665.

Thevet, André. *Cosmographie de Levant.* Lyon: Ian de Tournes et Guil. Gazeau, 1554.

Thuillet, Dom Vincent. "Mémoire pour un voiage littéraire de la Grèce et du Levant." In *Missions archéologiques françaises en Orient au XVIIe et XVIIIe siècles* edited by Henri Omont. 2 vols. Paris: Imprimerie Nationale, 1902.

Tiersot, Julien. *Les Fêtes et les chants de la Révolution Française.* Paris: Hachette, 1908.

Tilley, Arthur. *The Dawn of the French Renaissance.* New York: Russell & Russell, 1968.

Tsatsos, Constantinos D. "O romantismos, O Chateaubriand kai e Ellada." *Nea Estia* 74 (Christmas 1968): 174–83.

Tournefort, Joseph Pitton de. *Relation d'un voyage du Levant fait par ordre du Roy.* 2 vols. Paris: Imprimerie Royale, 1717.

Toynbee, Arnold. *The Greeks and Their Heritages.* Oxford: Oxford University Press, 1981.

Vakalopoulos, A. E. *Istoria tou neou ellenismou.* Thessalonike, 1973.

———. *E Poreia tou Genous.* Athens: Oi Ekdoseis ton Filon, 1966.

Vambas, Neophytos. *Retorike.* In *O Korais kai e epoche tou,* edited by C. Th. Dimaras. Vasike Vivliotheke, no. 9. Athens: Zacharopoulos, 1958.

Van Tieghem, Paul. *Le Préromantisme.* 2 vols. Paris: Librairie Félix Alcan, 1930.

Vandal, Albert. *L'Odyssée d'un ambassadeur: Les Voyages du Marquis de Nointel (1670–1680).* Paris: Librairie Plon, 1900.

Vial, André. *La Dialectique de Chateaubriand: "Transformation" et "changement" dans les "Memoires d'Outre-Tombe."* Paris: SEDES [Société d'Edition d'Enseignement Supérieur], 1978.

Villehardouin, Geoffroy de. *La Conquête de Constantinople.* Translated into modern French by Natalie de Wailly. Paris: Firmin-Didot, 1882.

Villemain, Abel-François. *M. de Chateaubriand, sa vie, ses écrits, son influence politique et littéraire sur son temps.* Paris: Michel Lévy, 1858.

———. "Essai sur l'état des Grecs depuis la conquête musulmane." In *Etudes d'histoire moderne.* New rev. ed. Paris: Didier, 1846.

———. *Lascaris, ou les Grecs du quinzième siècle.* 3d ed. Paris: Didier, 1837.

Villoison, D'Ansse de. "Observations faites pendant un voyage dans la Grèce et principalement dans les isles de l'Archipel. . . ." *Annales des voyages, de la géographie et de l'histoire* 2 (1809): 137–83.

Vogüé, Eugène. "Chateaubriand: à propos d'un livre récent [*Chateaubriand par M. de Lescure*]." *Revue des deux mondes* 90 (1892): 450–65.

Voltaire, Françoi-Marie Arouet de. *Candide and Other Philosophical Tales.* Edited by Morris Bishop. New York: Charles Scribner's Sons, 1957.

———. *Correspondence.* Edited by Theodore Besterman. 107 vols. Genève: Institut et Musée Voltaire, 1953–65.

———. *Dictionnaire philosophique.* Edited by Raymond Naves and Julien Benda. Paris: Garnier Frères, 1967.

———. "Dissertation sur la tragédie ancienne et moderne." In *Oeuvres complètes,* edited by Beaumarchais et al., vol. 3. Kehl: Imprimerie de la Société Littéraire et Typographique, 1785–89.

———. "Épître à l'impératrice de Russie, Catherine II (1771)." In *Oeuvres complètes,* edited by Beaumarchais et al., vol. 3. Kehl: Imprimerie de la Société Littéraire et Typographique, 1785–89.

———. *Essai sur les moeurs et l'esprit des nations.* In *Oeuvres complètes,* edited by Beaumarchais et al., vol. 16. Kehl: Imprimerie de la Société Littéraire et Typographique, 1785–89.

———. *Essai sur la poésie épique.* In *Oeuvres complètes,* edited by Beaumarchais et al., vol. 10. Kehl: Imprimerie de la Société Littéraire et Typographique, 1785–89.

———. "Ode pindarique à propos de la guerre présente en Grèce (1769)." In *Oeuvres complètes,* edited by Beaumarchais et al., vol. 13. Kehl: Imprimerie de la Société Littéraire et Typographique, 1785–89.

———. "Ode sur la guerre des Russes contre les Turcs en 1768." In *Oeuvres complètes,* edited by Beaumarchais et al., vol. 13. Kehl: Imprimerie de la Société Littéraire et Typographique, 1785–89.

Vourazele, Elene D. *O Vios tou ellenikou laou kata ten tourkokratian epi vasei ton xenon periegeton.* Athens, 1939.

Vyverberg, Henry. *Human Nature, Cultural Diversity, and the French Enlightenment.* New York: Oxford University Press, 1989.

Walker, Thomas Capell. *Chateaubriand's Natural Scenery: A Study of His Descriptive Art.* Baltimore: Johns Hopkins Press, 1946.

Ware, Timothy. *The Orthodox Church.* Baltimore: Penguin Books, 1963.

Weber, Shirley Howard. *Voyages and Travels in the Near East Made During the XIXth Century.* Princeton: American School of Classical Studies at Athens, 1952.

———. *Voyages and Travels in Greece, the Near ast and Adjacent Regions Made Previous to the Year 1801.* Princeton: American School of Classical Studies at Athens, 1953.

Weiss, Roberto. "Learning and Education in Western Europe from 1470 to 1520." In *The New Cambridge Modern History,* vol. 1, *The Renaissance 1493–1520.* Cambridge: Cambridge University Press, 1967.

———. *Medieval and Humanist Greek: Collected Essays.* Padua: Editrice Antenore, 1977.

———. *The Renaissance Discovery of Classical Antiquity.* Oxford: Basil Blackwell, 1969.

Wheler, George. *A Journey into Greece, by George Wheler, Esq., in company of Dr. Spon of Lyon.* London: William Cademan, Robert Kettlewell and Awnshane Churchill, 1682.

White, Florence Donnell. *Voltaire's Essay on Epic Poetry: A Study and an Edition.* 1915. Reprint. New York: Phaeton Press, 1970.

Winckelmann, Johann Joachim. *Histoire de l'art chez les anciens.* 2 vols. Paris: H. J. Jansen et Cie., 1793.

Woodhouse, C. M. *The Philhellenes.* London: Hodder & Stoughton, 1969.

INDEX

Library of Congress Cataloging-in-Publication Data

Augustinos, Olga.
    French odysseys : Greece in French travel literature from the
Renaissance to the romantic era / Olga Augustinos.
        p.   cm.
    Includes bibliographical references and index.
    ISBN 0-8018-4616-1
    1. Greece—Description and travel.   2. Travelers' writings, French—
History and criticism.   I. Title.
    DF721.A94   1994
    914.9504—dc20   93-8705